"WE FACE a dilemma in contemporary human studies," write the editors in their Introduction. "We cannot stop talking about the self (and its neighbors), but we cannot agree on our terms and their definitions." In an effort to alleviate that problem, *The Book of the Self* presents a number of unique psychological and philosophical discussions whose central concern is to clarify the language of the self and to establish a common framework from which this fundamental topic can be explored.

Polly Young-Eisendrath (a psychologist, educator, and writer) and James A. Hall (a Jungian psychiatrist and author) have assembled a distinguished group of contributors to address a series of fascinating topics. Here, the reader will find Donald Spence writing on the central role of the self in psychotherapy...Jane Loevinger on the concept of the self or ego...John Broughton on Piaget's concept of the self...and many others. These engaging essays offer provocative discussions for psychologists, psychotherapists, philosophers, and theologians, and will be useful to others who, in the editors' words, "earn their livelihood by solving personal dilemmas."

Also included are chapters on the self and Lacan, feminism, Christianity, and Jung.

Important, intellectually exciting, and highly appealing, *The Book of the Self* will provide scholars and professionals alike with intriguing, lively new perspectives on the self.

Polly Young-Eisendrath is Guest Lecturer in Human Development at Bryn Mawr College and Chief Psychologist at Clinical Associates West, Bala Cynwyd, Pennsylvania. A practicing clinical analyst and social worker, as well as a diplomate Jungian analyst, she is the author of *Female Authority* (with Florence Wiedemann) and *Hags and Heroes: A Feminist Approach to Jungian Psychotherapy with Couples*.

James A. Hall is Clinical Assistant Professor of Psychiatry at the University of Texas Health Science Center in Dallas and a Fellow of the American Psychiatric Association and of the American Academy of Psychoanalysis. He is the author of more than half a dozen books, including *Jungian Dream Interpretation, Clinical Uses of Dreams,* and *The Jungian Experience*.

THE BOOK OF THE SELF

THE BOOK OF THE SELF

Person, Pretext, and Process

POLLY YOUNG-EISENDRATH
and JAMES A. HALL
Editors

NEW YORK UNIVERSITY PRESS
New York *and* London

Library of Congress Cataloging-in-Publication Data

The Book of the self.

 Bibliography: p.
 Includes index.
 1. Self (Philosophy) 2. Self. I. Young-Eisendrath,
Polly, 1947– . II. Hall, James A. (James Albert),
1934– .
BD450.B59 1987   126   87–7813
ISBN 0–8147–9664–8

Book design by Laiying Chong.

To Edward Epstein, husband and dearest friend

POLLY YOUNG-EISENDRATH

To Suzi herSelf

JAMES A. HALL

CONTENTS

PREFACE AND ACKNOWLEDGMENTS

It seems impossible to remain outside contemporary debates about personal subjectivity—about self, intentionality, truth and death. Everyone is drawn into conversations about these topics in a radical way in this period of Western culture. So many aspects of personal being are under attack, the attack originating primarily in our ideals. Ideals formulated around personal freedom, individuation, empirical study of subjectivity, deconstruction of personal narratives, and so on are at odds with one another—and often at odds with personal experience. Even in everyday conversations, people are forced to question their conceptions of both self and world and to imagine new ones.

We, the editors, were drawn into some irresolvable conflicts about the nature of subjectivity at a conference held at Bryn Mawr College in 1983. (Young-Eisendrath planned and moderated the conference at which Hall was one of the speakers.) The conference was convened under the rubric of *Self* and we had anticipated a few dozen academic psychologists, philosophers, and humanists who might want to spend a day and a half listening to various theories about subjectivity. We were indeed shocked to encounter more than 350 people in our audience—people who had come to learn and discuss the construct of self. Throughout the reading and discussion of eight papers, we confronted an increasing frustration. No one shared a common language. People from different disciplines and theoretical perspectives were unable to understand one another, and were unable to translate specialized languages into ordinary concepts of everyday discourse.

This volume is partly the result of the confusion and frustration of attempted exchanges at that conference. A few months later, we met to ponder over what had happened—both in terms of the popularity of the topic and in terms of the problems of communication. We decided to invite scholars and practitioners from the human studies, people whose work we admired for its clarity and soundness, to enter into a dialogue with us. Our primary objective was to shape an arena for comparison and contrast of theories of individual subjectivity. What forms would discussion of self (and its neighbors) take if we were to put few constraints on our contributors? So we experimented. We invited our contributors to "write something about self" from the vantage point of their own discipline, practices, or research.

What we received was most gratifying and intriguing. Several themes emerged in a first reading of the papers: *person, pretext,* and *process* were the names we gave them. These themes encompassed regular and repeating subthemes: continuity, unity, stability, change, intentionality, and linguisticality. Versions of contemporary social constructivism were the mainstay of many interpretations of narrative and agency, but authors searched in diverse places for explanations adequate to the experience of unity, a coherent sense of being that is ubiquitous among persons.

The organization of the volume provides for both serious, academic readings and for more playful, aesthetic readings. The most serious academic approach would be to read through the first papers in each of the sections to get an overview of the terrain. Returning to other papers, in pursuit of subthemes in their connections to the section titles, would complete such an investigation of the entire scheme. Our introductory and concluding chapters attempt to trace the major topics surveyed by the papers. A more playful reading would evolve solely by interest, probably beginning with the essays in the section entitled Pretext because these present imaginative accounts.

In essence, collecting and editing these papers has been a pleasant task in more ways than one might expect for this sort of endeavor. Contributors have all been conscientious and responsive. Our editors at the Press, Kitty Moore and Despina Gimbel, have done an excellent job of copyediting. The two of us have met several times at Pendle Hill Quaker Study Center in Wallingford, Pennsylvania, to assemble and edit this work. The staff there provided the right combination of support and privacy, allowing us to engage in hours of rich conversation about the implications of these papers. To all of these people, we offer our appreciation. We also thank our family members for their tolerance and encouragement.

Polly Young-Eisendrath
James A. Hall

CONTRIBUTORS

AUGUSTO BLASI, Ph.D., is Associate Professor at the University of Massachusetts in Boston. His work has been in the areas of moral development, ego development, and the development of the self as subject.

JOHN M. BROUGHTON, Ph.D., is Associate Professor of Psychology and Education at Teachers College, Columbia University. He is the author of various articles on adolescence, the self, political development, fantasy, gender, and technology, and is the editor of two books, *The Cognitive Developmental Psychology of James Mark Baldwin,* and *Critical Theories of Psychological Development.* He is founding editor of the journals *PsychCritique* and *New Ideas in Psychology.*

WILLIAM R. CASPARY, Ph.D., is Associate Professor of Political Science at Washington University, St. Louis. His field is contemporary political philosophy.

HARRIET S. CHESSMAN, Ph.D., is an Assistant Professor of English and Women's Studies at Yale University. She has recently completed a study of Gertrude Stein, *The Public Is Invited to Dance: Representation, the Body, and Dialogue in Gertrude Stein.*

RICHARD deCHARMS, Ph.D., is Professor of Psychology and Education at Washington University, St. Louis. His primary interests are human agency and motivation, and new approaches to the study of human beings. He is author of *Enhancing Motivation* and *Personal Causation.*

CRAIG R. EISENDRATH, Ph.D., is Executive Director of the Pennsylvania Humanities Council. In addition to many articles on aspects of American culture, he has authored *The Unifying Moment: The Psychological Philosophy of William James and Alfred North Whitehead.*

MICHAEL FORDHAM, F.R.C. Psych., Hon. F.B. Ps.S., is an editor of Jung's *Collected Works.* Widely recognized as the founding figure of the *Society for Analytical Psychology* in England, he is noted for enlarging Jungian studies to include childhood development and for his concept of *de-integration* of the original self in the process of early childhood experience.

JUDITH KEGAN GARDINER, Ph.D., teaches English literature and Women's Studies at the University of Illinois at Chicago. Her previous publications and research focus on Renaissance English literature, modern writing by women, and psychoanalytic, feminist, and socialist theories of literary criticism. She is a member of a workshop in psychoanalysis and literature.

PETER GOLDENTHAL, Ph.D., is Assistant Professor of Human Development and Director of the Child Study Institute of Psychotherapy at Bryn Mawr College. For two years he was Postdoctoral Fellow at Judge Baker Guidance Center and Harvard Medical School. His current research focuses on the expectations and experiences of children and families as psychotherapy clients.

PAMELA WHITE HADAS, Ph.D., is the author of three volumes of verse, *Designing Women, In Light of Genesis*, and *Beside Herself: Pocahontas to Patty Hearst*, as well as one of prose, *Marianne Moore: Poet of Affection*. Most recently, she has been on the faculties of the University of California, Berkeley, Columbia University, the Bread Loaf School of English, and Princeton University.

JAMES A. HALL, M.D., is Clinical Associate Professor of Psychiatry at the University of Texas Health Science Center at Dallas and a Fellow of the American Psychiatric Association and the American Academy of Psychoanalysis. A Jungian analyst trained in Zurich, he is a founder and first president of the Inter-Regional Society of Jungian Analysts. Dr. Hall is author of *Jungian Dream Interpretation, Clinical Uses of Dreams, The Jungian Experience* and (with H. B. Crasilneck) *Clinical Hypnosis*.

ROBERT KRAVIS, Psy.D., is Assistant Professor of Mental Health Sciences and Director of the Charles Peberdy Jr. Child Psychiatry Clinic. He is also a practicing child and adult clinical psychologist.

PAUL K. KUGLER, Ph.D., is a Jungian analyst, graduate of the C. G. Jung Institute, Zurich, practicing in Buffalo, N.Y. He has taught at the State University of New York at Buffalo and is currently Chairperson of Admissions for the Inter-Regional Society of Jungian Analysts. He is author of *The Alchemy of Discourse: An Archetypal Approach to Language*.

FREDERIC J. LEVINE, Ph.D., is Professor of Mental Health Sciences at Hahnemann University, Philadelphia and Adjunct Associate Professor of Psychology in Psychiatry at the University of Pennsylvania School of Medicine. He is also a practicing psychoanalyst and clinical psychologist.

PHILIP LICHTENBERG, Ph.D., is Professor of Social Work and Social Research at Bryn Mawr College and Director of the Gestalt Therapy Institute of Philadelphia. A psychologist, he has published four books, mostly concerning psychoanalysis, and numerous articles on depression, mental health, and social issues informed by psychological theory. He is a practicing Gestalt therapist.

JANE LOEVINGER, Ph.D., is Professor of Psychology at Washington University, St. Louis, where for many years she directed the Ego Development Research Project. In addition to numerous articles and monographs, she has authored two books, *Ego Development* and *Paradigms of Personality*, as well as a two-volume scoring manual for her sentence completion test, *Measuring Ego Development I & II*.

JOSEPH MARGOLIS, Ph.D., is Professor of Philosophy at Temple University. He has authored *Persons and Minds, Culture and Cultural Entities, Philosophy and Psychology*, and coauthored *Psychology: Designing the Discipline*. His first volume of a three-volume project, *Pragmatism Without Foundations* has just appeared, soon to be followed by *Science Without Unity*.

ROBERT J. ORESICK, Ph.D., is Assistant Professor of Psychology and Counseling at Boston University. His research interest is in the psychology of personality.

ALBERT C. OUTLER, Ph.D., a graduate of Emory and Yale and a former professor at Duke and at Yale, is Professor of Theology Emeritus, Perkins School of Theology, Southern Methodist University. Dr. Outler is a former president of the American Theological Society and was a Delegated Protestant Observer at Vatican II.

JOSEPH W. T. REDFEARN, M.D., completed his medical training at Cambridge University and at Johns Hopkins and his psychiatric training at the Maudsley Hospital in London. After several years in psychiatric and neurophysiological research, he trained as a Jungian analyst. He is now a training analyst of the Society of Analytical Psychology, London.

SHIRLEY SANDERS, Ph.D., formerly with the University of North Carolina at Chapel Hill, is a former president of the American Society of Clinical Hypnosis. She has published widely in the field of hypnotherapy and is noted for her development of a self-administered dissociation rating scale.

DONALD P. SPENCE, Ph.D., is Professor of Psychiatry at the University of Medicine and Dentistry of New Jersey, Robert Wood Johnson Medical School, Piscataway. Formerly a Professor of Psychology at New York University, he is the editor of two books and the author of *Narrative Truth and Historical Truth.* He is a graduate of the New York Psychoanalytic Institute.

FREDERICK J. STRENG, Ph.D., is Professor of History of Religions, Perkins School of Theology, Southern Methodist University. His extensive publications include a study of Nagarjuna, *Emptiness: A Study on Religious Meaning.* A frequent contributor to Christian-Buddhist dialogue, Dr. Streng is currently teaching in Japan.

POLLY YOUNG-EISENDRATH, Ph.D., is Guest Lecturer in Human Development at Bryn Mawr College and Chief Psychologist at Clinical Associates West, Bala Cynwyd, Pennsylvania. Previously on the faculty of the Graduate School of Social Work and Social Research at Bryn Mawr, she is both a practicing clinical psychologist and social worker, as well as a diplomate Jungian analyst. In addition to articles and chapters on Jungian psychology, ego development, psychodynamic theories, and adult development, she has authored two books, *Hags and Heroes: A Feminist Approach to Jungian Psychotherapy with Couples,* and *Female Authority: Empowering Women Through Psychotherapy* (with Florence Wiedemann).

INTRODUCTION: A STUDY OF SELF

"No one ever told us we had to study our lives / make of our lives a study" (p. 73), says Adrienne Rich (1978) in her poem about the "transcendental étude" of separating and living as an individual after once having been contained in another. Any occasion in which we make a study of our lives is one for acute linguistic concern. When we speak as individuals about our shared experiences of being human, we are wary of our concepts and categories. We seem better equipped to investigate and represent the worlds of physical objects and biological organisms than the world of personal existence.

Why is this so? The intersubjective reality of self is the least consensual, the least accessible to shared construction; yet it is the tacit background, and fundamental ground, for all theorizing we do. Of the worlds we inhabit—the physical dimensions of time and space, the biological patterning of organic processes, and the cultural community of personal truths—the cultural is the most difficult to validate in a shared symbol system. An example may clarify. A small group of adults will typically have little difficulty agreeing on the dimensions of physical space surrounding them, the number and names of objects in the room, and even on the length of time or the particular moment of their meeting. Yet, they will likely be unable to agree on the nature of self (linguistic description of subjective experience). Even simple descriptions of "what it means to be a person" are likely to contradict one another and to vary considerably.

This kind of disagreement is expected in our contemporary culture. In fact, in most Western industrialized societies, we live within an ideology of self-reflective individualism. We expect to conceive of ourselves and others as independent "worlds," as unique, separate, and perhaps incompatible. Presumptions of separate, special, and different realities among adults are common in our encounters with each other, and we frequently find ourselves embroiled in conflicts (both formal and informal, both interpersonal and intrapsychic) about the truth of personal existence.

Many people, perhaps especially human service providers, philosophers, and social scientists, may doubt we could ever discover a common ground for dialogue about universal aspects of selfhood. Our
readers may be suspicious of terminology that implies universals, perhaps even of the term *self*. From the point of view of linguistics and
psychology, such suspicions are well founded, for there appears to be
little agreement for how to talk about the self. As John Broughton
(1984) reminds us,

> Even if we stick to English, in addition to self, ideal self,
> sense of self, subjectivity, intersubjectivity, the "I," the "me"
> and the ego, there is a host of hyphenated terms such as
> self-knowledge, self-control, self-realization, self-awareness,
> ego-ideal, and ego-identity. Even the shorter "Concise Ox-
> ford Dictionary" lists 150 different words formed with the
> assistance of the "self" prefix. (p. 130)

We face a dilemma in contemporary human studies. We cannot stop
talking about the self (and its neighbors), but we cannot agree on our
terms and their definitions. Epistemological and ethical systems of
selfhood provide no consistent basis for reasoning, making decisions,
or taking responsible actions. At root, theories should provide us with
some tools for doing things, with justifications for our actions, with
ethical constraints and explanations, as well as ideal methods for actions. Whereas we can take some comfort in our apparent consensual
agreement about the linguistically schematized view of our physical
world, and some satisfaction in our approach to a common ground
(for disagreement at least) about the organic nature of the biological
world, we have only dis-ease and distress in facing an apparently un-
schematized view of a personal world.

Many people may not feel a pressing need to rely on a schematized
view of a personal world, except in rare moments when they face a
choice that seems to require validation of personal truth. Other people—notably teachers, philosophers, theologians, lawyers, social workers, doctors, poets, artists, psychologists, and biographers—earn their
livelihood by solving personal dilemmas. For them, the dimensions of
personal reality are constantly focal in decision making. The crisis of
the personal becomes for them an ethical matter of everyday respect-
ability and responsibility. If I earn my living as a psychotherapist, for

example, I must justify the conditions under which I am paid and respected for my knowledge of the personal world.

Human service providers, philosophers, and theologians express concern and uneasiness about the chaotic state of affairs in the human studies. Multiplicity and incompatibility of personal realities can make even a simple conversation difficult. Philosophers especially have long recognized the dangers of speaking about the self as a universal subjective experience of unity and continuity: solipsism and/or useless generalizations. Language and descriptions used to schematize personal reality can lead us into confusions between the "thing in itself" and the intersubjectivity (the validity) of shared perspectives. When we infer a reality or world that cannot be directly observed and empirically described, we seem especially in danger of splitting off our terms from their references and/or reifying our terms as though they were the references themselves. The limitations of symbolization are especially apparent in the world of culture, the common experiences of personal life. When we assign terms to the unobservable and describe our intuitive apprehensions, we confront the limitations of our idiosyncracies and particular visions or distortions. One consequence of such limitations is a skepticism about our shared reality.

Discouraged by wasteful speculations and misleading dualisms— such as body-mind, subject-object, internal-external—some theoreticians in the human studies have abandoned the self as a topic for dialogue. Ultimately this kind of decision is both practical and ethical in its motivation. Such theoreticians assume that symbolic worldviews can be validated intersubjectively only for the physical and biological data that can be observed in personal life. They practice a disciplined skepticism and forcefully delimit their terms to exclude all inferences about subjective experience, all ideas generated from introspection. They refuse to talk about self or to pretend to any common ground for inferable characteristics of the personal.

An intellectual culture of skepticism about self theories has indeed been flourishing since Hume and has perhaps reached its peak in the humanities and arts in this century. Cartesian coordinates, Kantian categories, and Hegelian dialectics are out of fashion, if not out of mind, among historians and philosophers, even among many theologians and poets. Yet it is unlikely that the refusal to speak about theories of self has prevented anyone from speaking about self experiences. The most willful skeptic continues to phrase personal language in terms of "I," "me," "mine," and "myself."

One consequence of the skepticism about self theories in our society has been the confinement of introspection. Introspection and self-examination can rarely be employed as formal justification for publicly expressed truths in the academies of contemporary culture. Introspection has become a private matter, it seems. Looked at from another angle, however, the popular domain of the media is infused with ideologies of self-reflection: the culture of narcissism, romance with self-help programs, and prescriptions for self-control of habits are but a few examples. The "self" is popular in the media even if it is refused admittance to our academies.

Whether or not they like it, practitioners and theoreticians of the human studies must be concerned with the language of self. People will not stop talking about it. Confronted with the lack of consensual agreement and our reluctance to schematize shared experiences, many of us would echo Adrienne Rich (1978) when she describes our condition thus:

> No one lives in this room
> without confronting the whiteness of the wall
> behind the poems, planks of books,
> photographs of dead heroines.
> Without contemplating last and late
> the true nature of poetry. The drive
> to connect. The dream of a common language.
>
> (p. 7)

Our "dream of a common language" has motivated us to collect the essays in this volume and to bind them together as schematizations of self.

In this brief introduction we will give preliminary explanations for the categories we have chosen to organize the essays presented in this volume: person, pretext, and process. Each category constitutes a section of the book and is introduced with further explanation of the topics and papers that comprise it. Our final chapter, an attempt to schematize a common language for self theories, integrates the concerns presented in all of the sections.

The Person

Our first category is the "person," the particular world of self that is most obvious in our experience, but perhaps the last to be described.

Fundamental to the experience of being a person are two conditions: recognition of subjective coherence and enactment of agency. The subjective condition of experience as a coherent "I" or actor, as distinct from reactivity or adaptive conditioning to environmental stimuli, is the prerequisite of "I do."

Having an effect on the environment, recognizing the effect, and then anticipating it are probably the component steps to personal agency. The development of personality, or the recognition of personal characteristics in oneself and others, does not occur in isolation but, rather, is the development of both "self" and "other" constructions. In recognizing the personal causation of one's own actions, one endows the actions of others with similar intentionality. Others' attributions of intentionality and personal agency validate one's own intentionality.

The interpersonal construction of the person relies on the intersubjectivity of knowledge (representation) and action (reality). This framework implies a reality beyond hermeneutical interpretations, a reference system of intuitive apprehension—the positing of agency, responsibility, authority. The achievement of personality is gradual, and dependent on both a shared symbolic system and interaction with a physical-social environment.

Many adults do not achieve the integrity of linguistic representation and personal experience of agency. In other words, they are unconvinced or remain confused about the validity of personal agency, responsibility, and intentionality. Instead, they experience themselves in terms of another construction of self: as the product of an adaptive process or as the passive reactor to others' wishes and directives. Naturally, all these self-conceptions are also consensually validated within a shared linguistic system, and may constitute communal or shared theories of self among any array of persons.

Western cultural ideas of personhood—in terms of responsible choice and self-reflective morality—rest on the ground of intentionality. The psychoanalytic version of self gives prominence to person, and psychoanalytic therapy assists analysands in formulating a self as individually responsible:

> In the course of analysis, the analysand comes to construct narratives of personal agency ever more readily, independently, convincingly, and securely, particularly in those contexts that have to do with crucially maladaptive experiences

of drivenness. The important questions to be answered in
the analysis concern personal agency, and the important
answers reallocate the attributions of activity and passivity.
(Schafer, 1980, p. 42)

The Pretext

A more skeptical approach to the study of self is to assume that self
is essentially a construction or reflection, not a coherent experience of
unity or continuity. We chose the term *pretext* rather than *text* because
the former expresses the possibility that presuppositions of a continuous and unified self are illusory. The self may be a project of deception, a masking of discontinuity and disintegration. The "self" could
then be interpreted as a facade, a construction based on language, a
cultural point of view on human life, expressing a desire for unity in
the face of dissolution and death. From what does the desire arise?
Our authors answer differently the question of motivations for narrating or imagining a unifying principle of self.

Interpreting the self as pretext does not necessitate maintaining a
skeptical attitude. It is possible to regard the self as a representational
unity without assuming it is primarily a facade, a deception, or an
illusion. Accounts of self as pretext may rest on what Hans-Georg
Gadamer (1985) calls a "hermeneutics of trust." Because we talk about
ourselves and present a narrative and historical account of unity, because we assume that we can speak from the truth of personal experience, we have the basis for trusting each others' accounts of self.
The "self" as a representational construction of subjective unity and
agency is something like an ideal in speech. To speak about ourselves
as continuous, to construct life histories and pose questions of meaning, may constitute a belief in the validity of our effects rather than
an escape from our fate. Or it can be interpreted as a shared desire
for continuity—even immortality, as we shall see. Any effort to construct a hermeneutical account of a continuous self—either individual
or shared—requires a presupposition that understanding such an account is possible, a trust in the validity of a shared historical and
momentary construction of unity.

The self as pretext can then be seen as shared reality, founded on
linguisticality and desire for continuity rather than primarily on ex-

periences of integrity, intentionality, or agency. Although the origin of this pretext may be narrated differently by different theorists (e.g., it may be thought to begin with sensorimotor schemes that lead to language, with the unified image of the body reflected in a mirror, or with the social smile of the infant that is clearly directed as a communication to "another"), its context is uniformly recognized as the shared linguistic system of a culture. Not every pretextual account of self is a narrative theory, but each one relies primarily on a particular telling of self, a way of speaking about the self as continuous. As Schafer (1980) puts his theory of narration:

> We are forever telling stories about ourselves. In telling these self-stories *to others* we may, for most purposes, be said to be performing straightforward narrative actions. In saying that we also tell them *to ourselves,* however, we are enclosing one story with another. This is the story that there is a self to tell something to, a someone else serving as audience who is oneself or one's self. When the stories we tell others about ourselves concern these other selves of ours, when we say, for example, "I am not master of myself," we are again enclosing one story within another. On this view, the self is a telling. From time to time and from person to person, this telling varies in the degree to which it is unified, stable, and acceptable to informed observers as reliable and valid. (p. 35)

There are obvious standards for truth within a hermeneutical account of self. Unification, stability, and acceptability are three categories named by Schafer, and we will discover still others in the essays presented here.

The pretextual approach to self is not fundamentally grounded in skepticism. First of all, to assume that ideologies of self are merely distortions of some other reality is to presuppose a nondistorted understanding of self that underlies the presented account. To say that our tellings of a continuous self are simply defensive or delusional (concealing truer realities of death or alienation) is to privilege some standards over others (e.g., privileging disintegration or alienation over integrity and trust).

Second, that people talk about themselves as continuous and purposive is itself a basis for truth. That dialogue regularly occurs among

people with the common ground of shared assumptions about continuity and unity means we already have a linguistic system for interpreting self. What Robert Dostal (1987) says of Gadamer's account of
the "world" can also be said of the "self":

> The "world," or the narrower instance of the "text," is like
> a regulative ideal for speech. But it is neither the Kantian
> *Ding an sich* nor the neo-Kantian fiction. It is not a subjec-
> tive projection of total adequacy and coherence. It is rather
> the phenomenological thing itself. The world, *die Sacht
> selbst,* the text, is the end, the *telos.*(p. 428)

Our presentation of self as pretext is also a presentation of "self" as
telos, as the ideal constructed through the accounts of peoples' selves.
These accounts fall between the Kantian and neo-Kantian versions of
self. They are phenomenologically true because they are derived from
common assumptions about self as people talk about it.

The Process

The category of "process" in the study of self is most removed from
experience, more thoroughly abstracted, and often more structurally
formal in its approach. In depicting self as a process, theorists conceive
a map or schematization of functions or assume a continuum of integration and differentiation. This is not to say that the conceptualization of process excludes a discussion of experience. Experience of
self may be the central focus of a process approach, but the language
and representational images tend to be schematized and somewhat
distant from experience itself.

  On one extreme, we present theories of self that conceive of a unitary, inherent subject that unfolds and differentiates through a process of relationship to physical and interpersonal environments. On
the other extreme, we present theories that conceive of a subjectivity
of self (as an integration of perceptions and actions) without a subject,
without a presupposition of coherent or consistent unity. In the former
case it is the self (already unified) that is evidenced at the birth of
individuality of the infant, and at death in the integrity of the personal
spirit. In the latter, it is the process of structuralizing functions within

personality (representations of the physical world, for example) that imparts an apparent experience of unified subjectivity to human life.

The concept of self as process deemphasizes both intentionality and linguisticality of individual subjective experience. These qualifying characteristics of personhood and authorship are subsumed under a broader concern to map or trace a series of unfolding events as they appear to relate to each other. Examining the effects of a mother's particular patterns of communicative response and holding, in relation to the pattern of similar response and body-molding in her infant, is an example of a process approach to the study of self.

Our authors focus attention especially on cognitive, ethical, and religious process, distinguishing their models from analogies in the biological sciences. As Macmurray (1961) says, "We are not organisms but persons" (p. 46). We remind ourselves of this idea because the process model of self has sometimes been used to reduce persons to organisms, interpreting the "self" as primarily an adaptive process, reactive to conditions of the nervous system and the physical environment. Macmurray says further,

> The nexus of relations which unite us in a human society is not organic but personal. Human behaviour cannot be understood, but only caricatured, if it is represented as an adaptation to an environment; and there is not such a process as social evolution, but instead, a history which reveals precarious development and possibilities of both progress and retrogression. (p. 46)

The category of self as process takes its form from organic processes but is a locus for specifically human activities in the studies we present. Ethics, epistemology, theology, religion, and interpersonal communication are the contents shaped by the model of self as process in this volume.

References

Broughton, J. (1984). The psychology, history and ideology of the self. In K. Larsen (Ed.), *Psychology and ideology*. New York: Norwood.

Dostal, R. (1987). The world never lost: The hermeneutics of trust. *Philosophy and Phenomenological Research* XLVII, *3*, 413–34.

Gadamer, H-G. (1985). *Truth and method.* New York: Crossroad.

Macmurray, J. (1961). *Persons in relation.* Atlantic Highlands, N.J.: Humanities Press.

Rich, A. (1978). *The dream of a common language.* New York: W. W. Norton. Reprinted by permission.

Schafer, R. (1980). Narration in the psychoanalytic dialogue. *Critical Inquiry, 7,* 29–54.

PART I

Self as Person

Thus the world is the common ground, trodden by none and recognized by all, uniting all who speak with one another.
Hans-Georg Gadamer, 1985, p. 404

THE GOAL of describing and understanding personal life has long been sought by philosophers and psychologists alike. The task is to "say the obvious" while being adequate, systematic, and precise. In this part, the authors try to establish a language of personal life that is both common and formal enough to permit dialogue across disciplines—especially psychology, philosophy, medicine, social work, education, literature, history, and religion. We desire an ordinary language rooted in the common sense of shared experience in being human, one that would permit open dialogue between professor and student, psychotherapist and client, philosopher and layperson.

First we encounter a question of *necessity*. Why talk about self? Do we need a theoretical construct that refers to an experience hidden from perception but consensually inferred? Would descriptive language of action and thought better serve the purposes of dialogue among the human studies? Each author in this part argues for the necessity of the construct of self or person, a construct that refers to the "common ground" of continuity, self-reflection, and intentionality that we share in human life.

The reader will find various conceptual guides offered as launching points for a language and theory of self as person. The necessity of describing our particular collusion of body and psyche ("incarnate functionalism," as Joseph Margolis calls it) arises directly from personal references to intentionality ("I do") and truth ("I am"). While these references are constantly under revision in our personal lives, they are consistent enough to be pragmatic and determinate of everyday beliefs in human freedom, agency, and creative individuality. The authors in Part I refuse to ignore references to self in everyday life.

They seek to give an account of the purpose of such language and its counterparts in psychological and social theories of self, regarding such concepts as intentionality, agency, responsibility, self-reflection, and self-defense.

What is to be included in a theory of self? The answer depends on our purposes. As editors, we want to establish a basis for greater dialogue. Jane Loevinger reminds us that any theory or language system blocks out most of our ordinary awareness in favor of focal attention to particular relationships, configurations, or images. In theorizing about self, we immediately appreciate the barriers and limitations engendered by any language system, as well as the possibilities that are awakened.

Richard deCharms is acutely aware of the potential distortions that result from separating our understanding of body from mind, self from other, action from thought. The Cartesian throwbacks to misleading dichotomies plague any language of self. We can become logically committed to solipsism and defend the idea that the self is private, unknown to other selves, inconsequential, or hidden. Solipsism leads to other detours away from the unity of experience: for example, how can minds (persons) know each other when they are separately embodied? When intention is separated from action, individuality from relationship, and subject from object, we may commit our theoretical logic to confusing perspectives that distort our experience of consensual realities.

DeCharms argues for the construct of *person* as primary and unitary, as the fundamental groundwork for dialogue about action, continuity, and language in human life. Self, he says, is abstracted from person. DeCharms assists us in carefully recognizing the characteristics that qualify the human being to be a person (those characteristics that are shared with other person-alities).

Joseph Margolis further discusses the necessity of a construct of continuity and intentionality in human studies. He argues against Davidson's (1984) program for eliminating meaning and reference beyond the syntactical terms of language. Margolis advocates a theory of "incarnate functionalism." Among his fourteen points for conceptualization of self (stressing the linguistic character of personal life), he states that "linguistic aptitude is emergent with respect to more fundamental biological capacities for species survival, and so a theory of language cannot but be a part of a more inclusive theory of human behavior and cognition vis-à-vis an environing world, within which one's linguistic community is a part but only a part" (pp. 61–62). Wrestling both the remnants of logical positivism in contemporary psychology and current influences of structuralism and linguistics, Margolis rescues a construct of self that unifies culture and biology as a consensually interpretive community of human behavior.

The remaining essays in this part, introduced under the topic of *consistency,* stress psychological concepts of self. They concern issues of stability and change as these characterize development in adolescence and psychotherapy. A primary experience in personal development is the tension between stability and change. Many people, both professionals and laypersons, believe that the hallmarks of unique individuality are set early in life and do not change. How can I remain the same person and still change? Augusto Blasi and Robert Oresick provide answers regarding the changing structures of self experiences (i.e., ethical and epistemological). Loevinger develops the metaphor of self as immunological system, a defensive emotional and cognitive structure, designed to protect stability and limit change. Finally, Peter Goldenthal introduces a language system that can be used by psychotherapists to describe stability and change in the process of psychotherapeutic intervention.

As psychologists have become skeptical of introspection and self-report as empirical evidence, and as philosophers have rejected Cartesian and Kantian formulations of self, they also have tended to eliminate systematic discussions of anything tinged with the more ephemeral and unobservable qualities of psyche. As Donald Spence (1983) reminds us, the very people who are most committed to dialogues about self and person (e.g., clinicians and educators) are often also the greatest enemies of innovative theory.

Regarding psychoanalytic clinicians, he writes:

> . . . . each of us is always constructing a private narrative out of recent and outstanding details of our clinical experience and weaving these details into a private theory which best accounts for our recent successes and failures. In building this narrative, we are always bending the concept to fit the facts, bending the earlier account to fit some later retelling, and wherever possible, smoothing and polishing the story to give it the greatest coherence and the best ges-

talt. . . . Private narrative thrives on minimizing the surprise and the unexpected; it is essentially conservative and
quite content to stay with old and outmoded concepts; and
it has no patience with a first-time event or an unexplained
symptom. Public theory, on the other hand, thrives on the
unexpected because it is only from what cannot be explained that we have grounds for forming new constructs
and getting on with our theoretical work. (p. 476)

The ethical psychotherapist, like the angry teenager arguing stubbornly with parental injunctions, has a vested interest in using explanations that are on hand to give a plausible account of her or his own
decisions and actions. "Minimizing the surprise and the unexpected"
will be the first desire in anyone's private or pragmatic approach to
the theory of self.

It is only at the point of dialogue about differences and the testing
of theories against evidence (probing for their usefulness for further
discoveries) that private narratives can be translated into public theories. The essays in this part provide a framework for such translations.

References

Davidson, D. (1984). *Inquiries into truth and interpretation.* Oxford: Clar-
    endon.
Gadamer, H.-G. (1985). *Truth and method.* New York: Crossroad.
Spence, D. (1983). Narrative persuasion. *Psychoanalysis and Contempo-
    rary Thought, 6,* 3, 457–81.

SELF AND NECESSITY

Personal Causation, Agency, and the Self

RICHARD deCHARMS

WHO WROTE this paper? I did. There is no question in my mind about who wrote it. I caused the words to be put together this way; I typed the words into the computer. I am a cause and I am a person. Therefore I am a personal cause.

Who originated the thoughts in this essay? That is a different matter altogether. I often have great ideas that I later find in books that I had read years before. Or I remember very clearly a passage from a certain author expressing an idea and when I find the passage the idea is different.

Thoughts, information, and the processes that go into them are hard to attribute absolutely. Concrete, observable actions and outcomes are easy to attribute. My ability to attribute specific thoughts to you is nil. But my ability to attribute the cause of an event to you is great (though not infallible). My ability to attribute a cause to myself is almost (but not quite) incorrigible. The difference between my attributing causal power to myself and my attributing it to you is what makes the self unique. You may wonder whether I wrote this essay or just copied it from an old journal. If you had observed my struggles throughout the writing you would have little doubt. I am absolutely certain that I wrote it, because I was present throughout the writing—not as an observer but as the personal causal agent. The "I" to which I refer is my "self."

Apparently, thoughts are harder to attribute to selves than is personal causal agency. I must conclude that

(1) personal causation is primary and thought is secondary;

(2) personal causation is the core of the self.

What follows is an attempt to describe what led me to these conclusions.

Inadequate Information Processing

To a large extent, psychology and "self theory" have concentrated recently on cognition and neglected motivation. Thus we find conceptions of the self as an information processor (Markus and Sentis, 1982), an image that has roots in information theory (Miller, 1953) and systems theory (Miller, Galanter, and Pribram, 1960), similar to the roots of Artificial Intelligence.

The self is not just an information processor. The self experiences emotions, it feels, it has motives, purposes, and intentions. There is a motivational aspect of the self. Yet the self is not just motivation either. Perception, cognition, and motivation all are wrapped up in action, action that is intended by the agency of self. A scientific concept of self must combine cognition and motivation. Self as a personal causal agent combines cognitive and motivational aspects to present a more complete, more adequate conception of self.

A scientific concept of self that does not encompass personal causation is inadequate. Put more strongly, to comprehend the meaning of selfhood we must understand the self as a personal causal agent.

Wilder Penfield's Contribution

As a result of his widely acclaimed research on direct stimulation of the cortex of human epileptic patients, Wilder Penfield began, as the evidence accumulated, to wonder what held together the bits and pieces, strands (Locke's "thread of . . . ," Kant's analytic unity of apperception), and threads of memory elicited by the electrode—what held them together in some kind of coherent whole for the patient him(her)*self*. It is an obvious place to use the word *self* for the unifying something. When, for instance, Penfield could artificially interfere with the function of the speech mechanism, the patient could recognize a picture (butterfly) but could not name it. The patient then reported searching for other words. When the inhibition of speech was lifted the patient said, "Butterfly. I couldn't *get* that word 'butterfly,' so I tried to *get* the word 'moth'!" (Penfield, 1975, p. 52). Penfield hypothesizes two underlying mechanisms, a "concept mechanism" and a "speech mechanism." When the "concept mechanism" recognized a butterfly in the "stream of consciousness" but the "speech mechanism" failed to produce the word, some higher-level process then searched for another concept. When Penfield removed the inhibition the higher-level process showed through in behavior, and Penfield observed, "*He* got the words from the speech mechanism when *he* presented concepts to it" (p. 53). Penfield substituted the word *mind* for the *he* and courts transcendentalism and mysticism. We could substitute the word *self* and court reification and hypostacization. Still, there is a human phenomenon to be accounted for.

Self as mechanism, or better yet, as electronic phenomenon, that stores, retrieves, and coordinates "bits of data," traces, stored in memory banks, is explicated quite nicely by analogy to a computer and involves nothing extracognitive, nothing more than information processing, nothing demanding some concept of motive or agency. Further evidence from Penfield, however, forces on us a realm of phenomena not easily accounted for by a computer analogy.

Not only could Penfield elicit memory traces and inhibit verbal responses, he could also produce verbal responses and cause a patient to move parts of the body (the hand) by stimulating the motor cortex. He found that these elicited "activities" were experienced in a peculiar way by the "actor"—that is, the patient. They were not experienced as voluntary acts at all. "Invariably the response was: 'I didn't do that. You did.' When I caused him to vocalize, he said, 'I didn't make that sound, you pulled it out of me'" (p. 76).

If we compare the elicited vocalization to the patient's statement describing it, we have the contrast between a response and an action as distinguished by Macmurray (1957) and the philosophers of action (see White, 1968, and Mischel, 1969). The difference is between the voluntary vocalization of a person, a self, and the involuntary noise produced in the vocal cords of the person by an outside source. Compare the electrode-elicited hand movement with an intended hand movement authored by the patient and we have a graphic demonstration of what Wittgenstein (1953) meant when he asked: "What is left over when I subtract the fact that my arm goes up from the fact that I raise my arm?" What is left over in all these cases is the intention and motivation, the personal causation of the agent. This is what Penfield could not find or produce in the cortex.

Penfield concludes from his review of years of such research that electrical stimulation "from diencephalon to spinal cord" (p. 77) can cause a patient to move, to vocalize, to recall vivid experiences. "But *he* remains aloof. *He* passes judgment on it all" (p. 77, emphasis mine). The "he" I take to be the person of him*self*.

But Penfield went on to postulate that throughout his patients' introspective reports ran references to "I" the person, the self, that were never elicited by the electrode. Penfield could only conclude that this higher-level "mind-action" could not be found, by this technique, in the brain. "There is *no* area of gray matter, as far as my experience goes, in which local epileptic discharge brings to pass what can be called 'mind-action' . . . none of the actions that we attribute to the mind has been initiated by electrode stimulation" (p. 78). Penfield feels compelled to postulate two components, mind and brain.

> During brain action a neurophysiologist can surmise where the conduction of potentials is being carried out and its pattern. It is not so in the case of what we have come to call mind-action. And yet the mind seems to act independently of the brain in the same sense that a programmer acts independently of his computer, however much he may depend upon the action of that computer for certain purposes. (pp. 79–80)

Penfield finds himself uncomfortably taking a dualistic position (mind-brain) on what is basically a philosophical question. For our purposes, we will try to avoid the philosophical and stick to more clearly psychological issues. The psychologically present consciousness of an entity, a unity, a person, a self, though it contains memories and other cognitive phenomena that can be seen as analogs of computer function, contains something more, something "higher-level," something more primitive, more primary. The something is more agentlike, more motivational, more programmerlike; it is less cognitive, less programlike, with characteristics that are completely absent in either hardware or software. The computer analogy leaves us looking for the electricity and the programmer; the information-processing explanation of human behavior leaves us without motivation and agency. We have lost in the analogy the difference between behavior and action (Macmurray, 1957), between the arm going up and being voluntarily raised (Wittgenstein, 1953); we have lost the personal causal *self*.

The Primacy of Personal Causation

We are searching, then, for some primary, primitive central core of self, experienced in consciousness, that provides the unity, the organization, the direction, the intention, even the energy of action. But we are in danger of veering away from the monster Scylla just to be sucked into the whirlpool of Charybdis, and indeed emotional, motivational explanations have the force and danger of a whirlpool. Information processing is necessary but not sufficient for our understanding of the self.

Agent and *agency* are terms used (see, e.g., Macmurray, 1957, Harré, 1979, 1984) for a concept very similar to personal causation. I chose personal causation because (1) it restricts the concept to persons, (2) it has no implication of a little person (homunculus) hiding inside the person who does the causing, and (3) it explicitly restricts the search for the cause of action to a person and excludes a physical phenomenon or mechanism. An agent, on the other hand, is defined as "a person *or thing* that performs actions" (emphasis mine)—for instance, a chemical agent—or "a person . . . empowered to act for another." Is the self as agent empowered to act for the person? No.

Of great importance to our experience of self is our consciousness of the causal source of events. It makes a real difference, for example, whether a person is building a boat for his own pleasure, for the money he will get by selling it, or as a slave forced to work without compensation. Experience of self as a personal cause, in contrast with other people as personal causes or things as impersonal causes, is an everyday occurrence that helps to explain our actions. The contrast between self and other as cause is also a deep-seated, primitive distinction that is learned before the acquisition of more sophisticated cognitive discriminations based on verbal distinctions. Personal causation, experienced as either mine (self) or yours (other), determines the course of interaction and interdependence between me and you, my self and your self.

The above paragraph paraphrases one from Heider (1958):

> Of great importance for our picture of the social environment is the attribution of events to causal sources. It makes a real difference, for example, whether a person discovers that the stick that struck him fell from a rotting tree or was

> hurled by an enemy. Attribution in terms of impersonal
> and personal causes, and with the latter, in terms of intent,
> are everyday occurrences that determine much of our
> understanding of and reaction to our surroundings. . . .
> Also, one person can cause another person to cause a
> change by asking him to do something, or commanding
> him, etc. (p. 16)

The point of Heider's paragraph, which contains one of the original uses of the concept of personal causation (see also Kelley, 1971), is to distinguish it from *im*personal causation. This is the well-known distinction that formed the cornerstone of attribution theory. The point of my paraphrased paragraph is to suggest that a more primitive, developmentally prior, fundamentally more basic distinction is that between self-causation and other-causation. We are able to attribute personal causation to others and to distinguish personal causation from impersonal causation only after we have learned to distinguish other-causation from self-causation.

> Knowledge derives originally from sense perception.
> First we learn by feeling and then, in addition, by doing.
> At first the baby must learn to distinguish himself from
> other things and other people. The very small baby does
> not know that his foot is his, and may treat it rather badly—
> he puts it in his mouth and bites it. He senses immediately
> that something is wrong, and it does not take many repe-
> titions for him to stop biting.
> Another object in the environment, mother's breast, does
> not produce discomfort when bitten. Somehow it is differ-
> ent. Slowly the child discovers that, although his foot and
> mother's breast can both be looked at, tasted, and felt with
> his lips, he does not experience the subjective sensation
> from mother's breast of being bitten while he is biting.
> (deCharms, 1968, p. 258)

In a purely quantitative way, a baby has more sources of input when he bites his own foot than when he bites his mother's breast. In a meaningful yet elusive sense, he becomes conscious, in the first case (case 1), of himself both as agent of the act of biting and as object of being bitten. In the latter case (case 2), biting mother, he is the agent, with all its attendant active experiences, but not the object, with its passive receptive experience. Should the mother playfully (and one would hope, gently) bite the child's foot (case 3), he would have the reciprocal experience of case 2 (biting mother), with the attendant lack of self-causation but the passive experience of submitting to other-causation. But there is a fourth case: being acted upon by an impersonal object. To make the case clear and to maintain consistency with our example, we have to postulate that the baby has a mechanical toy dog—an object that can also bite his foot. Somewhere in the developmental (reciprocal, interdependent) scheme of things the baby will learn to distinguish between his mother's personal-causal-intentional biting and a mechanical toy's impersonal biting where no intention is attributed. There is, of course, an even more subtle distinction (call it case 3½) between mother's intentional biting and her accidental, unintentional biting.

Clearly the child learns to make all these distinctions early, for any normal adult can distinguish between biting himself; biting mother; being bitten by an angry other person; being bitten accidentally by a person; being bitten by a mad dog, a playful dog, a rattlesnake, a mosquito; or being caught in the jaws of a mechanical animal trap. We say a person learns to make these distinctions, assuming that they are not innate ideas with which human beings are born, although it is clear that persons must have the equipment to achieve the end before they can begin learning. Perhaps, for instance, a severely mentally retarded person never learns the distinctions.

> Countless material bodies may be observed by a given subject to be in, or to come into, contact with others; but there is only one body of which it is true that when that body is a party to such a situation of "establishing contact," then the subject normally has those experiences to which he alludes when he speaks of *feeling* some material body or other. The subject *feels* the dagger or the feather only when the dagger enters, or the feather lightly brushes, *this* body. . . . We may summarize such facts by saying that for each person there is one body which occupies a certain *causal* position in relation to that person's perceptual experience, a causal position which in various ways is unique . . . (Strawson, 1959, pp. 86–87)

Table 1–1   Agent and Recipient Actions

	Action	
	Done by	*Done to*
Case 1	Self (Self Agent)	Self (Recipient)
Case 2	Self (Self Agent)	Other Person (Recipient)
Case 3	Other Person (Other Agent) (Intentional)	Self (Recipient)
Case 3½	Other Person (Other Agent) (Not Intentional)	Self (Recipient)
Case 4	Physical Object (No Agent) (Not Intentional)	Self (Recipient)

Table 1.1 attempts to lay out the cases for quick reference. Note that self is involved as either agent or recipient or both in every case. These are the only cases involving self-experience.

If we assign primacy to self over other, to agent over recipient, to personal other over impersonal other (physical object), then the cases descend in primacy from case 1 to case 4. The fundamental assumptions underlying my position concerning personal causation are contained in the above statements. An adequate understanding of human action must take into account these assumptions. It must assume that agency is more fundamental than recipiency, that self is more fundamental than other, that personal others are more fundamental than impersonal objects. These are motivational assumptions applicable to understanding what we mean by self, but beyond that they are fundamental to the psychology of human action. The stress on the distinction between self and other in the experience of personal causation (self-causation) is what distinguishes my position from Heider's, from attribution theorists' (Jones and Nisbett, 1971; Kelley, 1971; Weiner, 1980; Weiner, Russell, and Lerman, 1979) and even from Bandura's (1982), despite his concept of self-efficacy.

Other Minds, Other Agents

As you sit reading this essay, suppose that I snatched the book out of your hands. Would you stop to wonder who caused the interruption in your reading? Of course not. Having physically experienced (as well as observed) my action, you would be absolutely certain that I did it. You immediately would know something about me as a causal agent directly. Examples containing some physical contact make this point most clearly. I jostle you out of line at a ticket office or shove you suddenly out of the path of a speeding automobile. You know me as the cause of your annoyance or your gratitude. You know immediately that I did it.

Why did I snatch your book or shove you? That involves my thoughts and, as we saw above, thoughts are another matter altogether. You cannot know my thoughts in any way directly or immediately. So again, in your knowledge of other "selves" their personal causation is primary, their thoughts are secondary. The philosopher's conundrum of the problem of other minds may still be puzzling—"What was he thinking that he pushed me?"—but that I pushed you is indubitable.

> Contemporary philosophers have exercised themselves with the problem of our knowledge of other minds. Enmeshed in the dogma of the ghost in the machine, they have found it impossible to discover any logically satisfactory evidence warranting one person in believing that there exist minds other than his own. (Ryle, 1949, p. 60)

This is the now classic statement of the "problem of other minds." Ryle argues that modern Western philosophy, with its roots in Plato and Aristotle but usually assumed to be most influenced by Descartes, incorporates a dualistic assumption, mind versus body, the ghost in the machine, that creates the problem of other minds—how do I know that you think since all I can observe is your behavior? The argument is that one person's thought, emotions, motives, intentions are totally private and hidden from another person's view. Such psychological states are private. According to Ryle, if we start with the radical separation of mind and body proposed by Descartes and the root of controversy in modern philosophy ever since, we end up logically committed to solipsism—the position that I cannot know that other minds, hence other selves or persons, exist. "I can witness what your body does, but I cannot witness what your mind does, and my pretensions to infer from what your body does to what your mind does all collapse" (p. 60).

We have seen Penfield confront the ghost, the higher-level something that he was forced to separate from the machinelike gray matter of the brain to account for the patient's "I" who did not move "my" hand or make that sound. Information-processing theories of psychology and of "self" can easily account, as we said above, for memories, storage, and so on, but to account for human action they resort to ghostlike higher-level concepts, such as "scripts" that cannot be seen and are not directly present in most introspective reports—and are inferences just like "other minds" (see Schank and Abelson, 1970, and Rommetveit, 1976). Personal causation as the central core of "self" avoids the ghostly problems by combining intentions as part and parcel of actions, and we experience actions, both our own and those of others, directly. We must guard against assuming that intentions are somehow hidden behind actions and inaccessible. They are usually manifest in the action; they are the action. But the most important difference between what we are saying and what has gone before is as follows: We do not learn about other people's emotions, motives, intentions by observing them. Rather, *we learn by acting,* by interacting with others, by shoving back. For me to act, someone or thing must be acted upon. For me to sell my boat, someone must buy my boat. Acting on things (painting my boat) tells me nothing about other selves. But interacting with other persons tells me directly about their actions and their intentions. There is a subtle distinction here that has revolutionary implications in the Kuhnian sense (Kuhn, 1970). We must try to spell this out more clearly and contrast it with most current thought implicit in information-processing theories, attribution theories, and indeed, most theories of psychology. Action is primary, thought is secondary; doing primary, observing secondary. Active learning involves the actor directly acted upon. Passive observation attempts to remove the observer.

The methodology of psychology dictates that the investigator remove himself from the phenomena and passively observe. The goal is to learn that so and so occurs. Knowledge (from learning) is equated with how to think about the phenomena. Active learning is quite different: its goal is to learn how to do something. In the old tradition, thought is primary. In active learning, action—"I do," to quote Macmurray (1957)—is primary; thought, and cognitive knowledge, are secondary. Doing is primary, observing is secondary. To find out about another person you act, primarily, and experience (possibly even observe) the other person's *reaction.* If I shove you, you shove back, and the result tells you of my intention. Do I persist or give way and apologize? A critical aspect is the reciprocality. To learn to act we must act on something. To learn about other persons (selves) we must act (as an agent), they must respond (as recipient), and they must act (as agent) and we respond (as recipient). It's like a good argument or chess game. We learn about the other, we learn his or her motives and intentions, directly by the opposition to our actions, motives, and intentions. We cannot understand selves without committing our "self" to action vis-à-vis at least one other. If I push, someone else must resist, otherwise pushing didn't occur. If I push an argument, it is always predicated on the assumption that some other will resist it.

Chess is a good example (Ryle's favorite) if you look at two players who are both acting. But notice, Ryle takes the example of an observer of a game and says that the observer can know what the goals, intentions, and purposes of the players are without inference to some ghost, *if the observer knows how to play.* But where did he learn to know relevant goals for chess? By playing with another person. By doing it himself, not observing. (For an excellent example of the development of agency in interaction between mother and child see Bruner, 1983).

So far we have sketched several diverse notions that point to the centrality of personal causation, agency, in our concept of the self. Apparently our scheme of things contains a concept of self, and central to it is personal causation. We have not, as yet, confronted the meaning of the word *self*.

How Can We Establish the Meaning of the Word Self?

For the most part scientific psychology, following the classic announcement by Stevens (1935) of operationalism (Bridgman, 1959), has considered operational definitions the bedrock of meaning. When a concept is needed, like length, that is not a thing to be pointed to, we solve the definitional problem by describing the operation involved in arriving at precise agreement—number of centimeters measured by a standard stick at the Bureau of Standards. This kind of definition can also be applied to observable behaviors—number of bar presses, number of drops of saliva, number of checks on a questionnaire, number of times a couple makes eye-to-eye contact. Some have assumed that ultimately, in principle, we will be able to reduce concepts like "self" to a countable set of behaviors.

Bridgman (1959) has offered us two types of operations—mental and physical. In verifying that X has a toothache, when X is self, use mental operations; when X is other, use physical operations, that is, observation. But this begs the question of the self. Can we verify that X is the self by one operation and that X is other by another? There must be some category prior to self/other to which both belong, namely, the concept of person. But person is not something that we can operationally define either.

Humanistic psychologists (Rogers, 1961, Maslow, 1968) have suggested that it is absurd to try to reduce "self" to specific behaviors. Self is somehow defined or known, not from objective observation but from subjective or personal knowledge (Polanyi, 1958). The problem with humanistic psychology is that we are told that we all know what *self* means, as in self-actualization, but we are not told how we know it. This is not very satisfactory for scientific purposes.

Accepting that we need to use such words as *self* and at the same time trading on the more scientifically respectable approach of objective observation, attribution and self-perception theories have attempted to have their cake and eat it too. Self is an inference that we all make from observing our own behavior just the way we observe others and they observe us. Some theorists emphasize the importance of others in our concept of self. You cannot really start with the isolated self and ever hope to reach other selves. But at the same time there is something absurd in assuming that I know myself exactly the way I know you or you know me (Bem, 1967). The immediacy of self-knowledge eludes us in the apparent objective rigor of self-perception and deludes us in the solipsistic Cartesian position that starts with the "I." How can we avoid the elusion and the illusion of self?

The upshot of this argument is that the meaning of words like *self, agency, action, personal causation,* and so on cannot be operationally defined either by mental operations (something like introspection) or by physical operations. They are contained within the structure of our ways of communicating—our language, our everyday scheme of things that we more or less agree upon as a basis for adequate communication.

A psychology adequate to include concepts like "self" must discipline itself in the use of words attributed uniquely to persons not by defining but by exploring the logic of how we use them and the way we learn to use them and their logic—the "forms of life," as Wittgenstein (1953) would say; the "architecture of intersubjectivity," as Rommetveit (1976) would say; the "scheme of things," as Strawson (1959) would say.

In short, we must aspire to a scientific rigor in the use of the word *self* by placing it in the context of an analysis of the logic of how we use it. Only then will we be able to relate it, and other such person-attribute words, to the empirically observable facts of interaction and interdependence between persons. We must resolve what Macmurray (1957) called the crisis of the personal, namely, the logic of the form of the personal. We will not do this by trying to define self operationally. "Rather conceptual clarification is a prerequisite for efficient experimentation" (Heider, 1958, p. 4).

We have worked hard on our methodology of experimentation and measurement but have ignored the methodology of conceptual clarification. The one exception is Heider's brief foray into "naive" psychology. Some of the descendants of this attempt, working on attribution theory, have proposed ad hoc schemes and immediately set out to demonstrate their schemes empirically. Thus Jones and Davis (1965) distinguish between actors and observers, Weiner (1980) distinguishes between internal/external and stable/unstable sources, and Kelley (1971) analyzes sources of variance observed by people in their worlds.

What these theorists have touched only slightly is the rigor of the logic of the form of attribution. We need to identify distinctions that we do make, such as the attribution of locus of causality. Some rules are needed to specify what Ossorio (1966) has called an adequate description of persons; that is, on the one hand we need enough distinctions for an adequate account, but on the other hand the number of concepts must conform to a principle of parsimony. As a result, the second needed step is to investigate the generality and fundamentality of concepts in a hierarchy so as not to make category mistakes (Ryle, 1949) or proliferate terms interminably.

By generality we mean that the concept would pertain to the largest possible segment of the universe under consideration. By fundamentality we mean that the concept should, in principle, support a wide range of other ideas so that if the fundamental concept is questioned many other ideas will be questioned in consequence, whereas questioning the other ideas does not touch the more fundamental concept. As an example, the concept "things" in general is a more fundamental concept than either living or nonliving things because it contains both living and nonliving things. Finally, as a third step, the logical structure of what characteristics apply to what categories forms the rigor of the conceptualization. When the logic of the conceptualization has been worked out we can avoid collecting data to demonstrate analytic propositions that must be true, such as "all bachelors are unmarried" (Ossorio and Davis, 1968). More important, we will have a rigorous conceptualization upon which to base our empirical research.

Toward an Adequate Conceptualization of Self, Person, and Personal Causation

Is "self" a fundamental concept? Is it more or less fundamental than "person"? If the word *self* has a unique use, then scientific psychology should be concerned to find the place of "self" in the structure of psychological concepts. The first step is to investigate what distinctions we can and do make. Is "self" an important category? Is there a hierarchy of concepts? Does "self" have a unique position in this hierarchy?

At the simplest level we can all distinguish among an object that is subject to mechanical laws, like a rock; a machine that runs on mechanical principles, like an automobile; a machine that runs on electronic principles, like a computer; an organism that runs on biophysical principles, like a pigeon; an organism to which we attribute something called consciousness, like a person; and a person with all the above characteristics whose consciousness I experience directly— namely, self.

But this list is not of separate categories. True, an organism is not a rock, but an organism is subject to the laws of physics. In moving from rock to person we have listed items in ascending order of complexity. Perhaps we should try reducing to the least complex concept. On the principle of parsimony, entities should not be multiplied more than necessary (*entia non sunt multiplicanda praeter necissatatem*). Logical positivism suggests that we reduce all science, in principle, to the laws of physics. If this is taken to imply that all the items on our list can be reduced to rocks or even, in principle, to the laws of physics it is manifestly absurd.

Another rule of logic suggests that with regard to a general-particular distinction the more general concept is the more fundamental one (Beardsley and Beardsley, 1965). As to the entities in our list, we might argue that the entity that contains the most properties is the most fundamental and the entity that contains the fewest properties is the least fundamental. By this criterion our list is in order of increasing fundamentality, because a person is subject to physical laws *and* biophysical laws and has consciousness, whereas a rock is only subject to physical laws. Macmurray (1957) used this order in his attempt to capture the logic of the form of the personal.

The inevitable question that arises when lists of this sort are made is, "What is the difference between persons and other organisms?" That is the wrong question. The critical question for the scientist is, "What is the difference between persons studying other persons and persons studying nonperson organisms or things?" The simple answer is obvious—the difference is that the scientist and the entity under study are both of the same class in the one case and not in the other. And this is unique as far as we know, unless unbeknownst to us some "scientist" porpoises are studying us (persons) objectively and also studying other porpoises.

There are, therefore, at least two guiding principles for the scientific study of persons: (1) "Person" is the fundamental primary concept that cannot, in principle, be reduced to organism or object (although its organismic and objectlike properties can be studied). (2) The scientific study of persons is different because of the relationship between the scientist and the entity being studied.

By now you will have noticed that my list runs in order from rock to self but that I have discussed "person" as fundamental and ignored "self." In fact, I will argue that "person" is more fundamental than "self." To do this we must investigate two distinctive characteristics of persons.

Two prime candidates for unique attributes of persons are (1) consciousness and (2) personal causal agency. When I jostle you out of line, the criterion that you use to attribute personal causal agency to me is my consciousness of jostling. Did I know that I did it? To attribute personal causation one must also attribute consciousness. Consciousness is implied by personal causation. Therefore, consciousness is secondary, personal causation primary. Personal causation is the more fundamental concept. The argument is parallel to that used above to distinguish personal causation from thought. Internal locus of causality is attributable to other organisms as well as persons, even organisms as humble as caterpillars, to which observers attributed "immanent" causality in Michotte's (1963) laboratory. Strictly speaking, we appear to attribute consciousness only to persons. Locus of causality for behavior appears attributable to other organisms as well. You can attribute "shoving" to an animal, hence attribute an internal locus of causality. Can you attribute altruism? Did the ape shove you out of the path of the speeding car to save your life? The crux of the *difference* between internal locus of causality and personal causation is the difference between an ape shoving you and a person shoving you. You can be much surer of the person than of the ape *because you are a person.* There is a unique relationship between you and another person, an interdependence and reciprocality that you can never have with an ape.

You might argue that our knowledge of an ape's "personal" causation is, in principle, the same as our knowledge of a person's. Many researchers and animal-lovers attribute intentional actions and emotional meaning to animals, especially the higher primates. Perhaps some animals have a kind of consciousness similar to persons, but why study vestiges of personal causation in nonpersons when we can study it directly in persons? I take the goal of psychology to be to understand persons, not apes. Why increase the danger of misattribution by studying organisms whose consciousness is certainly different from that of persons? We can answer the question "What is it like to be a person?" much more assuredly than "What is it like to be an ape?"

So again personal causation is more fundamental than consciousness, because personal causation implies consciousness. Consciousness can most safely be attributed to persons. But we attribute personal causation to persons and to self. Can we avoid the trap of assuming that we attribute it to others *because* we attribute it to ourselves? The answer hinges on our resolution of the relative fundamentality of person versus self.

Which Is More Fundamental: Person or Self?

At the most basic level we are concerned with how we can identify and communicate about different things in the world. By identify, we mean how one person can be sure that another person knows what is meant or is being talked about. Most important for our purposes is how we distinguish between persons and things, and then between self and other persons. We can attribute physical aspects, corporeal states, to both things and persons, but there is a class of attributes, call them "person attributes," that we only attribute to persons. Some person attributes are corporeal—she has red hair. But so does a red fox. The unique and distinctive person attributes imply consciousness. Although we may want to attribute consciousness to animals it is really only safe to do so with persons. We cannot really know what it is like to be a bat. For purposes of what follows, then, consciousness means person consciousness. *Persons are those bodies in the world to whom we attribute both person characteristics (those that imply consciousness) and physical characteristics (corporeal descriptions).* We learn to attribute characteristics to things and persons and to use names for them in childhood. At first blush it seems that there are two sources of learning: (1) learning by observation and (2) learning by experience. I learn what red hair is by observing it. I learn what pain is by experiencing it.

Here I want to give a slightly new meaning to the old distinction made originally by Koffka (1935, p. 80) between proximal and distal. I will use the term *distal observation* for the evidence for attribution to others as well as to self and the term *proximal experience* for that unique class of evidence for attribution to self. Proximal experience *cannot ever be* evidence, even by inference, for attribution to others.

This gives us a logically interlocking schema that singles out persons as the primary term and at the same time uses persons as those entities to which can be attributed both consciousness (person characteristics) and objectiveness (physical-corporeal characteristics). Animals and objects are exempt from consciousness and, therefore, from person characteristics.

(1) We attribute physical-corporeal characteristics to self and others on the basis of distal observation only. I can observe that I have red hair just as I can observe that you have a certain hair color. But I have no proximal experience of redheadedness.

(3) We attribute person characteristics to others on the basis of distal observation only. I see you holding your jaw and looking up a dentist's phone number. I attribute to you a toothache (Bridgman's [1959] example).

(3) We attribute some person characteristics to self on the basis of

distal observation. Having reviewed the facts of my past behavior, I now realize that I showed all the classic symptoms of depression although at the time I was unaware of it.

(4) But we attribute *some* person characteristics to self on a basis of *other than* distal observation, on the basis of what I have called proximal-immediate experience. Bridgman's classic example of the toothache shows the difference between proximal-immediate experience (it hurts me) and the evidence for your toothache that I cited above in (2).

We now have the schema for identifying what we mean by self—it is that entity to which we (1) can attribute personal characteristics by proximal-immediate experience. That, of course, is my self. Selves, in general, will be taken to be identical with "persons" as identified above.

This conception has the double advantage of being both logically consistent *and* commensurate with the commonsense, everyday way we as laymen (persons) use the ideas and language about persons and self.

We are now confronted with the classic example of private knowledge about pain and public knowledge about objective characteristics. Assuming the classic distinction between things and consciousness we are about to fall into a trap. I experience a toothache. I observe myself engaging in certain behaviors, including looking in the phone book for a dentist. I see you looking in the phone book at dentists. Ergo I infer that you have a toothache. Is this the only way that I can learn about consciousness in you and other persons?

This classical schema implies several separate things: (1) there is one process of learning private meanings of self-characteristics; (2) somehow I correlate this type of private learning with observations of my own behavior; (3) I observe similar behavior in you; (4) I infer that you have the same private meanings that I have.

But this is not all. It is also assumed that there are two other reciprocal processes: (1) I observe a certain set of behaviors in you; (2) you attribute them to characteristic X; (3) I observe a similar set of behaviors in myself; (4) ergo, by inference I must have characteristic X. For example, she was apathetic, a syndrome that she named clinical depression. On observing the syndrome in myself I infer, on those grounds alone, that I am clinically depressed.

The trap is the assumed leap of inference (faith) from my private sensation to my public behavior or the other way round, from your public behavior to an inference to your private sensation. Another part of the trap is the assumption that I know about myself and you in different ways. The trap leads to the irrelevant question: How do I know that your toothache feels like mine?

These assumptions make it sound as if I actually go through some absurd process of wondering, "Do I have a toothache?" and asking, "What do I do to find out?" This is absurd when applied to me, but quite reasonable when I want to know whether you actually have a toothache or are malingering to get out of work. To ask myself whether I have a toothache is like asking whether I have two hands. Normally, I *cannot* find out that I have two hands. "'But all you need is to hold them up before your eyes!'—If I am *now* in doubt whether I have two hands, I need not believe my eyes either. (I might just as well ask a friend.)" (Wittgenstein, 1953, p. 221).

Strawson (1959) has suggested a solution to this problem. We do not learn all these things separately and then put them together by inference. We learn them all at once. As children we learn how to attribute person characteristics to self and to others not separately but at the same time and by interaction with others. There is not one separate process of learning private meanings of self characteristics and then noting their correlation with one's own behavior and then another process of inferring similar characteristics to others when they display similar behavior; nor is there a separate process of applying a person characteristic to others on the basis of their behavior and then another process of applying the person characteristics to self by observing one's own behavior. To learn to use person characteristics is to learn to attribute them both to self and to others at the same time in interaction between self and others. If person characteristics were not of this sort then there would be no problem of what self is, but at the same time there would be no concept of persons as different from other animals (see Strawson, 1959, pp. 104–05).

Table 1.2 presents the discussion above in summary form. It highlights the most important fact that I attribute some identical person characteristics to self on the basis of immediate proximal experience and to you on the basis of distal observation only. The toothache example inevitably raises the issue of why and how I can attribute the same characteristic to me on one basis and to you on an entirely different one. Is your ache the same as mine? My evidence for your ache

Table 1–2   Attribution of Person Characteristics

	Characteristic	
	Person	Physical
Attributed to:		
Self	By observations By other than observation	By observation only
Other	By observation only	By observation only

is only circumstantial and not intrinsically part of it. This classic example leads us toward dualism of consciousness behavior, and all the problems of private experience and private language that we want to avoid.

Strawson (1959) has also suggested that there is a special person attribute that, so to speak, is both private and public. It is the attribution that a person is *doing something.* Strawson did not spell this kind of person attribute out in detail. Let us pursue his lead.

The Attribution of Personal Causation

Having presented the arguments that we have summarized in table 1.2, let us address the problem of personal causal agency by distinguishing a special class of person characteristics that involve doing something.

Let us move the attribution that someone is doing something to a central position. These "X does Y" attributions are of the type attributed to others on the basis of distal observation and to self by distal observation *and* by proximal experience. They are not aches, feelings, itches, and so on, but they also seem unique in that "one feels minimal reluctance to concede that what is [attributed] in these two different ways is the same" (Strawson, 1959, p. 108).

There are two striking characteristics unique to both "I do" and "you do" attributions. First, they have a public quality in being observable patterns of behavior, yet they are not, at the same time, a specific series of responses. If I am opening the door, I may do it with my right or left hand or even my foot. There is no one way to do it, but there is an observable pattern no matter how it is done. Second, any distinctive sensation or feeling is conspicuously absent. There is no distinctive "opening a door" feeling; the individual sensations are combinations found recombined in other cases of doing "the same thing." We have discovered the class of person characteristics that subvert dualism, that can easily be attributed to self without attempting to consult some inner private feeling (sensation, pain, drive, need, urge), and that at the same time can be observed in others without inferring their private experience.

The components of "doing" are the primary person characteristics, *and* the purpose or goal of action. They also describe personal causation (deCharms, 1968). In 1968 I tried to avoid the horns of the dualistic dilemma. On the one hand, I rejected the idea of personal causation as a drive or need; I tried to mechanize motivation in general with the concept of "affective mediating mechanisms," following a trend then current in learning theory, especially in Mowrer (1960) and early McClelland (McClelland, Atkinson, Clark, and Lowell, 1953). Yet I found these mechanisms inadequate. Personal causation turned out to be a characteristic that we can attribute to others on the basis of observation (an external-from-us yet, at the same time, personal locus of causality), and yet we can attribute it to ourselves *not* on the basis of observation but on the basis of a proximal-immediate experience. A proximal-immediate experience is not to be confused with a feeling or a perception, because it is neither an observation of one's self (if you stop to observe yourself while doing a skilled performance like landing an airplane or sailing a boat in heavy wind you will probably crash or capsize) nor a distinctive sensation or set thereof; it is not a feeling of innervation or a drive or a cognized intention. As Strawson points out, we don't see others doing movements. We see action. We don't either see or feel (perceive) our selves doing behavior; we experience ourselves involved in ongoing action. As I have argued elsewhere (1968, 1976), when we experience our actions as a sequence directed primarily by ourselves, the effects, in physical terms and on ourselves, will be different from when we experience our actions as a sequence directed primarily by some other person. This is the empirical benchmark of personal causation.

Such a guiding conceptualization has led to empirical confirmation (deCharms 1968, 1976, 1983), yet it has been logically incoherent in using unanalyzed terms—specifically *self* in attributing the locus of causality and *person* in the general category to which a special kind of causation is attributed. We now have a more coherent basis for using *self* (that to which can be attributed person characteristics on the basis of both distal observation and proximal-immediate experience) and *person* (the primitive concept of those entities in the world to which we attribute both consciousness [person characteristics] and corporeal descriptions [physical characteristics]).

Summary

Personal causation is the core of both the "self" and the "person" concepts. The primary concept is "persons," of which "self" is a subset.

Drawing heavily on the writings of Peter Strawson, we distinguished between "self" and "persons" as follows:

(1) "Persons" are those bodies in the world to whom we can attribute the person characteristic of personal causation, as well as physical characteristics.

(2) "Self" is that person in the world to whom we can attribute person characteristics by direct immediate experience.

The classic attempt to infer experience of others from their behavior was wrongheaded. It equated experience with sensation (e.g., pain) and tried to infer it from behavior. Personal causation (personally caused actions) typically has no unique sensation or behavior pattern, yet we can experience it directly in ourselves and also observe it directly in other persons without inference. We learn to attribute personal causation to ourselves and to others at the same time in the same way—in interdependent interaction with other persons by acting as a personal cause against the resistance of other persons acting as personal causes.

References

Bandura, A. (1982). The self and mechanisms of agency. In J. Suls (Ed.), *Psychological perspectives on the self*. Hillsdale, N.J.: Erlbaum.

Beardsley, M. C., and Beardsley, E. L. (1965). *Philosophical thinking*. New York: Harcourt, Brace and World.

Bem, D. J. (1967). Self perception: An alternative interpretation of cognitive dissonance phenomena. *Psychological Review, 74*, 183–200.

Bridgman, P. W. (1959). *The way things are.* Cambridge: Harvard University Press.

Bruner, J. (1983). *Child's talk: Learning to use language.* New York: W. W. Norton.

deCharms, R. (1968). *Personal causation.* New York: Academic press.

———. (1976). *Enhancing motivation.* New York: Irvington.

———. (1983). Motivation enhancement in educational settings. In R. E. Ames and C. Ames (Eds.), *Research on motivation in education.* Vol. 1. New York: Academic Press.

Harré, R. (1979). *Social being: A theory for social psychology.* Totowa, N.J.: Rowman and Littlefield.

———. (1984). *Personal being: A theory for individual psychology.* Cambridge: Harvard University Press.

Heider, F. (1958). *The psychology of interpersonal relations.* New York: Wiley.

Jones, E. E., and Davis, K. E. (1965). From acts to dispositions: The attribution process in person perception. In L. Berkowitz (Ed.), *Advances in experimental social psychology.* Vol. 2. New York: Academic Press.

———, and Nisbett, R. E. (1971). The actor and the observer: Divergent perceptions of the causes of behavior. In E. E. Jones, D. E. Kanouse, H. H. Kelley, R. E. Nisbett, S. Valins, and B. Weiner (Eds.), *Attribution: Perceiving the causes of behavior.* Morristown, N.J.: General Learning Press.

Kelley, H. H. (1971). Causal schemata and the attribution process. In E. E. Jones, D. E. Kanouse, H. H. Kelley, R. E. Nisbett, S. Valins, and B. Weiner (Eds.), *Attribution: Perceiving the causes of behavior.* Morristown, N.J.: General Learning Press.

Koffka, K. (1935). *Principles of gestalt psychology.* New York: Harcourt Brace.

Kuhn, T. S. (1970). *The structrure of scientific revolutions.* Chicago: University of Chicago Press.

Macmurray, J. (1957). *Self as agent.* New York: Harper.

Markus, H., and Sentis, K. (1982). The self in social information processing. In J. Suls (Ed.), *Psychological perspectives on the self.* Hillsdale, N.J.: Erlbaum.

Maslow, A. H. (1968). *Toward a psychology of being.* 2nd ed. New York: Van Nostrand Reinhold.

McClelland, D. C., Atkinson, J. W., Clark, R. A., and Lowell, E. L.

(1953). *The achievement motive.* New York: Appleton-Century-Crofts.

Michotte, A. (1963). *The perception of causality.* New York: Basic Books.

Miller, G. A. (1953). What is information measurement? *American Psychologist, 8,* 3–11.

———, Galanter, E. H., and Pribram, K. (1960). *Plans and the structure of behavior.* New York: Holt, Rinehart and Winston.

Mischel, T. (Ed.). (1969). *Human action.* New York: Academic Press.

Mowrer, O. H. (1960). *Learning theory and the symbolic processes.* New York: Wiley.

Ossorio, P. G. (1966). *Persons.* Boulder, Colo.: Linguistic Research Institute, Report #3.

———, and Davis, K. E. (1968). The self, intentionality, and reactions to evaluations of the self. In C. Gordon and K. J. Gergen (Eds.), *The self in social interaction.* New York: Wiley.

Penfield, W. (1975). *The mystery of the mind.* Princeton: Princeton University Press.

Polanyi, M. (1958). *Personal knowledge.* Chicago: University of Chicago Press.

Rogers, C. R. (1961). *On becoming a person.* Boston: Houghton Mifflin.

Rommetveit, R. (1976). On the architecture of intersubjectivity. In L. H. Strickland, F. A. Abund, and K. J. Gergen (Eds.), *Social psychology in transition.* New York: Plenum.

Rychlak, J. F. (1975). Psychological science as a humanist views it. In J. R. Arnold (Ed.), *Nebraska symposium on motivation.* Lincoln: University of Nebraska Press.

Ryle, G. (1949). *The concept of mind.* New York: Barnes and Noble.

Schank, R. C., and Abelson, R. P. (1970). *Scripts, plans, goals and understanding.* Hillsdale, N.J.: Erlbaum.

Stevens, S. S. (1935). The operational definition of psychological concepts. *Psychological Review, 42,* 511–27.

Strawson, P. (1959). *Individuals.* Garden City, N.Y.: Anchor.

Weiner, B. (1980). *Human motivation.* New York: Holt, Rinehart and Winston.

———, Russell, D., and Lerman, D. (1979). The cognitive-emotion process in achievement-related context. *Journal of Personality and Social Psychology, 37,* 1211–20.

White, A. R. (Ed.). (1968). *The philosophy of action.* Oxford: Oxford University Press.

Wittgenstein, L. (1953). *Philosophical investigations.* 3rd ed. New York: Macmillan.

———. (1982). *Last writings on philosophy and psychology.* Vol. 1. Chicago: University of Chicago Press.

CHAPTER 2

Eliminating Selves in the Psychological Sciences

JOSEPH MARGOLIS

I

WHEN WE THINK of human beings functioning as selves, we must admit how irresistible it is to think of their deliberate interventions in nature and the affairs of men, their technical inventions, purposive actions, projects held in mind, experience and use of feelings and physical energies, explicit and implicit reference to the things of the world through speech and behavior, and awareness of their own cognitive aptitude. The idiom of "selves" is at once noticeably odd and familiar—perhaps because we are so much a mystery to ourselves and because the physical sciences (and theories of science centered on them) have such obvious difficulty in reconciling the properties of selves with those of the phenomena of the physical world. Even more fundamentally, we must reckon with the huge and embarrassing fact that the natural sciences can hardly pretend to understand or explain the actual work and achievement of human scientists. Karl Popper has made the point memorably, if controversially: "We cannot predict, by rational or scientific methods, the future growth of our scientific knowledge." (He adds that "this assertion can be logically proved" [Popper, 1960, p. ix], by considerations that he adduces.) We need not follow Popper in his own claims, and we may safely leave unresolved the complex matter of what Popper terms "historicism." Nevertheless, he is surely right in claiming that no sanguine program of natural science and no program of inquiry fitting the unity of science model (leaving aside the additional, dualistic puzzles that interest Popper [1972], posed by Dilthey's and Collingwood's conceptions of history) has shown the slightest promise of being able to account for any part of the human achievement—in terms restricted to physicalist categories. For this reason, many of the strongest currents in the philosophy of science have, even to our own day, systematically sought to undermine or displace the central role of the concept of selves.

It has been an essential part of Popper's vision, however, to oppose the division of explanation (*Erklären*) and understanding (*Verstehen*), to reject the division between the sciences and the humanities, to insist on the symbiotic connection between the two, and to propose a deeper sort of common ground for both. "Laboring the difference . . . has become a bore"; "only a man who understands science (that is, scientific problems) can understand its history; and . . . only a man who has some real understanding of its history (the history of its problem situations) can understand science" (Popper, 1972, p. 185). The theme is a peculiar commonplace because it is so often ignored or denied by the self-appointed champions of the methods of the physical sciences. Popper argues convincingly that these partisans (notably the positivists) have simply misunderstood their own undertaking—which may be fairly confirmed without at all subscribing to Popper's own controversial views regarding conjecture and refutation. Their maneuver can hardly be serious if they cannot come to grips with the challenge Popper has laid down: to understand the physical sciences (Popper charges) we must understand the manner in which human physicists actually work; and to explain the stars we must understand and be able to explain our selves.

Rudolf Carnap, of course, was, in advance of his challenge, one of Popper's natural antagonists. For Carnap had affirmed, already in the early thirties, the universal adequacy of a physicalist language both for psychology and for science in general (Carnap, 1934). But although he never abandoned his conviction, Carnap did effectively abandon all efforts to demonstrate its full adequacy. Among the more recent beneficiaries of both positivism and the unity of science program—among theorists who hold such subtle commitments on pertinent issues that they often fail to draw our attention to their having actually taken sides in the contest Popper effectively focused, and often even fail to alert us that their seemingly tangential concerns really do bear in a central way on Popper's question—one should mention at least those who currently speculate about how to build a scientific account of language that obviates the need to depend on a theory of meaning or reference: for theories of meaning and reference risk admitting selves.

The best known current champion of such causes is Donald Davidson. Davidson's view is worth identifying because it helps see how and why seemingly technical theories of language both gain plausibility from, and lend plausibility to, deeper convictions about the nature of human selves. This may seem improbable, but it really is not: in fact, its seeming plausibility or lack thereof depends on whether we can recognize in it the clear analogue (that surely lurks there) of Popper's point about science and history. Roughly, what Davidson recommends is a program of analysis that treats language essentially in syntactic terms: if he were right, meaning and reference could, in a sense, be entirely obviated; or else, they could be benignly conceded to color in a picturesque way an otherwise (scientifically) sufficient explanation of the phenomenon of language. By parity of reasoning, the entire range of psychologically, culturally, historically, semiotically, intentionally rich characterizations of human selves are taken to be eliminable (or, decisively displaceable) in an adequate scientific psychology. Alternatively, such characterizations are regarded as part of a colorful (even efficient) idiom in which we move among our own kind, but which, in the eyes of a disciplined science (but only there) are entirely eliminable. This conceptual linkage helps explain Davidson's adherence to what he calls anomalous monism and to Tarski's Convention T (Davidson, 1980, 1984). Their union, in fact, is characteristic of much recent analytic philosophy of psychology.

This probably seems a strange way of boarding the question of the conceptual role of selves in the human sciences. But if we are looking for a sense of the entire range of possible strategies for excluding or diminishing that role—in the name of the normal constraints of science—we can hardly do better. Davidson's philosophical programs are surely among the more focused and influential in the current Anglo-American literature devotedly loyal to the most severe versions of the unity of science program; because of their precision, moreover, they supply a treasure of conceptual missteps and lacunae that inadvertently orient us with equal precision to the likeliest concessions, within the scope of the theory of science, the full acknowledgment of selves might extract. In pursuing his strategies, therefore, we must bear in mind that Davidson serves here as a stalking horse and that the point of contesting certain prominent conceptions of human psychology—

among which Davidson's is something of an inspiration—is to prepare the field for more promising candidate theories, *not* (at least here) to invent another contender.

Davidson's project is simplicity itself: "Words have no function save as they play a role in sentences: their semantic features are abstracted from the semantic features of sentences, just as the semantic features of sentences are abstracted from *their* part in helping people achieve goals or realize intentions" (Davidson, 1984, p. 220). But then, following Quine (even going beyond him), Davidson adds:

> . . . a translation manual is only a method of going from sentences of one language to sentences of another, and we can infer from it nothing about the relations between words and objects. Of course we know, or think we know, what the words in our own language refer to, *but this is information no translation manual contains.* Translation is a purely syntactic notion. Questions of reference do not arise in syntax, much less get settled. (Davidson, 1984, p. 221)

There you have the heart of the argument. Words have their function in sentences; sentences have theirs in the behavior of the members of human societies; and it is possible to provide an adequate schema for translation without any attention at all to the actual meanings and references of determinate discourse. The principal thing to understand is how entire languages function (or how the entire psychology of man is ordered), not the piecemeal meaning of this or that sentence (or the piecemeal intention and significance of this or that bit of behavior). Davidson himself hints at the analogy with a physics of psychology (Davidson, 1984, p. 222). And he concludes that "the theory gives up reference, then, as part of the cost of going empirical" (Davidson, 1984, p. 223); correspondingly, we may suppose, we give up, in psychology, intentions and beliefs (and intentionality) as well, as the same price of "going empirical" (Margolis, 1984b). In Popper's terms, this, precisely, is once again to segregate science and history.

It is extremely important to fix the trouble with Davidson's program, because in resisting it—which, in a sense, is entailed by insisting on the scientific relevance and ineliminability of selves—we are led to see one of the deepest and most universal intellectual contests that underlie nearly all the speculative quarrels of philosophy and science in our own day. More to the point, that contest is very nearly invisible in the smaller projects of every discipline. Without wishing to exaggerate the actual force of Davidson's strategy (as opposed to the importance of the contest that it takes its place in and that may never be entirely settled), one may say that the essential issue concerns the prospects of a comprehensive extensionalism or, alternatively, of the possibility or impossibility of eliminating intensional complexities at the very heart of science and rational inquiry. Davidson's proposal is to treat meaning (and reference) solely in terms of truth; treat truth entirely in *syntactic* terms, conformably with Tarski's (1983) satisfaction condition (actually apt, in Tarski's opinion, only for suitably formalized languages); and construe the *scientific* (genuinely "empirical") interest in the phenomenon of language as restricted to such matters only (Hacking, 1975).

No doubt the bearing of these matters on the theory of selves will seem quite remote. But that is their attraction. If one asks how, on what grounds, Davidson can defend his confidence that, conformably with scientific concerns, meaning can (in theory) be adequately captured by truth, and truth, adequately captured by an extensional syntax, the entire house of cards will collapse; with this collapse, the full significance of insisting on the function of selves emerges with surprising clarity. The trick rests on a very simple maneuver—that, almost isomorphically, appears in theorizing both about language and about human action and human psychological states. The connection is natural, for one cannot interpret linguistic behavior without making ascriptions of beliefs and intentions and the like, and, in the human (the paradigm) case, one cannot ascribe beliefs and intentions without both modeling such ascriptions linguistically and construing them as naturally manifested in linguistic utterances.

Davidson concedes quite straightforwardly that his "Tarski-like theory of truth *does not* analyze or explain either the *pre*-analytic concept of truth or the pre-analytic concept of reference" (Davidson, 1984, p. 239). He means by the "preanalytic": (1) whatever concepts of truth and reference can be fitted to the linguistic and linguistically informed behavior of human agents normally acknowledged in the practices or forms of life of natural societies (whose members acquire their linguistic and cultural aptitudes merely by growing up in a community of apt adults) *and* (2) whatever may be the adequate story of the semantic and pragmatic function of words, sentences, utterances, acts generated by such agents *within* such practices. In defending "a version of the holistic approach" (Davidson, 1984, p. 221), Davidson means to exclude such factors from his linguistic and psychological theories. Alternatively put, he distinguishes sharply

> between explanation *within* the theory and explanation *of* the theory. Within the theory, the conditions of truth of a sentence are specified by adverting to postulated structure and semantic concepts like that of satisfaction or reference. But when it comes to interpreting the theory as a whole, it is the notion of truth, as applied to closed sentences, which must be connected with human ends and activities.

II

Let us now reconsider what's at stake. We have been picking up in a somewhat anecdotal way a number of current clues about the essential puzzles posed by the concept and phenomena of selves. But we have not yet ordered those clues—as we shall, very shortly—so as to display nearly all the principal strategies currently favored for eliminating or disarming the systematic import of introducing selves in a central and potentially irreducible way in the human sciences. Popper recognized and featured the symbiosis between science and history, which, rightly perceived, challenges at its core all reductive conceptions in which the vocabulary of physics (or the larger vocabulary of the physical and life sciences, excluding language and intentional states) is taken to be entirely adequate for all the descriptive and explanatory work of science itself (Davidson, 1984, pp. 221–22). Carnap represents the most sanguine embodiment of all "simple" reductive programs, because he believed that psychological predicates could actually be translated without remainder by a purely physicalist idiom. Carnap retreated from the required labor, but his more resilient followers realized that translation, predicate by predicate, was both quite unlikely and unnecessary. Hence, J. J. C. Smart's well known effort to defend so-called type identity represents the usual direction in which a broadly Carnapian program has been pursued (Feigl, 1967). But, as is also well known, Smart's argument begs the question and depends entirely on a presumption in favor of the reductive objectives of the unity of science program and on examples of theoretical identity drawn exclusively from the physical sciences—where the question at stake is simply not raised at all (Smart, 1962, 1963). By contrast, though it also favors a version of the identity thesis (so-called token identity, a concept that denies psychophysical laws while admitting the identity and causal interaction of mental and physical states "token" by "token"—so-called anomalous monism, a thesis that ultimately proves to be formally incoherent [Margolis, 1984b]), Davidson's strategy is a paradigm of "sophisticated" reductive programs. That is, it proposes to show that the closure of science itself—the very condition for the adequacy of the scientific explanation of all empirical phenomena—does not require the regimentation of the idiom the simple reductionists had labored so fruitlessly to achieve. Davidson concedes the irreducibility and the useful function of psychological idioms: he "merely" disallows their having any essential function as such within the bounds of science. To anticipate a little, all strategies that would eliminate or reduce the function of selves in accord with the assumed adequacy of a physicalist idiom are either of the "simple" or "sophisticated" sorts (or a mixture of the two). The counterstrategy, intended to save the full conceptual role of selves in the human sciences, must (1) disarm or defeat those options and (2) resist, in restoring their functions, assigning those functions to systems that are not selves.

We are now effectively launched into the center of the controversy. If there were irreducible psychophysical laws, or if there were psychophysical causal processes (even if we were unable to formulate their covering laws), the physicalist closure of science would be empirically untenable: we should then need to reinstate the concept of selves once again within the "space" of science. To meet the challenge, Davidson divides his strategy. He argues as a "simple" reductionist, in advancing his doctrine of anomalous monism; he argues as a "sophisticated" reductionist, in drawing out the full import of his extension of Tarski's Convention T; and he supports each project by appeal to the work of the other. This is a most complex matter, of course: we shall have to be brief in marshaling arguments against Davidson if we are ever to supply, here, a reasonably succinct picture of the larger contest at stake. But there is no escaping some detail—and the dialectical play involved is most instructive.

The countermoves to Davidson's theory of psychology (anomalous monism) are extremely powerful. First of all, the usual simple theories

(Davidson's, Carnap's, Smart's, Feigl's) are committed to a realist interpretation of psychology: they concede causal processes involving the psychological and attempt to save the reductive undertaking by supporting some version of the identity thesis. There is no other option under the simple realist concession. The only other prospects are these: (1) treat psychology solely as an idiom that has had its innings for historically contingent reasons and that may now be retired, in principle, by a physicalist idiom with respect to whatever (neutrally identified) is empirically real; (2) treat psychological descriptions and explanations as lacking any realist import at all, as falsely appearing to have referred to what is actual. Both alternatives have of course been pursued, and both (generously construed) may be taken as instances of "sophisticated" strategies replacing the "simple."

The first of these is notably associated with the views of Wilfrid Sellars and of such advocates of the unity of science orientation as May Brodbeck and Stephan Körner (Sellars, 1963; Brodbeck, 1966; Körner, 1966). In a sense, it obviates the need for supporting an identity thesis, since (on the argument) what is real *is* physical (in whatever sense may be defended) since the picturesque idiom of the mental proves scientifically otiose. The trouble is that this has never actually been shown to be true and, conceding a realist view of the phenomena of linguistic and psychological behavior (however provisionally identified by means of an idiom that does employ semantic, pragmatic, or mental predicates), must (somewhere) be shown to be suitably characterized in terms of a (scientific) idiom that eschews such predicates. The second option is notoriously associated with an early version of Paul Feyerabend's views, with the early views of Richard Rorty, and, more recently, with those (oscillating somewhat between the two options) of Paul Churchland and Stephen Stich (Feyerabend, 1963; Churchland, 1979; Stich, 1983). Here again, the trouble is that there is no known or remotely promising way to specify any physicalistically real set of phenomena able to explain whatever may be salvaged as real (that the psychological idiom may be supposed to have luckily identified) and able, at the same time, to vindicate discarding as illusory or a mere artifact of the idiom whatever else that idiom mistakenly took to be real.

Dialectically, the prospect of psychophysical laws and psychophysical causal processes poses the most troublesome threat. Curiously, the proponents of a reductive psychology—notably, Davidson again—tend to be rather orthodox or vague about the nature of scientific laws (Davidson, 1980; Cartwright, 1983). It is, however, a dogma of science that causal contexts (as and if distinct from contexts of causal explanation) invariably behave extensionally (Davidson, 1980). This is simply the nether side of the thesis of the scientifically closed physical universe: if there were psychophysical causal processes, and if the psychological were not reducible in physicalist terms, then it would be impossible (by any "simple" strategy) to avoid the peculiar intensional, semantic, pragmatic, semiotic, historical, and cultural complexities that are introduced by acknowledging the reality of human selves. In that case, causal contexts would not behave extensionally only—which is to say there would be no operable basis on which to reidentify all causes extensionally (since, on any theory, causes remain self-identical). That would lead to a stalemate regarding all efforts to reduce or eliminate selves or else oblige us (supporting the reductive objective) to seek subtler versions of the "sophisticated" strategy meant to provide the needed supplement.

As far as we have gone, it should be clear that the Freud of the *Scientific Project* at least was a "simple" reductionist, honorably baffled by the emerging complexities of his own clinical practice, which would not behave conformably with his Helmholtzian views (Margolis, 1978), and that B. F. Skinner, through his entire career, has rather cavalierly shifted between the simple and sophisticated reductive strategies (Margolis, 1984b). We should be able to see, also, that functionalism may be reconciled with the reductive undertaking only if the intentional idiom it permits is treated heuristically—which is to say, either as a *façon de parler* or as falsely descriptive of what is real (Fodor, 1981; Dennett, 1969). Otherwise, it would confirm once again the ineliminability of selves: either dualistically (Eccles, 1953, 1970, 1977) or by means of a more complex monism of a nonreductive sort. Our map of the alternative possibilities of psychological theories is now nearly complete.

III

It is at this point that Davidson shifts, effectively, to advocating his special extension of Tarski's Convention T. His theory rests on certain technical considerations. But what we need to bear in mind, reviewing it here, is that the merest retreat from its quite severe constraints along specifiable lines would utterly disable its prospects for bringing a psychology within the competence of the physical sciences. This can readily be shown to be a devastating weakness. The point of pressing the required analysis is simply that Davidson's strategy is without a doubt a version of the minimal ("sophisticated") strategy regarding the theory of language that could bring a scientific account of the phenomena into accord with something like the anomalous monism intended. Furthermore, to grasp the reasons for the failure of Davidson's option is to be able to map the remaining possible strategies regarding the methodological fortunes of the concept of selves.

Concede, then, for the sake of the argument, Davidson's characteristic conditions. For one thing, as we have already seen, Davidson brackets all questions on explaining the truth of individual sentences using "the semantic features of words" (psychologically descriptive terms, say) within the scope of the linguistic theory he advances; he considers only the explanation of the theory en bloc. On this view, as he says, "words, meanings of words, reference, and satisfaction are posits we need to implement a theory of truth. They serve this purpose without needing independent confirmation or empirical basis" (Davidson, 1984). What this means, evidently, what it can only mean, is that categories of these linguistic sorts are introduced in a purely formal way, that they are either syntactic, semantically uninterpreted categories (with respect to their distributed instantiations) or else completely explicable (as to their function with regard to sentences) in terms of purely syntactic or formal distinctions. Anything else would smack of apriorism—and Davidson can hardly be accused of that. But if it turned out that that maneuver was not semantically neutral as supposed (in the very sense Davidson means to favor), then the planned extension (or adjustment) of Tarski's account would fail—as arbitrary, undefended, a priori, or question-begging; as a result, we should find ourselves quite reasonably obliged to restore the full pivotal function of the concept of selves—which, as suggested, captures the essential point of Popper's original challenge to positivism and reductive materialism. Furthermore, the beauty of proceeding in this way is that it permits us to grasp, without any partisan doctrine of human nature whatsoever, that Davidson's way simply cannot manage to describe and explain the psychologically real phenomena that all theoretical hands acknowledge "preanalytically."

A second condition is more problematic. Davidson admits that "a general and preanalytic notion of truth is presupposed by the theory" itself, in order that "we can tell what counts as evidence for the truth of a T-sentence" (that is, a sentence cast in the extensional, syntactically canonical form the Tarskian theory affords—which, on the first condition, does not affect empirical questions at all). Davidson warns us that such a notion is not required for merely introducing the concepts of satisfaction and reference (which are, when used distributively, systematically tied to the admission of selves): "Their role is theoretical, and so we know all there is to know about them when we know how they operate to characterize truth." It is in this sense—an entirely fair sense—that "we don't need the concept of reference" (Putnam, 1983; Davidson, 1984). Consequently, we don't need the concept of selves. Obviously, Davidson would expect to capture the pre-analytic consideration introduced for T-sentences by a higher-order application of the same theory—and would hope, in doing so, to exhaust all interesting challenges to his account. Perhaps. But it may be noted, in allowing the point, that the implied regress does not actually show how, in real-time terms, to escape relying on semantically rich notions of satisfaction (or truth) and reference. It looks as if the very formality of Convention T confirms our ultimate dependence on (semantically pertinent applications of) satisfaction and reference, whether for the truth of our object-language sentences or for their T-sentence replacements—hence, confirms our ultimate dependence on the concept of selves. We must bear in mind that to postpone the application of the concept is hardly to attenuate its critical role.

Here, a third consideration of a most troublesome sort arises, which may be conveniently clarified by recalling some observations of Hilary Putnam's with which Davidson seems to agree. "'True,'" on Tarski's account (also, on Carnap's, Quine's, Ayer's and others'), "is, amazingly, a philosophically neutral notion. 'True' is just a device for 'semantic ascent': for 'raising' assertions from the 'object language' to the 'metalanguage,' and the device does not commit one epistemologically or metaphysically" (Putnam, 1975, p. 76). If we put quotation marks around the sentence *Snow is white* and adjoin the words *is true*, "the resulting sentence is itself one which is true if and only if the original sentence is true. It is, moreover, assertible if and only if the original sentence is assertible; it is probable to degree *r* if and only if the original sentence is probable to degree *r*; etc." So, "to understand P is true, where P is a sentence in quotes, just 'disquote' *P*: take off the quotation marks (and erase 'is true')" (Putnam, pp. 75–76). This surely raises the puzzling question of how, on a realist reading of empirical assertions, satisfaction (or truth) and reference can be avoided; more significantly, it raises the question of how the formal adequacy of any would-be T-sentences (as replacements for natural language sentences) could be decided without invoking, at that very level, the original worries about satisfaction and reference. Here, one might even invoke the so-called antirealist strategy introduced by Michael Dummett, with which both Putnam and Davidson appear somewhat sympathetic (Dummett, 1978). For, in raising the decidability question, antirealism poses the issue once again of the eliminability of personal agents or selves (the very agents *who* decide)—which agrees in effect with Popper's challenge, regardless of technical disagreements elsewhere. To put it another way, a T-sentence must be strictly constructed in an extensionally satisfactory way in accord with Tarski's view of a suitably formalized language. Tarski believed that natural languages could not be completely regularized to this end. This is most important, for if "true" is "philosophically neutral" as Putnam says (and Davidson obviously believes), then quotation and disquotation are not conceptually linked with Tarski's account of the conditions on which "true" is a predicate of sentences admissible in his theory (T-sentences); and if they are so linked, then "true" is not in the least philosophically neutral. Either way, Davidson cannot use Tarski's theory to strengthen the empirical adequacy of any form of simple or sophisticated reductionism. More pointedly put, whether sentences describing or explaining psychologically real phenomena can be extensionally construed or are irreducibly complex in nonextensional ways is itself a substantive question that needs to be independently addressed. Either Davidson must already have succeeded in his theory of psychology (anomalous monism or some other "simple" reductive account) in demonstrating an extensionally adequate analysis of the relevant phenomena (which he has merely chosen to cast in terms of T-sentences), or else the project has already been aborted by the failure of the antecedent psychology. Either the empirical psychology must precede the formal linguistics or the intended linguistics is itself empirical and cannot be known in advance to be congruent with Tarski's formal constraints. Here is the most salient version of the conceptual lacuna of all formal versions of extensionalism. The irony is that it was already anticipated by Tarski.

There simply are no other options, though it is possible to flesh out variations of the options already considered. What we have exhibited, therefore, is a reasonably complete map of the essential strategies— on the side of theorizing about psychology or about science or about language—that may be thought to bear on the reducibility or eliminability of the concept of selves; and we have been able to begin to assess the likelihood of realizing that objective by pursuing any empirical or formal strategy that we can imagine.

But we have not yet exhausted the advantages of what may still seem an oddly indirect way of pursuing the analysis of selves. Davidson is candid enough to say that the Tarski-like theory of truth he favors can "at best" give "the extension of the concept of truth for one or another language with a fixed primitive vocabulary" (Davidson, 1984, p. 221). It cannot explain the truth of semantically rich individual sentences. If there were an empirically available primitive vocabulary, and if all complex concepts could be extensionally treated in terms of such a vocabulary, then either type or token identity might ultimately be empirically defended. As it happens, this is precisely the undertaking that Jerry Fodor (1975, 1981) favors, and it has become extremely influential in current cognitive psychology. Unfortunately, Fodor's theory is cast in an extremely unlikely platonist (or nativist) form and is utterly inexplicit about the actual extensional reduction of complex concepts (along Tarskian lines) to some original core of putatively primitive concepts.

A somewhat analogous (but differently motivated) strategy is advocated by the champions of Artificial Intelligence (AI) modeling of human psychology. For those partisans, it is unnecessary to posit an original or nativist supply of primitive concepts; all that is required is that, for any range of empirically true ascriptions made of human agents, some AI simulation would as such be indistinguishable in input-output terms, precluding differences in intervening (internal) processing or of testing extensions or continuations of the simulation indefinitely beyond the finite segment of behavior examined (in whatever terms that segment is said to be modeled). A dual response is the proper answer to their alternative: we must concede that any finite segment of behavior can be simulated by an extensionally defined program if we disregard the forms of intervening processing (between input and output), and the success of such simulation (the Turing game, so to say) does not as such signify psychologically pertinent performance or capacity of any sort. These results are reasonably widely accepted (Putnam, 1975; Block, 1978; Searle, 1980).

But it may be (and is sometimes) thought that, if such simulation can be effected, then intentional attributions made at the molar level for systems that function as selves can, progressively, be factored in such a way (in accord with the fine tuning of AI simulation) that, at some point in the analysis, a completely extensional replacement of the admittedly intentionally complex molar characterizations of the states and behavior of selves or persons could be achieved. The inference is a non sequitur. But the program is the nerve of Daniel Dennett's version of cognitivism, which of course trades heavily on the extensionalist presumptions of Quine's and Davidson's views about the eliminability of intensional contexts (Margolis, 1984b).

Only such a dependence could possibly explain the peculiarly optimistic tone of Dennett's substantive views about persons within the psychological sciences: "the personal story [the "story" of a person's mental states, the "story" of selves] has a relatively vulnerable and impermanent place in our conceptual scheme, and could in principle be rendered 'obsolete' if some day we ceased to treat anything (any mobile body or system or device) as an Intentional system—by reasoning with it, communicating with it, etc." (Dennett, 1969, p. 190). Certainly, what one sees at once is that if a program of semantically focused translation (Carnap's option) did not succeed in providing the conditions for the truth of individual sentences, then at least a syntactically governed program of translation (a Tarski-like program, favored by Davidson and Quine) could be counted on to succeed in an empirically pertinent way (if the semantic could be antecedently regimented in an extensional way, syntactically): the semantic or intensional complexities of empirical concepts would then, à la Davidson (1984) be entirely managed by "adverting to [further] postulated structure" (p. 221) within the theory, which would permit an "indirect" but not "direct" assignment of empirical content "to relations between names or predicates and objects" (p. 223). So it could not be supposed (and normally is not supposed) that the extensionalist treatment of language is a purely formal matter (as Davidson had alleged). To be pertinent to empirical science at all, it is and must be an empirical matter itself. That is, the putatively "amazing" neutrality of Tarski's notion of "true" is at best a desperately equivocal reading, and the purely formal reading of "true" has as such absolutely no (a priori) bearing on paraphrastic programs—direct or indirect—within the empirical sciences. This is why Dennett correctly observes that "the task of avoiding the dilemma of Intentionality is the task of somehow getting from motion and matter to content and purpose—and back" (Dennett, 1969, p. 40).

Davidson, of course, again shows the way; for, as he puts it, "our primitive actions, the ones we do not do by doing something else, *mere movements of the body* [that is, movements extensionally identifiable]— these are all the actions there are" (Davidson, 1980, p. 59). If the thesis held (independently of the program involving Convention T), then it would be reasonable to extend it to the rest of human psychology. A suitably reductive account, whether "simple" or "sophisticated," must center on empirical psychology itself. But this is also precisely why Dennett's sanguine view about the elimination of selves depends on filling a lacuna that no one has as yet filled. There is no known way to regiment the intensional complexity of natural languages and natural cultures extensionally.

Ironically, the full difficulty of linking the two approaches is fixed by an essential equivocation in Davidson's own "sophisticated" account. For, as you will remember, Davidson treats words, meanings, reference, and the like (in a formal sense) as theoretical "posits" that need no empirical backing. Nevertheless, he also remarks (as already cited) that words and their semantic features and the like are "abstracted" from sentences, and their features are abstracted from human behavior at large. Now, if they are "posited," they are completely formal—and lack empirical import altogether; but if they are "abstracted," then they are empirical—and then whether tailored T-sentences can be provided for sentences occurring in natural contexts becomes a distinctly empirical question. One cannot have it both ways. Fodor and Dennett and Davidson, however, are obliged to assume the empirical adequacy of the device introduced by the merely formal account. This may well be the most widespread lacuna or question-begging maneuver of all current reductive psychologies.

IV

The alleged mutual independence of anomalous monism and the empirical application of Convention T suggest further substrategies within a generously construed range of psychological theories. For it is sometimes thought that the intensional complexities of linguistic and cultural behavior can be favorably managed by first ascribing information, intentional properties, or the dependence of semantic factors on syntactic factors, within systems that are not characterized as selves. It suggests a way of introducing these features in extensionally controlled ways—which proves to be a surprisingly popular and variable strategy. But it is also doomed for elementary reasons that bear on the conceptual linkage between psychology and linguistics. In any case, to tolerate what would otherwise seem to be the misascription of personal attributes or processes to systems not suitably endowed demands its own conceptual reassurance. The maneuver is a sort of halfway house between the full-fledged admission of selves and the selective use of certain highly structured features of the world of selves without the conceptual and methodological encumbrances that their admission normally entails. Gibson, for instance, advances a straightforward version of the maneuver by attributing ecologically relevant information—what he calls "affordances" (more or less in the Gestalt sense)—to the perceptually ambient world in which living creatures (including man) find their niches (Gibson, 1966, 1979). On Gibson's view, organism and environment exhibit a preestablished harmony, in virtue of which no cognitive agent (a fortiori, no selves) need be postulated in order to account for the successful "use" of ambient information. To Gibson, there is no interpretive processing of information internal to the living creature—hence, there are no selves. But, as is generally known, Gibson's efforts came to grief (on this score at least) in his increasingly strained attempts to make sense of two-dimensional paintings (which can't harbor ecologically accessible information in the way required by the theory, that is, without independent cognitive processing or interpretation) (Gibson, 1960, 1971). Fred Dretske has generalized a related account by introducing information pervasively through the natural world as logically prior to, and conceptually independent of, all forms of cognition and interpretation. The intensional complexities of human selves are, then, treated essentially as restrictions of one sort or another *within* a (perfectly) extensional informational network that is not in any way encumbered by psychological complexities. The trouble, again, is that information (even on Dretske's view) is propositionally modeled; but there is no effective way of treating information propositionally without construing it linguistically, and doing that (in empirically relevant ways) effectively reverses the conceptual connection between information and the behavior of human selves: propositionally construed, information cannot fail to be a cognitively dependent interpretation (shall we say, an "abstraction," in the empirical sense bearing on Davidson's view of language); it must, therefore, be governed by whatever semantic or intensional complexities are rightly attributed to human agents (Dretske, 1981).

Three other examples should provide reasonably complete closure for our survey. First of all, analytic structuralism—in particular, the structuralism of Lévi-Strauss, modeled on Saussure's theory of *langues*—both construes the semantic or interpretative analysis of anthropological phenomena as conceptually subordinate to some putatively totalized system of syntactically defined possibilities and transformations within a given domain, and construes the resultant system as not rightly ascribable to any human agents at all and as not capable of being fully internalized by any such agents. (How Lévi-Strauss finally conceives his own grasp of this system of possibilities is an utter mystery) (Derrida, 1976). He is of course entirely explicit:

> I believe the ultimate goal of the human sciences to be not to constitute, but to dissolve man. . . . Ethnographic analysis tries to arrive at invariants beyond the empirical diversity of human societies. . . . [A] good deal of egocentricity and naivety is necessary to believe that man has taken refuge in a single one of the historical or geographical modes of his existence, when the truth about man resides in the system of their differences and common properties. (Lévi-Strauss, 1966, pp. 247, 249)

Nevertheless, rather more comfortably than Saussure before him, Lévi-Strauss fails to explain the conceptual source of the totalized invariances he pursues, the evidence that he has formulated a genuine "system" in the structuralist sense, the relevance of his would-be schema with regard to fitting the interpreted details of actual societies, and where, in what world, these purely formal rules of formation and transformation may be supposed to obtain (Bourdieu, 1977).

Nearly the inverse of Lévi-Strauss's account is provided in the work of Noam Chomsky. Chomsky holds that the universal grammatical invariants of all natural languages are genetically determined: "universal grammar is an element of the genotype that maps a course of experience [some contingent society's development of a natural language, say] into a particular grammar that constitutes the system of mature knowledge of a language, a relatively steady state achieved at a certain point in normal life" (Chomsky, 1980, p. 65). The fact remains that both Lévi-Strauss and Chomsky violate (in their own rather distinctive extensions of the unity of science program) the symbiosis between science and history that Popper was so insistent on; and both characteristically fail even to locate satisfactorily or explicitly the semantic or intensional complexity of the actual, historically contingent practices of human persons or selves—*paroles,* in Saussure's sense. There is no genuine attention paid in either's account to the behavior and the social and historical conditions of individual agents, although it is quite impossible to account empirically for the invariances adduced without a developed theory of the performance of persons or selves.

Another false division between the linguistic and the psychological appears in the literature centered on the unusual phenomena elicited following commissurotomies. A curious tendency has developed among brain surgeons and experimenters theorizing about the human mind: they often construe personal attributes straightforwardly as hemispheric attributes (Gazzaniga, 1970; Bogen, 1969). It has in fact become normal to hear of calculations, inferences, interpretations, thoughts, even linguistic acts of the left and right halves of the cerebral cortex. But although this way of speaking does concede the contribution of the concept of selves, it also confuses subfactors of personal functioning with such functioning, and it fails to grasp the fact that neurological ascriptions cannot, except by first conceptually bridging the difference between the neurological and the personal, be interpreted as subfunctional contributions to whatever functional unity may be ascribed to molar selves. When, for instance, it is said (with commendable caution) that "while it might have been concluded, just a few years ago, that the right hemisphere was completely devoid of linguistic ability, it is now apparent that this view requires some modification" (Marin et al., 1979, p. 193), that very caution ignores the critical fact that there is and can be no independent basis for making molar or submolar attributions to parts of the brain except (paradoxically) by pirating ascriptions originally made of molar selves. These speculations have even led to construing each hemisphere as embodying a distinct self—which, it should be emphasized, is quite a different matter from what the phenomena of dissociation, schizo-

phrenia, amnesia, hypnosis, and even ordinary forgetfulness may en-
tail (Pucetti, 1973). Also, the conceptual propriety and import of
displacing personal attributes to the physical brain is neither pursued
in the literature nor explicitly resolved in terms of extensional-
intensional puzzles.

All of the last three proposals (Lévi-Strauss's, Chomsky's, and the
split-brain enthusiasts') simply fail to come to terms with the conceptual constraints binding on ascriptions normally made of human persons or selves—in that strongly "preanalytic" sense already admitted
that no one will deny. What this signifies is that the submolar import
assigned the functioning brain need not be restricted at all to whatever
submolar factoring applies to human agents in naturally acquired cultures. For instance, how to construe neurological processes in molar
calculation need not be restricted to the idiom of submolar calculation
intuitively identified at the level of molar reflection. The point bears—
with equal force—on AI simulation, the neurophysiology of the brain,
sociobiology, Chomskyan genetics, ecological optics, the original Gestalt psychology, and structuralist studies of language and social existence. It's clear in fact that to restrict such (effectively, homuncular)
categories thus is to impoverish the pertinent sciences, at the cost of
anthropomorphizing systems that are not persons at all. The idioms
in question, however, are all relationally dependent on a molar language: the contribution of the relevant sciences is, on the gathering
argument, invariably subservient to the descriptive and explanatory
vocabulary initially addressed to molar selves, even when (on empirically reasonable grounds) they force a revision in that vocabulary.
They baffle us by selectively preserving the ascriptions, but without
the normal referents (and without a full excuse).

The entire array of possibilities that we have now considered does
seem, on any reasonable view, to have collected just about all the
pertinent moves that could be and have been made to eliminate, attenuate, reduce, or displace the descriptive and explanatory resources
the pivotal concept of selves effectively affords. We have of course
done no more than clear the decks; we have not attempted to provide
the "correct" account. In fact, there is every reason to believe we have
barely begun to grasp the complexity of the conceptual role of selves.
So let us be content, here, with some very general—some strenuous
and hard-won—points of strategy that have the grace at least to be
hospitable to as many lines of theorizing as may now promisingly arise.

All in all, theories of the self designed to fit a fresh picture of the sciences, freed from the pressures of the various reductionisms, must come to grips with a number of themes that are most conveniently collected by reflecting on the nature of language. They include at least the following: (1) selves are languaged entities or systems, for language is the precondition of cultural and reflexive aptitudes as well as the paradigm of the cultural (Feigl, 1967); (2) the linguistic designates real attributes of human behavior and real capacities for behavior; (3) the linguistic is sui generis, hence emergent, for its intensional complexities, inseparable from and symbiotically linked to the syntactic, appear inexplicable in sublinguistic terms of any sort; (4) the linguistic is identified and analyzed functionally, in terms of such abstractable properties as the syntactic, the semantic, the pragmatic, the representational, the purposive, the interpretive; (5) the emergent functional properties of the linguistic must, on pain of failing to avoid a Cartesian dualism, be (abstracted) "aspects" of indissolubly complex properties—not independent properties themselves—from which, similarly, physical or biological "aspects" may also be abstracted (Margolis, 1984a); (6) the functional properties of the linguistic cannot be mapped or generated or systematically predicted solely from any subaltern physical or biological systems, that is, without reference to sui generis regularities bridging the linguistic and such systems; (7) language is an idealization of some sort, of regularities among its (putative) functional properties, ascribed to entire societies only, whose individual members are judged to be members and to be linguistically apt insofar as their aggregated behavior justifies the idealization imputed; (8) linguistic behavior is ascribed only to individuals, who are (or emerge as) persons or selves in virtue of their acquired linguistic aptitude; (9) linguistic idealizations over aggregated behavior exhibit, over time, regular, continuous, open-ended changes of an intensionally complex sort not generable solely in terms of diachronically earlier phases of the linguistic behavior of a given society; (10) a society shares a history, that is, an intensionally complex sequence of temporal changes, insofar as the aggregated behavior of its members justifies diachronic changes in the idealization of its language; (11) the diachronic movement of the idealized regularities of a language entails consensually interpretive behavior among its communicating members; (12) the perception of, and apt response to, linguistic behavior obtains only in the idealized space of a shared language; (13) linguistic

aptitude is emergent with respect to more fundamental biological capacities for species survival, and so a theory of language cannot but
be a part of a more inclusive theory of human behavior and cognition
vis-à-vis an environing world, within which one's linguistic community
is a part but only a part; and (14) what holds for the linguistic holds
for all manifestations of the cultural.

These fourteen themes are hardly uncontroversial, although, with
some ingenuity, they may reasonably be extracted from the argumen-
tative setting in which the reductionisms considered have been defeated or stalemated. In any case, they surely include the central
themes of nearly all current theories of the human sciences that are
opposed to the reductionisms canvassed.

One can see their integrative virtue in such events as the remarkable
recent flurry of heterodox new interpretations of Freud's metapsychology. The essential clue is adumbrated in Freud's own reflections,
in his utter bafflement (for instance in his letters to Fliess) following
his surprise at how the narrative work of psychoanalysis inevitably
drew him further and further away from the reductive presumptions
of his Helmholtzian days (Freud, 1893–95, pp. 160–61; 1954). These
reflections continue to reverberate in astonishingly vigorous ways
among widely (even wildly) diverging readers of Freud—for instance,
in Samuel Weber's rather Derridean reading, Vološinov's Marxist critique, Neal Bruss's and Anthony Wilden's Lacanian constructions,
Paul Ricoeur's hermeneutic version, Roy Schafer's Rylean narrative
(and later, more narratological account), Jürgen Habermas's treatment of Freud as anticipating Frankfurt critical themes, Julia Kristeva's semiotizing of Freud (Weber, 1982; Vološinov, 1976; Bruss,
1976; Wilden, 1968; Ricoeur, 1970, Schafer, 1976, 1983; Habermas,
1971; Kristeva, 1980). There's no prospect of pursuing these latest
hares here, and perhaps there is no need to. The principal finding
collecting them all (as well as more "professional" emendations within
the practice of psychoanalysis itself) concerns understanding the con-
vergent powers of cultural history, social membership, and interpretive work affecting the functional unity (or whatever there is of such
unity) in the aggregated lives of humans. In fact, an incarnate functionalism appears to offer the only way in which to concede sufficient
unity to support such processes as speech, action, fantasy; at the same
time neither Cartesianism nor reductive materialism is forced on us,
nor less conceptual flexibility than what is needed to accommodate
psychic development and the contingent disunities of psychic life itself.

Selves, then, are the distributed members of a society construed as agents—capable of certain functional unities (as of articulate speech or choice or fantasy) within such constraints as (the fourteen points) we have just enumerated. But what it is to be a self, and what its distinctive dynamics are, is—as the gathering Freudian corpus attests—endlessly disclosed by the accumulating theories and studies of every human literature.

References

Block, N. Savage, C. W. (Ed.). (1978). Troubles with functionalism. *Minnesota studies in the philosophy of science* (Vol. 9). Minneapolis: University of Minnesota Press.

Bogen, J. E. (1969). The other side of the brain II: An appositional mind. *Bulletin of the Los Angeles Neurological Society,* XXXIV.

Bourdieu, P. (1977). *Outline of a theory of practice* (R. Nice, Trans.). Cambridge: Cambridge University Press.

Brodbeck, M. (1966). Mental and physical: Identity versus sameness. In P. K. Feyerabend and G. Maxwell (Eds.), *Mind, matter, and method.* Minneapolis: University of Minnesota Press.

Bruss, N. H. (1976). V. N. Vološinov and the structure of language in Freudianism. In V. N. Vološinov, I. R. Titunik and N. H. Bruss (Eds.), *Freudianism: A Marxist critique.* (I. R. Titunik, Trans.). New York: Academic Press.

Carnap, R. (1934). *The unity of science* (M. Black, Trans.). London: Kegan Paul, Trench, Trubner.

————. (1959). Psychology in physical language (G. Schlick, Trans.). In A. J. Ayer (Ed.), *Logical positivism.* Glencoe, Ill.: Free Press.

Cartwright, N. (1983). *How the laws of physics lie.* Oxford: Clarendon.

Chomsky, N. (1980). *Rules and representations.* New York: Columbia University Press.

Churchland, P. M. (1979). *Scientific realism and the plasticity of the mind.* Cambridge: Cambridge University Press.

————. (1981). Eliminative materialism and propositional attitudes. *Journal of Philosophy,* LXXVIII.

Davidson, D. (1980). *Essays on actions and events.* Oxford: Clarendon.

————. (1984). *Inquiries into truth and interpretation.* Oxford: Clarendon.

Dennett, D. (1969). *Content and consciousness*. London: Routledge and Kegan Paul.

———. (1978). *Brainstorms*. Montgomery, Vt.: Bradford Books.

Derrida, J. (1976). *Of grammatology* (G. C. Spivak, Trans.). Baltimore: Johns Hopkins University Press.

Dretske, F. I. (1981). *Knowledge and the flow of information*. Cambridge: MIT Press.

Dummett, M. (1978). *Truth and other enigmas*. Cambridge: Harvard University Press.

Eccles, J. C. (1953). *The neurophysiological basis of mind*. Oxford: Clarendon.

———. (1970). *Facing reality*. Berlin: Springer.

———, and Popper, K. R. (1977). *The self and its brain*. Berlin: Springer International.

Feigl, H. (1967). *The "mental" and the "physical": The essay and a postscript*. Minneapolis: University of Minnesota Press.

Feyerabend, P. K. (1963). Materialism and the mind-body problem. *Review of metaphysics*, XVII.

Fodor, J. A. (1975). *The language of thought*. New York: Thomas Y. Crowell.

———. (1981). *Representations*. New York: Thomas Y. Crowell.

Freud, S. Bonaparte, M., et al. (Eds.) (1954). *The origins of psychoanalysis* (E. Mosbacher and J. Strachey, Trans.). New York: Basic Books.

———. (1955). *Standard edition of the complete psychological works of Sigmund Freud* (Vol. II, 1893–95) (J. Strachey et al., Trans.). London: Hogarth Press and the Institute of Psychoanalysis.

Gazzaniga, M. (1970). *The bisected brain*. New York: Appleton-Century-Crofts.

Gibson, J. J. (1960). Pictures, perspective, and perception. *Daedalus*, Winter.

———. (1966). *The senses considered as perceptual systems*. Boston: Houghton Mifflin.

———. (1971). The information available in pictures. *Leonardo*, IV.

———. (1979). *The ecological approach to visual perception*. Boston: Houghton Mifflin.

Habermas, J. (1971). *Knowledge and human interests* (J. J. Shapiro, Trans.). Boston: Beacon Press.

Hacking, I. (1975). *Why does language matter to philosophy?* Cambridge: Cambridge University Press.

Harman, G. (1974). Meaning and semantics. In Milton I. Munitz and Peter K. Unger (Eds.), *Semantics and philosophy*. New York: New York University Press.

Körner, S. (1966). *Experience and theory*. London: Routledge and Kegan Paul.

Kristeva, J. Roudiez, L. S. (Ed.). (1980). *Desire in language* (T. Gora et al., Trans.). New York: Columbia University Press.

Lévi-Strauss, C. (1966). *The savage mind*. Chicago: University of Chicago Press.

Margolis, J. (1978). Reconciling Freud's scientific project and psychoanalysis. In H. T. Englehardt, Jr., and D. Callahan (Eds.), *Morals, science and sociality* (Vol. III: *The foundations of ethics and its relationship to science*). Hastings-on-Hudson: The Hastings Center.

———. (1984a). *Culture and cultural entities*. Dordrecht: D. Reidel.

———. (1984b). *Philosophy of psychology*. Englewood Cliffs: Prentice-Hall.

———. (in press). In F. S. Zucker et al. (Eds.), *Goethe and the sciences: A reappraisal*. Dordrecht: D. Reidel.

Marin, O. et al. (1979). Origins and distribution of language. In Michael S. Gazzaniga (Ed.), *Handbook of behavioral neurobiology*, vol. 2. New York: Plenum.

Popper, K. R. (1960). *The poverty of historicism*. 2nd ed. London: Routledge and Kegan Paul.

———. (1972). *Objective knowledge*. Oxford: Clarendon.

Pucetti, R. (1973). Brain bisection and personal identity. *British Journal for the Philosophy of Science*, XXIV.

Putnam, H. (1975). The mental life of some machines and The nature of mental states. *Philosophical papers*, vol. 2. Cambridge: Cambridge University Press.

———. (1983). Beyond historicism. *Philosophical papers*, Vol. 3. Cambridge: Cambridge University Press.

Ricoeur, P. (1970). *Freud and philosophy: An essay on interpretation* (D. Savage, Trans.). New Haven: Yale University Press.

Schafer, R. (1976). *A new language for psychoanalysis*. New Haven: Yale University Press.

———. (1983). *The analytic attitude*. London: Hogarth Press.

Searle, J. R. (1980). Minds, brains, and programs. *Behavioral and brain sciences*, III.

Sellars, W. (1963). Philosophy and the scientific image of man. *Science, perception and reality*. London: Routledge and Kegan Paul.

Smart, J. J. C. (1962). Sensations and brain process. In V. C. Chappell (Ed.), *The philosophy of mind*. Englewood Cliffs: Prentice-Hall.

———. (1963). *Philosophy and scientific realism*. London: Routledge and Kegan Paul.

Stich, S. P. (1983). *From folk psychology to cognitive science*. Cambridge: MIT Press.

Tarski, A. (1983). The concept of truth in formalized languages. *Logic, semantics, metamathematics* (J. H. Woodger, Trans.). Indianapolis: Hackett.

Vološinov, V. N., Titunik, I. R., and N. H. Bruss (Eds.). (1976). *Freudianism: A Marxist critique* (I. R. Titunik, Trans.). New York: Academic Press.

Weber, S. (1982). *The legend of Freud*. Minneapolis: University of Minnesota Press.

Wilden, A. (1968). Lacan and the discourse of the other. In J. Lacan, *Speech and language in psychoanalysis* (A. Wilden, Trans.). Baltimore: Johns Hopkins University Press.

SELF AND CONSISTENCY

The struggle to establish a continuous and coherent account of personal identity over time is a significant aspect of contemporary life in our culture. Photographs, observations, and personal journalistic accounts of any individual's early childhood and adolescent years present evidence of discontinuity. The helpless infant in mother's arms, the chubby and awkward four-year-old, the self-conscious and shy preadolescent, or the silly preoccupation of a romantic fantasy life with a teenage idol are in direct contrast to the contemporary physical appearance, psychological stance, and predominant ideas of a forty-five-year-old woman. Yet, when she examines these data of her personal history, when she questions family and friends about herself in the past, she will undoubtedly strive to make her personal account continuous and coherent, to fill in gaps and inconsistencies with details that provide coherence in her sense of self. In other words, she will strive (from her current perspective on self and world) to tell her own story so that the photographs and journal accounts are not ambiguous and meaningless but serve to explain and reveal herself at the moment, no matter how incongruent the facts may be.

Why do people struggle to achieve such continuity? Why is discontinuity so troubling that some people spend years in psychotherapeutic treatment in an effort to make sense of a personal life narrative? From what does this desire arise and how does it function in personality?

The following three essays present evidence and argument for stability and consistency as fundamental concepts in a psychological theory of self. Blasi and Oresick use data from research, on taking responsibility and on ethical dilemmas in adolescence, to unfold a new approach to the topic of self-inconsistency. Rejecting the concept of "cognitive dissonance" as inadequate to a theory of integrity or integration of self, these authors explore a new conceptual approach to understanding both the motivations and phenomena of self-consistency. Primarily, they employ Loevinger's (1976) stages of ego development in tracing out the dimension of self-consistency. Loevinger's own essay follows, with her parsimonious account of self in personality development: the self system as resistance to change. Her approach presents us with an unexpected explanation for stability of self over time.

Finally, Goldenthal takes up the problem of developing a language for clinical descriptions of change in psychotherapy. Eschewing metapsychological approaches but embracing the necessity for explaining connections between personal self-images, Goldenthal uses Rotter's (1982) language of need potentials, freedom, and goals to sketch out a scheme that could become the basis for systematic record keeping among psychological clinicians.

References

Loevinger, J. (1976). *Ego development.* San Francisco: Jossey-Bass.
Rotter, J. B. (1982). *The development and application of social learning theory.* New York: Praeger.

Self-Inconsistency and the Development of the Self

AUGUSTO BLASI and ROBERT J. ORESICK

A N IMPORTANT ELEMENT in human experience is the experience of self-inconsistency. While the phenomenon is clear enough descriptively, at least to those who have undergone it (and who hasn't?), it is less clear how self-inconsistency should be viewed in terms of psychological processes, to what other processes it should be assimilated, and what its theoretical implications are. For instance, it is quite possible to try to understand self-inconsistency as a case of internal contradiction or conflict. But, as we shall argue, in doing so, one misses just what is most characteristic (and unique) about it, namely, that it is a manifestation of the structure and functioning of the self.

The purpose of this essay is precisely to analyze the experience of self-inconsistency as a manifestation of the self and to use it as a springboard to discuss how the self should be understood in psychological terms and what developmental vicissitudes would be required for the experience of self-inconsistency to be possible.

Examples of Self-Consistency and Self-Inconsistency

We begin with two literary descriptions of self-consistency. They may be more dramatic than those we find in our own lives, but they include perceptions that highlight the essential features of the experience.

In *Marie: A True Story* (Maas, 1983), Peter Maas describes the courage of a young woman, chairman of the board of pardons and paroles of the State of Tennessee, who decided to fight political corruption, even when it directly involved the governor who had appointed her.

In doing so she risked not only losing her job and her ability to support her three children, but public disgrace (a slanderous campaign against her was inspired by the administration) and even her life (witnesses had been killed, and the FBI had learned of a murder contract against her). The author asked what motivated her to pursue her fight despite her own fears and the advice of all her friends. In answering the question, he reported an entry in her diary:

> I thought back to all the hard times that the kids and I had known . . . and thought, too, of all the dates I was asked for, and the marriage proposals, and the other proposals, and how *easy* it would have been, at any time, how *easy* it would have been to "sell out," to let some poor fool spend all his money on me and the kids, if I would lead him on, or sleep with him—but for me, in my simplistic fashion, it all boils down to a question of love and integrity: I couldn't let anyone spend money on me or my children unless I *loved* him, otherwise, it would have been a lie, a prostitution of myself and my little ones.
>
> And so it is today. Even to "look the other way" when all this dirt is flying through the air would be to prostitute myself and my integrity. (Maas, 1983, p. 204)

A classic example of the opposite behavior, self-inconsistency, is the theme of Joseph Conrad's (1981/1920) *Lord Jim*. Jim, the protagonist of the story, grew up dreaming of adventures and heroic deeds and preparing himself, in his heart and imagination, to overcome obstacles and difficulties in the service of other people and of the country. The very first opportunity to prove himself, to be faithful to his ideal for himself, came shortly after he had enlisted in the merchant marine as a mate, and it was a tragic, crushing failure. The ship of which he was an officer was traveling with several hundred people aboard, when a collision occurred and water began to rush in, rapidly endangering the ship and the lives of everybody on board. While the passengers slept, ignorant of the imminent danger, all the crew feverishly tried to free the few lifeboats and to leave the sinking ship. Jim was disgusted by the behavior of the crew, but at the same time utterly paralyzed. At last, without realizing what he was doing, he jumped ship and joined those that he so intensely despised. He felt dejection, despair, disbelief at what he had done; he felt completely unworthy, as if his life, the person he was, had disappeared forever with the lost opportunity and with the ship. Conrad's novel is a description of how Jim, slowly, clinging stubbornly to a basic sense of dignity, attempts to recover first a sense of balance, by searching for jobs that would fit his sense of unworthiness, and finally his sense of self and his ideal, by dying to vindicate the trust that others had placed in him and to remain faithful to his ideal.

The Experience of Self-Inconsistency

We begin with a conceptual distinction between self-inconsistency and internal contradiction.[1] One normally speaks of internal contradiction in relation to a theory, a logical system, or a book, when they are internally inconsistent, namely, when they contain logically contradictory statements. It would be inappropriate to speak of self-inconsistency in these cases, because such systems do not have a self.

On the other hand, internal contradiction is not a necessary characteristic of self-inconsistency. For example, Jim, in Conrad's novel, was self-inconsistent, but without internal contradiction: there was no logical incompatibility among his heroic values and aspirations, though his behavior failed to express them.

It would not be sufficient to claim that self-inconsistency pertains only to people, while internal contradiction refers only to systems and books, since both concepts may at times apply to people. For example, we may suppose that Marie would want to keep her job and her ability to support her children and that these important goals were in conflict with her sense of integrity. Despite such internal conflict, she is an exemplar of self-consistency.

Self-inconsistency is clearest in those cases in which a person's action contradicts beliefs of that person about the same action. Jim deeply believes in heroic actions, overcoming obstacles in the service of others; he is self-inconsistent because he fails to act according to these beliefs. Conversely, Marie values integrity and acts accordingly. Though these are dramatic examples, we are all personally familiar with this type of situation. But we may not be fully aware of how broad this first category of self-inconsistency can be. Examples of self-inconsistency would include acting against one's moral principles, compromising one's ideals, lying, and self-deception.

The important role that beliefs play here should be emphasized. Unlike any other human behavior or process, beliefs seem to act as links connecting actions to the self. Both a central self and beliefs are required for the very possibility of self-inconsistency. Not all beliefs, however, have the same value and the same effects. Some are only peripherally related to our identity. If one acts against such beliefs, one is inconsistent, but in a *weak sense*. On the other hand, certain beliefs are so central to one's identity that one is compelled to act in accordance with them by psychological necessity; if one fails to do so, one is inconsistent in a strong sense.

In its strong sense, then, self-inconsistency involves a failure to act in accord with one's self-defining beliefs, those that determine one's basic self-ideals, most cherished goals and ambitions. For example, Marie believes in having a job, in being loyal to her employers, in self-preservation, and in protecting her children. Her actions are inconsistent with these beliefs, according to the earlier definition, but this is only a relatively weak sense of self-inconsistency. Instead, her beliefs that corruption must be exposed and that marriage requires love are more central to her sense of identity. Her actions were weakly inconsistent with the former beliefs, and so she felt they were difficult; but had she acted against the latter beliefs, her actions would have been strongly inconsistent with her essential nature—as Marie put it, she would have become a prostitute who sold her self.

So far we have discussed one group of self-inconsistency examples, those involving a contradiction between an action and its corresponding belief. But there could be a different kind of self-inconsistency, in which action is not directly involved but there is, instead, some sort of split in the personality itself—for example, among different desires, among desires and duties or desires and values, among tendencies. These cases are typical examples of internal conflict. From a more objective standpoint, one may wish to speak of internal contradiction and of lack of internal coordination. Since in these instances the various elements of one's personality (traits, tendencies, desires, etc.) are not adequately coordinated with each other or subordinated to more encompassing regulatory principles, smooth psychological functioning becomes difficult or impossible. In these cases, however, there is no obvious self-inconsistency. For instance, there is conflict but there is no self-inconsistency in wanting and striving for independence, while, at the same time, desiring to be taken care of, or, as in Maas's (1983) hero, in aspiring to be a loyal employee and providing mother, while wanting to maintain one's integrity.

In one instance of internal conflict, however, it is possible to speak of genuine self-inconsistency. There is a point in development, when internal conflict may be experienced as relevant to the self. When a child begins to look at himself or herself as having stable characteristics and no longer as a series of actions, the realization becomes possible that some of these stable tendencies are an obstacle to the realization of other traits he or she may desire to have. In this case, there is self-inconsistency: when a trait is a part of a person's self-definition or of his or her ideal self, when a second trait interferes with the actualization of the first, and when the person could eliminate the conflict but prefers to do nothing. For example, in the case of *Lord Jim*, Jim's lack of control and courage was in conflict with his heroic ideals; the movement of the novel follows his efforts to remove this contradiction within his personality, and the resolution of the plot lies in the final correspondence between his beliefs and actions. But, then, this type of self-inconsistency is related to, and derives from the first type, that is, the contradiction between one's beliefs about oneself and one's actions.

According to our description, then, the experience of self-inconsistency involves two essential psychological elements: first, a contradiction between one's basic identity, what one knows one's essential self to be, and its expression in action; second, the realization that one is responsible for the inconsistency, namely, that the inconsistency was intended at some level and could have been avoided by the agent.

A necessary prerequisite for the possibility of these two psychological elements is a certain type of self: the person needs to have

> such a sense of self that allows for the perception of identity
> as a principle of internal unity and for the understanding
> of agency as involving responsibility both for the expression
> of oneself in action and for those internal conditions that
> would guarantee the fidelity of one's self expressions. (Blasi
> and Oresick, 1986)

This type of self is not a natural endowment of all human beings and cannot be assumed to be present in all individuals; rather, it seems to develop slowly through childhood and adolescence and to be achieved

only by some people. In what follows we will try to clarify what we mean by self and to describe what appear to be its main developmental vicissitudes.

The Self as Subject

The term *self* is being used in psychology with two very different meanings and in two contexts. The most frequent use is to indicate the self-concept, namely, the set of more or less organized ideas and judgments and more or less conscious perceptions and attitudes that each person has of himself or herself. The second use is to indicate the concrete person as object of reflexive activity, or, sometimes, the overall personality. The latter use, rather common in literature and in literary criticism, is relatively infrequent in psychology and of rather recent origin, probably following the resurgence of interest in the self that can be observed in our culture as a whole.

Our own use of the term *self* refers to neither of these two meanings. On the one hand, we are referring not to the set of ideas, perceptions, and evaluations that people have of themselves, but to the constructor, organizer, and holder of these ideas and evaluations. Following William James's (1950/1892) distinction, we are referring not to the self as object (self-concept) but to the self as subject. On the other hand, we are not identifying the self as subject with the concrete person or even with the individual's psychological makeup or personality. As we understand it, the self as subject is only one aspect, though a central one, of the concrete individual person. The aspect here called the subjective self is what is immediately experienced *in* and *through* every intentional action, in each act of desiring, wanting, knowing, and making. Even though it is possible to reflect on it and to formulate concepts and judgments about it (and, therefore, to integrate it in one's larger self-concept), the subjective self is not discovered through reflection and introspection; its grasp is immediate and indirect, namely, in the direct knowledge of all the objects of our cognitive and noncognitive activities.

When one carefully observes a rose and notices its vivid colors, the shape of its petals, and its intense smell, the rose is the direct object of one's perception, the "intention" of one's cognitive act. One's awareness also includes as direct, though secondary, objects the green of the bush on which the rose stands, the play of light and shadow on the meadow, and so on. But one's experience also includes the awareness of seeing, smelling, and attending and the awareness that the acts of seeing, smelling, and attending are one's own, that one and nobody else is doing them. Even though one is aware of one's acts and of oneself as agent, one's acts and agency are not *objects* of experience. They are unintended, necessary concomitants of experiencing the rose.

A similar kind of analysis can be done of all experience of intentional acts, of wanting, hoping, thinking, deliberating, making, including the experience of reflecting on oneself as agent. In each instance, there is awareness of an object, which is directly intended by the act, and awareness of one's act and of oneself, but indirectly, as subjects, not as objects. These two awarenesses—or, rather, these two aspects of awareness—are inextricably bound in experience; in fact, they are constitutive of human experience, whenever it occurs and whatever its contexts might be.

In this respect, then, what is described here as the immediate but "unintended" grasp of the self is quite different from William James's introspectionistic account of the awareness of the "core self." For James, what one reaches are movements, mostly located in the head or upper neck, differing according to the type of experience (1950/ 1892, pp. 296–305). For us, what is being grasped in experience is fundamentally the same in all experiences and could be considered as the defining form of experience.

Even though the awareness of the self as subject is present in any experience, the self that is so grasped is not abstract in the same sense that general concepts are said to be abstract, but a very individual, concrete reality; similarly, it is not so "pure" (in William James's words) or "empty" (in Sartre's, 1947, words) that we cannot identify some of its central characteristics.

Four such characteristics seem essential in any grasp of the self as subject: the first is the experience of agency, namely, the unreflected realization of the action as belonging to the agent and having the agent as its source, experience not to be confused with the awareness of movements occurring in the body. The second is the experience of identity with oneself, of the fact that the self as agent is grasped as identical with the aware, grasping self. This experience, sometimes expressed by the metaphors of transparency and immediate intimacy, is the ground for genuine reflection, namely, for the creation of distance from that very self which is experienced as identical. The third characteristic is the experience of unity of the self as the one source of the various present activities—seeing the rose, remembering another experience, searching for details, and so on, including the action of reflecting on one's seeing and remembering. Closely related to these characteristics is a fourth, the experience of separateness, of emerging from the field of objects and causes in which one's action is being produced.

In sum, the fundamental structure of the self as subject, as immediately grasped in every intentional action, includes the experience of an agentic center, of identity with oneself, and of otherness from all that does not share in its agency. More concretely, the subjective self includes the immediate experiences of self-consciousness and self-scrutiny, of internal unity and identity; of self-control, self-monitoring, responsibility and autonomy; of internal divisions and splits in the use of distorting processes; of self-inconsistency and inner conflicts; of individuality and pride. It becomes clear, then, in what way the self as subject is different from either the self-concept or the concrete person as object of reflection. The self as subject is not a concept or a set of concepts but a concrete reality immediately grasped in experience, from which a number of self-concepts may be constructed. This reality, moreover, is much more limited than the person of which it is a part; more important, it radically differs from any other part of the person, as it is immediately grasped in every single experience.

This fundamental structure of the subjective self is common to all experience, but it may take different forms, determining the various ways in which different people experience their own self. Moreover, these different forms of self-experience may gradually emerge, one from another, in the course of a person's development. The following pages will attempt to identify the specific developmental forms of the subjective self that seem to be required for the experience of self-inconsistency.

The Development of the Subjective Self and Self-Inconsistency

Recently, Blasi (1983) attempted to outline some of the forms in which the self may be experienced at different points in development. The categories that Loevinger and her coworkers constructed to score sentence completions for ego development (Loevinger, Wessler, and Redmore, 1970; Redmore, Loevinger, and Tamashiro, 1978) were used as the empirical basis for reconstructing the experiences of the subjective self. During the past twenty years Loevinger and her colleagues have attempted to define a concept of ego and to describe its developmental forms (Loevinger, 1976). By ego they refer to the attempt to make personal sense of oneself and of the world with which one interacts as well as one's fundamental personal, interpersonal, and social meanings. These meanings would then determine the individual's deep preoccupations and motives, self-control and character, attitudes toward others and toward interpersonal relationships, and moral understanding. Using sentence completions from large samples as raw data, Loevinger and her team described a series of ego developmental stages and constructed scoring manuals to reliably assess ego development. In their work they relied on a cyclical interpretive process, using the theory of ego development to make sense of the data and the data to progressively refine the theory. Very abbreviated descriptions of ego stages are reported in table 3.1.

Table 3–1   Ego-Development Stages, Modes of Self Experience, and Self-Inconsistency[a]

Impulsive

Psychological characteristics of ego development
Impulsive; egocentric, dependent in interpersonal mode; preoccupation with bodily feelings

Modes of self experience
Monolithic, physicalistic self; little or no capacity for reflectivity; agency and mastery over one's feelings are not experienced

Self-inconsistency
Experience of self-inconsistency is not available

Self-Protective

Psychological characteristics of ego development
Opportunistic; manipulative, wary in interpersonal mode; preoccupation with "trouble" and control

Modes of self experience
same as Impulsive

Self-inconsistency
same as Impulsive

Conformist

Psychological characteristics of ego development
Respect for rules; interpersonally cooperative, loyal; preoccupation with appearance, behavior

Modes of self experience
Distance vis-à-vis oneself is achieved through internalization of social roles; sense of agency, control, and limited responsibility; mediating self remains external

Self-inconsistency
Inconsistency with social roles is not really felt as self-inconsistency

Conscientious-Conformist

Psychological characteristics of ego development
Exceptions allowable in rule following; interpersonally helpful, self-aware; preoccupation with feeling, problems, and adjustments

Modes of self experience
Creation of the self as independent psychological reality; internal self is real self; givenness of the self; social orientation

Self-inconsistency
Self-consistency is very important; it is viewed as rigid fidelity to unquestioned identity

Conscientious

Psychological characteristics of ego development
Self-evaluated standards; self-critical; intense, responsible interpersonally; preoccupation with motives, traits, achievement

Modes of self experience
Identity is extended in action; action is to be guided by life ideals; one is not responsible for ideals but for shaping identity according to them

Self-inconsistency
Self-consistency is fidelity to ideals rather than to fixed identity

Autonomous

Psychological characteristics of ego development
Coping with conflict; interdependent interpersonally; preoccupation with self-fulfillment, psychological causation.

Modes of self experience
Self and identity must be personally discovered; search is guided by spirit of autonomy and objectivity

Self-inconsistency
Self-consistency as fidelity to reality and to one's search for authenticity

Integrated

Psychological characteristics of ego development
Cherishing individuality; preoccupation with identity

Modes of self experience
Self is responsible for distortion and compromise

Self-inconsistency
Self-consistency as fidelity to reality and to one's search for authenticity

[a]Parts of the table are adapted from Loevinger (1979).

Because of the way they are constructed, the scoring manuals for ego development lend themselves particularly well to secondary analyses and even to reinterpretations and extensions of Loevinger's own descriptions of the stages. In fact, these categories cover a rather narrow and well-defined semantic field, remain close to commonsense meanings, and, finally, are ordered by stage. It is possible, therefore, to read together the various categories that represent the same ego stage, either within or across items, and to ask what kind of self experience seems to be presupposed by them. In other words, the sentence completions were not interpreted for what subjects directly intended to say about themselves and their experience or about their understanding of themselves and others. Instead, through some sort of "oblique interpretation" (Blasi, 1983), an effort was made to capture that basic experience of oneself which subjects may not intend to convey but which seems to be required in order for their completions to make psychological sense.

For instance, the statement "When I am nervous . . . I can't concentrate" suggests, without intending to communicate, a certain stance of the person toward her or his actions, namely, the experience of mastery and control as well as the experience of loss of control in spite of one's effort to maintain it. Similarly, the completion "The thing I like about myself is . . . that I am not phony," suggests that the person experiences the self as divided between an inside and an outside, but also that these two parts are experienced as unified in some way, as belonging to the same subject.[2]

During the first three of Loevinger's ego stages, the self seems to be experienced in such a way that self-consistency or self-inconsistency seems hardly possible as subjective reality. At the Impulsive and Self-Protective stages (only a small percentage of early adolescents or older subjects are typically classified in these two stages) the self is experienced as monolithic and physicalistic: that is, there is very little distance vis-à-vis oneself or capacity for reduplicative reflectivity, while the few reported emotions and internal movements are presented in physical or behavioral terms (swelling, trembling, getting hot, fighting, etc.). The experience of the self has not yet emerged from the experience of one's body. Moreover, the experience of agency, for instance, in the form of control over oneself, seems to be lacking, while responsibility for one's actions is frequently projected on to the environment. Feelings, emotions, desires, and impulses seem to be exclusively felt as occurring in oneself, and the self seems to be experienced as a helpless spectator. Under these conditions, the essential prerequisites for self-inconsistency (i.e., the division of self into parts, the possibility of unity among the parts, and responsibility for accomplishing this unity) are entirely missing.

This is also true at the next stage, the Conformist, but for different reasons. The self is no longer physicalistic; elementary feelings are reflected upon and appropriated. More important, a split begins to occur between two parts of one's personality: between, on the one hand, one's actions and habits and, on the other, the set of social standards, expectations, and roles that one has internalized and with which one identifies. It is as if the individual were now viewing himself or herself from the perspective of these rather stereotypical social expectations. What could be called the "social look" has been internalized, producing a cleavage between the self that acts and the self that compares and criticizes; social appearance has become the mediating system occupying the inner space. As a result, distance is created from one's actions, feelings and motives; a genuine, though simple, sense of agency, self-control, and responsibility begins to be felt.

At earlier stages, the self was a self of bodily impulses, experienced as oneself, but almost in spite of oneself. Now there is control of one's actions, but the mediating system with which actions are considered and evaluated (the internalized social look) remains somewhat extraneous, received rather than constructed. Peripheral in both its emphasis (namely, roles and behaviors) and its perspective, the social look is both too external and too solidly given to generate experiences of self-inconsistency.

From the perspective of the self there is a radical change at Loevinger's Conscientious-Conformist ego stage, typically characterizing middle adolescents as well as most adults. One can speak now of the creation of the subjective self, in that what was formerly simply lived in an unreflected mode (namely, the agentic source of intentional action, the identity of the source of action and awareness, thus its unity and its separateness from others) now seems to emerge from action, is unified, isolated and differentiated from other internal processes, and experienced as a psychological substance in its own right. For the first time one seems to experience oneself as having an intimate center, and this center is felt as the real part of one's being, the source of one's individuality. It becomes possible, then, to scrutinize this new psychological reality and to create around it a new set of feelings, motives, and evaluations.

In a parallel move, the feelings of agency, mastery, and responsibility are extended from one's actions and habits to one's stable emotions, attitudes, traits, and abilities. As a result, agency begins to involve not only what one does but also what one is.

From now on both the experience of self-inconsistency and the motives for maintaining self-consistency will be part of one's psychological repertory. In fact, all the psychological prerequisites are now present: a sense of self in the form of identity; the realization that the self has different components which may contradict each other and, finally, the realization that one may be responsible for the contradiction as well as for keeping that internal unity that constitutes one's identity. However, self-inconsistency seems to be experienced differently and to have different meanings at each of Loevinger's later ego stages.

At the Conscientious-Conformist stage self-inconsistency is seen as a gap, a contradiction, between one's external face (what one says, how one looks and behaves) and one's real internal self. Here lies the importance for the middle adolescent of being phony and insincere or frank, "real," and sincere. Sincerity, now, does not simply mean telling the truth, but it involves, instead, being one with oneself. At this stage, however, concern for self-consistency is characterized by two aspects: the unquestioned givenness of one's identity, still largely guided by social expectations and socially derived standards; and its social orientation, namely, the concern for presenting in public what one really is, for giving others the true picture of oneself, without the distorting interference of roles and role-playing. These two characteristics, particularly the felt givenness of one's identity, may explain a certain degree of rigidity and even righteousness with which adolescents approach the issue of self-consistency.

At the next ego stage, the Conscientious, the self seems to be felt no longer as a given identity but as an identity that is extended in action and needs to be worked out in action. Identity is not yet understood as something to be discovered and chosen, a characteristic only of the most advanced ego stages. Instead, the self seems to be understood as having to be shaped around life goals and ideals; while these goals and ideals still are rather conventional, they are accepted as guiding one's lifelong construction of what one actually is.

Action, then, becomes both the material from which one's actual identity is fashioned and the testing ground for one's unity and integrity. The important agentic virtues now may appear to have an instrumental quality: ability to decide, tendency to avoid procrastination and inefficiency, perseverance, and courage. Their deeper meaning, however, is far from instrumental and lies in the search for integrity and in being faithful to one's ideal identity. It should be stressed that, at this stage, one owns one's self in a way that could not have been possible at the previous stage. One does not yet choose one's identity, but one must decide, execute, and be responsible for the actions that create the sense of internal consistency and real unity.

At the following two ego stages, labeled by Loevinger Autonomous and Integrated, and apparently represented only by a small proportion of the American adult population, self-consistency has no longer the meaning of being faithful in action to a basically conventional ideal self. Rather, it mainly indicates one's fidelity in the construction of an identity for which conventional guidelines are no longer available. Being true to oneself seems to consist now in the pursuit of a project whose outcome is not at all clear at the starting point: a project of questioning not only conventional wisdom but also that very identity which used to feel obviously true and which one may still find familiar and comfortable; a project of searching not only within oneself but in the broadest surrounding world for what should become one's authentic self.

In order to be true to oneself, the pursuit of this project seems to require two complementary characteristics: freedom from internal and external pressures and, most important, from accepted "truths"; and also a spirit of objectivity not only in one's attending to and judging external reality, but also in controlling one's internal sources of distortion.

Self-inconsistency, conversely, while still including one's deliberate contradictions with one's identity, also covers one's lack of autonomy in the pursuit of one's authentic self and one's more or less conscious acquiescence with one's own distorting processes.

In one respect, the adolescent rigidity in confronting possible compromises seems no longer present, probably because what constitutes one's self is now much more ambiguous than it ever was. In another respect, however, fidelity and self-consistency run much deeper and invest one's responsibility in a way that was not possible at earlier stages. In fact, identity is one's own, not only because one has accepted it but because one has personally discovered it and found it to be uniquely authentic. Responsibility covers one's deliberate contradictions in action, but also one's semiconscious complacencies and one's spontaneous, almost automatic attempts to avoid and distort reality.

To summarize the above descriptions, an analysis of Loevinger's ego development data seems to yield a series of steps through which the subjective self progressively emerges and the forms of its experience gradually change. During the first two stages, the self seems to be lived in the experience of one's body and is not yet differentiated in one's consciousness. The identification with social roles and expectations at the Conformist stage introduces a cleavage within one's personality and establishes a perspective from which distancing becomes possible. At the Conscientious-Conformist stage the subjective self becomes a psychological reality in its own right, but this reality is mostly experienced as a given, unquestioned true self. During later stages the self is extended to one's actions and finally becomes the object of questions and doubts in the search for authenticity.

The experience of self-consistency and self-inconsistency seems to follow these vicissitudes: this experience is initially impossible or of little personal importance; starting at the Conscientious-Conformist stage, however, self-consistency becomes of overwhelming importance as it is tied to the unity of one's identity. At the Conscientious stage, self-consistency lies in the progressive realization of an identity that one already knows to be true; later, it consists instead in maintaining one's freedom and objectivity in the search for one's uniquely authentic self.

These descriptions are given as tentative and uncertain for at least two reasons: they are based on interpretive reconstructions of data that were not originally gathered for the study of the self; more important, these data only rarely contain information about self-inconsistency. Obviously a more direct empirical approach is needed to test the accuracy of our interpretations and inferences. This type of research is at present missing. At least one study, however, seems to give a general confirmation of what we have been saying about the experience of self-inconsistency.

In the context of a larger research project on the development of responsibility (Blasi, 1984), groups of sixth and eleventh graders were interviewed and presented with hypothetical situations in which consistency with one's personal moral standards was pitted against obedience to institutional rules and laws. For what concerns us here, the most important response categories were the following: (1) There is no recognition that consistency with one's moral beliefs has moral value; only objective rules and commands can be the basis for morality. (2) Being consistent with one's moral standards has a genuine moral value; however, this criterion is subordinated to objective criteria and is purely a matter of good will, without establishing any strict obligation. (3) A person's moral judgment and standards are among the most important criteria. The importance of self-inconsistency, however, lies less in fidelity to one's self than in its potential to elicit emotions that may impair the subjective sense of happiness and well-being. (4) Consistency with one's moral philosophy, particularly when the latter has been carefully thought out, is the ultimate criterion, because one cannot go against one's own self.

We found that sixth graders reason mostly according to the first two categories, with emphasis on the first. These children understand quite well what internal conflict is and also what it means to be self-inconsistent, at least descriptively; self-inconsistency, however, is not viewed as a moral issue and does not elicit any significant emotional response. The more frequent responses of high school students correspond to categories 2 and 3; self-consistency may be understood in its moral value, but not for its importance in the preservation of one's identity. Only a small group of high schoolers viewed consistency with one's principles as an absolute for which no compromise is admissible; their responses seem to indicate that they understand the self as being so central to the person and fidelity in action as being so central to one's identity that they experience self-inconsistency as total loss, as spiritual death.

Conclusion

The phenomena of self-consistency and self-inconsistency are important from a variety of perspectives. For existential philosophers and writers they indicate at its clearest the nature of the human predicament; for moralists and ethics philosophers they manifest the nature of moral commitment. From the perspective of psychological theory, these experiences seem to be particularly significant for what they reveal about the self, its development and functioning.

Although psychologists, from the early days of their discipline, had been made aware by William James of the important distinction between self as object and self as subject, they neglected almost completely the second member of the distinction. As a result, most psychological accounts of self-consistency and self-inconsistency are inadequate to represent these experiences, and the inadequacy is fundamental rather than marginal.

When self-consistency is viewed in terms of correlations, as in the trait approach, the essentially subjective nature of the phenomenon is disregarded; in fact, it even becomes impossible to determine what should count as inconsistency. The various accounts based on a defensive understanding of congruency, as an attempt to reduce anxiety, not only do not clarify the psychological nature of self-inconsistency but end up missing its central aspect of fidelity.

Cognitive approaches to self-consistency, relying on the logical relations among self-concepts, may be able to account for the reality value of self-concepts and also for their subjective nature, at least in one sense of subjectivity. However, they tend to confuse self-consistency with internal contradiction, miss the crucial relation between identity and the experience of self-inconsistency, and overlook the fact that this experience involves the recognition of personal responsibility.

This is also true when the self is construed as a system of schemata guiding the processing of information (e.g., Markus and Sentis, 1980) or as a Piagetian cognitive structure. In these versions, one may argue, it is possible to account not only for the outcome of self-knowledge as reflected in self-concepts but also for the processor of information and the constructor of the self as known, namely, for the self as knower or the "I" of Mead's theory. At bottom, in fact, all cognitive approaches seem to forget that cognitive processes, schemas, structures, and self-concepts do not simply *occur* in a psychological context defined by a variety of processes including emotions and attitudes but are experienced as being of a subject (with emphasis on the possessive meaning of *of*). In other words, they seem to forget that this subject is experienced with varying characteristics and that these characteristics (of internal unity, intention, control, and responsibility) are relevant to the very nature of one's cognitive activity.

Self-inconsistency, as it is described in this essay, primarily occurs in the context of action and involves a conceptual construction of one's action. In many instances, however, one's action seems to be conceptually processed as self-inconsistent, and yet the typical experience of self-inconsistency, with the set of attitudes and feelings that define it, does not occur. As we pointed out in our developmental reconstruction, in these cases the self is not experienced with that special sense of unity and ownership that we call identity, nor is responsibility understood to extend to one's identity.

Of course, identity and responsibility are also concepts and, sometimes, self-concepts. One could, therefore, conclude that the self is a set of concepts and develops by adding new concepts or by organizing them in different ways. This reductive strategy, however, ignores that intention, ownership, responsibility, identity—in sum, the self as subject—are *stances* or attitudes vis-à-vis oneself and one's actions (see Blasi, in press). Stances and concepts, whatever their relations may be, seem to be primary psychological elements, irreducible to each other. As the experience of self-inconsistency reveals, the study of the self must begin with the analysis of this special set of stances, particularly those that are implicit in, but give meaning to, one's intentional activity.

Notes

1. The following discussion of the concept of self-inconsistency is borrowed, in a somewhat modified version, from Blasi and Oresick (1986).

2. Eight of Loevinger's items were selected because they seem to frequently evoke subjective experience: "The thing I like about myself is . . ." and "I am . . ." elicit the ways in which the self establishes distance from itself and articulates it in self-concepts; "When I get mad . . ." and "When I am nervous . . ." bring out the ways in which self-control is experienced; "What gets me into trouble . . ." and "My main problem is . . ." evoke self-criticism and, again, the experience of distance from oneself and others as well as of mastery and control; finally, "When they avoided me . . ." and "When I am criticized . . ." bring up preoccupations with social rejection and self-protection, but also the experience of separateness.

The categories of these eight items, grouped by ego stage, were then reinterpreted using as guidelines the descriptions of the subjective self and of its four essential components that were presented earlier in this essay.

References

Blasi, A. (1983). *The self as subject: Its dimensions and development.* Unpublished manuscript, University of Massachusetts, Boston.

———. (1984). Autonomie im Gehorsam. (Autonomy in obedience: The development of distancing in the process of socialization.) In W. Edelstein and J. Habermas (Eds.), *Soziale Interaktion und soziales Verstehen.* Frankfurt am Main: Suhrkamp Verlag.

———. (in press). The self as subject in the study of personality. In D. Ozer, J. M. Healy, Jr., and A. J. Stewart (Eds.), *Perspectives in personality,* Vol. 3, Greenwich, Conn.: JAI Press.

———, and Oresick, R. J. (1986). Emotions and cognitions in self-inconsistency. In D. Bearison and H. Zimiles (Eds.), *Thought and emotion: Developmental perspectives.* Hillsdale, N.J.: Erlbaum.

Conrad, J. (1981). *Lord Jim.* New York: New American Library. (Original work published 1920).

James, W. (1950). *The principles of psychology.* New York: Dover Publications. (Original work published 1892).

Loevinger, J. (1976). *Ego development: Conceptions and theories.* San Francisco: Jossey-Bass.

———. (1979). Construct validity of the sentence completion test of ego development. *Applied psychological measurement, 3,* 281–311.

———, Wessler, R., and Redmore, C. (1970). *Measuring ego development. II. Scoring manual for women and girls.* San Francisco: Jossey-Bass.

Maas, P. (1983). *Marie: A true story.* New York: Random House.

Markus, H., and Sentis, K. (1980). The self in social information processing. In J. Suls (Ed.), *Social psychological perspectives on the self.* Hillsdale, N.J.: Erlbaum.

Redmore, C., Loevinger, J., and Tamashiro, R. T. (1978). *Measuring ego development: Scoring manual for men and boys.* Unpublished manuscript, Washington University, St. Louis.

Sartre, J.-P. (1947). *Baudelaire.* Paris: Gallimard.

CHAPTER 4

The Concept of Self or Ego

JANE LOEVINGER

M Y THINKING on the topic of the self has some points of affinity with several other essays in this volume. The closest tie is with the essay of Pamela White Hadas. Her topic, as I interpret it, is the terror one feels as one peers over the abyss into nonself. The fear of death, powerfully invoked by the poets she quotes, is not the only manifestation of that terror. Any major change—in particular, the changes brought about in intensive psychotherapy—has the potential to invoke a fear that partakes of that terror.

Having paid my respects to poetry, I propose next to pay my respects to biology, by showing that the self-system (to borrow Harry Stack Sullivan's term, 1953) is a branch of the immune system, or, if that is too bold an assertion, at least an interesting analogue of it. Let me begin with a story. Recently, a visiting psychoanalyst gave a talk to a psychoanalytic society on the fear of change, which, he asserted, is an important but little-recognized and little-discussed factor in treatment, especially in the early stages of psychoanalysis. He told of a vivid dream occurring early in the analysis of a young physician. The patient dreamed he was being operated on in an especially gory way. The visitor interpreted the gruesome operation as symbolizing the patient's fear of the radical changes that analysis might bring.

Ordinarily psychoanalysts commenting on visitors' talks are effusive in their praise, to a degree almost objectionable. On this occasion, however, after the obligatory praise and expressions of gratitude, one of the host analysts got up to comment, shaking with rage. The interpretation of the dream was wrong, he said. It should have been interpreted in terms of the id and the superego and castration anxiety and I forget what all else (for something in my "head" switches off when people start repeating those textbook interpretations).

The visitor replied mildly that the patient wasn't yet ready for such deep interpretations. Indeed, that was the point of his talk. Then, said the critic, that interpretation should have been given two years later, else the patient was being deceived and even cheated. He demanded that the visitor answer for his conduct. Had he made such interpretations? The visitor, somewhat shaken, replied, "Not perhaps to your satisfaction."

No one present had the courage to stand up and say, "Exhibit A. Here you see how afraid of changing his ideas even a normal person, even an eminent psychoanalyst, can be."

How shall we read the structure of the human soul? Shall we read it as the critic psychoanalyst does, as ego, superego, id, period? Or shall we add, as some psychoanalysts do, the ego ideal, or even add further an ideal ego? Or with Kohut and his followers, shall we add also a self, or several selves? Do we include or discard the original psychoanalytic system of the unconscious, the preconscious, and the conscious? There are advocates of each of those variant readings of the basic structure of personality.

And what of the Jungian version? Can it be that each person possesses (or carries, or comprises) all of those and also a persona, a shadow, an anima and animus, and a collective unconscious or "objective psyche"? Surely we cannot burden each person with all of the Freudian *and* all of the Jungian entities.

Closely examined, the disagreements among the Freudians are almost as striking as those between Freudians and Jungians. (I am unaware of whether there are equally striking variations among the Jungians *inter se*.) Surely some of those entities are dispensable without hampering our ability to give a relatively complete account of behavior, just as complete an account as with the added entities.

The fundamental problem, the factor that has brought self and ego theory to something of an impasse, is, in my opinion, the belief of the critic (and many like him) that what he sees and reports is both necessary and justified because it is the truth. A person who sees "how it truly is" must speak out for that truth, no matter how many entities already occupy the same "space," a figurative space, of course, as both Jaynes (1977) and Schafer (1978) insist. If there really and truly is a thing called the "self," that must be proclaimed, even if it treads on the toes of an ego already there.

The ego theorists and self theorists may or may not be misreading the human soul; I am certain that they misunderstand the nature of theory. All theories are, in principle, false. A theory is only a map, and no map reproduces the terrain exactly. A two-dimensional map, for example, cannot preserve both angles and distances. As a mathematical physicist once said about his kind, a physicist is a device for screening out most of the universe. If we understand the nature of theories in general, we should be inclined to hold particular theories more lightly.

So far I have done no more than give my own elaboration of one point which has been made by many others: There is no one true theory. As Jaynes (1977) has portrayed it, the self is a fairly recent invention of a species that over a million or two million years developed sense organs to survive in forest and field, not to introspect. Introspection is a phenomenon of only a few millenia at most, and introspection about the self, a phenomenon of only a small fraction of the species. Normally humans are well equipped to apprehend the world about them, but hardly equipped at all to apprehend their selves, assuming that there is a definite something that is a self, waiting to be apprehended.

And yet, finally, I cannot go all the way with Schafer's thesis (1981) that the self is no more than a set of narratives that we tell ourselves. I return to my little story. The patient, in enough pain to commit his time, money, body, and soul to psychoanalysis, is still so terrified of change that he depicts it as a horrifying surgical assault. Something must be postulated to account for the strength with which he had to protect himself from the assault and the damage that he anticipates at the same time that he asks for change (Vergote, 1957). (And what patient has not felt that fear, even terror?)

Look, too, at the psychoanalyst critic, and the fervor, the anger, one might guess the "fear and trembling," with which he defended his classical drive-theoretical interpretations from any dilution by the almost common-sense considerations of fear of change. Those classical interpretations that he invoked to account for the dream are the kind of thing on which he has staked his treatment, teaching, and writings for decades. He is not playing games or just telling stories. He is completely sincere in his beliefs. Like most or all of us, his deeply rooted beliefs have entered the fundamental structure of his personality, and he will defend that structure, exactly as the patient will defend the structure of *his* personality. No matter that one of them is, presumably, in principle, "healthy," the other, "sick."

I doubt that fear of change is less strong in the healthy soul. This conclusion for me is purely theoretical; however, James Hall (1977) appears to be making a closely related point on the basis of his clinical experience when he states that the anxiety that accompanies an incipient ego change seems independent of whether the change is regressive or progressive. I would go farther and say that although fear of change does not sound particularly healthy, that is just what it is. Is it not another name for, or perhaps another aspect of, what Freud called resistance? At the same time, as Sullivan (1953) vividly described, it is a manifestation of what he called the self-system.

Sullivan conceived of the self-system as the template or frame of reference within which each of us perceives and conceives the interpersonal world. It is the gatekeeper (Loevinger, 1976, Ch. 12). Any perception or conception that is at variance with our present framework causes anxiety; the discrepancy threatens our framework, our structure, our being. The most usual ways of meeting that threat are distortion of the perception so as to bring it within our current compass or, alternatively, "selective inattention" to the event. Only under special circumstances is any of us induced to change fundamentally. Those circumstances may be extended psychotherapy, particularly psychoanalysis or some variant, or unusual vicissitudes of life, especially during periods of rapid growth in other respects. That is the essence of Sullivan's theory, or at least of the aspects relevant to my discussion.

This dynamic of stability, movingly and brilliantly described by Sullivan, has never found a secure place in orthodox psychoanalytic theory, though surely many psychoanalysts understand it. Rapaport (1960) said (and was often approvingly quoted to this effect) that aspects of personality, or of the person, if you will, that changed slowly were therefore structural. Sullivan's theory is the converse. The self-system, Sullivan's name for what the psychoanalysts call structural, is part of the person's frame of reference; it screens out inconsistent observations and so can only change slowly. This dynamic I miss in the account of those theorists who oppose the postulation of a self or ego.

A few years ago I became fascinated with an account of multiple selves by Mardi Horowitz (1979) that presents a graphic and visual alternative to the Sullivanian concept of the self-system. There is potentially much clinical wisdom and much that is worth exploring in that way of looking at personality. But one way of looking at personality is just that: one way. It does not exhaust the possibilities. To me, Sullivan's way also seems valid, and the most straightforward way to account for both the thesis of the visitor and the reaction of his critic in my cautionary tale.

Whether we talk of the "self-system," as Sullivan did, or "stability of the ego," as many psychoanalysts would be inclined to do, or "resistance," as Freud did, or "fear of change," as the visitor did, or even, paradoxically, of "the power to die," as Hadas does, seems to me at least partly arbitrary. There really is something there, something all those ways of speaking reflect in various ways, all perhaps carrying other implications and "surplus meanings" that may be gratuitous, unverifiable, or even untrue. But there is a solid core of meaning, a solid set of phenomena, that are not conveyed by the image, or story, of a multiplicity of selves. The multiplicity of selves, in turn, represents other aspects of reality that are not conveyed by any rendering of a stable self or ego fearing its own annihilation. I see no way to dispense with either set of implications while being true to the data.

In short, while vividly aware of more or less contradiction and conflict in each of us, I still need a concept of ego or self to account for the stability that is to me the foremost fact about personality, at least after early childhood. I may have twelve selves at war with one another, but if I do, I will wake up tomorrow with the same twelve selves engaged in the same war. The fact remains that giving up the war of those "selves" or even surrendering any one of them is potentially a fearful experience.

As between calling this fact ego stability or a self-system, I have no strong preference. Take any such term and translate it into one language, then another, then back to English, and such distinctions will be lost anyhow. Freud's term was never *ego* but *das Ich*, which in French becomes *le moi*. More than one commentator (Bettelheim, 1983; Brandt, 1961, 1966; Kaufmann, 1981) has protested the travesty of translating these homely and childish words by the sophisticated *ego*. The only cure is to hold our terminology lightly, to constantly look through the words to the thing signified. Schafer would no doubt insist that it is the *person* who defends himself against change, not the self or ego, and I concur completely. I find the term *self* or *ego* convenient not for what is being defended so much as for the process of defense, a point exactly analogous to Jaynes's description of consciousness as a process. Fingarette (1963) long ago defined the ego as the process of making meaning out of experience and anxiety as the obverse face, meaninglessness; that is another way of expressing Sullivan's theory. In any case, the difficulty one has in rendering its fundamental terms into English testifies to the fact that terminology is not of the essence of psychoanalytic theory.

Lewis Thomas (1983), the biologist and poet, has had a lifelong interest in the immune system. One of its functions, he says, is to make the distinction between what is self and what is not self. What is not part of the organism it vigorously rejects or destroys. Moreover, in his opinion, and surely we will defer to his judgment on the point, some diseases and the most harmful symptoms of others result not from an invading organism but from a mistake on the part of the immune system, which treats a relatively harmless invader as if it were a noxious agent. As is well known, overreaction of the immune system is the major problem in surgical transplants. Thus, although the immune system is absolutely essential for the integrity of our physical being, and a person with a grossly defective one ordinarily soon succumbs, it can also be a source of trouble, including severe chronic diseases and even death.

My point is that Sullivan's conception of the self-system is similar. It too has the function of distinguishing the perceptions and conceptions that are assimilable to or by the self from those that are not so assimilable and rejecting or distorting those that cannot be assimilated. The problem of the psychotherapist, who faces the patient's resistance to change as the greatest obstacle to his work, is precisely that this stabilizing and homeostatic force, absolutely necessary for self-preservation, now stands in the way of attempts to bring about salutary change.

Thus the problem of resistance in therapy and the fear of change can be recast as a kind of autoimmune reaction of the self. Indeed, may we not include repression and the original formation of symptoms as autoimmune reactions? Whether this suggestion is a source of insight or is only a play on words I leave for others to judge.

References

Bettelheim, B. (1983). *Freud and man's soul*. New York: Knopf.
Brandt, L. W. (1961). Some notes on English Freudian terminology. *Journal of the American Psychoanalytic Association, 9*, 331–39.

————. (1966). Process or structure? *Psychoanalytic Review, 53,* 374–78.

Fingarette, H. (1963). *The self in transformation.* New York: Basic Books.

Hall, J. A. (1977). *Clinical uses of dreams: Jungian interpretations and enactments.* New York: Grune and Stratton.

Horowitz, M. J. (1979). *States of mind.* New York: Plenum.

Jaynes, J. (1977). *The origin of consciousness in the breakdown of the bicameral mind.* Boston: Houghton Mifflin.

Kaufmann, W. (1981). *Discovering the mind. Vol. 3. Freud versus Adler and Jung.* New York: McGraw-Hill.

Loevinger, J. (1976). *Ego development: Conceptions and theories.* San Francisco: Jossey-Bass.

Rapaport, D. (1960). The structure of psychoanalytic theory. *Psychological Issues, 2* (2, Whole no. 6).

Schafer, R. (1978). *Language and insight.* New Haven: Yale University Press.

————. (1981). *Narrative actions in psychoanalysis.* Worcester, Mass.: Clark University Press.

Spence, D. P. (1982). *Narrative truth and historical truth: Meaning and interpretation in psychoanalysis.* New York: Norton.

Sullivan, H. S. (1953). *The interpersonal theory of psychiatry.* New York: Norton.

Thomas, L. (1983). *The youngest science: Notes of a medicine-watcher.* New York: Viking.

Vergote, A. (1957). Psychanalyse et phenomenologie. *Recherche et débats, 21,* 125–44.

CHAPTER 5

A Language for Systematic Eclectic Psychotherapy

PETER GOLDENTHAL

MANY WRITERS and clinicians have come to realize that methods of effective psychotherapy conducted under the aegis of a variety of approaches may have more in common than is apparent from an examination of the discursive theoretical writings produced by these various schools. Writers such as Frank (1961), Goldfried (1982), and Kendall (1982) have called for investigations into the curative elements common to various forms of psychotherapy. While investigators differ in the precise language used to describe these common elements, there is widespread agreement that such commonalities do indeed exist. As early as 1936, Rosenzweig discussed the role of the therapist's theoretical orientation.

> Whether the therapist talks in terms of psychoanalysis or Christian Science is from this point of view relatively unimportant as compared with the *formal consistency* with which the doctrine employed is adhered to, for by virtue of this consistency the patient receives a schema for achieving some sort and degree of personality organization. (p. 414)

If effective psychotherapy relies on the same common curative elements regardless of the theoretical orientation of the clinician, it might be suggested that to be most effective, the clinician should abandon all specific theoretical orientations in favor of a model based only on the common curative factors discussed by Frank (1961) and others.

Such an approach, however, while theoretically appealing, has a major risk. As Rosenzweig states, while the specific orientation of the clinician may not be important, it is critically important that the clinician's thinking and activities be based on some specific, systematic, and consistent theory of personality and psychotherapy. There are several reasons for this. First of all, if Rosenzweig, Frank, and others are correct, part of the psychologically disturbed individual's problems stem from a lack of cohesive understanding of him- or herself, of the ways in which other individuals function, and above all of the source of his or her difficulties. After all, the goal of psychotherapy is not to produce problem-free living for the client—an impossible task—but rather to aid the client in developing more effective mechanisms and strategies for dealing with life's unavoidable difficulties.

Second, it must be remembered that the clinician too needs a structure in order to operate successfully. This is perhaps most obvious when one considers the training and supervision of beginning psychotherapists. It is certainly true that neophyte clinicians need experience with clients and practice in applying specific psychotherapeutic techniques. More than that, however, beginning clinicians need ways to think about clients and clients' problems, ways of thinking that foster organization of clinical observations, historical information, hypotheses regarding dynamics, and choices regarding intervention. In short, psychotherapists need sufficiently specific theories to guide their work. Without these, psychotherapy becomes a random series of behavior-change interventions. Many predominant theoretical approaches to psychotherapy differ from other approaches either by using unique, theory-specific therapeutic techniques or by explicitly avoiding the use of techniques that are inconsistent with that particular approach (Klerman et al., 1979). Psychoanalysis, for example, is characterized by the analyst's neutrality, by the use of interpretations of resistance and transference, and by the absence of direct instruction and advice giving or the assignment of therapeutic "homework" (Menninger, 1958). Much the same may be said of psychoanalytically oriented psychotherapy (Luborsky, 1984). Carl Rogers's client-centered approach (Rogers, 1942, 1951) utilizes the techniques of active listening and reflection of the client's feeling statements but does not employ interpretation—that is, the assignment of meaning or the explication of causal, dynamic connections among various statements or experiences. Behavior therapy (e.g., O'Leary and Wilson, 1975) utilizes a wide variety of techniques such as systematic desensitization but, while recognizing the need for a supportive therapeutic relationship, avoids a direct focus on the therapeutic relationship itself.

Clinicians who wish their work to reflect an awareness of the common elements that cut across the various psychotherapies are in a difficult position. Choosing to work solely from one of these theoretical orientations provides a clear structure and a systematic framework, while sacrificing considerable flexibility with regard to the intervention techniques that can logically be employed. Inextricably tied to selecting a specific psychotherapeutic approach is a choice to include some strategies to bring about the common curative elements (Frank, 1961) described above, while explicitly avoiding other specific methods and techniques.

One solution to the dilemma of maintaining both a specific theoretical orientation and flexibility with regard to specific interventions has traditionally been to engage in some form of eclecticism. Garfield and Kurz (1977) conducted a survey of eclectic views and found that some clinicians specifically combine elements of two or three theories, while others may pragmatically select the method or theory that seems to fit a particular client's problem or problems. Still another approach involves utilizing an amalgamation of theories or aspects of theories. Finally, some who describe themselves as eclectic work more pragmatically than theoretically, selecting individual techniques in accordance with their individual judgments.

An eclectic approach may, in fact, be the only way in which a practitioner can flexibly adjust techniques to fit individual clients. Yet such an approach loses something in terms of efficiency, in ways in which clinical experience can contribute to theory, and in the ability to provide the client with a united framework of the sort discussed by Rosenzweig (1936). The problem, then, is how to operate from a unified theoretical framework without sacrificing flexibility and clinical eclecticism when it is called for to respond best to clients' needs. This situation argues for a theoretical framework broad enough to incorporate the technical innovations of the various schools of psychotherapy and yet specific enough to utilize and integrate these techniques. Perhaps the needed framework is best thought of as a language chosen to fit the therapeutic process to guide the choice of intervention techniques and to analyze their effects.

Here *language* refers to a body of constructs incorporating those phenomena important to understanding clients and to conducting psychotherapy with them. Any construct, of course, represents an aspect of reality from only one of infinitely many possible perspectives. In abstracting from the ongoing phenomena of interest, much more must be left out of a selected or developed construct than can be included (see Johnson, 1946, for a comprehensive discussion of the process of abstracting). The choice of any construct does not rely on whether it is true or false, since no construct is either totally "true" or totally "false"; and since the most any construct can do is to capture some aspect of reality, never its entirety, the choice ultimately rests on its degree of usefulness. Thus, the choice of a set of constructs for a systematic eclecticism depends on a consideration of those aspects of clients' lives and of the psychotherapy process that are most crucial to understanding and planning the unique kinds of interaction we refer to by that name, as well as on the systems of interconnections among those constructs. What are these aspects of clients' lives and of the psychotherapeutic process? First, as clinicians we are clearly concerned with the things clients tell themselves, their hopes, aspirations, dreams, and plans for the future—that is, their life goals, as well as their evaluative statements about themselves, about their intellectual capabilities, interpersonal style, and personal concerns. Included here are such statements about oneself, usually made only to oneself, as "I am a weak person" or "I always have trouble coping with stress," as well as "I feel like I'm growing stronger and more autonomous." Certainly there are also many such self-evaluative statements of which individuals are unaware and yet which are of great influence.

Inasmuch as a great deal of psychotherapy focuses on what clients do, say, and feel in response to some external or internal event, there is a clear need for a construct or several constructs reflecting these activities. The kinds of activities or behaviors referred to here include some that are predominantly emotional, such as sadness, anger, anxiety, and joy, as well as verbal statements reflective of these emotional experiences. Overt, observable activities like running on a track, operating a lathe, or performing an experiment would also be included here. The psychotherapist is not only concerned, however, with easily observable activities. The person who labels her emotional state "I feel sad" or "I feel joyful" engages in a self-evaluative process related to, but different from, the experience of the emotion itself.

In addition to these statements, actions, and feelings, the ideas, activities, and relationships that clients value also figure importantly in their life decisions and determine in large part the extent to which they will find satisfaction in life. These values include preferences for certain kinds of rewards that may be available in life—financial, interpersonal, spiritual, aesthetic, to mention only a few examples. Values are also preferred ways of relating to the world. Thus an individual may value the opportunity to contribute to society above all else. She or he may equally value personal freedom or religious service in a similar manner.

However rich our understanding of intrapersonal dynamics, clients' lives cannot be fully understood without reference to context. Their relationships with others, both intimate and casual, have as meaningful an impact on their lives as do their private thoughts and feelings. The experience and meaning of depression, for example, can differ widely depending on contextual and relationship factors. Two people may feel lonely, sad, isolated, and hopeless, yet one may in fact be socially isolated while the other may have many interpersonal relationships.

In addition to constructs referring to specific elements of clients' lives, a systematic eclectic model of psychotherapy will need to include language useful for examining and describing the process by which individuals change, both in and out of therapy. A number of criteria seem indicated. First, the chosen language should be a language of change, one with an explicit model of process. While content categories for individual variables (for example, interpersonal style, self-confidence, aggressiveness) are clearly needed, the process of acquiring and changing these variables is most salient in conducting effective psychotherapy. Ideally, this language should reflect the learning process occurring in all forms of psychotherapy. Franz Alexander, one of those who have contributed most to modern revisions of classical psychoanalysis, conducted a fine-grained analysis of therapist-patient interaction using psychoanalysts as judges. In discussing his preliminary findings, Alexander comes "to the conclusion that the therapeutic process can best be understood in terms of learning theory" (1963, p. 446). Although there may be argument over the details of the kind of learning theory best suited to this task, it is clear that the process of psychotherapy provides a variety of new experiences for the client, who then changes in various ways as the result of the experiences. And, as Alexander goes on to state, "Learning is defined as a change resulting from previous experience" (p. 446).

Second, in order to enhance its utility to the clinician in formulating diagnoses and treatment strategies, the language should be as clear and as free from ambiguity as possible. Third, the language will best serve the purpose of guiding psychotherapy if the constructs can be tied to observable aspects of the client's world. This will help avoid the problem that arises when hypothetical constructs are defined only in terms of other hypothetical constructs, but never in terms of phenomena that the clinician can observe.[1] Fourth, a successful language for systematic eclecticism will describe the ways in which the constructs are linked, how changes in one aspect of a client's perceptions, thoughts, and feelings as actions may lead to changes in other areas. Fifth, this language will optimally function at a middle level of generality, neither so specific as to be restricted to a narrow range of interventions nor so general as to fail to provide any real guidelines for therapist activity.

The social learning theory developed by Rotter (1954, 1982) has the potential to serve as the framework for a truly systematic eclecticism in ways that may not be generally recognized. In what follows I shall briefly sketch some of the tenets of Rotter's theory and then indicate how they may be used to meet the criteria outlined above. Social learning theory draws on and combines aspects of both the cognitive, or "field" theories (e.g., Kantor, 1924; Lewin, 1935; Tolman, 1932), and the reinforcement, or "R-S-R," theories (e.g., Hull, 1943; Thorndike, 1932) dominant at the time of its development, and so may properly be considered an expectancy-reinforcement theory (Rotter, 1954, p. 80). Rotter discusses four classes of variables or factors that need to be considered in order to understand fully an individual's life, life situation, and, most important, conception of himself or herself. First, the individuals' thoughts about themselves, be they evaluative, descriptive, or phenomenological, are incorporated in the construct of *freedom of movement*. Their activities—including both observable and unobservable behavior, as well as the experience and expression of emotion, that often have both observable and unobservable components—are discussed using the construct of *need potential*. The extent to which individuals value various aspects of their lives are discussed here as *need values*. Finally, the contextual factors in individuals' lives are incorporated as the critical concept of the *psychological situation*, which, like need value, has a different meaning from those given to it in other personality theories.

This theory thus provides clearly defined and well-articulated constructs referring to clients' beliefs, thoughts, feelings, hopes, aspirations, goals, plans, dreams, urges, and strivings, as well as to their observable and unobservable behaviors and their personal values. In addition, as will become clear, social learning theory provides a way that clinicians can explicitly incorporate situational and contextual factors, the importance of which is now widely recognized, in their formulations and treatment plans. Most important, the theory operates at a middle level of generality, and so provides a clear guiding framework while permitting a wide latitude in the choice of specific therapeutic techniques.

It may appear that a number of theories of personality and psychotherapy might equally well be utilized as models for a systematic eclecticism. Certainly psychoanalytic theory provides a wealth of constructs for individual intrapsychic experiences of the sort referred to above. Humanistic approaches, such as client-centered therapy, also focus on the individual's inner subjective life in great detail. These two theoretical orientations, as well as others, meet many of the six criteria outlined above. In fact, from some perspectives they may offer a richness and a clinical lore not commonly associated with social learning theory. Hence, it may be unclear what advantages accrue to the systematic eclectic psychotherapist operating from a social learning perspective as opposed to one working within a psychoanalytic, client-centered, or other orientation.

There are several reasons why a truly systematic eclecticism cannot be based as readily on these models as well as it can be on social learning theory. First, the ultimate goal of the kind of eclecticism described here is to provide flexibility in the choice of interventions while conveying the benefits of a single, unified, organized, and systematic theoretical framework. This requires that the chosen framework be broad, process-oriented, and free of specific restrictions with regard to techniques. As noted earlier, however, many models of psychotherapy define themselves through just these kinds of restrictions. Clinicians choosing these models can gain flexibility only by violating the parameters of their chosen models.

Thus a client-centered therapist, for example, can choose to give advice, to praise a client openly, or to offer an interpretation only by stepping outside the theoretically specified framework. Gains in flexibility or breadth are thus offset by losses in theoretical purity and efficiency. The theoretical base of client-centered therapy gives no guidance on when to give advice, interpret, or praise exactly because it explicitly excludes these techniques. This argument applies equally to psychoanalysis or psychoanalytic psychotherapy. Psychoanalytically oriented clinicians who wish to apply nonpsychoanalytic techniques have no framework to guide them in choosing these techniques or in integrating them theoretically with other aspects of treatment. Such techniques might include, for example, the use of direct praise, advice giving, behavioral rehearsal, or hypnosis for purposes other than enhancing associations. Psychoanalytically oriented therapists are free to use these and other techniques, but, like their client-centered colleagues, only by stepping outside the therapeutic framework.

Strict behavior therapists are equally restricted in the range of interventions available to them if they wish to maintain theoretical purity. Many techniques that have no theoretical place in client-centered or psychoanalytic therapy are central to behavioral approaches. These include behavioral rehearsals, the use of homework, advice giving, desensitization procedures, and others. But behavior therapists wishing to acknowledge and interpret client statements and beliefs indicative of unconscious motivational processes in ways that will lead to insight must abandon their behavioral framework. Similarly, interventions focused on the therapist-client relationship have no theoretical place in behavior therapy per se. The same is true of Rogerian active listening techniques.

The second difficulty in developing a model for systematic eclecticism stems from the need for a genuinely eclectic therapist to account for both intrapersonal and interpersonal, contextual factors in maintaining and changing aspects of clients' lives. Psychoanalytic and humanistic theories tend to focus almost solely on intrapersonal, subjective aspects of clients' lives, seeing the interpersonal, environmental factors as stemming from intrapsychic realities. Behavior therapies, on the other hand, focus almost solely on environmental factors, neglecting or disregarding intrapersonal dynamics. Family systems approaches, too, relegate individual dynamics to the world of the unknowable, instead focusing on interpersonal (i.e., situational and contextual) variables exclusively. Clinicians operating from one of these frameworks who want to encompass factors not recognized by their models can do so only by abandoning those models (at least temporarily).

Social learning theory (Rotter, 1954) provides solutions to these two problems confronting would-be systematic eclectic psychotherapists.

The first problem, that of maintaining flexibility, is solved by having the theory operate at a middle level of generality. Other theoretical approaches (e.g., psychoanalytic, client-centered, behavioral) guide the practitioner toward narrowly limited ranges of techniques while excluding other, potentially very useful techniques from consideration. Social learning theory, on the other hand, in providing a more general framework, neither requires the use of specific techniques nor eliminates the use of others. It provides, rather, a set of theoretical tools for the analysis of individuals' problems and for the choices of functionally related groups of techniques to accomplish theoretically meaningful goals. In this model, insight, direct praise, and other techniques used by practitioners of all schools of psychotherapy can be utilized. Even more important, these techniques can be meaningfully integrated into a theoretically coherent whole; this is a model that clinicians need not abandon or step outside of in order to function flexibly. The second problem—that of being responsive to both the situational, contextual factors stressed by behavior therapists and systems theorists as well as the intrapersonal and subjective factors stressed by psychoanalysts and humanistic theories—is solved in social learning theory by using both individual and situational constructs. The constructs of freedom of movement, need value, and need potential refer to individuals' internal beliefs, expectancies, and goals, while the construct of the psychological situation refers explicitly to the role of environmental context, interpersonal as well as situational.

Several common misconceptions about social learning theory (Rotter, 1954, 1982) need to be addressed before its utility in guiding psychotherapy and in understanding individual differences in personality can be appreciated. First, social learning theory, unlike the learning theories of Hull or Skinner, for example, takes a holistic approach to understanding the individual. The concern is with understanding people as complete individuals in their intrapersonal and interpersonal contexts rather than with understanding isolated bits of behavior. Influenced by Kantor (1924) and Lewin (1935), Rotter defines the locus of personality to include both person and meaningful environment. "The unit of investigation for the study of personality is the interaction of the individual and his [sic] meaningful environment" (Rotter, 1954, p. 85). Here we are interested in the person in context—that is, the whole person—not just some pieces of behavior "emitted" by the person. Furthermore, social learning theory, like most theories of personality, assumes that "personality has unity" and that "new experiences are a partial function of acquired meanings" (p. 94). In this sense, social learning theory, at least at a high level of abstraction, shares much with the stated goals of those who present their views as antithetical to a "learning" or "behavioral" perspective, a concern for individuals examined and understood holistically with an awareness of the complexities of their cognitive and affective lives and experiences.

The second major misconception regarding social learning theory (Rotter, 1954) involves the extent to which individuals are "mechanistically" controlled by environmental factors, the extent to which the person can be thought of as analogous to a laboratory animal. Social learning theory focuses not simply on what happens to a person, but most importantly on how the person experiences, perceives, and thinks about what has happened. More important than knowing an individual's reinforcement history is knowing what decisions and conclusions the individual has made based on previous experiences. More crucial still for the clinician is understanding what the person hopes for and expects in the future. In short, social learning theory takes as its explicit concern an understanding of the individual's inner life with a focus on his or her inner cognitive life.

Three of the constructs noted above, freedom of movement, need potential, and need value, stem from the constructs of *expectancy, behavior potential,* and *reinforcement value.* Rotter (1954) defines behavior potential as "the potentiality of any behavior's occurring in any given situation or situations as calculated in relation to any single reinforcement or set of reinforcements" (pp. 50–51). Here Rotter (1954) defines any action that can be observed directly or indirectly and that occurs in response to a meaningful stimulus as behavior. Rotter makes it clear that he uses the term *behavior* in a much broader sense than is typically understood. Many psychoanalytic and Adlerian defense mechanisms—emotional activities and such cognitive activities as looking for alternatives or waiting for more data before making a decision—are all considered to be behaviors. Because *behavior potential* refers to the potential for the occurrence of a single specific behavior, the discussion of clinical problems is facilitated by the use of the term *need potential,* which refers to the potential for the occurrence of any one of many related behaviors.

Need potential, then is the potential for feelings that an individual may experience, activities in which an individual may engage, and, in the broadest possible sense of the word, behaviors that are part of the person's life. The likelihood of any set of related feelings—or actions occurring as part of a response to any set of thoughts, feelings, or actions that have meaning for the individual—would be conceptualized as need potentials. These behaviors may be directly observable, such as a student studying hard for an examination or a child learning to ride a bicycle, or they may only be implicitly observable, through their behavioral manifestations. So while we cannot observe another's emotional experience directly, we may be able to observe changes in skin tone, facial expression, and vocal intensity. These behaviors may be the feelings of affection between two lovers, the feelings of animosity between two competitors, or the feeling of despondency experienced by a characterologically depressed individual. Needs can also be individuals' private thoughts, feelings, hopes, plans, and goals, as well as cognitive appraisals or evaluative statements about themselves. The psychoanalytic defense mechanisms such as projection, rationalization, and displacement are also examples of need.

An expectancy is defined (Rotter, 1954) as "the probability held by the individual that a particular reinforcement will occur as a function of a specific behavior on his part in a specific situation or situations" (p. 50). Inasmuch as this concept of expectancy focuses on the individual's subjectively held probability rather than on objective "reality" is it much closer to the expectancy construct proposed by Lewin (1935) than to that utilized by Brunswick (1951). While individuals may incorporate what they know of an occurrence's objective probability into the expectancy they subjectively hold, this will not necessarily dominate their expectancy of such an occurrence. An individual's expectancies for the occurrence of a variety of related reinforcing events in response to any of several related behaviors in any of many related situations can be less awkwardly referred to by the term *freedom of movement*. Rotter (1954) explains that his choice of this term, when *mean expectancy* would have perhaps been clearer, was designed to indicate its relationship to other concepts of maladjustment; that is, an individual with a high freedom of movement would have relatively high expectations for success in a variety of life situations.

Freedom of movement refers to three kinds of inner cognitive activities, all of which involve overt or implicit decision making on the part of the individual. The first and simplest category involves descriptions or labeling statements such as "I am hungry" or "There is a restaurant." The second involves the individual's subjectively held judgment about the relationship between any of the kinds of activities described above as need potentials and their various possible consequences. Included here would be beliefs such as "If I work hard, I will succeed" or "If I am too successful, my parents will reject me." The third category is actually a subset of the second: subjectively held beliefs about whether the occurrence of a desired outcome increases the likelihood of another such desired outcome in the future.

The youngster who thinks, "If I work hard in school, I will succeed," for example, may or may not also think, "If I succeed in school, then I will become rich. My parents will be happy, and I will be content." Or, in the case of the child learning to ride a bicycle, "If I ride my bicycle everyday, soon I will be allowed to take off the training wheels." Freedom of movement, then, refers to the individual's expectations about what is and what is not possible for him or for her to achieve at a given time in a given situation. It is important to emphasize time and situation because, as noted above, social learning theory does not presume that an individual in one situation or at one time is exactly the same person as he or she is in another situation or at another time (see also Johnson, 1946).

While social learning theory does not explicitly address cognitive aspects of development, the freedom of movement concept provides a vehicle by which the clinician can explicitly integrate what has been learned by Piaget and his colleagues (Piaget, 1936/1952, 1937/1954) about developmental changes in the ways individuals perceive and understand events in the world. Inasmuch as expectations arise out of a personal process of abstracting from experience, the manner in which an infant, toddler, young child, school-age child, adolescent, or adult develops knowledge may greatly affect the expectancies that these individuals develop about actions and their consequences. A youngster who is able to handle abstractions comfortably, for example, will engage in a process of generalization from one experience to another that differs from that of a child who has not yet developed this kind of abstract thinking about cause-and-effect relationships. These conclusions about causes and effects and about the similarity of classes of events or behaviors strongly influence expectations about the relationships among active behaviors and the attainment of personal goals. Clearly, then, an individual's freedom of movement regarding the relationship between classes of behaviors and classes of outcomes will depend to a large extent on the way in which the individual abstracts similarity across events, as well as the manner in which she understands cause and effect.

Considering a person's subjective understanding of the possibility of the occurrence of certain events or experiences has a wide range of utility. It is possible to discuss a student's freedom of movement regarding the probability that if she studies hard she will get an A on an English exam. Freedom of movement does not apply only to such discrete situations, however. It also makes sense when applied to an individual's subjective beliefs that if she acts throughout life in a way consistent with her personally held values—that is, with some personal moral code—she will ultimately have fulfilled her life in a manner consistent with her religious beliefs.

The construct of freedom of movement can also be used to conceptualize discrete events as well as large, broad, abstract categories of events, both internal and external to the person. Implicit in the construct is the idea first introduced by Tolman (1932) that individuals are goal-oriented. These may be short-term goals, as in the case of the high school student who hopes to get an A. They may be goals of moderate duration, as in the case of an executive who hopes to have a certain contract accepted by a client. They may also be goals at a very high level of abstraction and with a very long time frame, as in the case of the individual who wants to lead a meaningful life and to contribute to society in some way that may not be evident until after his or her death.

Freedom of movement, then, refers to the individual's subjectively held belief that behaving in certain ways will, to a greater or lesser extent, lead to a desired goal. The behaviors may or may not be discrete. Individuals hold implicit beliefs about the likelihood that certain behaviors, in the broadest sense of the word, will lead to certain goals in the short or long term. There is no need to assume that individuals are always aware of these goals or even that persons are aware of their own subjectively held belief about the probability that these goals will be achieved.

The third major construct in social learning theory is that of reinforcement value, which is defined as the degree of preference for a specific potential reinforcer if all possible reinforcers were equally likely to occur (Rotter, 1954). As was the case for expectancy and behavior potential, it is convenient to be able to consider related sets of reinforcers having identical or highly similar preferences. In social learning theory these sets of related reinforcers are referred to as needs and an individual's preference for one set of needs over another is referred to as a need value, essentially a mean reinforcement value for a set of reinforcements. An individual's need value for a goal depends on how important that goal is to the person. Considering the high school senior who hopes to get an A on her English exam, the need value that coincides with the grade of A refers to how important the individual feels it is to achieve an A as opposed to a B. In the case of the person who wants to be remembered for contributing to society, need value refers to the importance the person places on achieving this goal. The importance of achieving interpersonal goals similarly can be construed in terms of need value. Once again, it is not at all necessary that individuals be totally aware of holding these values. Some people may at times be aware of some goals, while at other times these goals may be totally out of awareness.

The fourth variable, and in some ways the most unique to this theory, is that of the psychological situation. It is here perhaps that the language of social learning theory most clearly contributes a dimension to the understanding of individual experience and functioning absent from many theoretical descriptions of personality currently used to guide clinical practice. Social learning theory clearly acknowledges that individuals behave in more or less consistent ways across a variety of situations and across relatively long periods of time. To truly understand another's experience, however, one must realize that individuals live not in isolation but in complex interpersonal contexts. The psychological situation refers to those aspects of an individual's environment at a given time that make a psychological difference in the individual's experience and awareness. This implies two things. First of all, some physical, environmental changes may make no difference, psychologically speaking. To take a trivial example, there is no reason to believe that the high school student's feelings about an examination depend substantially on whether the exam is taken in a cafeteria, in an auditorium, in a small classroom, or in a large classroom. On the other hand, situations may differ psychologically in important ways while still being physically very similar. For example, the student may have very different feelings about the likelihood of achieving her goal depending on whether this examination is in English literature or chemistry, even though the two examinations are taken in the same room, sitting at the same desk, and so on.

The psychological situation not only refers to psychological aspects of environmental change but also includes other people who figure importantly in the individual's context. For example, while a child's psychological situation certainly includes the fact that the child is at a day-care center or at home, it also includes the context defined by the child's family—parents, siblings, grandparents, and other relatives. The concept of psychological situation also refers to the fact that while parents, for example, influence children by providing the context for their development, children in turn influence parents, providing a context for their development as well. In fact, the complex pattern of interaction and reciprocal influence that occurs in a family might easily be conceptualized as consisting of the interplay of the ways in which individuals in the family play important roles in the construction of the psychological situations in which they and other family members function. In this sense, the concept of the psychological situation is not linearly causal; rather, it implicitly refers to a circular system of interaction.

In general, the greater the individual's freedom of movement and need value for one of a related set of behaviors (using the term in its broadest possible sense) in a certain psychological situation, the more likely the person will be to behave in those ways. In other words, the higher an individual's subjectively held belief (freedom of movement), be it conscious or unconscious, that engaging in one of a related set of behaviors will ultimately lead to a desired goal, and the more the individual values that goal, the more likely it will be that the individual will behave in those ways. As before, behavior here refers to observable behaviors, inner thoughts, feelings, defense mechanisms, and all other forms of action. An individual client may be able to explicate his or her need values and freedom of movement for some kinds of behaviors; considerable work may be necessary to lead to insight into the active factors in maintaining other sets of behavior.

Consideration of the relationship between an individual's freedom of movement for a set of needs relative to that individual's value for those needs is particularly critical for clinical practice. Some individuals feel a great need to attain a goal or a set of goals and, at the same time, feel incapable of doing so. For example, many students experience an exceedingly high need for outstanding academic achievement.

Such individuals have very high minimal goal levels; only the very highest grades (for example, straight A's) are experienced as positive, while other moderately high grades (for example, B's) are experienced as failure. Other individuals may place a high value on goals that are unobtainable, or at least unobtainable in our culture, such as being liked by everyone, or having all of one's dependency needs met all of the time, or having a marriage in which there is never any disagreement or conflict. Individuals in situations like these are most likely to engage in the defensive, avoidant behaviors that interfere with achieving satisfaction in life and that manifest themselves as various forms of psychpathology. From a social learning perspective, then, the goals of psychotherapy are to help clients increase their freedom of movement, to modify inappropriate need values, and when possible, to restructure psychological situations to permit them to have more positive, rewarding life experiences. This approach is distinguished from other forms of psychological treatment neither by the techniques it employs nor by the techniques it specifically avoids. It is distinguished, rather, by the method of analysis it brings to clinical problems. The analysis of a client's need potentials, need values, freedom of movement, and the psychological situations in which they occur leads to certain implications at a middle level of generality for treatment goals, but not to specific treatment techniques. The clinician chooses the specific treatment techniques only after developing a thorough understanding of the client's problem, personal values, needs, goals, perceptions of the world, and life experiences. Of course, the clinician's choice of techniques will also be guided by personal values. The middle level of generality at which a social learning language operates makes it well suited to an integrated systematic eclecticism. A wide range of techniques, drawn from an equally wide range of psychotherapies, may be employed to help the client change. Active listening, interpretation of underlying unconscious motives, and behavioral homework all have equal places in this eclectic approach to psychotherapy. These techniques, and an unlimited array of others, may be chosen to lead to changes in freedom of movement, need potentials, need values, and psychological situations. In every case, the specific techniques are chosen, according to a social learning analysis, to fit the particular client, problem, situation, and context.

No two individuals are identical, no two life problems are identical, and from the perspective outlined above, no two clients are treated identically. Most interventions will be chosen to facilitate change in need values or freedom of movement. Because individuals are unique, it is not possible to draw up firm rules for selecting the specific techniques which will best facilitate these changes for clients. Some clients may be able to make significant life changes in response to a commonsense educative approach. With others, the clinician may find it necessary to engage in considerable historical and dynamic exploration.

The manner in which a systematic eclectic approach combines a wide variety of therapeutic techniques is best explicated through example. The following brief case descriptions illustrate how the rationale of social learning theory facilitates selection of techniques to fit a case. The techniques themselves are in no way unique. What is unique is the manner in which a systematic eclectic approach guides the clinician in selecting techniques to fit individual clients, based on a social learning analysis of the individual, not on a preconception of what is "good for everyone." Thus, this model provides a truly client-focused psychotherapy.

J. S. is an electively mute five-year-old boy. His parents report that he began to speak normally at about one year of age and that his speech appeared to develop normally up until the age of two and a half. At that time, his father experienced a serious reversal in his business, putting the family under considerable stress. J. became more and more reticent outside the home, finally refusing to speak at all to anyone other than his parents and maternal grandparents.

At the time of referral, J. was enrolled in kindergarten in a suburban public school outside Boston. His presentation during the initial therapy session, which he attended with his parents, was of "a little old man," a phrase echoed by his teachers and parents. J. maintained a very stiff posture throughout the initial hour. He was totally silent and constantly maintained a serious, somewhat gruff facial expression. He sat in an adult-sized chair, nonverbally refusing the offered child-sized chair. During the hour, he did not move from his chair to explore the play materials conspicuously displayed throughout the consulting room. Neither did he remove his jacket, although the room was quite warm. He also protested vigorously, through gesture and by refusing to move, the suggestion that he and the therapist might spend some time together while his parents sat in the waiting room. J. did not respond to the therapist's questions and remarks, either nonverbally or verbally.

Mr. and Mrs. S. were also noticeably restrained in their style of

interaction. While both expressed concerns about J.'s reticence, neither was predisposed to overt manifestations of their feelings. Mr. S.
stated that he was extremely concerned about J., but did so with considerable affective control. Mrs. S. was relatively quiet throughout the
meeting. Both Mr. and Mrs. S. felt that the business difficulties of
several years earlier figured importantly in their son's current problems. Both also acknowledged that the problem was theirs as much as
it was his. Mr. S. further stated that J. had "no need to talk" because
he and his wife had learned to "read" his wishes and to anticipate his
needs. Observing J.'s stoic manner, his refusal to acknowledge questions or comments, his expressionless features, and the way his parents' interventions obviated his need to communicate, the therapist
conceptualized the case as one in which the child J. S. experienced
low freedom of movement, not just for speaking outside the home but
for any kind of display of emotion or interest in others. The therapist
also hypothesized, based on Mr. S.'s statements, that his son behaved
similarly in all extrafamilial situations, that speaking outside the home
generally had little value for J. S. The role of the psychological situation was particularly salient in this case; J. was apparently discriminating between situations in which he was alone with his family and
those in which others were present in addition to, or instead of, his
parents or relatives. Furthermore, it was clear that Mr. and Mrs. S.'s
need values regarding their son's beginning to speak in public were
ambivalent. For this reason, the therapist's initial formulations involved the entire family system.

At this point, the therapist hypothesized that, in addition to having
relatively low freedom of movement with regard to talking, J. S. was
experiencing low freedom of movement for any activities (for example,
facial expressions of emotion, free body gestures, unguarded posture)
that might lead to engaging in interaction with non–family members.
The therapist further hypothesized that this constriction might reflect
the current functioning of the family, more specifically of his parents.

The first strategy was to conduct a series of family interviews to
learn more about the patterns of family interaction and about J.'s
parents' expectations and feelings regarding his beginning to speak
outside of the family. This focus was based on the therapist's understanding of the important role parental wishes play in the lives of all
young children. J. S. could be expected to experience very little freedom in speaking to the therapist, to his schoolmates, or to anyone else,

if his parents, perhaps unwittingly, communicated to J. that they placed a high value on his remaining relatively immature and dependent in interpersonal situations. The therapist adopted two strategies based on these initial formulations. First of all, he wanted to increase J.'s freedom of movement for engaging in some form of communication with nonparental adults. In order to do so, he adopted a very free, permissive, nondemanding stance. J. was encouraged to explore the toys in the therapy room and to engage in puppet play and drawing as modeled by the therapist, but was not pushed into any of these activities. Similarly, he was asked if he would like to "play" with the therapist alone while his parents waited outside, but was not pushed into doing so. The technique of allowing this youngster to choose his own activities and to control the extent of his involvement with the therapist is similar to that utilized by Allen (1942). The rationale for its choice, however, is quite different from Allen's and illustrates the utility of the sort of eclecticism advocated here. Allen believed that all troubled children, whether fearful or aggressive, benefited from free, relatively unrestricted activity in the play or counseling room. In the case of J. S., this set of techniques was chosen as a means of enhancing this child's freedom of movement for expressing feelings, thoughts, and wishes outside of his family. These techniques would not have been employed so extensively if J. S. were less timid, and not at all if he were aggressive. This then, is one illustration of the way a set of techniques derived from a specific perspective (Rankian in this case) can be most effectively applied after a social-learning-based analysis of the individual in treatment.

The systematic eclectic psychotherapist has a great advantage not enjoyed by clinicians who restrict their interventions to those promulgated by one "school." Unlike Allen (1942), J. S.'s therapist was committed not to a set of techniques but to developing and utilizing whatever techniques would enhance this child's freedom of movement for the desired behaviors. Operating from this framework, the clinician was able to incorporate forms of intervention usually associated with clinicians who have adopted a family systems perspective (e.g., Haley, 1976; Minuchin, 1974; Selvini-Palazolli et al., 1978). The therapist also began to meet with Mr. and Mrs. S., both with and without J. In these sessions, the goal was to clarify their freedom of movement and the value they placed on J.'s speech. The therapist was also interested in discerning the ways Mr. and Mrs. S. influenced the psychological situation in which J. functioned, and vice versa. It soon became clear that Mr. and Mrs. S. preferred not to discuss many aspects of their lives, supporting the hypothesis that they may have unconsciously encouraged their child's elective mutism.

It also became clear, however, that discussions of their marital relationship drastically lowered their freedom of movement for obtaining satisfaction from the therapeutic relationship as it had come to be defined. Mr. and Mrs. S. began to cancel sessions, to express unhappiness at how therapy was progressing, and to be even more reluctant to discuss their concerns openly. At the same time, there had been no noticeable improvement in J.'s interpersonal constriction. For these reasons, the therapist decided to abandon the technique of conjoint family interviews. The therapist did not reject the probability that parental concerns were strongly influencing J. It did appear clear, however, that those particular techniques were unlikely to be helpful.

Inasmuch as Mr. and Mrs. S. felt strongly that J. should be seen alone, arrangements were made to do so. Because of the child's continuing discomfort, Mrs. S. was encouraged to sit in on his first session. This was done to increase both mother's and son's freedom of movement in the therapy situation. J. did not speak in the first session with his mother. She too was quite reserved, similar to her behavior in the family sessions where her husband tended to speak for both of them. The therapist's goal was twofold. He hoped to increase Mrs. S.'s freedom of movement for sharing her thoughts and feelings, so that she might demonstrate these to J. and so increase his freedom of movement, and to enhance the value she placed on seeing changes in J.'s interpersonal behavior. The primary technique employed to attain this goal was active listening. After the first month, Mrs. S. became much more active verbally. During the third month, she described in detail some of the financial difficulties the family had recently experienced. During the same session, J. began, for the first time, to whisper to his mother. While he did not direct his speech to the therapist, some of it was audible.

Over the next several months, as Mrs. S. became more comfortable in talking to the therapist, J.'s whispering to her became more frequent and more audible. School personnel reported that he had begun to participate more actively in classroom activities, to smile more, and to respond (nonverbally) to questions. His freedom of movement for interpersonal exchange had apparently begun to increase. The therapist responded to Mrs. S.'s reports of these changes with direct praise. This technique is inconsistent with the Rogerian approach used up to this point, but totally consistent with the goal of enhancing Mrs. S.'s value for increasing her son's interpersonal involvement.

After several more months, Mrs. S. reported that J. had begun to talk occasionally to a boy in the neighborhood. School personnel continued to report improvement in his interactions with other children. J.'s whispering continued to increase and was joined by occasional laughter and giggling. He began first to be willing and then apparently to look forward to spending at least part of his session alone with the therapist. Therapy continued, relying mostly on permissiveness, freedom from demands, and following the child's lead—all employed as tactics for enhancing his freedom of movement.

The second illustrative case shows how the same theoretical framework can lead the clinician to choose quite different techniques. S. N. is a ten-year-old boy referred for treatment by his teacher, who had been concerned for some time about his unusual behavior. At the time of the referral, she explained that he avoided eye contact, especially with adults, refused to shake an adult's hand, frequently made odd noises, and often walked with an odd apelike gait, his arms hanging down at his sides. Above all, he avoided friendly interaction with other children, and, in the weeks preceding the referral, he had been involved in two incidents that she found particularly disturbing. The first involved pushing a girl down a short flight of stairs after accusing her of "yelling at him." The second incident, even more disturbing both to school personnel and to S.'s parents, occurred in response to teasing by another boy. According to his teacher, S. N. put his hands around the boy's neck, appeared to be attempting to strangle him, and in fact reportedly said that was exactly what he was trying to do. S.'s teacher also reported that he had asked her if she ever thought of killing herself, stating that he often thought of such things.

S. appeared to be moderately depressed at an initial interview with his parents. When seen alone, S. said that he felt "sad all the time" and that he wished he could be "somebody else," "an actor," and "strange." He explained that he was really "strange" and "weird" and that he liked being that way. S. also described himself as being dumb and terrible at sports. Mr. and Mrs. N. expressed unhappiness with S.'s slight overweight and with his poor achievement in school. Mr. N., who also has a weight problem, described his academic achievement as a youngster by noting that he outperformed all his peers in every academic area. Mrs. N. described herself as having done reasonably well in school but as having had, and continuing to have, problems interacting socially with groups of individuals.

The therapist's initial formulation involved several elements. First, he hypothesized that S. might have very little freedom of movement in the academic sphere, which, coupled with a very high value placed on equaling his father's academic performance, tended to lead to his sadness and depression as well as to his avoidance of academic tasks. In other words, S. was viewed as having a high, and perhaps unrealistic, academic minimal goal level, probably maintained by that of his parents or at least by his perception of his parents. The therapist further hypothesized that a similar set of factors operated for S. in a very different psychological situation, that of interpersonal peer relationships. It seemed likely that his relatively constrained freedom of movement in this aspect of his life, combined with a normal value for friendship, might have led him to engage in various avoidant behaviors including ostensibly adopting a desire to be different from his peers.

The initial goals of treatment were to enhance S.'s freedom of movement in both the academic and interpersonal psychological situations and to help him to lower his minimal goal level for academic achievement. The treatment strategy was based on a belief that there was a great deal of connection between these two aspects of S.'s life and that improvement in one would likely lead to improvement in the other. After talking with S., the therapist determined that he believed his parents would be angry if he did not produce stellar academic performance, and that he was incapable of producing this. The therapist then discussed the matter with Mr. and Mrs. N., who explained that while they had never explicitly demanded an extraordinary level of performance from S., they had done so from his three older brothers. They both agreed that S. could easily have drawn the conclusion that similar standards were being held out for him. The therapist directly encouraged them to help S. understand what their expectations really were and to help him to lower his demands on himself. Over time, this approach was successful.

S.'s lack of awareness of any connection between his unusual behavior and goals and a desire for satisfying peer relationships ruled out the direct, educative approach taken with regard to his academic problems. Active listening techniques of the sort typically associated with Rogers's client-centered therapy were used to enhance S.'s freedom of movement in the therapeutic situation in general and for expressing his feelings in particular. Unlike therapy conducted solely from a client-centered framework, however, the systematically eclectic therapist utilized other sets of interventions to achieve the desired goals of enhancing S.'s freedom of movement and clarifying the value peer acceptance held for him. Interpretations of J.'s symbolic, idiosyncratic, and metaphoric communication, more congruent with psychoanalytically oriented psychotherapy than with Rogers's approach, were also utilized. These insight-oriented interventions were utilized to change S.'s freedom of movement by helping him to speak directly about his personal concerns. For example, S.'s often expressed desire to own an underground cave with elaborate machines responsive to his wishes was interpreted as his wish to have a place where he could get away from everybody, where he would be safe and in control. Since wishes of this sort were repeatedly expressed, interpretations of their hidden meaning were also made regularly in the first months of treatment. In addition, S.'s repeated assertions that he was somehow different from his peers in a negative way were interpreted as a desire to be special. Observing that S.'s "weirdness" seemed to be quite consciously adopted, the therapist suggested that S. wanted to be seen as special, and because he felt unable to be especially popular or athletic, chose to be especially strange.

Learning that swimming was one area in which S. both excelled and felt confident, the therapist encouraged him and his parents to devote energy to this activity. Mr. and Mrs. N. found a swim club where S. could receive recognition for his ability without being prematurely pushed into a competitive situation. In doing this, they provided a new psychological situation for S., one in which he could experience success and specialness based on ability, not self-imposed disability. The therapist also directly praised S. for his swimming ability, at the same time challenging his view of himself as being strange. This use of direct praise, a technique advocated by both Adler (Ansbacher and Ansbacher, 1979; Dollard and Miller, 1950), provides another example of how a systematic eclectic approach can utilize a wide variety of techniques while maintaining a unified conceptual framework.

As treatment progressed, S.'s use of metaphoric language to express his concerns diminished as his direct expression of them increased.

He rarely displayed the unusual facial expressions and bodily postures that had so worried his teacher. His use of animallike noises disappeared totally. He no longer looked depressed or spoke of wishing to die. While he continued to experience some difficulties in making friends and in getting his school work finished on time, it was possible to deal with these in a straightforward manner.

It is not possible, within two brief case examples, to illustrate all, or even a significant number, of the techniques that an eclectic psychotherapist may employ. The cases just described utilized Rogerian active listening, interpretation of unconscious motives, direct praise by the therapist, direct suggestion, and educative parent guidance. Clearly these techniques come from a very disparate group of psychotherapies, and yet they have been utilized within one integrated and systematic framework. In each case the choice of techniques was based on a social learning analysis and not on a preconceived notion that a specific technique or set of techniques should be utilized in working with all clients. In principle, any technique that the clinician has found effective may be utilized in this manner. Dream interpretation, hypnosis, and relaxation training—all can be employed to aid clients in changing their freedom of movement, need values, and psychological situations.

The goal of achieving maximum flexibility in the selection of psychotherapy interventions can lead to an atheoretical, technique-centered approach, or it can, as has been advocated here, lead to a truly systematic eclectic psychotherapy. Rotter's (1954, 1982) social learning theory provides a broad process-oriented framework that, by operating at a middle level of generality, facilitates the selection of appropriate intervention strategies from among those typically associated with psychoanalytic, humanistic, behavioral, and other therapies. The advantage of this approach to eclecticism stems from the way in which social learning theory provides an interrelated set of constructs for analyzing people's problems and for planning intervention strategies. Social learning theory differs from other theories, however, in that it neither prescribes a specific set of techniques nor proscribes the use of others. While it is not currently possible to delineate guidelines for the matching of techniques to clients and to specific problems, the development of such guidelines represents a logical next step in the development of this model. A wide variety of techniques associated with various forms of individual therapy are, however, readily subsumed under this theoretical framework. In addition, those associated with systems approaches are also encompassed by the construct of the psychological situation. The way in which social learning theory can systematically organize the most useful interventions of a variety of therapies has only been suggested in this paper. The approach outlined here could also potentially be productively utilized to integrate approaches, such as individual psychodynamic and family systems, heretofore regarded as basically incompatible.

Author's Note

The model proposed here represents an extension of ideas suggested by J. B. Rotter in his writings and in many discussions. Any misinterpretation or inaccuracy, however, is entirely the responsibility of the author. I also thank George J. Allen, Len Milling, Judith Goldberg, and Rob Wozniak for their comments and suggestions on an earlier draft of this paper and Harper Reno for her assistance in manuscript preparation.

Notes

1. This is the problem that Wendell Johnson (1946) refers to as "short circuited abstraction."

References

Alexander, F. (1963). The dynamics of psychotherapy in the light of learning theory. *American Journal of Psychiatry, 120,* 440–48.

Allen, F. H. (1942). *Psychotherapy with children.* New York: W. W. Norton.

Ansbacher, H. L., and Ansbacher, R. R. (1979). *Alfred Adler: Superiority and social interest.* New York: W. W. Norton.

Bandura, A. (1977). *Social learning theory.* Englewood Cliffs, N.J.: Prentice-Hall.

Brunswick, E. (1951). The probability point of view. In M. M. Marx (Ed.). *Psychological theory.* New York: Macmillan.

Dollard, J., and Miller, N. E. (1950). *Personality and psychotherapy: An analysis in terms of learning, thinking, and culture*. New York: McGraw-Hill.

Frank, J. P. (1961). *Persuasion and healing*. Baltimore: Johns Hopkins University Press.

Garfield, S. C. (1982). Eclecticism and integration in psychotherapy. *Behavior Therapy, 13,* 610–23.

——, and Kurtz, R. A. (1977). A study of eclectic views. *Journal of Consulting and Clinical Psychology, 45,* 78–83.

Goldfried, M. R. (Ed.). (1982). *Converging themes in psychotherapy*. New York: Springer.

Haley, J. (1976). *Problem-solving therapy: New strategies for effective family therapy*. San Francisco: Jossey-Bass.

Hull, C. L. (1943). *Principles of behavior*. New York: Appleton-Century-Crofts.

Johnson, W. (1946). *People in quandaries*. New York: Harper and Row.

Kantor, J. R. (1924). *Principles of psychology* (Vols. 1–2). New York: Alfred A. Knopf.

Kendall, P. C. (1982). Integration: Behavior therapy and other schools of thought. *Behavior Therapy, 13,* 559–71.

Klerman, G. L., Rounsaville, B., Chevron, E., Nev, C., and Weisman, M. (1979). *Manual for short term interpersonal psychotherapy (RPT) of depression*. Unpublished manuscript.

Lewin, K. (1935). *A dynamic theory of personality*. New York: McGraw-Hill.

Luborsky, L. (1984). *Principles of psychoanalytic psychotherapy: A manual for supportive-expressive treatment*. New York: Basic.

Menninger, K. (1958). *Theory of psychoanalytic technique*. New York: Basic.

Minuchin, S. (1974). *Families and family therapy*. Cambridge: Harvard University Press.

O'Leary, K. D., and Wilson, G. T. (1975). *Behavior therapy: Application and outcome*. New York: Prentice-Hall.

Piaget, J. (1936/1952). *The origins of intelligence in children*. (M. Cook, Trans.) New York: International Universities Press.

——. (1937/1954). *The construction of reality in the child*. (M. Cook, Trans.) New York: International Universities Press.

Rogers, C. (1942). *Counseling and psychotherapy*. Boston: Houghton Mifflin.

———. (1951). *Client centered therapy.* Boston: Houghton Mifflin.

Rosenzweig, S. (1936). Some implicit common factors in diverse methods of psychotherapy. *American Journal of Orthopsychiatry, 6,* 412–15.

Rotter, J. B. (1954). *Social learning and clinical psychology.* Englewood Cliffs, N.J.: Prentice-Hall.

———. (1982). *The development and application of social learning theory: Selected papers.* New York: Praeger.

Selvini-Palazolli, M., Lecchin, G., Prata, G., and Boscolo, L. (1978). *Paradox and counterparadox: A new model in the therapy of families in schizophrenic transaction.* New York: Jason Aronson.

Thorndike, E. L. (1932). *The fundamentals of learning.* New York: Columbia University Press.

Tolman, E. L. (1932). *Purposive behavior in animals and men.* New York: Appleton-Century-Crofts.

PART II

Self as Pretext

Nietzsche . . . considers what may have been the original motive toward this moral enterprise. He admits, first of all, the self-protective nature of simulation, the need to protect one's "true" or naked being by little fibs; then, this being so easy to do, one may be tempted to go further, to increase one's estate by gratuitous or malicious misrepresentations. Nietzsche goes on to suggest that "because man, out of need and boredom, wants to exist socially," he will try to make a "peace pact" with his fellow human beings through semantic constancy.

Pamela White Hadas, this volume, p. 215

A PRETEXT IS an account that does not precisely mean what is said—a cover or facade behind which other meaning is hidden. Ideological statements, dreams, and self reports can be readily interpreted as pretexts, in that they conceal certain undesirable interests or situations in favor of more desirable ones. Every speaker or writer communicates through some vested interest linked to ideology or identity. Every text, especially every text involving self and its description, can be read as a pretext, an effort to create a consistent meaning structure to conceal experiences of discontinuity, alienation, or death.

Essays in this section make claims for the primacy of discontinuity in human experience, the effects of inexplicable happenings and accidents, the everyday deaths that are beyond our control. Approaching the topic of self from a hermeneutical premise—that all understanding is interpretive—the essays give accounts of self as ways of speaking or knowing that arise in our efforts to conceal a lack, gap, or ignorance.

The problem of interpreting expressions of self is the problem of understanding what its references are. These accounts move beyond the Wittgensteinian position of relating language games simply to each other. These authors presuppose both a historical context and the possibility of truthfulness in their accounts. They favor a dialogical basis of trust regarding self texts, although they assume that the text conceals and pretends a reality which does not exist, the continuous self. Whereas Wittgenstein addresses the necessity of understanding competing realities of textual interpretations, these authors assume the necessity of understanding the common grounds that permit a dialogue of differences.

In this way, we could say that the essays here present a text as well as a pretext for self. While they privilege no correct interpretation of self, within or outside of a particular culture, they search for what is purposive and explanatory in addressing accounts of a self. This interpretive approach to pretext and discontinuity is similar to what Robert Dostal (1987) asserts about the hermeneutics of Gadamer: "Though the hermeneutical experience of understanding is universal, texts are not the universal and sole objects of the understanding. . . . The task of the interpretation of a text is to once again bring to speech what is fixed in the text" (p. 6). The task of interpretation—"to once again bring to speech"—is to reveal the foundation for dialogue, the common ground against which conflicts take place. Within such a spoken dialogue, or a written effort to establish its basis, there emerges some kind of shared framework (however implicitly) that Gadamer calls the "fusion of horizons." Grounded in what is spoken about— the self, in this case—authors herein reveal the representations and rules that allow us to talk about intentionality, rationality, style and action in the face of alienation, despair, and discontinuity. Refuting a unitary construct of a core self, they embrace a search for meaningful explanations for the project of self, whether the project is conceived as "vicarious introspection" (empathy), self-deception, or mirroring self-reflections.

The first three essays are organized around the theme of *meaning* as introduced by Donald Spence. He focuses our attention on the narrative function of self: the search for general principles (substituting the abstract, coherent, and rational for happenstance and chaos) that assist us in turning away from what is too painful and immediate. Such a search, Spence says, can potentially be demonstrated to follow "a limited number of patterns, which have been used over and over again" (p. 146). Potentially only, however, because he anticipates our self-deception even in the search for dramatic and mythological accounts of self (the "deep structures" of self narrations) that may obscure the actual narrative function of self stories.

> If the self is in the business of emphasizing sense over ref-
> erence and if it relies primarily on narrative modes of
> thought, then almost by definition, it cannot be reduced to
> a standard schema or represent one out of many possible
> templates. . . . Ideographic rather than nomothetic, the sci-
> ence of the self may slip between our fingers until we in-
> terrupt our search for regularities and turn to more
> primitive forms of description and illustration. (p. 147)

By primitive forms, Spence means the more immediate and observable
details of particular life histories or narrative accounts. Rather than
impose a pattern (of regularities), Spence would have us establish "the
transformation rules that are used to turn happenings into meanings.
. . . We aim not to reduce a lived life to a set of standard patterns but
to discover something that has never been described" (p. 148). Thus,
from Spence we gather an orientation to biographical and psychobio-
graphical accounts that urges us to be alert to new meanings in both
the narrative inventions and other descriptive accounts of self.

This is precisely the approach taken by Craig Eisendrath in his
interpretation of Kafka's autobiographical and fictional selves. By entertaining several descriptions of Kafka "as a person"—for example,
classification of him as a personality disorder and journalistic impressions written by his friends—Eisendrath allows us to discover something we have not previously known about Kafka: the paradox of his
self-abnegation. Many of us believe we know the "true Kafka" as the
prototype of alienated man. As Sharp (1980) puts it, "Kafka did not
go insane, but he was certainly suffering . . . for he was caught in what
Jung called 'the provisional life': one's lot is not what one really wants;
one is always 'about to' take the step into real life; some day one will
do what is necessary—only not just yet" (p. 75). From Kafka's fictional
and journalistic accounts, we may become convinced that he did indeed only pretend to an existence and that his experience of alienation
was so profound as to make him somehow exempt from responsibility
and intentionality. Curiously, Kafka moves us to accept a depoten-
tiated and tortured self as the true version of himself—when we are
suddenly aware that Kafka has revealed his private sufferings boldly
and explicitly in a way that contrasts with his own claims.

Moreover, Eisendrath shows us descriptions of Kafka from friends
and publisher that provide images of a charming and warmly engaged

person, thoroughly at odds with Kafka's own self-narratives. The "transformation rule" for Kafka's life turns on the irony of his self-abnegation. Convinced of his inferior masculinity and prowess, Kafka constructed a world wherein he achieved status and meaning by weaving the fabric of self-depreciation and despair. As Eisendrath says, ". . . we cannot know the arrangement of his conscious field, but we can see vividly in his writings how he has appropriated the world into a complex presentation . . ." (p. 171). This presentation, his pretext of self, is finally the self-image retrieved in its opposite, fame and acceptance. Kafka's self-depreciating pretext is the vehicle by which he converts his personal suffering into public displays, achieving eventually such broad acceptance that even his name is used as an English adjective (Kafkaesque). Clearly his fame and acceptance came late, much of it after his death. All the same, it was contained in his writing, repressed in his autobiographical accounts, in the desire for public recognition in many of his characters as they search the world for reflections of themselves.

Jacques Lacan privileges a particular moment in the human life cycle as the birth of self: the reflection of oneself as an Other, the image in the mirror. This is the original paradox that binds one forever to the world: we can see ourselves only through reflections. The unification of subjectivity can never be directly known but is always repressed and projected onto the Other. Consequently, we are caught in a hermeneutical circle. Condemned to seek ourselves in what we cannot see, we can see ourselves only as we are reflected. Paul Kugler, in the next essay, extends our understanding of Kafka's life by showing us how Lacan's psychology plunges us into a Kafkaesque series of inescapable deceptions that constitute the drama of self. From Lacan's point of view, the narrative of self must be read from three perspectives of competing self-constructions: the real, the imaginary, and the symbolic.

Kugler directs our attention especially to the problems in imagining the self as Other, both in terms of this unitary construction of self-experience and in Lacan's refusal to apply his own methods to his psychology. By valuing the unitary and the visible, over and above the discontinuous and invisible, Lacan's account excludes what is mysterious and unseen.

The next essay, by Pamela White Hadas, turns us directly toward the problem of what is unseen and obscured by any account of a continuous self: *death* in both its momentary and its final forms. Freud viewed all interest in immortality as motivated by compensation, the setting up of illusory and wishful defenses against disintegration. White Hadas also persuades us that the self is an account of immortality and continuity, a pretext of power displays over against our experience of powerlessness, but she approaches her subject matter (death, disintegration, and stasis) from a different premise than did Freud. Self is a play on words whose scenes are captivating precisely because they are self-limited and transitory rather than because they are a compensation for our fears. Her project of self is a play space of words and images that inform us and are informed by finitude.

Her chapter is central to the orientation of this section because it draws on both psychological and literary explanations for the creation of self as pretext. White Hadas's self is recreative and recreational, provoked by moments of disintegration and despair, and ever revisable in its imaginary space. Perhaps the vitality of personal causation (as depicted by deCharms in the earlier section) is, in our experience, the freedom to construct and revise the symbolic forms of our own immortality. Our reflections on death command our attention and grip our imaginations in a constantly recurring fashion that becomes the self of daily life.

The freedom to create self out of experiences of disintegration may be directly connected to the esteem we feel for our individual worth and ability. The next two essays, under the heading of *gender*, speak in different ways about the condition of women in a male-dominated culture. Relating especially to the psychoanalytic interpretation of self, Judith Kegan Gardiner and Harriet Chessman are united in one theme only: let us not privilege the phallus (as the monotheistic and singularly known) as the epitome of self. Unless the female experience of the unseen and the unknown (e.g., the space within, the vagina, the servant, or the unnamed) is included in our account of self, we are at odds with experience. Thus autonomy, the ideal of ego psychology, is not a primary goal in a feminist account of self, whether the text is psychological (Kegan Gardiner) or literary (Chessman).

The conclusion of Chessman's essay turns us back again to the problem of interpretation. She says "All this, of course, is not to say that interpretation is impossible. Perhaps what we mean by interpretation must be transformed to include the kind of interpretation that is not 'claiming anything,' but is guessing at 'anything'" (p. 268). Her state-

ment echoes Spence's central interpretive rule to discover the unexpected meaning as one of the very "hallmarks of truth telling" in a
hermeneutics of self.

References

Dostal, R. J. (1987). The world never lost: The hermeneutics of trust.
    Philosophy and Phenomenological Research, XLVII, *3,* 413–434.
Sharp, D. (1980). *The secret raven: Conflict and transformation in the life
    of Franz Kafka.* Toronto, Ont.: Inner City Books.

SELF AND MEANING

CHAPTER 6

Turning Happenings into Meanings: The Central Role of the Self

DONALD P. SPENCE

I

PUTTING THINGS into words is a serial activity that funnels a multivariate reality into an ordered stream of language. Grammar requires selection: present is distinguished from past, actions are supplied with motives, mother is separated from father, and "perhaps" is separated from "absolutely." No telling can be faithful to the life being described.

> The art of reflecting that is essential to conscious awareness [and to the logic of putting things into words] is transferred, by a kind of unavoidable optical illusion, back to the stage of the event iself . . . autobiography [and free association] is condemned to substitute endlessly the completely formed for that which is in the process of being formed. (Gusdorf, 1980, p. 41)

The need to impose order, rationality, coherence, and causality on the fabric of life has been described as the original sin of autobiography (see Gusdorf, 1980), and the same argument applies to the productions of patients in psychotherapy and psychoanalysis. It could be argued that Freud hoped to escape from this inadvertent ordering with his new invention of free association, but he could not escape the necessary ordering imposed by grammar and syntax; truly free associations are incomprehensible and are quickly interpreted as a form of resistance. And even a moderate degree of free association still cannot recover the uncertainty of lived time; the patient can never

recapture the sense of events unfolding or reconstruct the uncertainty
of what tomorrow will bring because at the time of telling, he is looking
back at a completed past and he knows what happened. He may remember the excitement of going off to college or the fear of leaving
home to join the paratroops, but he can hardly recapture the suspense
because he knows how the story came out.

There is also reason to question the usual model of remembering
in which previous happenings are faithfully stored and unerringly
retrieved. If we question the permanence of memory traces (see Loftus and Loftus, 1980), if we realize that the remarkable recoveries
described by Penfield (1958) apply to only a small fraction of his patients, and if we take seriously the discrepancy between the accounts
of the same event by the same person at different points in time, then
a good part of free association may be more composition then recovery. The patient is not "playing back" a childhood tape, but is attempting to attach words to a series of mere impressions.

The narrative smoothing that we see in any attempt to represent
the world, whether in the form of memories, free associations, or case
histories, can be looked at from two quite distinct points of view. Describing autobiography as an original sin directs our attention to the
way in which smoothing leads to error and gets in the way of a veridical
report. From another point of view, however, the nature of the narrative construction and the particular form it takes may be more important than its truth value. What Gusdorf has called the original sin
of autobiography may be more benignly described as a signature or
a fingerprint. The way a life is conceived or described tells us something important about the teller that he very likely does not know
himself. Signature, fingerprint—or more abstractly, the self—becomes
the organizing subject of this essay, and we will consider whether signature, fingerprint, or perhaps some other metaphor is the best way
of representing the central topic.

II

To bring meaning out of confusion can be described as one of the
central missions of the self. The concept of self reminds us that a
certain structured constellation of attitudes, principles, and values
contributes to our view of everyday happenings and affects the way

these happenings are represented in memory and recovered over time. What Gusdorf has identified as an interference with recall is perhaps the structure of recollection itself, which comes into being long before the autobiography is begun.

The concept of self as a signature or structure has some clear advantages over the metaphor of computer as mind. To think about intercourse with the world as a species of "input" and "output"—a species of "information processing"—is to suggest that stimuli are faithfully registered in this transaction. Left out of this account is the fact that stimuli are rendered into input, that input is not permanently stored over time, and that the act of retrieval may often influence the contents of what is retrieved. There seems nothing in the brain that in any way resembles the fixed and faithful "read-only memory" of the computer. Conversely, there seems nothing in the computer that represents the consistent "input-output mismatch" of human interactions—error, perhaps, but not random error.

In an essay on autobiography, Elizabeth Bowen gives us an even further reason for being dissatisfied with the computer metaphor. "The 'I' in the narrative," she writes, "stands for something more than consistent viewpoint or continuity; it provides the visionary element, in whose light all things appear momentous and fresh—though they may not be new, though they may have happened before" (Bowen, 1962, p. 71). The all-seeing "I" that gives form and substance to observed happenings is visionary because it goes beyond the data and provides order to chaos and meaning to random occurrence. There may be an important connection between the visionary function of the self and the possibility (about which more later) that meanings and happenings are essentially distinct and nonoverlapping. It could be argued that the self functions *primarily* to give meaning and organization to a largely ambiguous world; thus it carries an adaptive advantage and might even be studied from an evolutionary point of view. Need for the self and its meaning-generating function is perhaps uppermost in man, for whom both the inner and outer environment carry a wide range of different possibilities. Other species, because they are more stimulus-bound, tend to respond to their surroundings in more immediate and "hard-wired" fashion and thus have less need of a system that can be used to supply meanings and choose among alternatives.

At the core of this conception of the self stands the function of language. It is by means of a continuous dialogue with ourselves—in daydreams, partial thoughts, and full-fledged plans—that we search for ways to interact with our environment and turn happenings into meanings, and we organize these interactions by putting our reactions into words. Daydreaming may be thought of as a way of applying the selective and categorizing functions of the self to the outside world, and even though visual, our daydreams also have significant verbal fragments: I have interior dialogues with significant people, I begin or continue important letters, I hear myself reacting to possible questions or situations. Even the more visual pieces of the daydream may be initiated by language and owe their organization and mode of representation more to grammar than to the purely visual features of the world. Language offers a mechanism for putting myself into the world, as Heidegger might phrase it, and for making the world part of me; and language very likely determines the way in which experience will be registered and later recalled. To see the importance of language is to understand why the poet has always been a potential enemy of the state: his verbal gift allows him to see things in an original way and to communicate this vision to others. If we are right in assuming that meaning is imposed from without and if certain governments have a vested interest in imposing only one meaning, then the poet is perhaps one of the few who can see a different meaning and make others see it too.

The visionary function of the self, mentioned above by Bowen, is clearly conveyed by language. The novel turn of phrase allows us to see the ordinary in a fresh light, and a rich stock of figurative language can turn the ordinary into the fantastic (as in Shakespeare). We see things in a new way because someone before us—a poet or novelist—has found the right words and his vision becomes ours. Whether we are talking about metaphor or aphorism or narrative, each new usage supplies a new set of meanings and enriches our outlook. This store of images becomes a critical part of the self and the way it brings order into the sheer *thereness* of the world.

III

We have been arguing that a central function of the self is to bring meaning out of chaos. At this point, it might be useful to look more closely at how much order actually exists in the everyday world. We will take the position that a faithful description of this world would realize less patterning than is commonly assumed, and we will make the rather strong claim that the world is composed of two domains—meanings and happenings—that are essentially distinct and non-overlapping. "Events," writes the archeologist and philosopher Paul Veyne, "have no natural unity; one cannot, like the good cook in Phèdre, cut them according to their true joints, because they have none . . . events do not exist with the [consistency] of a guitar or a soup tureen" (Veyne, 1984, p. 37). "Facts," he says in another place, "do not exist in isolation" (p. 32); in other words, a fact becomes a fact only when embedded in a certain context.

One of the characters in the novel *V* by Thomas Pynchon tells us that "there is more accident to [life] than a man can ever admit to in a lifetime and stay sane." Many events, as we will learn later from "flashbulb memories," have their significance problematically attached to them after the fact, whereas other, less significant happenings may be given an arbitrary meaning at the time they occur, a meaning that will be revised later as a new context develops. While some attempts have been made to formulate a taxonomy of events that depends on their formal properties (see Gibson, 1975) and to argue that we look for the appearance of natural forms in nature as a guide to understanding, there is no clear evidence that meaning is inextricably linked to happening. "Social actions," writes Gergen,

> appear to carry little in the way of intrinsic meaning; the conceptual categories or meaning systems into which they are placed appear primarily to be products of social negotiation. The fact that a given stimulus pattern falls into the category of "humor," "aggression," "dominance," or "manipulativeness," for example, depends not on the intrinsic properties of the relevant pattern but on the development of a community of agreement. As a result, the labeling of any given action is forever open to negotiation among interested parties, and the legitimacy of any observation statement is continuously open to challenge. (Gergen, 1978, p. 1350)

At times there may be less agreement than we assume and the "pattern" is simply imposed by the observer.

It can be argued that, far from being transparent and open to immediate classification, the great majority of events are without clear meaning or pattern and that a full description would disclose a surprising degree of ambiguity and unpredictability, which makes them impossible to classify or remember or interpret. Happenings appear all around us; they are what we see if we see clearly; but their meaning is not immediately given because meanings belong to a different domain. Happenings tend to be physical events that are "out there," and describable. But where happenings are pictorial, sharp-edged, and concrete, meanings are verbal and often abstract. To put things into words is to endow a happening with a meaning; to remember something is to supply a meaning to an event; to forget something may be to lose the meaning of an event.

Happenings as a description of sheer events or sheer thereness have much in common with Heidegger's *facticity*—the idea that we are cast into a world of things not of our own making, coming to us from the past. These things, for Heidegger, are always understood in personal terms; we project meanings onto them without being aware of it, and as a result, happening is almost never seen apart from meaning. But Heidegger is also sensitive to the fact that many of these meanings are false simply because they are subjective, and that we are, as a result, enslaved by the things of the world because we do not see them in their true state. To this extent, he would agree with our thesis that meaning and happening are not two sides of the same coin and that in many cases enslavement comes about because the meaning imposed on a happening is not the true meaning but the result of custom, tradition, official account, or some other institution that gets in the way of seeing clearly. To the extent that meaning is imposed from without, we may lose part of our freedom and our ability to see clearly and without preconception or subjective delusion.

Some have said that happening alone in its sheer thereness cannot be stared at in isolation; we always thirst after meaning because we are pattern-finding creatures. As a result, we are always on the lookout for covering narratives that will describe and/or explain what are essentially empty or ambiguous sequences, and endow them with meaning. But to the extent that these covering narratives are not part of the happening itself and to the extent that they come from a completely different domain, then the covering narrative may prevent us from seeing the happening in its pure state. What is more, it is no longer possible to turn back and recapture the pure state, because of the way that meaning participates in memory. This is the danger of narrative smoothing—it not only supplies a simplified description for a more complex happening, but in many cases, the description, or covering narrative, takes the place of the original happening and makes it impossible ever to see it clearly again. To make matters worse, description is then mistaken for explanation so that we delude ourselves into thinking that we understand something that never occurred in the first place.

The loss of freedom brought about by narrative smoothing is balanced by the terror brought about by seeing the sheer thereness of the world. The central drama of *The Iceman Cometh* deals with the need for pipe dreams, the need to have some kind of narrative smoothing, to have some kind of rose-colored glasses; scorn and anger were heaped on Hickey when he tried to take them away. He is surprised by the anger because he believes that people are grateful when they are no longer being deluded; he does not understand that delusions are needed because a world without meaning is too much to bear.

If we understand the deep-seated need for pattern and order, we can begin to see how necessary is the narrative-building function of the self and, from the side of the listener, how quickly we grasp at any kind of explanation. The untrustworthy teller of stories is in a position of enormous power and influence; in the world of story-telling, it is always a seller's market. I have written elsewhere (see Spence, 1983) about the grounds for narrative persuasion, and at least four principles seem important. There is, first, a clear advantage to the first account; if I can explain something that has never been explained before, then my story will always carry a certain kind of conviction regardless of its truth value. This kind of argument can be called argument from exclusion (see Quine and Ullian, 1970), but it carries an obvious danger: if almost any account is better than no account, then the way is open to almost any kind of irresponsible explanation.

Second, we are influenced by the range and scope of the narrative account.

> If I can show that your life can be reduced to a limited number of significant themes, variously repeated and transformed, then it follows that this account will tend to be more persuasive than a formulation which must invent a

new reason for each new [happening]. The rule of limited reasons (extended scope) draws some of its appeal from a mistaken analogy with the natural sciences. It is as if I have found a basic law that can be applied to a wide range of situations. Apart from this dubious comparison, however, there is the undoubted aesthetic satisfaction in finding that one theme continues to appear and reappear in a person's life; this kind of dramatic parsimony is the basis for great literature and one of the appeals of famous autobiographies. (Spence, 1983, pp. 461–62)

Third is the principle of frequency and familiarity. This principle gives priority to narrative accounts that contain arguments we have heard before, and once again, we have a mistaken analogy to the natural sciences. To invoke a familiar explanation has the look of replicating a known principle; the analogy fails because to invoke an argument says nothing about whether it is true or false. Nevertheless, there is an appeal in the familiar, and the more frequently it is invoked as an explanation, the more persuasive the appeal. Despite the principle of argument by exclusion, there is a certain distrust of novelty, and familiar explanations, though wrong (consider the "laws" of "common sense"), often fare better than "blue sky" arguments, even when right.

Fourth (in the case of psychoanalytic patients in particular), there is the principle of here-and-now fit.

A given narrative account that meshes with the current experience of the patient in the transference (what might be called its "real-time" component) will tend to be more compelling than an alternative that does not. If the patient is experiencing (and is aware of) angry feelings toward the analyst, he is likely to be more persuaded by an account of his past organized around similar feelings than by a similar account in a period of positive transference. Under conditions of positive feeling, the angry narrative may be intellectually understood but only superficially experienced and, moreover, may run a substantial risk of being forgotten. Under conditions of negative feeling, it not only meshes more exactly with the patient's ongoing experience; it may also bring into awareness pieces of the past which support the narrative and which have remained out of awareness until that moment. (Spence, 1983, pp. 462–63)

What do these principles of narrative persuasion tell us about the difference between meaning and happening? That, first, because all of us are more charmed by order than by disorder, we are in a poor position to separate plausible from actual accounts, particularly when the latter are illogical and quixotic. Nor (in the clinical situation) should we be taken in by so-called confirming associations, because these may simply mean that the patient has learned to see his past in a new manner and not that this new discovery is necessarily causal or of primary significance. Third, it would seem a mistake to use confirming associations as proof of a theoretical proposition, because to use such statements as evidence would seem to disregard the many demand characteristics of the treatment situation and the degree to which all of us are constantly searching for the best-fitting explanation.

IV

The difference between meanings and happenings also has clear implications for our theory of memory. Even if it is less a collection of traces than we like to think, *something* is evidently preserved over time, and there is more and more evidence to support the idea that images are stored in a different (and perhaps more lasting) fashion than words. What has been called the dual-coding theory of memory (see Bucci, 1985) suggests that specific pieces of the world—in particular, concrete images of common objects—are stored in one modality and verbal traces in another. Other evidence suggests that pictorial representations may be more distinctively coded and more subject to retrieval, whereas verbal traces may be coded with respect to length of word, number of syllables, and initial letter and thus may be more easily confused (see Brown and McNeil, 1966; Shepard, 1967).

Visual storage allows us to collect appearances—but not necessarily meanings. Visual storage seems more resonant with happenings. The more concrete the item, the more we can capture its surface size, shape, and texture and the less we need to embed it in a particular context—an elephant is always an elephant. Thus it may happen that memories in the visual mode are relatively innocent with respect to meanings. The flashbulb vividness of visual memory makes it possible to remember pieces of the past but not necessarily remember what they represent, because meanings tend to be abstract and are often hard to represent in visual form. As a result, a given visual memory can be woven into any number of narratives, and if the visual quality is uppermost, there is nothing in the recovered memory to confirm or disconfirm one interpretation over another.

The dual-coding theory also implies that verbal memories are distinctively coded and stored separately from visual memories. This theory supports the hypothesis that the meaning of an event is not necessarily attached to its visual icon (the happening). As a result, the original meaning need not be recovered with the original image. It would also follow that new interpretations will not necessarily be disconfirmed by original meanings, because the latter are stored in separate codes and probably in separate locations.

If we focus now on the verbal store, we find that certain systematic changes take place over time. The specificity of a one-time event tends to be transformed into a general set of rules that cover a number of occasions but lose the hard edge of the particular occasion. What are called episodic memories (concrete events—e.g., I went to the store yesterday for a jar of marmalade and three papaya) tend to become consolidated into semantic memories (abstract principles—e.g., a representation of what season is best for good tropical fruit). It seems as if the general features of a series of activities become organized into an abstract schema that provides information about the underlying common denominator. Suppose I make regular trips to the opera. The episodic memory of going to see *Carmen* on a particular Saturday afternoon in November is gradually transformed into an abstract schema that provides information about optional routes, best times for departure, what time the garage closes, good neighborhood restaurants, and so forth. Much less available are memories about particular performances, or the plot and cast of a particular opera.

It can be argued that episodic-to-semantic transformations also take advantage of the dual-coding system. What is initially an episodic event is probably highly saturated with visual features—the color of the seats in the first-visited opera house, the spectacular rising chandeliers, the specific texture of the applause. These and other sensory surfaces are captured and preserved in visual memory. But as we make repeated trips to the opera and build up an opera schema, it becomes more abstract and semantically articulated, and as the schema becomes more extended, it begins to lose its concrete, visual features. Episodic memories are partly visual and are probably stored in a visual mode; semantic memories are more abstract and are probably stored in a verbal mode. The resulting recoding detaches them from a particular time and place; thus I may know that access to the garage is problematic after 12:30 but no longer remember just when I became aware of this fact.

Marigold Linton's research on memory in everyday life (1982) contains many useful examples of these transformations. She first made a record of each day's most salient experiences over a period of six years (e.g., "I go to New York for the first time"; "I xerox the final draft of the statistics book and mail it to Brooks/Cole"). She then sampled these events in semirandom fashion by drawing two items each month from the accumulating pool, estimating their chronological order, and attempting to reconstruct their dates. She often found it impossible to distinguish items that described the same general event; for example, she mailed off the "final draft" several times and had no way of dating the entries. Even more striking, some entries made no sense at all, suggesting that the context assumed at the time of writing the entry had disappeared by the time of recovery. In the first case, the episodic nature of mailing off the "final draft" had been transformed into a general schema of mailing off manuscripts, and the specific features of the particular event had been forgotten; in the second case, the specific nature of the item (its episodic signature) had been eroded—probably because it did not belong to a general category of repeated activities, it ceased to make sense.

Linton's findings suggest that semantic memory of repeated experiences is far superior to episodic: her general store of information was far greater than specific memories of specific happenings. Her findings have important implications for what might be called the original sin of psychotherapy. On the one hand, the vividly remembered detail may appear in isolation, deprived of an enabling narrative context, and thus be particularly vulnerable to an after-the-fact reconstruction. On the other hand, a well-preserved schema of abstract information (in the summer we used to visit my grandfather in Wisconsin) may bring with it an accumulation of images from different periods of time, some of them specific to Wisconsin, some specific to other trips, and some pseudo-images that belong to pieces of the family romance (stories about trips to Wisconsin, sometimes fanciful and embellished, may be recoded as visual images). In either event, a specific visual icon is not necessarily attached to its original meaning or its original place in my particular life, and thus becomes freely available, subject to the beck and call of the most compelling narrative.

V

We have seen how verbal memories may be stored separately from visual and how, within the verbal store, semantic memories tend to be extracted from episodic. It now remains to be seen how these two processes affect our store of meanings. Both the separation of verbal from visual and the gradual shift from concrete to abstract would tend to make meaning less and less relevant to happening. Knowing something about the specific transition of episodic memories into a semantic trace may provide us with the detailed knowledge of just how the self comes into being. One person, for example, may maintain an episodic memory much longer than another; one person may separate meanings from happenings much sooner than another. If the self represents a collection of organizing principles, we should be able to find consistency at the lower level, and a careful study of the way experience is transformed into memory, à la Marigold Linton, should give us insight into the rules by which the self comes into being. But as we will see, it is possible that only a certain number of principles will be uncovered because of the essentially ideographic nature of the self. We will have more to say on this topic later.

We are now in a position to return to the self and its relation to memory, meanings, and happenings. It can be seen that our sense of the self is intimately connected with our store of current memories. At the same time, we see that the self is closely connected with the formation of these memories. We have defined remembering as the joining together of meaning and happening. More specifically, an episodic memory comes into being when meaning is joined with happening. Notice that the meaning may be either true or false; in other words, there is nothing inherent in the act of "remembering" that tells us we are retrieving something that really happened—we could be simply imagining a nonevent. Thus we can define remembering as primarily an achievement of the self—the act of linking meaning with happening—but not necessarily an act of information retrieval. The act of remembering is entirely subjective and has no necessary reference to the outside world.

What happens as time passes and episodic memories become semantic? The original memory, which was a linkage of meaning and happening, is now decomposed into a largely abstract "meaning" (the quotation marks are used to indicate that it may have nothing much to do with the original event). Happening has been removed; that is why Linton may have a memory of "mailing off the manuscript" but have no recollection of which event she is describing.

It now becomes clear that forgetting can result from separating meaning from happening, and this can take place in one of several ways. It may happen that the meaning becomes too abstract, as with semantic memory, and in that case we have lost the details of the original incident; the Linton example comes to mind. Second, the meaning may be simply lost, and because we have no access to the happening per se, we have the subjective sense of having forgotten it. Third, the happening may remain intact but linked up with the wrong meaning; in this case, we "remember" what never happened, and we forget the original event. The last case fits the description of Freud's screen memories.

I have written elsewhere that

> we are all the time constructing narratives about our past and our future and that the core of our identity is really a narrative thread that gives meaning to our life, provided— and this is the big if—that it is never broken. Break the thread and you will see the opposite side of the story. Talk to patients in a fugue state, to patients with Korsakoff's syndrome or Alzheimer's disease, and you will sense the terror that lies behind not knowing who you are, what happened yesterday, and what will happen tomorrow. (Spence, 1983, p. 458)

The terror stems, in large measure, from a view of the world consisting of separate domains of meanings and happenings. Our need to find a meaningful story about the world makes it extraordinarily difficult to see a lived life as merely a series of discrete happenings; not only do we automatically impose a structure on random events, but the anxiety aroused by their randomness makes it difficult to concentrate on them for any length of time. "I don't care what you call it," says the protagonist in the recent novel *Waterland* by Graham Swift,— "explaining, evading the facts, making up meanings, taking a larger view, putting things into perspective, dodging the here and now, education, history, fairy-tales—it helps to eliminate fear."

It would seem that the self provides us with an extended grammar by means of which we can "parse" the world, select the most convenient units, and impose the necessary meanings on these units to preserve them in memory. The most dramatic example of this activity is seen in the generation of "flashbulb memories" (Brown and Kulik, 1977). "Memories become flashbulbs," writes Neisser, "primarily through the significance that is attached to them afterwards; later that day, the next day, and in subsequent months and years" (Neisser, 1982, p. 45). This is a good example of how meaning linked to happening can generate a memory. The apparent veridicality of these memories, sharp-edged and visually impressive, probably stems more from the attachment of meaning than from the fact that they really happened. We see once again that subjective clarity should not be confused with correspondence to reality.

If the self contributes to the formation of memories, particularly episodic memories, it can be seen to repair the split between meanings and happenings. We began with the assumption that much of the external world carries with it little in the way of inherent meaning. In order to have dealings with this world, however, we must find some way of assigning meaning. These assignments can be neither totally arbitrary nor unnecessarily short-lived. We have argued that the self provides the invariance over time that allows the world to be seen as less random, less fragmented, and less episodic than it really is. We have argued that the self does the work of choosing appropriate units, assigning meaning, and discovering entry points in the world of happenings, and that this search for meaning determines much of what we remember. Language in general, and daydreams in particular, seems to play a principal role in this search for meaning.

We have noted that the self is nourished by memories, particularly by episodic memories. But since many of these "memories" are actually constructions of the self, we see a second function at work. The self not only contributes meaning to the world by joining meanings with happenings but also contributes meaning and organization and some kind of enduring permanence to itself. In a certain sense, then, the self is more real, more constant, and more internally consistent than the so-called reality "out there," and if the self possesses this advantage, we see another reason why loss of self—and by accompanying loss of memory—seems so catastrophic. By the same token, we see the dangers produced by an unstable sense of self. Take the self away—or replace it by another, less familiar—and we are faced again by a world of meanings and happenings that only now and then overlap. In extreme situations, we are confronted by chaos.

What makes it so difficult to study the self is that it can never be seen clearly, that it varies so much from one person to another, and that its organizing principles are largely implicit. A specimen of self-reports or daydreams or childhood memories from different subjects would contain differences as well as similarities, and perhaps that is the reason why, up to now, the self has been little more than a metaphor—comforting as a piece of folk wisdom but not very useful as a model. Only by staying with the same subject over time—in the manner of Murray's *Explorations in Personality* (1938), the developmental studies of Jack Block (1971), and the first-person reports of Marigold Linton (1982)—only by gathering repeated attempts to classify the world *by the same person* will we learn much of importance about the implicit grammar of the self, because the family of self language is probably as large as the family of man.

If each person sees the world in his own fashion and if there is no definable reality to be seen, then we are tempted to return to autobiography as a rich source of data—but with a slightly different twist. What Gusdorf has called the "original sin" becomes a kind of Holy Grail, not something to be discounted as we read over or around it, but something to be teased out, precisely identified, and elaborated into a predictive mode.

Consider *The Education of Henry Adams* and what it tells us about his self. We discover that he says nothing about the occurrence of his wife's suicide. Instead of asking what really happened, we can look at the ways in which he avoids this and other tragic events. We discover that he substitutes the abstract for the concrete and (in all likelihood) focuses on the sweep of history in a search for general principles as a means of turning away from what is painful and immediate. We have a good example of this reaction in the way he describes his sister's death from lockjaw; after a short description of her painful suffering, we find the following epiphany:

Death took features altogether new to him, in these rich

and sensual surroundings. Nature enjoyed it, played with it, the horror added to her charm, she liked the torture and smothered her victim with caresses. Never had one seen her so winning. The hot Italian sun brooded outside, over the market place and the picturesque peasants, and in the singular color of the Tuscan atmosphere, the hills and vineyards of the Apennines seemed bursting with midsummer blood. (Adams, 1918, p. 288)

Here is a sample of the self—Adams's self—at work as it attempts to cope with the raw and helpless experience of watching his sister die and reshape it into something more artistic and larger than life. "Never had one seen her so winning" sounds suspiciously more like denial than a sincere reaction. But putting the event in these words is an example of the way he is trying to give meaning to a senseless accident and embed it in an informing narrative. Close study of his autobiography would reveal other transformation rules that are used to give meaning to events; these rules would appear in Adams's style, in the form of his narrative, and in the nature of his memories. Certain kinds of regularities, identified by computer, might point to less obvious transformations. Once a tentative grammar had been assembled, it might be possible to make predictions about other works by the same author and ask whether certain transformation patterns might be discovered in certain periods of life and whether these patterns show a shift over time.

What, finally, can be said about the generality of these patterns? The study of comparative mythology provides some evidence that there are a limited number of patterns, which have been used over and over again. Schafer (1976) gives us one list of four "visions" of reality: the comic, the romantic, the ironic, and the tragic. Jung (1916) has presented us with an archetypal structure of Self via repeating sociocultural motifs. Bruner (1984) gives a general template:

Most narratives that create an aura of believable life-likeness involve a recounting of an initial canonical steady state, its breach, an ensuing crisis, and a redress, with limited accompanying states of awareness in the protagonists. This has led various literary theorists (Turner, Todorov) to suggest that there is a highly constrained deep structure to narrative, analogous to the deep structure, say, of a gram-

mar, and that good stories are well-formed surface realizations of this underlying structure. (p. 6)

We may find that the classification of patterns is more elusive than
the identification of genre and that a central organizing feature of the
self structure is its dependence on the narrative mode of thought.
This mode can be defined as a kind of description that emphasizes
sense at the expense of reference and can be contrasted to the paradigmatic mode of thought, which emphasizes reference at the expense
of sense (see Bruner, 1984, p. 13). The shift in mode may influence
the formation of memories. It can be seen that in our initial recollection of a happening, we may try to stay pretty close to the "facts" and
emphasize what happened at the expense of why it happened. But
over time and over the course of repeated retellings, we may shift to
a more narrative mode of description and emphasize sense over reference. As episodic memories are transformed into semantic, they may
acquire more features of the narrative mode of thought; as our self
evolves into a coherent set of principles, it seems to dwell more on
making sense than on veridical report. Its reliance on the narrative
mode gives us another reason why the self metaphor is clearly quite
discordant with the computer metaphor and why our sense of self is
not captured by either "software" or "hardware."

From another point of view, the search for repeated pattern may
end in frustration because it marks the persistent quest for underlying
regularity and uniformity. This is a key attribute of the paradigmatic
mode of thought, and the self, as just described, may depend primarily
on the narrative mode. Part of the frustration in defining the self and
part of the failure to reach even an approximate model may stem
from the belief that we can discover an underlying regularity under
all the confusion. But we may be looking under the wrong lamp post.
If the self is in the business of emphasizing sense over reference and
if it relies primarily on narrative modes of thought, then, almost by
definition, it cannot be reduced to a standard schema or represent
one out of many possible templates. Bruner (p. 26) has argued that
narrative and paradigmatic modes complement each other and that
one cannot be translated into the other. Ideographic rather than nom-
othetic, the science of the self may slip between our fingers until we
interrupt our search for regularities and turn to more primitive forms
of description and illustration.

If it is true that neither narrative nor paradigmatic modes can be reduced to the other, then this axiom has some important consequences. First, it calls into question any attempt to search for regularity and lawfulness in the self system and its development because the more rules we have uncovered, the less we have captured the narrative essence of the thing we are trying to describe. Second, it would suggest that the rules that emerge cannot be used to predict the more important aspects of the phenomenon, because prediction implies the lawful transition from one mode into the other and Bruner's axiom states that they are complementary. Third, it seems clear that a fully fleshed-out description of the self as it develops, matures, and learns to interpret the world is far more revealing than any set of rules or universal patterns, and that a fuller understanding (and more complete description) of this structure may be a necessary preliminary to the better understanding of remembering and forgetting.

The need for a fuller description of the self in operation brings us back to autobiography and psychobiography—this time with a second twist. Whereas the usual example of the latter tries to establish the reasons for a man's life and thus tries to reduce his life to a series of regularities, the newer approach would be more descriptive and comparative. Rather than trace the loss of innocence or the development of professional competencies, for example, the newer biography would try to establish the transformation rules that are used to turn happenings into meanings. Some of these rules may have never been seen before. We aim not to reduce a lived life to a set of standard patterns but to discover something that has never been described. Success in this endeavor might be measured by surprise, as with a new piece of art or fiction, and not by recognition, as with a new piece of science.

It is in keeping with this spirit that many surprises lie ahead. Some descriptions of the self to be encountered in the chapters to come may seem quite unlike the self you are used to. But it should be clear by now that this very feature may be a hallmark of truth telling in this new endeavor. What is being described should *not* feel familiar, because if it does, it probably leans more on what is shared than on what is individual. It is the latter that stands to teach us the most.

References

Adams, H. (1918). *The Education of Henry Adams*. New York: Houghton Mifflin.

Block, J. (1971). *Lives through time.* Berkeley: Bancroft Books.

Bowen, E. (1962). *Seven winters and afterthoughts.* New York: Knopf.

Brown, R., and Kulik, J. (1977). Flashbulb memories. *Cognition, 5,* 73–99.

———, and McNeil, D. (1966). The "tip of the tongue" phenomenon. *Journal of Verbal Learning and Verbal Behavior, 5,* 325–37.

Bruner, J. (1984). Narrative and paradigmatic modes of thought. Presented at the American Psychological Association Annual Meeting, Toronto.

Bucci, W. (1985). Dual coding: A cognitive model for psychoanalytic research. *Journal of the American Psychoanalytic Association, 33,* 571–607.

Freud, S. (1899). Screen memories. *Standard Edition,* Vol. 3. Ed. and trans. James Strachey. London: Hogarth Press, 1962.

Gergen, K. (1978). Toward generative theory. *Journal of Personality and Social Psychology, 36,* 1344–60.

Gibson, E. (1975). A classification of events for the study of event perception. Presented at the American Psychological Association Annual Meeting, Chicago.

Gusdorf, G. (1980). Conditions and limits of autobiography. In J. Olney (Ed.), *Autobiography: Essays theoretical and critical.* Princeton: Princeton University Press.

Heidegger, M. (1962). *Being and time.* Trans. John Macquarrie and E. Robinson. London: SCM Press.

Jung, C. G. (1916). *Psychology of the unconscious.* New York: Moffat, Yard.

Linton, M. (1982). Transformations of memory in everyday life. In U. Neisser (Ed.), *Memory observed.* San Francisco: W. H. Freeman.

Loftus, E. F., and Loftus, G. R. (1980). On the permanence of stored information in the human brain. *American Psychologist, 35,* 400–20.

Murray, H. (1938). *Explorations in personality.* New York: Oxford University Press.

Neisser, U. (1982). Snapshots or benchmarks? In U. Neisser (Ed.), *Memory observed.* San Francisco: W. H. Freeman.

O'Neill, E. (1946). *The Iceman cometh.* New York: Random House.

Penfield, W. (1958). *The excitable cortex in conscious man.* Liverpool: Liverpool University Press.

Pynchon, T. (1963). *V.* Philadelphia: Lippincott.

Quine, W. V., and Ullian, J. S. (1970). *The web of belief.* 2nd ed. New York: Random House.

Schafer, R. (1976). *A new language for psychoanalysis.* New Haven: Yale University Press.

Shepard, R. (1967). Recognition memory for words, sentences, and pictures. *Journal of Verbal Learning and Verbal Behavior, 6,* 156–63.

Spence, D. P. (1983). Narrative persuasion. *Psychoanalysis and Contemporary Thought, 6,* 457–68.

Swift, G. (1983). *Waterland.* New York: Poseidon Press.

Todorov, T. (1977). *The poetics of prose.* Ithaca: Cornell University Press.

Turner, U. (1982). *From ritual to theatre.* New York: New York Academy Performing Arts Journal Pub.

Veyne, P. (1984). *Writing history.* Trans. Mina Moore-Rinvolucri. Middletown, Conn.: Wesleyan University Press.

In Search of the Self:
The Case of Franz Kafka

CRAIG R. EISENDRATH

O UR PURPOSE is to attempt to answer two sets of questions. Many writers, such as Franz Kafka, have left us a wealth of material about themselves: letters, journals, and fiction. Additionally, we have records of others' impressions in biographies, history, and journals. Is there some way of ranking this evidence as more or less truthful about the personality and motivation of the writer? Can we arrive at an agreement about a method that can be used to distill the evidence about a person's life, that will guide toward truthfulness of one or another account?

In 1919, when Kafka was thirty-six (he was to die in 1924), he wrote a book-length *Letter to His Father* describing what he called his "incapacity for life" and tracing its origins to a ruinous relation with his father (Kafka, 1953). We begin with this document because it has the look of the primary and supremely credible piece of evidence we are seeking: It was written by the author himself; it is self-deprecating— always a winning feature—for it enhances our sense of superiority; and so it must be true, else why would the author deprecate himself? The *Letter* is long and intimate and abounds with telling detail, so that one feels it is the result of a lengthy search into Kafka's memory, a careful sifting of evidence, illustrated by anecdotes too specific to invent.

In the *Letter,* Kafka writes of himself:

> I remember, for instance, how we often undressed in the same bathing hut. There was I, skinny, weakly, slight; you strong, tall, broad. Even inside the hut I felt a miserable specimen, and what's more, not only in your eyes but in the

eyes of the whole world, for you were for me the measure
of all things. (p. 19)

The father's power, the *Letter* says, was so complete that the son was
virtually paralyzed in his very processes of thought:

> All these thoughts, seemingly independent of you, were
> from the beginning burdened with your belittling judg-
> ments; it was almost impossible to endure this and still work
> out a thought with any measure of completeness and per-
> manence. I am not here speaking of any sublime thoughts,
> but of every little childhood enterprise. (p. 23)

Behind the power was the father's threat of punishment, all the
more horrifying because usually not executed (p. 37). Like Dostoevski,
condemned to death by the czar and put through the preliminaries
of execution, Kafka represented himself in the *Letter* as damaged permanently by a sentence that would never be carried out in the objective
world, but only in the mind, and by Franz himself, not his father. This
is the origin, as we will see, of Kafka's seminal short story "The Judgment."

But the *Letter,* which translates so easily into his early fiction, does
not adequately represent Kafka's interpersonal presentation of himself as reported by friends or as implied in many of his other letters
(Kafka, 1973, 1977). This Kafka had an immense capacity for friendship, he could laugh at himself, he could travel well, he could give
and accept criticism, he could generously applaud his friends' suc-
cesses, and he could take his friends into his confidence at times of
stress. With young people, he could be fatherly and nurturant. With
his editors, he could be clear and direct concerning the handling of
his work. Max Brod (1963), his lifelong friend, biographer, and literary executor, objects to Kafka's self-representation as a nebbish in
the *Letter*:

> To those who knew him closely, at least, he presented quite
> a different picture from that of a man haunted by the "fa-
> ther-image"; they had the picture of a man glowingly under
> the impulsion of form, the desire and power to mold things,
> the urge to know, interest in observing life, and the love of
> humanity. (Brod, 1963, p. 24)

Here we have some contradiction, but if we consider the two sets of evidence on the same level, we have no basis of making a judgment. Perhaps a better tack is to assume for the moment that all evidence is true in its way, that the *Letter* is a true description of Kafka of his life up to his thirty-sixth year and Brod's assessment is also "true." How can the discrepancy be resolved?

Beyond this, we may need a line of thinking about Kafka's personality in which discrepancies are reconcilable, a theory of interpretation in which the various representations can fit, just as a theory in physics provides a lens that encompasses different perspectives, a theory like that for the various positions and times of falling bodies or quantum mechanics for the otherwise irreconcilable differences in observations concerning waves and particles.

Suitably prompted to look for a theory, we can return to the evidence of the *Letter* and see whether it will begin to yield one about the character or evolving character of Kafka. He writes:

> Jewish schoolboys in our country often tend to be odd; among them one finds the most unlikely things; but something like my cold indifference, scarcely disguised, indestructible, childishly helpless, approaching the ridiculous, and brutishly complacent, the indifference of a self-sufficient but coldly imaginative child, I have never found anywhere else; to be sure it was the sole defense against destruction of the nerves by fear and by a sense of guilt. All that occupied my mind was worry about myself. . . . (p. 89)

This passage reminded me of a character in literature, the Marcel in *Remembrance of Things Past,* and his author, Marcel Proust. Proust was able to create his character fairly directly in his work; Kafka, we will find, was not; but differences aside, we have from Heinz Kohut the suggestion that in Proust's case we are dealing with a narcissistically wounded person (Kohut, 1977, pp. 180–82), a description that also fits Kafka. Indeed there are great similarities between these two hypersensitive, neurasthenic, gifted, and contemporary Jewish writers. Nevertheless we should keep a difference in mind: Kafka's persistence in transmuting or displacing his personality into an entire dream landscape (as opposed to the strictly sociological world of Proust), particularly in *The Trial* and *The Castle* (Kafka, 1969, 1974). In these works,

Kafka's personal mask is that of a somewhat purposive, egocentric professional, precisely the mask Kafka could imagine himself wearing in the bureaucratic world of his "career," if he were not Kafka.

Kafka's employment was of a quasi-public nature, in an insurance office where he investigated and reported industrial accidents and working conditions. Kafka was considered an excellent employee, was frequently commended for his reports (he wrote well), and was regularly promoted. He wrote in his *Diaries* (1965):

> If I have written something good one evening, I am afire the next day in the office and can bring nothing to completion. This back and forth continually becomes worse. Outwardly, I fulfill my duties satisfactorily in the office, not my inner duties, however, and every unfulfilled inner duty becomes a misfortune that never leaves. (vol. 1, p. 59)

Here the obvious statement is that Kafka hated his work, but it was on the job that he learned firsthand about bureaucracy and the hopeless, almost despairing relations between peoples and governments that form the fabric of *The Trial* and *The Castle*. He learned about the tearing of the flesh and the wounding of the spirit when human bodies are mutilated by machines, a learning Kafka transformed almost directly into "The Penal Colony" but applied metaphorically throughout his writings (Kafka, 1961). Thus from his *Diaries* in 1913:

> Always the image of a pork butcher's broad knife that quickly and with mechanical regularity chops into me from the side and cuts off very thin slices which fly off almost like shavings because of the speed of the action. (vol. 1, pp. 286–87)

Is such a sentence conceivable without the experience provided by his employment, and were Kafka as committed to writing as he says— "My talent for portraying my dreamlike inner life . . . Nothing else will ever satisfy me" (vol. 2, p. 77)—must there not have been some appreciation of the value of his job for that process? None that I have found in his writings, but might there not have been some unconscious appreciation left unsaid because so much depended on his identity as a writer and nothing really need be said about the other half of his life, his "career," because by necessity and in fact he had one?

Not surprisingly, when we begin to look at his writings we see that different categories of writings give evidence, as we have seen, of an almost fanatical sense for objective detail. We can read in his *Diaries* the same obstinacy, now turned to recording everything in his inner life, every emotion, every conflict, every indecision, every failure, fueled by his already overdeveloped self-criticism. In 1915, Kafka wrote:

> At a certain point in self-knowledge, when other circum-stances favoring self-scrutiny are present, it will invariably follow that you find yourself execrable. Every moral stan-dard—however opinions may differ on it—will seem too high. You will see that you are nothing but a rat's nest of miserable dissimulations. (vol. 2, p. 114)

In fact, he swamped himself in introspective detail, frustrating his capacity to act. But this process operated in an intermediate zone— that of his diaries and letters. The fiction, by maintaining some free-dom from his day-to-day turmoil, allowed him larger, more inclusive constructions—Joshua (his letters and diaries) battling on the plain, Moses (his fiction) holding up his arms on the hill.

Writing served Kafka as a simulacrum for the processes of life, much as chess can serve those in power as a prototype of politico-military strategy. Writing gave Kafka an area of activity removed from immediate connections and casual contingencies, one in which he could pick and choose possibilities and strike on a particular path. Writing thus formed a pattern for decision making that Kafka could continuously perfect through the years and that itself could offer through the evidence of its own success the possibility of greater de-cisiveness in his life as a whole.

Writing not only contained the functional discrepancies in Kafka's life but also provided a clear avenue for personal agency. For however painful the writing might be, it was the writer Kafka who controlled it; and this sense of mastery together with an ongoing occupation of writing (a sense of what you do with your life) united with the praise and admiration from friends, and then readers and publishers, was the foundation of Kafka's effectiveness as a writer. If we are secretly urging our subject toward health, we can see a way out of Kafka's miseries: community with other writers and literary people, as well as publication, royalties, and financial independence. But here we are defeated, and again must look for a theory, because throughout his life, Kafka made clear that he did not wholly believe in the public nature of his work, but rather considered it the artifact of a private struggle, and with few exceptions, to be burnt and buried with the life with which it was intimately and hermetically bound. He was not sufficiently aware of his own relation to humanity to see just how communicative his writing was to others.

Still, we might have consoled him, it was not an altogether bad life. His work was dull but the hours were short (he was finished at 2. P.M.); he wrote; he took outings and vacations with his friends; he pursued interests, such as various literary enthusiasms and the Yiddish theater; he engaged in flirtations—he was quite attractive to women, as are his heroes in *The Trial* and *The Castle,* and occasionally visited whores. His health, while somewhat delicate—he was an exercise and food faddist—was not particularly bad in his early years.

What disrupted this not altogether unsuccessful adaptation was the expectation of his class, family, and particularly himself that to be a fully realized man, one of his age should marry and have a family. Far from seeing the venture as an easing into comfort and domesticity, Kafka took it as a supreme challenge. "Marriage, founding a family," he wrote in his *Letter,* "accepting all the children that come, supporting them in this insecure world and perhaps even guiding them a little, is, I am convinced, the utmost a human being can succeed in doing at all" (p. 99).

The effort to marry proved his undoing, or perhaps, for we are beginning to catch the possibility of a theory, it proved his lack of worth; indeed, his manner of pursuing marriage seemed calculated to achieve that objective. The prospect was threatening and potentially defeating on three levels: First, it clearly involved a reawakening of rivalries with his father, a contest that he would certainly lose as he was already defeated in it. Second, it threatened the possibility of a genuinely close relationship with another human being, an exposure of self, and here we must guess at Kafka's terror—that he had no self to expose, or that self would not bear scrutiny. And last, it represented the swamping of his precarious identity as a writer by the expectation of his living a middle-class life.

His father, as always, played a double role in the dramas of Kafka's engagements. His sarcasms provided an incentive. In the *Letter,* Kafka reports his father's comments on one of his engagements: "She probably put on a fancy blouse, something these Prague Jewesses are good at, and right away, of course, you decided to marry her" (p. 107). No, Kafka would show him, but in the end the certainty of failure was preferable to the strain of attempting success:

> The simile of the bird in the hand and the two in the bush has only a very remote application here. In my hand I have nothing, in the bush is everything, and yet—so it is decided by the conditions of battle and the exigency of life—I must choose the nothing. I had to make a similar choice when I chose my profession. (p. 119)

The hundreds of pages of letters to Felice Bauer testify to how hard Kafka tried to fail (Kafka, 1973). The letters throb with romance and profess a longing for intimacy, but what is disconcerting is that Kafka secretly found Felice unattractive. In his *Diaries,* he describes her "bony, empty face that wore its emptiness openly," and notes again and again how little Felice cared for or understood his writing (vol. 1, p. 268). Yet he went on with the relationship, professing his longing for the marriage while using any device he could think of to subvert it. He dwelt endlessly in the letters on his illnesses, his skinniness; he did everything to disappear, even to having his name at the end of his letters get smaller and smaller.

What soaks through the letters to Felice—and later to Milena (Kafka, 1962), who, unlike Felice, was beautiful and intellectually stimulating—is fear. As the letters record his essentially epistolary romances (Kafka was generally successful in avoiding contact), the "fear" achieves the tangibleness of a beast and Kafka's defenses rise to meet it, the endless and sometimes boring defenses of powerlessness of which he was a master. Fear, he wrote to Milena, "is really mysterious, I don't know its inner laws, I know only its hand at my throat . . ." (Kafka, 1962, p. 106).

The compulsion to marry was put to rest at this point in his life by his perception that he had tuberculosis, although the disease was confused in his mind with his spiritual or emotional problems. As it progressed, Kafka drifted into a kind of neurasthenic self-enclosure. He was obsessed with noise—the slightest sound left him desperate and insomniac, and one thinks again of Proust. Visits to him at the sanatorium proved upsetting and letters became "ghosts"—words like *intolerable* and *unbearable* abound in his letters.

As the time passed, he began to disintegrate into psychosis, and in January 1922, he wrote:

> This past week I suffered something very like a breakdown.
> . . . Everything seemed over with . . . impossible to sleep,
> impossible to stay awake, impossible to endure life. . . . The
> clocks are not in unison; the inner one runs crazily on at a
> devilish or demonic or in any case inhuman pace, the outer
> one limps along at its usual speed. What else can happen
> but that the two worlds split apart, and they do split apart,
> or at least clash in a fearful manner. (vol. 2, pp. 201–02)

Thereafter he became increasingly depressed. He shunned people, read little, spoke of having irrevocably wasted his life.

This was Kafka's state of mind when, already quite ill, he met a young woman named Dora Diamant and fell in love. It was in July of 1923. Kafka was forty. Soon after meeting her he decisively cut all ties with his employer, and over the objections of his family moved with Dora to Berlin to live on his pension as a writer. Despite physical distress, he wrote quite well. He seemed, Brod says, "blissfully happy." But his health was broken. Bravely, he wrote to Dora's orthodox father asking for Dora in marriage, explaining that although he was not a practicing Jew in her father's sense, he was nevertheless a "repentant one, seeking to return," and therefore might perhaps hope to be accepted into the family of such a pious man. He wasn't. The father turned him down cold. On June 3, 1924, Kafka died painfully of tuberculosis in a sanatorium near Vienna.

We have yet to take up in any detail a powerful resource about Kafka—his fiction. Here, it seems, we are dealing with a person who incessantly told a nonrational, repetitive story, a kind of dream depicted in engrossing and often exhausting detail. Of course, the characters in the works are not dreaming, they are living in the dream, or rather they are caught in the nightmarish landscapes of the works, which like dreams unite the uncanny with the routine and predictable.

One can also characterize Kafka's fiction as exaggerated metaphorical inner spaces, or mind spaces, that seem fairly psychotic. There is a kind of detachment in these extended metaphors with a corresponding gutting or devaluing of the central character that is symptomatic of someone with a personality disorder, someone who has a problem of thinking of himself as real or worthwhile and having continuity in time (Kohut, 1971, 1977).[1]

The child, as we mentioned, was overwhelmed and seemingly disintegrated by his insensitive, aggressive, disparaging father and insufficiently protected by his mother, who gave over to the father. One consequence, which the literature supports, was a genuine fear that inside Kafka was nothing, or nothing good, that he was worthless. This could have resulted in an unwillingness to look inside himself for fear of what he would find, and indeed in *The Trial* and *The Castle* this option is explored through his central characters, who are generally incapable of self-analysis.

But such analysis does occur in the letters and diaries, where we can see its anxious importance for him, and by the same token, its exhibitionism, its exaggeration and repetitiveness, his eagerness to display his flaws. There is a narcissistic preoccupation with being flawed, an anxiety that great damage has already been done, that perhaps no self has survived the early beating, that its influence continues to be the dominant causative factor in his life, that he himself has no will.

The most poignant result of this early deep wounding is his fear of a close relationship. Without a sense of being someone himself, he could not enter into a relationship with another in which his self would be wounded. The connection between the destruction of self by his father and this fear is reinforced by his father's ability to preempt Kafka's eroticism, as will be seen in "The Judgment."

When the personality is organized around self-rejection, as Kafka's was, a person tends to split apart and wholly dichotomize the good and the bad. The bad is "out there," inexorable and terrifying, and the good is "inaccessible" but potentially "in here" if one exercises, diets, disciplines oneself enough to get at it. Kafka's experiences in his early years at home—experiences, as will be seen, mirrored exactly in his fiction, particularly *The Trial* and *The Castle*—seem to have resulted in ritualized attempts to get the good.

Because Kafka was unsure of his individual worth, he couldn't see his own meaning and worth to others. Hence the somewhat vapid central characters in Kafka's works. Other characters have more energy or interest, but not the representatives of self. Suffering from a personality disorder, Kafka tends to disclaim his ability to create something worthwhile and to construct a continuous sense of being acceptable as a person. Writing (out there) is the effort to constitute being in the world, but it does not succeed, precisely because writing replaces his real story.

This is an operating theory, supported by all categories of Kafka's writing. It explains the seeming contradiction of Kafka's *Letter to His Father* and his relation to Max Brod or his publishers. For what touches the central narcissistic hurt (his father, the engagements) will elicit a "different" Kafka from what does not (Brod, publishers, children), or not in as threatening a way. But in finding confirmation of Kafka's personality disorder in his fiction, we discover something that could not have been altogether predicted. True, we find the personality disorder united with the extraordinary talent to create the literature we know, a literature of alienation and despair that seems at the heart of the modern world (although ironically almost by accident, for it is based more on Kafka's writing about himself than about the world). But we also find in his writings an unsteady but discernible process of repair, perhaps achieving in the end an uncertain kind of redemption.

Kafka wrote in his diary that writing is

> a leap out of murderers' row; it is a seeing of what is really taking place. This occurs by a higher type of observation, a higher, not a keener type, and the higher it is and the less within reach of the "row," the more independent it becomes, the more obedient to its own laws of motion, the more incalculable, the more joyful, the more ascendant its course. (vol. 2, p. 212)

The first story that Kafka felt truly represented him as a writer was "The Judgment," dated 1912 (Kafka, 1961). Its story is quickly told: A young man, Georg, lives with his widower father and has successfully taken increasing responsibility for managing the family business as the powers of his father have declined. In writing to a friend, who has been living some years in Russia, Georg delicately hesitates to tell him of his engagement because the friend has been both a social and commercial failure. Inexplicably, when Georg shows his father the letter, the old man questions the friend's existence. Georg's response is to assume his father is even weaker and more senile than he had supposed, and he gently lifts the old man into his bed. At that point, the father suddenly rears up huge and powerful, denouncing his son and his engagement in every way.

> "Because she lifted up her skirts," his father began to flute, "because she lifted up her skirts like this, the nasty creature," and mimicking her he lifted his shirt so high that one could see the scar on his thigh from his war wound, "because she lifted her skirts like this and this you made up to her, and in order to make free with her undisturbed you have disgraced your mother's memory, betrayed your friend and stuck your father into bed so that he can't move. But he can move, or can't he?" (p. 60)

Totally dominating the scene, rendering Georg powerless, the father ends by saying:

> So now you know what else there was in the world besides yourself, till now you've known only about yourself! An innocent child, yes, that you were, truly, but still more truly have you been a devilish human being!—And therefore take note: I sentence you now to death by drowning! (pp. 62–63)

As his father crashes on the bed, Georg runs out of the room to the bridge that spans the river near his home. As he lets himself drop over the side, he says, "Dear parents, I have always loved you, all the same." The story ends with this sentence: "At this moment an unending stream of traffic [*verkehr*, "intercourse"] was just going over the bridge" (p. 63).

Here all the themes we have identified: the dreamlike and inescapable character of the story, the aggression and rage of the father, the corresponding sense of worthlessness in the son, the agentive ability of the father to condemn him to death, his corresponding acquiescence and willessness, the father's usurpation of erotic attachment and capacity to eliminate Georg's other relationships, the exhibitionism of the story, and so on. It was, Kafka felt, his first real breakthrough as a writer, and in reading it, he could barely keep from tears. So from the beginning we can see perhaps the seeds of his writing's transformative power, because he could, in this story, put to paper this terrible experience. In a very limited sense, Kafka was able to lift the verbal expression of his disorder into what Jung once called the "current conscious attitude," and so perhaps to deal with it.

In "The Metamorphosis" (Kafka, 1961, pp. 67–132), which immediately followed "The Judgment," Kafka was repeating the original family setting—in this sense, the story is regressive rather than looking ahead to any resolution of problems. In this story, perhaps his most famous, the hero finds himself inexplicably transformed into a gigantic dung beetle. Before his transformation, Gregor had sacrificed a great deal to support his father, mother, and sister; now, transformed into a bug, he has become an increasingly objectionable burden. Throughout the story he retains his ability to understand what his family says, but he cannot make himself understood. His death comes psychically from a sense of total abandonment; physically, from a festering wound, an apple thrown at him by his enraged father that lodges in his back.

During the attack, his mother tries to save Gregor:

> . . . he saw his mother rushing towards his father, leaving one after another behind her on the floor her loosened petticoats, stumbling over her petticoats straight to his father and embracing him, in complete union with him—but here Gregor's sight began to fail—with her hands clasped round his father's neck as she begged for her son's life. (p. 110)

Here again are the basic themes of personality disorder, but with a few new elements in the foreground. The body image has taken a psychotic transformation into a dung beetle. The apple that sticks in his back is an image which expresses both his distrust of nurturance, experienced as aggression, and his rationale (suspicion) for abstemious eating habits maintained throughout his life. An erotic but powerless mother is incapable of protecting her son's life against the aggression of the father's nurturance. The son is himself powerless to sustain himself through the comic/tragic transformations of his existence.

In *The Trial* (Kafka, 1969), begun in 1914 though not published during the author's lifetime, the familial setting is replaced by an entire landscape, the kind of psychotic mindscapes mentioned earlier. Here, for the first time, Kafka has metaphorized his condition into a total world.

"Someone must have traduced Joseph K.," the novel opens, "for without having done anything wrong he was arrested one fine morning" (p. 3). K. never learns what crime he has committed, never confirms the Law under which he is arrested by determining whether it is a valid part of the objective world. Instead, the accusation of his guilt confirms the Law. He is not incarcerated; he is allowed to be at large, to walk about with a sense that he is accused and probably guilty. Indeed, as the novel develops, K. becomes increasingly desperate to clear himself, although he has no idea of what. At one point he contemplates writing a defense of his entire life moment by moment, although he realizes the effort will be exhausting and probably futile.

The entire novel is a testimony to an unspecified guilt, an ontological sense of abasement of K.'s being. There is no crime, no crime is necessary—he is simply no good. He can protest forever, he can write out his entire life, but it will not help—it would help only were he guilty of a particular crime. Ontological guilt has no expiation, although the need for expiation is inexhaustible. Hence the continuous state of guilt and the continual expiatory acts.

As in "The Judgment," the bad is inexorable and terrifying, and the good is "inaccessible"—the mysterious Law. The splitting off of evil from good is expressed in how Kafka distributes accusation—the hero doesn't accuse himself so much as others, and these take on his own attributes. In "The Judgment," Georg clearly internalizes his father's opinion of him and carries out his sentence. In *The Trial*, he is killed by lowly court officials. The despicableness of the court officials might be understood as a displacement of the author's own opinion of himself.

Alienation, and the consequent need for displacement, is further suggested by K.'s character in both *The Trial* and *The Castle*. K. is a relatively competent, somewhat officious professional; he is virtually without quirks or problems, and is unremarkable physically and ethnically. He does not draw attention to himself, because there is nothing to draw attention to. Indeed the hero thinks, at least initially, that the reasons for accusation lie not in himself but in a system of courts or the Castle. The very mechanism of displacement that renders the agency of guilt—the courts, the Castle—alien to the hero divests him of those qualities that the author had in real life.

Very much in the modern style, Kafka's novels have replaced psychoanalytic history with existential guilt and have created a landscape or world to replace the guilt-generating family. It is as if in "The Judgment" the true source of guilt has subtly shifted from the father to the son himself; it is the son who in each moment generates the feelings he has. The sources of judgment and acceptance have both been infinitely removed. K. does not reach the higher courts and he never enters the Castle.

Toward the end of his life, in 1922, Kafka wrote "A Hunger Artist" (Kafka, 1961, pp. 243–56), which repeats most of the major elements of "The Judgment" and "The Metamorphosis," but with significant transformations. "A Hunger Artist" is the story of a man whose profession it is to fast in a circus as a public act or spectacle. In contrast to "The Metamorphosis," the starvation results from a choice rather than from an affliction. Like the bug, the hunger artist is an object or spectacle rather than a person, but his audience has widened from a family to a general public. The sensuality and cruelty of the father, which appear in "The Judgment" and "The Metamorphosis," have now been assumed by the warders (usually butchers, strangely enough) who guard the hunger artist.

The end of the story comes not from abandonment or total despair, as in the earlier stories, but from an act of will. The hunger artist believes that he can now achieve a record for fasting that has never been reached; he will not be bound by the customary limit of forty days. Now he begins to fast forever; but soon, as in "The Metamorphosis," he is totally forgotten. As he dies, the overseer of the circus finds him lying in the straw. The following dialogue ensues:

> "I always wanted you to admire my fasting," said the hunger artist. "We do admire it," said the overseer, affably. "But you shouldn't admire it," said the hunger artist. "Well then we don't admire it," said the overseer, "but why shouldn't we admire it?" "Because I have to fast, I can't help it," said the hunger artist. "What a fellow you are," said the overseer, "and why can't you help it?" "Because," said the hunger artist, lifting his head a little and speaking with his lips pursed, as if for a kiss, right into the overseer's ear, so that

no syllable might be lost, "because I couldn't find the food I liked. If I had found it, believe me, I should have made no fuss and stuffed myself like you or anyone else." These were his last words, but in his dimming eyes remained the firm though no longer proud persuasion that he was still continuing to fast. (p. 255)

Here, again, the hero has asked forgiveness; but now, even if it was given indifferently, he has received it. He has engaged in an activity for which he seeks admiration, as had Georg and Gregor in their support of the family, but this time he has received it without enmeshment in a family setting, although again qualified with indifference. He has starved himself, an act indirectly similar to Georg's suicide and directly similar to Gregor's starvation, but this time the act seems transcendental; it is in the service of some higher ideal, despite the hunger artist's own statements.

Rather than a repetition of the original problem, we see the beginnings of a transformation. The writing seems to have changed in some sense from being the regressive reflection of a personality problem to some progressive vision of the future, however tragic. There is the glimmering of a realignment of psychic forces under the guidance of art, rather than Freud's picture of art as symptom of disorder.

During the last nine months of his life, Kafka wrote a number of short stories that were burnt, at his request, by Dora Diamant. (We owe the survival of most of Kafka's writings, letters, and diaries to the fact that Max Brod, his literary executor, failed to honor Kafka's request to burn the works in his care.)

His last surviving story, "Josephine the Singer, or the Mouse Folk" (Kafka, 1961, pp. 254–77), represents a final attempt at imagining himself in preparation for death. The story stands in that class of works, such as Shakespeare's *The Tempest* or Beethoven's sixteenth quartet, by which their authors take a final, unexpected step through lightheartedness and humor. For Kafka, the comic was almost always present; it is a gentle, playful element that appears directly in letters and as an often unnoticed baseline in his works of fiction. Kafka himself felt it there; he frequently giggled when he wrote and would often laugh when he read his work to friends. Humor allowed him distance, a position from which he could achieve some larger perspective and some safety from depressing implications. From that position he could transform powerlessness into whimsy and abjection into absurdity. It was in this comic mode that, in "Josephine the Singer, or the Mouse Folk," he wrote his epitaph.

The story begins as follows: "Our singer is called Josephine. Anyone who has not heard her does not know the power of song" (p. 254). Here, whatever subsequent irony is introduced, is an immediate affirmation of the power of art and the artist. The people for whom Josephine sings are so described that in some ways they are mice (the most helpless and powerless), in others they are Jews, and in most ways they are humankind. (It is impossible to read this story without thinking of the fate of the "mouse folk" in the years that followed Kafka's death.) The ironic element is quickly introduced when the narrator asks if Josephine sings at all, for all she seems to do is pipe, which, we are told, is what all mice do. Her piping, moreover, has a "quite ordinary piping tone, which at most differs from the others through being delicate or weak" (p. 258). What is it then that distinguishes her? She sings with such intensity,

> as if she has concentrated all her strength on her song, as if from everything in her that does not directly subserve her singing all strength has been withdrawn, almost all power of life, as if she were laid bare, abandoned, committed merely to the care of good angels, as if while she is so wholly withdrawn and living only in her song a cold breath blowing upon her might kill her. (pp. 260–61)

So like the dying Kafka himself.

Then the story takes a turn that moves it beyond the drama of the individual artist. It attempts to describe, however ironically, the relation between the artist and the people. In "A Hunger Artist," this relationship is negative; the hunger artist amuses or entertains, but then is forgotten. In "Josephine" the relation between artist and people is explored far more thoroughly in passages of pure epic poetry. The people feel that Josephine is their charge, that they are responsible for taking care of her; ironically, however, it is Josephine who thinks she protects the people. In times of trouble, the people gather together and Josephine sings for them. In reality, they are sitting in the stillness she creates.

> Josephine's thin piping amidst grave decisions is almost like

> our people's precarious existence amidst the tumult of a
> hostile world. . . . Something of our poor brief childhood
> is in it, something of lost happiness that can never be found
> again, but also something of active daily life. . . . here pip-
> ing is set free from the fetters of daily life and it sets us
> free too for a little while. (pp. 265–66, 269)

Nevertheless, the narrator says, "it is a long, long way to Josephine's
claim that she gives us new strength" (p. 269).

The denouement occurs when Josephine claims exemption from
daily work because of her singing, just as Kafka would have wished
to have avoided work at the office. But here, as in his life, the people
refuse to offer their support. Despite her threats to change her singing, in practice Josephine seems to go on piping just as before. However, after many strategems, she simply disappears; "this time she has
deserted us entirely" (p. 276), the narrator says.

In the final passages, Kafka achieves a redemptive vision. This is to
claim for his art the power not to cure him but rather to alleviate and
transfigure his pain. In his modernity, Kafka never wavers.

> Josephine's road, however, must go downhill. The time will
> soon come when her last notes sound and die into silence.
> She is a small episode in the eternal history of our people,
> and the people will get over the loss of her. Not that it will
> be easy for us; how can our gatherings take place in utter
> silence? Still, were they not silent even when Josephine was
> present? Was her actual piping notably louder and more
> alive than the memory of it will be? Was it even in her
> lifetime more than a simple memory? Was it not rather
> because Josephine's singing was already past losing in this
> way that our people in their wisdom prized it so highly?
>
> So perhaps we shall not miss so very much after all, while
> Josephine, redeemed from the earthly sorrows which to her
> thinking lay in wait for all chosen spirits, will happily lose
> herself in the numberless throng of the heroes of our peo-
> ple, and soon, since we are no historians, will rise to the
> heights of redemption and be forgotten like all her broth-
> ers. (p. 277)

This working sketch of a biography of Kafka differs markedly from the univocal, reductive tendencies of some accounts. For us, the letters, diaries, and fiction, as well as personal relations, are not just a manifest layer of expression pointing to a latent or basic set of concepts (e.g., "Kafka suffered from an unrealizable homosexual attachment to his father" or "Kafka's life is an expiation for the death of his two brothers"), or a single "true" or most likely narrative, were it to have been constructed in cooperation with a skilled therapist. Rather, it is a skein of expressive lines involving various social relations, letters, diaries, and fiction—each in turn concerning different situations, different people, including Kafka's own perception of himself as an object, each with its own developmental route, each with distinct functional roles, each representing real, felt experience—that together constitute the felt expressive history of Kafka. In this skein, we can discern one line particularly—fiction, which played for Kafka a developmental role that was purposive, that is, served in some way as a final cause perhaps subtly, complexly influencing all the other lines of expression.

For this level of our biography, the role of theory, as we developed it in this case, was to suggest some evolving metastructure—a personality disorder resulting from a narcissistic hurt—that contains or makes plausible the wide variations of behavior and expression evinced by our evidence. Thus it will be clear why Kafka is a "different person" for Max Brod than for Milena Pollak; it will also suggest why identification as a writer could initiate a process of repair. At this level we can begin the process of emphatic understanding, that is, begin to reconstruct from the expressive evidence some suggestions for what it might have felt like to be Kafka at any particular time.

But in attempting this task, we feel something is missing, some process for which we are lacking a basic term. Initially we asked ourselves if Kafka in representing himself in words had not by this very act distorted or attenuated a continuing basic, personal experience at the core of his personality, a central component of which writing or verbal expression was only an emanation or reflection?

We can see now that this question is not well put, however suggestive. There is no gainsaying an experience, such as writing a diary or talking with a friend, by calling it epiphenomenal, manifest, and so on. To do so is perhaps the most persistent fallacy of Freud, a fallacy that William James has called the "nothing but" fallacy. No, the experience is real in its own terms; indeed, its own terms define it. Moreover, we have suggested that a particular line of expression for

Kafka—fiction—had efficacy in effecting change discernible in other lines of expression or behavior.

But there must be something to which his various moments of expression or experience related, something that went beyond the immediate evidence, some ground upon which we were able to build a theory—a theory of narcissistic wounding. Let us call this ground the self.

Let us be clear that we are now moving into an area of constructs rather than direct experience. We do not have a diary of the self, we have only a diary. The self, like other concepts such as the ego, is a useful construct only if it explains what we know about Kafka better than anything else we might devise.

Thus admonished, we will posit a complex scheme of identification called the self. It will be the function of this scheme to initiate activity that expresses itself in a particular context or circumstances or with a particular person. It will also be its function to create a sense of continuity or ownership of experiences by differentiating those in the primary memory (the just past) that conform to it (what Sullivan would call the Me) and those that do not (the not-Me) (Sullivan, 1953, ch. 10; Neisser, 1967, pp. 225–26). This scheme will be the central structure of the personality and will be subject to change as it or parts of it are added to, enhanced in value, hurt, or reconstellated. We are thus dealing with what might be called a "living structure" or "intentional scheme" (Miller, Galanter, and Pribram, 1960, ch. 2). It is clear from this brief description that the self is not a neutral cognitive construct but a set of interrelated valued ideas with a highly idiosyncratic composition (Neisser, 1967, pp. 3–11).

William James wrote that *"a man's Self is the sum total of all that he CAN call his,* not only his body and his psychic powers, but his clothes and his house, his wife and children, his ancestors and friends, his reputation and works, his lands and horses, and yacht and bank account" (James, 1890, vol. 1, p. 291). This empirical self in James's account is not a collection, however, but an intensively interrelated evolving structure built up in the course of one's life.

The internal process of "experiencing Kafka" or "Kafka things" would then be a relational experience rather than, say, a simple continuous pulse of identity (Eisendrath, 1971, pp. 84–99). One term would be the complex concept of the self, and the other would be an experience in the recent past, something held in the primary memory, that is, the cognitive mechanism holding material for attention. For example, were Kafka to see his skinny figure in a mirror, he would know it was his—he would be having an experience of being Kafka because the image would correspond with his schematic sense of his own body, which would be a central component of the self. The experience might be depressing, for it might confirm the negative valuation he had of his body, but it would be his. Were Kafka to sit down at his desk and write something in his diary about himself, and it was not true, the sense of its not being true would be a felt lack of conformity between the concept of self and what he had written. If he were to find himself unable to tolerate the idea of seeing Milena, and if he were to reflect on this experience, it, too, would be found to be his, however painful.

The self as a cognitive intentional scheme is not necessarily directly expressible in conscious experience, and indeed, it has been the object of a hundred years of psychiatry to show us that parts of it may be unavailable for such expression. (We are also suggesting that it is not consciously experienced at all, but only as expressed.) In certain kinds of neurosis, this expression through symptoms is quite oblique. What is remarkable about Kafka is that he seems to have had the capacity in one form or another, be it diaries or letters or fiction, to express his self. Indeed, one way of defining the difference between narcissistic personality disorder and neurosis is just this capacity or lack of it.

The self also controls perception in that it selects from the environment those things, including things about the self, that conform to it, and rejects or does not attend to those things that are not part of the self, that have no "interest" for it or threaten it. Sullivan's selective inattention (Sullivan, 1953, pp. 170, 233–34) is the propensity not to see what is threatening to the self, namely, material that confirms negatively valued elements of the self that are in conflict with positively valued but frail elements. Existential anxiety would then be the persistent feeling that positively valued elements are not strong enough, that they will be overwhelmed, or that the core elements themselves are negatively valued—persistent experiences that Kafka lived with most of his life.

Finally, we need to say that the scheme of the self is not a dead letter, as some Jungians would have us believe, a diamondlike core of the personality that must be found. Wounded or enhanced by experiences—some generated out of the self—it wills for the future; it is, in modern language, an intentional scheme. Consciousness and, more radically, art are the fields where perception and ideality are united. What one arranges for attention in the conscious field and what one organizes for artistic display or narration are creatures of the self, as we have described it (Eisendrath, 1971, pp. 100–27). Thus in the case of Kafka, we cannot know the arrangement of his conscious field, but we can see vividly in his writings how he has appropriated the world into a complex presentation that is at once description (like consciousness) and intention (the movement toward redemption we traced from "The Judgment" to "Josephine"). The mistake is to assume that by attempting to construct the scheme of the self we have the deeper experience of the author; we do not, but we do have one of its terms and thereby we can emphatically perceive how this term operates in the world—to perceive selectively, as did Kafka, and to create intentionally, as did Kafka. The construction and development of this scheme and the re-creation of its continuously changing role in the world in all its various lines of attention (including what is not seen), activity, and expression is the final goal of biography, one whose difficulty renders the goal highly elusive, however worthwhile.

Notes

1. I am indebted to Polly Young-Eisendrath for her suggestions for this section of the essay.

References

Brod, M. (1963). *Franz Kafka: A biography.* New York: Schocken Books. (Reprinted by permission of Schocken Books, Inc. Copyright © 1937 by Heinrich Mercy Sohn, Prague.)

Eisendrath, C. R. (1971). *The unifying moment: The psychological philosophy of William James and Alfred North Whitehead.* Cambridge: Harvard University Press.

James, W. (1890). *The principles of psychology,* 2 vols. New York: Henry Holt.

Kafka, F. (1953). *Letter to his father* (E. Kaiser and E. Wilkins, Trans.).

New York: Schocken Books. (Reprinted by permission of Schocken Books, Inc. Copyright © 1953 by Schocken Books, Inc.)

———. (1961). *The penal colony: Stories and short pieces* (W. and E. Muir, Trans.). New York: Schocken Books. (Reprinted by permission of Schocken Books, Inc. Copyright © 1948 by Schocken Books, Inc.)

———. (1962). *Letters to Milena* (T. and J. Stern, Trans.). New York: Schocken Books. (Reprinted by permission of Schocken Books, Inc. Copyright © 1953 by Schocken Books, Inc.)

———. (1965). *Diaries 1910–1913* and *Diaries 1914–1923* (M. Greenberg, Trans.). New York: Schocken Books. (Reprinted by permission of Schocken Books, Inc. Copyright © 1948, 1949 by Schocken Books, Inc.)

———. (1969). *The trial* (W. and E. Muir, Trans.). New York: Vintage Books.

———. (1973). *Letters to Felice* (J. Stern and E. Duckworth, Trans.). New York: Schocken Books. (Reprinted by permission of Schocken Books, Inc. Copyright © 1967 by Schocken Books, Inc.)

———. (1974). *The castle* (W. and E. Muir, Trans.). New York: Schocken Books. (Reprinted by permission of Schocken Books, Inc. Copyright © 1926 by Schocken Books, Inc.)

———. (1977). *Letters to friends, family and editors* (R. and C. Winston, Trans.). New York: Schocken Books. (Reprinted by permission of Schocken Books, Inc. Copyright © 1958 by Schocken Books, Inc.)

Kohut, H. (1971). *The analysis of the self*. New York: International Universities Press.

———. (1977). *The restoration of the self*. New York: International Universities Press.

Miller, G. A., Galanter, E., and Pribram, K. H. (1960). *Plans and the structure of behavior*. New York: Henry Holt.

Neisser, U. (1967). *Cognitive psychology*. New York: Appleton-Century-Crofts.

Sullivan, H. S. (1953). *The interpersonal theory of psychiatry*. New York and London: W. W. Norton.

CHAPTER 8

Jacques Lacan: Postmodern Depth Psychology and the Birth of the Self-Reflexive Subject

PAUL K. KUGLER

> When I prepared this little talk for you, it was early in the morning. I could see Baltimore through the window and it was a very interesting moment, because it was not quite daylight and a neon sign indicated to me every minute the change of time; and naturally there was heavy traffic; and I remarked to myself that exactly all that I could see, except for some trees in the distance, was the result of thoughts, actively thinking thoughts, where the function played by the subjects was not completely obvious—perhaps only transmission organs. In any case, the so-called *Dasein*, as a definition of the subject, was there in this rather intermittent or fading—or perhaps "irrealizing"—spectator. The best image to sum up the unconscious is exactly Baltimore in the early morning.
>
> (Lacan, 1983/1966, p. 845)

PERHAPS NO PSYCHOANALYST has had greater influence on postmodern analytic theory and clinical practice than Jacques Lacan. While it is practically impossible to define just what is meant by postmodernism, it is possible to note that at its heart lies a deep concern with the self-reflexive subject (Lyotard, 1984). And it is precisely around the issue of a self capable of self-reflection that postmodernism intersects with the work of Lacan. This chapter focuses on Lacan's theory of the mirror stage of psychological development and its function in the birth of a self capable of self-reflection. We will look at how a self becomes divided from itself and in the process capable of differentiating the literal from the metaphorical, the real from the imaginal, the conscious from the unconscious. But first, in order to gain a better understanding of Lacan's significance for critical theory and clinical practice, we will review his role and place in the psychoanalytic movement.

The history of Freudian psychoanalysis is characterized by a variety of shifts in theoretical and clinical focus. At the beginning of the century, Freud's focus was on the Oedipus complex and the vicissitudes of id psychology. The central issues of human life were packaged into the resolution of critical childhood relationships between the ages of three and five. With Freud's death in 1939 came the end of the dominance of id psychology and psychoanalytic history.

The publications of Anna Freud's *The Ego and the Mechanisms of Defense* (1946) and Heinz Hartmann's *Ego Psychology and the Problems of Adaptation* (1939) inaugurated a new era of ego psychology. Their work shifted the clinical emphasis away from a psychology of the unconscious to a focus on the ego and its various functions in organizing psychic processes. The development of ego psychology in the 1930s through what became, at least in America, almost an obsession with the notion of identity in the 1940s and 50s to the present, has been accompanied by another movement within psychoanalysis toward exploration of earlier and more archaic relationships in human life. In general, this second historical development in depth psychology has been away from a focus on relationships that are triangular and include questions of the role of the father, toward a focus on relationships that are dyadic and concern the mother-child interaction.

Over the next twenty-five years, the role of the father in the formation of personality has been almost completely excluded by object relations theory through its focus on the mother-child dyad. In the history of psychoanalysis, nearly a quarter of the time has involved an eclipse of the Oedipus complex. But what was gained through neglecting the role of the father was an intense focus on the earliest and most archaic aspects of child development in regard to the grounding of self in relation to (M)other. The focus of clinical attention on the earliest phases of psychological development has led to an elaboration and refinement of psychoanalysis as a perceptual theory of personality. It has extended Freud's structural conceptualization by stressing the effects of much earlier perceptions and interpersonal relations.

The clinical focus on object relations was most intense in England and South America, especially through the works of Melanie Klein, Fairbairn, Bion, Guntrip, and Winnicott. Although orthodox psychoanalysis included the emphasis on ego psychology after Freud's death, it did not admit object relations theory to its inner circle until the 1970s. In the 1970s the "new theory" of object relations began to gain ascendancy as the central focus of psychoanalytic theory. The two figures most responsible for bridging classical psychoanalysis with object relations theory were Margaret Mahler, with her studies on autism, infants, and early object relations, and Edith Jacobson, with her book *The Self and the Object World* (1964) and her many volumes on depression.

By the mid-1970s object relations theory was being imported into the United States through Heinz Kohut's and Otto Kernberg's work on narcissistic disorders and borderline conditions. Initially, Kohut (1971, 1977) presented his ideas within existing psychoanalytic theory, but he later replaced traditional structural and metapsychological theory with his new "psychology of the self." Kernberg (1975) on the other hand, has attempted to make his contributions to narcissistic and borderline disorders within the mainstream of psychoanalytic theory. His description of self and object representations is in line with the more orthodox formulations of Jacobson; the theories of Mahler, Hartmann, and Rapaport; and the techniques of Stone and Lowenstein.

The 1970s were marked by another significant shift in clinical and theoretical focus that called into question the very foundation of psychoanalysis. While psychoanalysis was clinically based on the "talking cure," it was theoretically based on a biological and economic model: the theory of drives and libido. The decade of the 1970s witnessed movements from various quarters to substitute linguistics for biology and economics as the scientific foundation and model for psychoanalysis. Marshall Edelson (1976) replaced the economic model with generative grammar; Roy Schafer (1976) substituted "action language" for Freud's metapsychology; and Jacques Lacan (1977, 1978) exchanged the biological foundation for a foundation in structural linguistics.

Attention to theoretical foundations shifted again in the 1980s, this time to a questioning of the very notion of theory itself. Perhaps nothing is more characteristic of depth psychology in the 1980s than the movement toward deliteralization of theory. The traditional notion of theory as a concrete explanation of original facts is being replaced by the notion of theory as a constructive narrative; consequently, the view of personality as originating in literal events is giving way to the view that personality is self-reflexively constructed through narrative. This theoretical shift has become pervasive in psychoanalysis. Today it is practically impossible to pick up a depth psychology text without seeing an almost hyper-self-consciousness of the constructed and re-flexive dimension of both theory and personality. This focus on the constructive, fictional dimension of personality inevitably led to the question of the origin of the human subject and its characteristic re-flexivity. This question now occupies the central stage of contempo-rary psychoanalytic theory and is one of the main reasons for the interest among psychoanalysts in the work of Jacques Lacan. The question of what constitutes the reflexive subject is the central question in all of psychoanalysis. How is a reflexive subject possible in the first place? Under what conditions is human reflexivity defined? Under what conditions is it reversed?

These questions originated with the realization that the reflexive subject is created, not given. Today, in psychoanalytic circles, concern about the origin of self-consciousness has assumed such overriding importance that it has led to the further question of how the construc-tion of human personality occurs in and through the various systems of representation available in any given space and time. And the ques-tion of the origin of self-consciousness itself has become so strangely reflexive that the very theories in which we talk about the construction of personality have themselves become self-consciously constructed. We have begun to see the fictionality of the theories through which we construct our "myths of human personality" (Hillman, 1972, 1975, 1979, 1983).

This realization has come about in England and the United States partly through systematic and empirical work with mothers and in-fants. It has happened in other countries by other means. In France, among the Lacanians, the same issue was raised not through empirical data but in much more theoretical terms and through philosophical lenses. But the issue remains the same: How can we understand hu-man subjectivity so as to account for both the presence and the absence of reflexivity in human beings? How can we define the human subject so as to account for both its reflexive possibility and the possibility of its loss?

Traditionally, psychoanalysis has defined the origin of the reflexive subject in terms of the biological substrata of instinctual drives. The radicalism of Lacan's move was in his substitution of linguistics for biology as the scientific model underlying psychoanalysis. Lacan emphasizes the process through which personality development is dependent on and invented in a matrix of cultural signs and signifiers. The human subject does not come into being without the participation of an elaborate linguistic universe; the cultural matrix is there from the beginning, analogous to the cultural base in which a bacteria originates.

Lacan's most important contributions to psychoanalysis are his reflections on the mirror stage of psychological development and its function in the birth of the human subject. The human subject is a self characterized by an inherently divided psychic reality. Throughout the history of psychoanalysis, there has been the assumption that psychic life is inherently a divided or double kind of reality. "Divided" because psychic conflict has to do with experiencing the personality as divided, whether into consciousness and unconsciousness, or into various complexes, or as divided more elaborately and topographically into a conscious, preconscious, and unconscious. On the other hand, "double" means divided in a very different sense: capable of, and in a sense doomed to, a kind of self-reflection. How does this "divided subject" doomed to self-reflection come into being?

The drama of the mirror stage and its function in the birth of subjectivity, as narrated by Lacan, is not so complicated. The scene is set in the home and the principal actor is an infant, six months to a year in age, not yet able to talk. All at once, the child, who has never before hesitated in passing before the mirror, stops and smiles, for this is the first time it has recognized itself in a mirror. Lacan, following Hegel, insists that this initial identification with an image is the action upon which all subjectivity is based; it is the moment human reflexivity is born (Casey and Woody, 1983). The infant's discovery of and identification with its image in the mirror, or in a mirroring relationship, signifies the splitting of the subject into other and self, into unconscious and conscious. The childhood scenario is described by Lacan in the following passage from his book *Ecrits*:

> This development is experienced as a temporal dialectic that decisively projects the formation of the individual into history. The "mirror stage" is a drama whose internal thrust is precipitated from insufficiency to anticipation—

and which manufactures the subject, caught up in the lure
of spatial identification, the succession of phantasies that
extends from a fragmented body-image to a form of its
totality that I shall call orthopaedic—and, lastly, to the assumption of the armour of an alienating identity, which will
mark with its rigid structure the subject's entire mental
development. (Lacan, 1977, p. 4)

Lacan's text pushes the reader to the limits of comprehension, to
the place where unconsciousness begins and the inaccessible is to be
found. The first close encounter with Lacan's writing style often leaves
the reader feeling lost, confused, even angry. Lacan's writings are
impossible to understand fully, impossible to master, for they always
seem to allude to something behind, beyond the text, to an elsewhere,
to a truth that the texts do not quite yield. To read Lacan, it is necessary to tolerate the frustration of misrecognition, misapprehension,
and misunderstanding and to live into the experience of the inaccessible. To read Lacan is to experience the unexplainable and the unknowable. His texts defy literal readings and fixed interpretations
through a continuous subversion of the reading subject: the cogito,
the subject supposed to know. Through a close psychological reading
of these enigmatic texts, the reader is driven closer to a psychological
reading of his or her own enigmatic text. A close reading of Lacan is
a close encounter with the Other in ourselves.

With this qualification, allow me to turn elsewhere for an errant
reading of this critical passage from *Ecrits* describing the mirror stage.
It is a reading invented by the Other (Derrida, 1983) about a mirror
stage whose silvering and drama should not be taken too literally. At
the moment of the infant's inaugurating look into the mirror, the child
is captivated in an image by the specularization. The reflecting mirror
produces an imaginary duplication of the child, an originary reflexivity that divides the subject into unconscious and conscious, into other
and self. The image in the mirror actually "belongs" to the same child
viewing and experiencing the image as other. Octavio Paz describes
the subject's experience of otherness this way: "'Otherness' is above
all the simultaneous perception that we are others without ceasing to
be what we are and that, without ceasing to be where we are, our true
being is in another place" (Paz, 1975, p. 245).

As the infant for the first time views its own image as other in a mirroring relationship, that very act of viewing simultaneously brings into being the "subject" of the viewer doing the viewing. The event of the mirror stage is the first instance of the infant's psyche imagining itself. It is the first conscious experience of a psychic representation. The occasion of the first self-reflection is the specular experience of the imaginary and the real separated only by the amount of time it takes the reflected light to return to the child's eye. The act of reflection mixes up the two heterogenous "subjects," the imaginary and the real, the other and the self, the fictional and the autobiographical, at a speed no less than the speed of light. We can, therefore, no longer speak of one event initiating the other, for at the speed of light, physical, logical, and explanatory causality breaks down. We can no longer with any degree of certainty decide whether the imaginary initiates the real or the real initiates the imaginary, whether the other initiates the self or the self initiates the other, whether the fictional initiates the autobiographical or the autobiographical initiates the fictional. These two heterogenous subjects are now separated only by the speed of light.

This infinitely fast oscillation between the imaginary and the real constitutes the birth of the divided subject and its inherent reflexivity. The extraordinary economy of such an allegorical event—a child looking in a mirror, perfectly normal in its drama and staging—spontaneously deconstructs the oppositional logic that lies in the Western categorical distinctions between imaginal and real. The "first act" of self-reflection in a mirroring relationship produces the very drama it re-views. It is the play and the re-play, the action and the re-action, the cognition and the re-cognition in an infinitely fast oscillation contained within a single event. The child's dramatic performance of the mirror stage consists simply in producing "itself." It is a reflection that creates the self of self-reflection by creating the drama in the very act of re-viewing it.

The mirror stage is a paradigmatic metaphor for the birth of self-reflexive consciousness and the mutual dependence between the imaginary and the real. There can be no reflection without the real child, and there can be no consciousness of the real child without the imaginary child. The real and the imaginary are coterminous: each implicates the other.

The realization of the morphogenetic role played by the mirror image on personality development led Lacan to differentiate three orders of psychic experience: the Real, the Imaginary, and the Symbolic. For Lacan, the Real order is the world as such, while the Imaginary order is constituted during the mirror phase and consists of imagos. On the other hand, the Symbolic order comes into being with language and social exchange. Musing on the difference between the imaginary and the real, Lacan (1977) writes: "The mirror would do well to reflect a little more before returning our image to us" (p. 138).

Prior to the mirror stage, the child lacks the capacity to distinguish the objective from the subjective, the real from the imaginary. If there is hunger, it is not the child's hunger, because the infant is incapable of conceiving a "self" separate from the world. But during the mirror stage, this unity of experience is split and the child develops the capacity to recognize "its self" in a mirroring relationship.

This split, between the actual infant and the mirror image with which the infant identifies is only the anticipation of a more profound splitting of the subject, which will occur during language acquisition. This later process only replaces the mirror image of the body with the linguistic image, the first-person pronoun (e.g., *I* in English). This linguistic image is all the more deceptive in that it does not signify the particular individual infant at all, but only whoever is speaking. With the acquisition of language comes the rupture that, so to speak, lies between narrative truth and historical truth, between the description and the event, between language and metalanguage (Spence, 1982).

Through the acquisition of language the child is ushered into an elaborate linguistic universe, a collective matrix of signifiers. The importance of this linguistic entry into a system of representations cannot be overemphasized. For in acquiring linguistic competence, the infant (Lat. *infans*, "not speaking") learns to speak to the world through a network of collectively determined symbols. The human subject becomes possible during the mirror stage, when neurological development allows the infant to distinguish objects, and the human subject becomes actual when the child acquires the code of language and customs used consciously and unconsciously to order and construct itself and its world (Kugler, 1982).

The realization that subjectivity is constructed leads to the awareness that we are in language and creating metaphors of ourselves, as well as of our understanding of ourselves, all the time. Subjectivity is not given, nor are the myths we have of it. Subjectivity is something constructed continuously through metaphorizing in every dimension of our existence, including theory making, free associating, and every other dimension of representation that exists after the advent of language. Whether this constructing and metaphorizing activity exists before the psyche is structured through language is impossible to say, but certainly it is an irreversible fact once we live in the world of language.

The main critique of Lacan's work has come from Jacques Derrida (1975). Through a deconstruction of Lacan's psychoanalytic discourse, Derrida has revealed how despite Lacan's fiercely antihumanistic claims for having decentered the sovereign Cartesian subject, his psychoanalysis still remains caught in the tradition of Western ontological thought, trapped in the metaphysics of presence. Lacan's analysis aims at unveiling the "truth" (although, by his own confession, not the "whole truth"), and his theory adheres to a paradigm requiring a transcendental signified, a basic "god" term, to which each clinical case, each text, is reduced.

For Lacan, the phallus is the new transcendental signified to which all signifiers, every word and image, must ultimately be reduced. Consequently, Lacan's theory is still caught in the history of Western ontological thought with its dominant belief in an external meaning existing prior to signification. In the metaphysics of presence, this transcendental signified has traditionally been called "Being" or "Truth." Rather than escaping the trap of Western metaphysics, Lacan instead has only renamed the previous transcendental signified, thereby falling himself back into the same metaphysics. Lacan is trapped in his phallocentric logos, merely a new metaphysics of presence.

A second critique of Lacan's work has come from French feminism (Irigaray, 1985a,b). The feminist critique questions Lacan's system of representation, the discursive system at work in Lacan's writings. The feminists ask: To what extent does Lacan's language and style facilitate the "translation" of desire into representation? To what extent does it preclude the translation of desire, especially feminine desire, into representation? Is it possible, they ask, that Freud's "penis envy" and Lacan's notion of "woman as lack" refer to a lack existing not on the anatomical level or on the psychological level but on the linguistic level? For example, in French, the word *jouissance* is of feminine gender and refers to a specific pleasure experienced just prior to orgasm.

In English there is no specific word to accurately translate and represent this form of feminine desire. English lacks the capacity to represent the experience of *jouissance*. Similarly, Lacan's discursive system apparently lacks the capacity to represent feminine desire.

A second critique by the French feminists is of Lacan's theoretical model itself (Irigaray, 1985a,b). In Lacan's reformulation of the psychoanalytic model into three orders, the Symbolic, the Imaginary, and the Real, there is an implicit formalism that leads to an obscuring of phenomena and a formalizing of the uniqueness of the clinical case. When Lacan interprets the unconscious by, so to speak, ordering it into preexisting theoretical models—the Oedipus complex and the Symbolic, the Imaginary, and the Real orders—is he interpreting the patient's unconscious material phenomenologically or formally? For example, does not Lacan's assertion that the Oedipus complex and his three orders are a priori universal truths subvert the intention of psychoanalysis? When the analyst listens to the analysand, ideally there should be no a priori truths. The actions and words of the person being analyzed, and the transfer of meaning, cannot be ordered into any predesignated structure, any predetermined interpretation.

To this critique, I would add that instead of giving orders to the psyche through what Lacan calls "the law of the Father," we might analyze Lacan's theory of "the law of the Father" from the perspective of the unconscious, from the point of view of the Other, other-wise. This would involve analyzing Lacan's theory of unconscious fantasies for the unconscious fantasies, the implicit metaphors, structuring the theory itself. By this I am not suggesting that Lacan's theory, or any other theory, must be free from implicit philosophical assumptions, tropes, and dreams but only that we subject Lacan's text to the same self-reflexive reading to which it subjects dreams and other texts. Lacan, as is well known, was one of the first analysts to read a theoretical text as a dream. Lacan reads Freud as Freud reads dreams. Lacan rereads Freud for the "dreams" in Freud's writings, for an analysis of Freud's textual metaphors.

With his reflections on the mirror stage of psychological development, Lacan gives birth to the "subject" of postmodern depth psychology; but he, like all fathers, does not go far enough. He does not reveal the whole truth. For while Lacan turns the silvery mirror on his patients, Freud's writings, literary texts, and social events, he does not turn the mirror structure on his own theoretical work.

Lacan does, however, pursue and encourage "the analysis of the analysis"; he encourages the analysand to analyze his or her previous analysis with another analyst. But he does not pursue the psychoanalysis of his own theory of analysis; he cannot "see through," deconstruct, his own analytic theory.

Lacan's failure to "see through" all his implicit philosophical assumptions, all his textual metaphors, is, however, not criticized here. For, as analysts know only too well, self-analysis is impossible, just as a complete analysis of another is impossible. Psychoanalysis is an impossible profession. And I would add, depth psychology loses nothing by admitting that it is impossible. Those analysts who precipitously content themselves with this view lose nothing from having to wait for the final analysis. For the subject of postmodern depth psychology, possibility would rather be the danger: a danger of becoming a veritable set of rule-governed procedures, methodic practices, formalized techniques, uniform standards, accessible approaches. The interest in postmodern depth psychology, of such force and desire as it may have, is a certain experience of the impossible. It is the experience of the other subject, the experience of the other as the creation, the construction, of the impossible subject. The impossible is the only possible place, the only imaginable topos, out of which to create a new subject.

References

Casey, E., and J. M. Woody. (1983). "Hegel, Heidegger, Lacan: The dialectic of desire." In J. Smith and W. Kerrigan (Eds.), *Interpreting Lacan*. New Haven: Yale University Press.

Derrida, J. (1975). "The purveyor of truth." *Yale French Studies, 52.*

———. (1983). "Psyche: Invention of the other." Series of lectures given at Cornell University.

Edelson, M. (1976). *Language and interpretation in psychoanalysis.* New Haven: Yale University Press.

Freud, A. (1946). *The ego and mechanisms of defense.* New York: International Universities Press.

Hartmann, H. (1958). *Ego psychology and the problem of adaptation.* New York: International Universities Press.

Hillman, J. (1972). *Myth of analysis.* Evanston: Northwestern University Press.

————. (1975). *Re-visioning psychology*. New York: Harper & Row.

————. (1979). *The dream and the underworld*. New York: Harper & Row.

————. (1983). *Healing fictions*. Station Hill: Station Hill Press.

————. (1983). *Interviews*. New York: Harper & Row.

Irigaray, L. (1985a). *Speculum of the other woman*. Ithaca: Cornell University Press.

————. (1985b). *This sex which is not one*. Ithaca: Cornell University Press.

Jacobson, E. (1964). *The self and the object world*. New York: International Universities Press.

Kernberg, O. (1975). *Borderline conditions and pathological narcissism*. New York: Jason Aronson.

Kohut, H. (1971). *The analysis of the self*. New York: International Universities Press.

————. (1977). *The restoration of the self*. New York: International Universities Press.

Kugler, P. (1982). *The alchemy of discourse*. Lewisburg: Bucknell University Press.

Lacan, J. (1977). *Ecrits: A selection* (A. Sheridan, Trans.). New York: W. W. Norton.

————. (1978). *The four fundamental concepts of psychoanalysis* (A. Sheridan, Trans.). New York: W. W. Norton.

————. (1983). Sur un terrain en friche: Liminal note, lecture translated and transcribed by R. Macksey, held at Johns Hopkins University, 1966. In *Lacan and narration*, R. C. Davis (Ed.). Baltimore: Johns Hopkins University Press.

Lyotard, J. (1984). *The Postmodern Condition: A Report on Knowledge*. Minneapolis: University of Minnesota Press.

Mahler, M. (1968). *On human symbiosis and the vicissitudes of individuation*, Vol. 1, *Infantile psychosis*. New York: International Universities Press.

Paz, O. (1975). *The bow and the lyre* (R. L. C. Simms, Trans.). New York: McGraw-Hill.

Schafer, R. (1976). *A new language for psychoanalysis*. New Haven: Yale University Press.

Spence, D. (1982). *Narrative truth and historical truth: Meaning and interpretation in psychoanalysis*. New York: W. W. Norton.

SELF and DEATH

According to Robert Jay Lifton (1983), death represents "essentially
. . . a compelling universal urge to maintain an inner sense of continuous symbolic relationship, over time and space, with the various elements of life" (p. 31). The following account of the pretext of self
follows a similar theme and considers self to be a series of playful
deceptions filled with color and distraction. Pamela White Hadas's
version of self does not mix readily with the serious claims to intentionality and integrity made by authors in the first section of the book.
Even so, she explores self-reference when she takes on a variety of
voices that repeat a central theme: ". . . a particular 'interval / Experience between,' about profound experiments within finitude, within
parentheses chiseled or inked definitively after a name; this telling,
any telling, tends to place a period on one of many possible life sentences, neat as a pin at the throat, yet revisable as an unfashionable
ruffle" (p. 202). We witness the self as a symbolic continuity in the
face of extinction, as the product of desire for symbolic immortality,
a term coined by Lifton (1983).

Interpreting both the experiential and the narrative context of self
as a linguistic project, White Hadas brings us to encounters with all
three "subparadigms" of death as described by Lifton: separation,
disintegration, and stasis. These processes are forever recurring in
daily life as they become the basis for our narratives of attachment,
integration, and agency. In contrast to any single interpretation of self
as primarily compensation and defense, White Hadas offers multivarious images of self as a creative project emanating out of death
experiences.

References

Lifton, R. J. (1983). *The life of the self*. New York: Basic Books.

CHAPTER 9

"Because It Hath No Bottom": Self, Narrative, and the Power to Die

PAMELA WHITE HADAS

I. Nothing to Speak of

TO SPEAK OF the "self," as if I knew whereof, in any technical sense, I speak, fills me with the unease I imagine proper to a novice criminal embarking solo on a major-league scam. I am not prepared to offer a "concept of self" in terms of psychosocial conundrums or clinical data; nor shall I speculate, with any authority, as to how the kernel of our human kindness first took root in the primate psyche, or how the embryonic "I am I" may have incited the hominid aspirations of *australopithicus afarensis* or may have stipulated our upright gait. It does occur to me, though, in my simple capacity as participant/spectator in this arena of "self," that the distinction of a conscious "human" self from the felt integrities of other creatures may well have originated in the ends of play rather than in the latter-day beginnings (only some four million years ago) of our "sagacity." The human knack for numbers hacked in a bone, say, or for minding a brainstorm's oracles (as accidentally sparked as dry brush by bad weather), seem less a matter of the "self's" mysterious mastery than of zoological mechanics, less indicative of self-conscious intent than of an accidentally practical flap among internuncial neurons.

The constructive "work of self," and the kinds of play that are to be the subjects of this essay, will look to the spectacle of *homo ludens* rather than to the probity of *homo sapiens*. I shall consider the "self" principally as a maker of narratives that, though they may be sapiently crafted toward aesthetic ends, reveal their sources in the inventive desperation and serious silliness of child's play. The aim is to concentrate some light on a suspected nexus of self-constructive processes that have been artfully "coated" (as elusive objects are for electron microscopy), such that certain functional aspects of the hidden "self" may, in the sharpened edges of a cast shadow, be more clearly surmised. Throughout, I shall qualify (or clothe) the particular, narrative "self" in inverted commas, serving partly to protect its privacy, partly to say: "I must distance this object from my sense of its inconstancy."

The "self," most habitually free in its associations, is "like that," or "like this"; it is also the "very thing" that makes us *us,* me *me,* the rest of you *them.* But what in the world is the *sed per se?* Simply some *quid pro quo?* Or, as James Joyce's Molly Bloom asks her wandering spouse, of the word *metempsychosis* stumbled upon in her latest "smutty" novel, "Who's he when he's at home?" Mr. Bloom, caught up in his own soul's gadding, has heard of the concept of "the transmigration of souls," but he cannot say, in so many words, or even a few, who "he" is "when he's at home." Regarding such a personal "concept," in a word, or in a work of art, we may—by chance, choice, or need—begin to understand it as expressive of a "something in progress" that "behind the scenes," so to speak, defines a particular being as "unto-itself-but-among-others."

The nature of art (no less than that of Nature, save in the latter's randomness perhaps) is to accrete where possible and to contain by necessity; if, as we like to say, art "works," we probably mean, among other things, that the work's implicit struggle between elaboration and restraint, its solution to the primary problematical injunction to "say something" but to "stop in time," are recognized by the consumer no less than realized by the maker. The nature of a human "self" is like that too, tending to fill up available space, to kill vacant time, and to play with and/or against the natural limits of the spaces and times that invite our most creative acts of obliteration.

Both "self" and "art," along with the "naked truths" we may ask for them to tell us, do arise mysteriously from the basic "thingness" of the world, and neither can materially represent their hidden, perhaps ultimately unpresentable, origins or ends. Narratives that engage us on levels not readily available to reason often have a "telling" propensity to conceal their real sources, or to "forget" exactly what "it" was all about in the first place. Nevertheless, despite the fictive intent to "fill in the blanks" with any old thing, to reveal sources and satisfy curiosities—all of course within the bounds of common proprieties, consciously observed—the deepest, most "original" truths about ourselves (not so nice, maybe, not so comforting) often do get told. The specific resources of a proper "self," given the truth of this hypothesis, may be most clearly seen in certain aesthetic properties and in the management by artifice of what otherwise is "improper to be shown," if not "impossible to be known." The "let's pretend" of art displays, in other words, and in the safety of art's inconsequence, our most common human predicaments and powers. But to tell the truth . . .

II. Magical Extents

To be faced with the singular prospect of "self"—one's oddly reversed visage in the mirror, or an other, even stranger, whose oddity must be (but politely) remarked ("Grandmother, what big eyes you have!"), or (God forbid) the "concept" at large—is to risk being taken in, possibly taken aback. To be struck by the relatively ordered result of any creative effort, in fact, from human evolution to a child's cornhusk doll, what is "it" exactly that strikes us? captivates us? Why are we gathered together, after all, to ask and answer for our "self" and the selves of others, what processes determine our sense of being, in or among those selves, subject-matters, objects of interest? By what spell are we fascinated, bound, by this thoroughly natural phenomenon of our separateness, its maintenance, its haunting dependencies? What work of consciousness or unconsciousness results in the certainty that a "self" is with us—too much, or too little, like the world; or behind us—about to catch us in our fall, or to ambush . . . ? In the sounds we make, to protect or to provoke . . . Is anybody home?

"One need not be a Chamber—to be Haunted," suggests Emily Dickinson (1959),

> One need not be a House—
> The Brain has Corridors—surpassing
> Material Place—
>
> Ourself behind ourself, concealed—
> Should startle most—
> Assassin hid in our Apartment
> Be Horror's least.
>
> The Body—borrows a Revolver—
> He bolts the Door—

O'erlooking a superior spectre—
Or More—
(#670)

And yet, to mitigate the fear of what we are "in truth" up against, alone with, in our solitary chambers, Dickinson notes the redeeming fact that

Contained in this short Life
Are magical extents
The soul returning soft at night
To steal securer thence. . .
(#1165)

The duties of self or art are constantly subject to shifts, as are the moods, from Gothic to Mother Goose, in the verses of Dickinson just cited; as are voices and attitudes, between passive and active responses, toward being in the world. An art that is felt to move through time and seen to occupy space would seem best to comprehend the "self" that goes along as witness or protagonist. The purpose of "narrative," as it relates particularly the movement of a physically encumbered mind (or mentally encumbered body) from here to there, is to make actual, in the end, what began as no more than potential.

A storyteller may be said to be masterful in the degree that she is able to to manipulate the potentialities of various losses, entailing them by acts of choice as well as by chance; the narrative containment of losses prepares for inevitable actualities, both within and beyond a "story." These rehearsals, including all possible constructions and revisions of what the conscious mind senses to be true, are central to my sense not only of how a work of art gets made but of the "work of self" required of all of us. As in learning to play any game or musical instrument, to play one's "self" at any imaginable moment takes practice; one may "get it right" by accident the first time, and miss the point of one's own profound experiment or joke; or one may finally "get it right" only to realize that the "it" is much more, or less, than one had bargained for.

In a recent novel by Joanna McClelland Glass, *Woman Wanted,* the protagonist recalls herself at the age of four, hiding in the back seat of her parents' car as they drive through a customs gate at the Canadian border. She is under a blanket, ostensibly scared by the officer's demand for declarations of goods. The officer asks, reasonably enough,

> "And what's that wriggling in the back?"
> "Oh, that's our daughter. She's scared."
> "Little girl? Why are you scared?"
> "Because," said she, "I'm alive."
> They had a good laugh over that, the three adults. A good, middle-aged guffaw.
> "She'll grow out of it," said the officer. (Glass, 1985, p. 133)

Relegated to the back seat, the child's body may be found among the boughten goods, but in an important sense, and she knows it, she's not "duty-free." She is in possession of her own secret life and consciousness as if these were a sort of contraband. If discovered, this bright child figures, the somehow illegally purchased booty of her very aliveness, her "self," might properly be confiscated at the border. How is a child to distinguish her "self" from the other undeclared properties belonging to her parents? Is she susceptible to their being dispossessed of her? Might they have to render her unto an unknown Caesar along with the booze and jewelry? The answer to the child's reasonable anxiety, it seems to me, will lie in her gradual and continuous re-creation and repossession of her person as a "self" that is not tradable, not "fixed" in value as long as it is (dangerously still) alive. The corollary, the price of self-possession, will be realized, too: that the "self" she treasures must be rendered as she goes, in order to keep on going.

To tell the truth, particularly in narrative works, the child buried in us may return, like any object repressed, to enlighten, disrupt, or haunt a maturer sense of continuity; the child in us comes also to confirm ownership of *this* "self" and may come to protect it, by recollection, from experiencing unremittable loss. The eventual mastery of language (such that the "joke" may be understood at last, the passage be retold unto its perfect end) seems to me to stem from the most secret and eventful condition of childhood.

Suppose I dare to commit the simplest of definitions: the "self" is any true "I" in a story, the "true I" being the one that can say with conviction, "I am alive," or with trust in its own vision, "the emperor has no clothes." But does the "self" need to tell a story to be true to itself? Or to be definitive? And what, necessarily, marks a story as "true"? Whatever is not "self-contradictory," shall we say? At any given moment? But to tell the truth, the "self" wrapped up in its event is not *just* that, nor *all* there—nor infinitely more, either.

All differences between our "self" and its so-called truth are, one supposes, rightly to be made up in the end. Through its magical extents, as well as within its haunted chamber, however, the "self" may be less deliberate in its discoveries than we would like to think. Still, a poem or narrative from which any "self" looks back, or looks out, for what comes next, may show us at least a momentarily true reflection of our own privately felt predicament, if not the "real thing"; for instance, Emily Dickinson admits that

> I never hear that one is dead
> Without the chance of Life
> Afresh annihilating me
> That mightiest Belief,
>
> Too mighty for the Daily mind
> That tilling its abyss,
> Had Madness, had it once or twice
> The yawning Consciousness,
>
> Beliefs are Bandaged, like the Tongue
> When Terror were it told
> In any Tone commensurate
> Would strike us instant Dead
>
> I do not know the man so bold
> He dare in lonely Place
> That awful stranger Consciousness
> Deliberately face—
>
> (#1323)

In any case, no matter in what realm or in what form each "self" is to be found and rendered, the act of self-possession or self-definition involves rehearsals of an "original" scene, such as the child faces at the customs gate, or faces with the fact of another's funeral. Our certainties no less than our believed-in possibilities are subject to rehearsals. *Imagine* the coming of the IRS: be audited, defend, pay up.

Or, here is the page of the *Times* devoted to obits: read 'em and weep. The hood the self customarily wears is of whole cloth—a weave of variations, improvisations, and the revisions enforced by time, Mad Ave. promo, and forgetting. Like the hood of the condemned, our selfhood is worn not only to protect its wearer from the sight of a firing squad, but to protect the "consciousness" of the surviving potential assassin from the face of its victim. The mirrors in a house of mourning, in at least one sensitive tradition, are customarily sheeted when a death occurs. Thus, at the feast following the funeral, none shall contemplate his own face, or arrange her own hair upon some fleeting, vain reflection.

III. To Tell the Truth

Can the "self" appear at all without disguise? If not, how can we speak of a "true self" at all? Nietzsche plays with notions of self and simulation in a fragment, "On Truth and Lie in an Extra-Moral Sense," and begins by posing, or postulating, the following:

> In some remote corner of the universe, poured out and glittering in innumerable solar systems, there once was a star on which clever animals invented knowledge. That was the haughtiest and most mendacious minute of "world history"—yet only a minute. After nature had drawn a few breaths the star grew cold, and the clever animals had to die.
>
> One might invent such a fable and still not have illustrated sufficiently how wretched, how shadowy and flighty, how aimless and arbitrary, the human intellect appears in nature. There have been eternities when it did not exist; and when it is done for again, nothing will have happened. . . . But if we could communicate with the mosquito, then we would learn that it floats through the air with the same self-importance, feeling within itself the flying center of the world. . . .
>
> The intellect, as a means for the preservation of the individual, unfolds its chief powers in simulation. . . . In man this art of simulation reaches its peak: here deception, flattery, lying and cheating, talking behind the back, posing,

living in borrowed splendor, being masked, the disguise of convention, acting a role before others and before oneself— in short, the constant fluttering around the single flame of vanity is so much the rule and the law that almost nothing is more incomprehensible than how an honest and pure urge for truth could make its appearance among men. . . . Moreover, man permits himself to be lied to at night, his life long, when he dreams, and his moral sense never even tries to prevent this. . . .

What, indeed, does man know of himself! Can he even once perceive himself completely, laid out as if in an illuminated glass case? Does not nature keep much the most from him, even about his body, to spellbind and confine him in a proud, deceptive consciousness . . . ? She threw away the key; and woe to the calamitous curiosity which might peer just once through a crack in the chamber of consciousness and look down, and sense that man rests upon the merciless, the greedy, the insatiable, the murderous, in the indifference of his ignorance-hanging in dreams, as it were, upon the back of a tiger. In view of this, whence in all the world comes the urge for truth? (Nietzsche, 1982, pp. 242–44)

How the "self" as credible narrator is to proceed, to tell "the truth," or at least "it like it is" with regard to a very conditional existence, is without doubt one of the "self's" definitive, and definitively secretive, properties. Shall the truthfulness of the hero be shown best by stages, or circuitously? Shall a narrator's true motives be fugally chased to a single resolution, as in a Bach prelude, or be masked for good and simple, like the Lone Ranger? Or might our "true self" come dressed to kill, perhaps, as cannily convincing as Little Red Riding Hood's local wolf? Whether the "self" makes moral points, subversively or clearly as any fairy tale; whether it fills its plots with showy creative efforts gone right, or amok, or just plain wrong; whether it kills time in anticipation of the "big fish" it knows is lolling just under the surface, "it" does know this: "it" is *after* something.

The dedicated fisher (let's say) for self-images knows, in a way indistinguishable from hopeful belief in its own past or the oft-repeated experience of others, that her prey is there, just below vision. This slippery, finned self-image is most likely (why else wait fly-bitten and hungry on the shore?) just dying for the mind's proffered bait, hidden hook and all, hankering for the history it will become when caught, brought home.

To begin, then, again, toward "getting to the bottom" of our narrative predilection, even its passion, for "telling it *like* it"—was or is, may be or, most particularly, might have been—I shall offer three literary examples of our self-regarding nature at work, the "self" in play. All have to do with the author's self-conscious exploitation of illusion, the uses and risks of verbal precision; the wish to tell some deeply felt truth, as will be seen in these passages, is inseparable from the author's fears of self-exposure and the consequences not of being misunderstood so much as of telling too much too truly. All these passages present reflective or reflected selves engaged in their acts of telling; all suggest poignantly their awareness of the true monsters just behind or beneath their aesthetically controlled, reflective surfaces.

My first example is from Shakespeare's *A Midsummer Night's Dream*. The play as a whole is a concatenation of unsettling and settling arguments; wedding imbues its air from the outset, but none of the play's apparent subjects, players or playthings, are certain of their proper mates. The marriage between King Oberon of Fairyland and his Queen Titania (the invisible potentates of the play's space) is on the rocks; among the mortals, Duke Theseus is engaged to his former enemy, the Amazon Hippolyta; and two young couples, from a privileged but not noble class, must endure uncommon muddlings of their affairs before achieving their proper couplings. Posed against all this "romance," whose end is of course the legitimization of sexual creativity, is a group of craftsmen, "rude mechanicals," who are intent on the purely cultural creation of an amateur play, which they mean to present at court upon the occasion of the Duke's marriage, should everybody survive the formidable hodgepodge of the intervening "dream."

One of the "mechanicals" at the bottom of the play's heap of uncertain characters, significantly Bottom by name, is by trade a master weaver; most childlike among the characters, he plays a crucial part in creating the "play within the play." In the second scene of the first act, the craftsmen begin to plan their presentation of "Pyramus and Thisby" (the prototype of Shakespeare's own *Romeo and Juliet*). Their exuberance in deciding to represent doomed lovers on the felicitous occasion of Duke Theseus's marriage more than mitigates their hilarious lack of dramatic savvy and the inappropriateness of their choice; their devotion to their play is the proper and polymorphously perverse antidote to the marriage-bound society and postoedipal sexual tensions inherent in the surrounding plots.

SCENE II.—Athens. A Room in QUINCE'S House.
Enter QUINCE, SNUG, BOTTOM, FLUTE, SNOUT, and STARVELING.

QUIN. Is all our company here?

BOT. . . . Now, good Peter Quince, call forth your actors . . .

QUIN. . . . Nick Bottom, the weaver.

BOT. Ready. Name what part I am for, and proceed.

QUIN. You, Nick Bottom, are set down for Pyramus.

BOT. What is Pyramus? a lover, or a tyrant?

QUIN. A lover, that kills himself most gallantly for love.

BOT. That will ask some tears in the true performing of it: if I do it, let the audience look to their eyes; I will move storms, I will condole in some measure. To the rest: yet my chief humour is for a tyrant. I could play Ercles rarely, or a part to tear a cat in, to make all split.

> The raging rocks
> And shivering shocks
> Shall break the locks
> Of prison gates:
> And Phibbus' car
> Shall shine from far
> And make and mar
> The foolish Fates.

This was lofty! . . . This is Ercles' vein, a tyrant's vein; a lover is more condoling.

[Quince proceeds to call the players by name and assign them roles. Flute is asked to play Thisby and tries to protest as a man, as he has "a beard coming." Bottom interrupts.]

BOT. An I may hide my face, let me play Thisby too. I'll speak in a monstrous little voice, 'Thisne, Thisne!' 'Ah, Pyramus, my lover dear; thy Thisby dear, and lady dear!'

QUIN. No, no. . . . Snug, the joiner, you the lion's part; and, I hope, here is a play fitted.

. . .

BOT. Let me play the lion too. I will roar, that I will do any man's heart good to hear me; I will roar, that I will

make the duke say, 'Let him roar again, let him roar
again.'

QUIN. An you should do it too terribly, you would fright
the duchess and the ladies, that they would shriek; and
that were enough to hang us all.

ALL. That would hang us, every mother's son.

BOT. I grant you, friends, if that you should fright the
ladies out of their wits, they would have no more discre-
tion but to hang us; but I will aggravate my voice so that
I will roar you as gently as any sucking dove; I will roar
you as 'twere any nightingale.

[Quince instructs Bottom that he must play Pyramus, "a
sweet-faced man; a proper man, as one shall see in a summer's day," and Bottom proceeds to consider what color
beard he will dress up in. Quince cuts in to ask the players
to meet in the wood outside the town, by moonlight the
next night.]

BOT. We will meet; and there we may rehearse more ob-
scenely and courageously. Take pains; be perfect; adieu.

                                                                 (I.ii.1–109)

This scene, presumably a parody not unrelated to the improvisatory
methods of Shakespeare's Globe company, may be read as representing a common "collective self," with Bottom representing its "bottom
nature" (to borrow a phrase of Gertrude Stein's), ego-wise. The other
representatives of this common body may be "rude" as well as "mechanical" regarding notions of performance, yet as a whole, this "self"
is touchingly innocent, sensitive to the problems of presenting "reality"
in a way that will be both credible and unthreatening.

Emily Dickinson, two and a half centuries later, offers the following
advice regarding the representation of "Truth," a view not all that
different, at bottom, from the resolves of Shakespeare's troupe:

                    Tell all the Truth but tell it slant—
                    Success in Circuit lies
                    Too bright for our infirm Delight
                    The truth's superb surprise

                    As Lightning to the Children eased
                    With explanation kind

> The Truth must dazzle gradually
> Or every man be blind—
> (#1129)

The "awful truth" that lovers who die and tyrants who exact death, that the tragic and romantic, the illuminating and the blinding, are somehow interchangeable as agents of murderous (forbidden) knowledge, cannot be communicated, believed, and survived without recourse to illusion. The most famous early example of this is Perseus's use of a mirror to circumvent the "reality" of the Medusa's monstrous head of snakes, the direct sight of which turns the witness into stone. To do away with this paralyzing embodiment of evil, female power, is something the hero *must* do to get on with his life. Perseus comes up with the trick of approaching his Gorgon backwards, guiding his regressive steps and his sword to its mark by regarding, not the Medusa herself, but her image as reflected in his bright shield. Having no real substance there, she is as good as dead.

Sylvia Plath, in this century, offers yet another Persean slant on the way a "self" might come to terms with terror through terror's reflection. Here too, the lethal aspect is measured out so as to alert, without in one fell swoop murdering, the protagonist-audience. Like Shakespeare (through the character of Bottom), and like Bottom imagining his "lion's part," Plath defends against the appearance of monstrousness by giving the monster in her poem, the "Mirror," her own, but "aggravated," voice.

> I am silver and exact. I have no preconceptions.
> Whatever I see I swallow immediately.
> Just as it is, unmisted by love or dislike.
> I am not cruel, only truthful—
> The eye of a little god, four-cornered.
> Most of the time I meditate on the opposite wall.
> It is pink, with speckles. I have looked at it so long
> I think it is a part of my heart. But it flickers.
> Faces and darkness separate us over and over.

The "little god" that swallows everything it sees here, despite the precise language to which it is given (by art, not nature), is newborn, the clean-slate infant "self"—consequently, it is the engulfer, as well as the accuser—of its author, its mother, and the mature "self" of which it can have, as yet, no preconceptions. This human "mirror" is not only the miniature reflector of the "monster" who fills and abandons its frame at will, but a monster in its own reflective right as it "shows" its witness what she herself has been, and will become through her narcissistic attachment to this "thing," this intractable and "perfect" body. The irresistible image invites one to take a plunge; it is a "self," in other words, worth diving down for, even, as Narcissus found out, if the consequence is drowning. Plath's mirror quite flatly states:

> Now I am a lake. A woman bends over me,
> Searching my reaches for what she really is.
> Then she turns to those liars, the candles or the moon.
> I see her back, and reflect it faithfully.
> She rewards me with tears and an agitation of hands.
> I am important to her. She comes and goes.
> Each morning it is her face that replaces the darkness.
> In me she has drowned a young girl, and in me an old woman
> Rises toward her day after day, like a terrible fish.

Following a Dickinsonian slant, Plath's "Mirror" comes full circle, without the whole and dazzlingly horrible truth of the matter, the fishy "catch" at the bottom of the reflective pool, being realized. The full realization takes time, time and reversals, cold slants, hot denials. Quite as ruthlessly, but without the deflective ritual of a "fairy tale," Plath's "Mirror" speaks of what is as unfair as it is unmentionable in polite company. The "spitting" image douses its source; the child is, in other words, mother to the woman, and the play between them prefigures the obliteration of these roles at the same time as it occasions their creative relation to each other. As Plath admits in the poem "Morning Song," on the same subject:

> I'm no more your mother
> Than the cloud that distills a mirror to reflect its own slow
> Effacement at the wind's hand.

The reflection of Plath's "Mirror" is unmitigated by heroic dreams or sexual intents. Decidedly lacking in courtly graces or prophylactic illusions, it flatly assesses its object, penetrates the curiously inflated "other" with pointed affronts, says: "This is it, baby, the image stops here."

Shakespeare's "mechanicals" have the charm of their mindless spontaneity; Dickinson reflects on the danger of exposing "children" to
verbal "lightning" without some insulating artifice; and Plath, too,
seems to be getting at a "source" of creative relation that abjures not
only sophistication and straightforwardness but any mature capacity
for evaluating "things as they are." Is responsible or truly informed
thought possibly no more relevant to the general "work of self" than
it is to the selves represented here by the "work of art"? How come
we think we want or need to know these things anyhow? I think . . .

But once I begin to *think*, possibly *therefore*, "I" no longer *am* . . .
quite . . . graspable, and yet . . . this "I" beneath or beyond or behind
it, has it not? And specifically *in order* to tell, well, "something like"
the truth? I might ask, then, is this "likening" tendency all that the
"work of self" will turn out, fundamentally, to be *about*? But to tell
the truth . . .

The "self" is "such stuff as dreams are made on," the stuff and
stuffing, so to speak, of our capacity for "suspended disbelief." Even
in the midst of reeling in its "catch," the "self" may be planning its
subsequent pose, framing the event destined to be a conversation piece
at home. By its trophies, or such tropes as it places in evidence, the
"self" should be self-evident. "It" says, here am "I" in my *having*, in
my having *been*, in my having been *there*. And *then* . . .

IV. A Potential Abyss

What most deniably (I nearly said "undeniably" and caught myself in
the act) belongs to an as yet unreflective and unreflected "self," and
to no "other," may be one's initial, internal experience of trauma.
"Trauma implies," according to D. W. Winnicott, "a break in life's
continuity" (Winnicott, 1971, p. 97). The *echt* traumatic experience
would seem to come from nowhere, without reason or definition in
itself, without relation to previous events (that one can tell) or expectations. Emily Dickinson, of all poets supremely obsessed with the
traumas of separation and death, warns that

> To fill a Gap
> Insert the Thing that caused it—
> Block it up

> With Other—and 'twill yawn the more—
> You cannot solder an Abyss
> With Air.

> (#546)

This "fact" of a Gap's intractability regarding the makeshift, mournful as this reality is for all its would-be subverters, may be the primary virtue (as well as a definitive property) of such an Abyss. Such gaps are provocative; the void calls for words, mouthfuls of immaterial definition, and for a kind of play that devotes itself to linking the "edges" (or at least "selving" the loose threads) surrounding any perceived hiatus in the fabric (or fabrication) of our lives. Purposeful play, investigating or recreating the nature of the "something missing," fills vacancy with activity, if nothing else; the inadequacy of this attempt to "solder" the raw edges of experience may be redeemed through the corollary means to that end, those of discovery and exploration. And then, in the end, perhaps the potentiality of the interval, and not its "true" character (missed at all, and at great costs) is what we are here to embody, to "explain."

The lamentable circumstance of a "Gap," along with the mastery required to "insert" some representation of the willfully departed object, are, as one of Parnassus's myths would have it, attributable to a self-same Olympian source. This high mind, having invented the flying horse of poetry, is accidentally gashed by Pegasus's careless hoof. The wound and the lyric are linked from the earliest appearance of the latter. As Sylvia Plath puts it in the poem "Kindness," "The blood jet is poetry / There is no stopping it." This "wounded" consciousness has occasion, then, to explain its injury, make a bandage of anecdote: consequently, Pegasus is off again, and flying.

Emily Dickinson presents this paradoxical predicament of "Consciousness" in terms of a not-very-sentimental journey:

> This Consciousness that is aware
> Of Neighbors and the Sun
> Will be the one aware of Death
> And that itself alone

> Is traversing the interval
> Experience between
> And most profound experiment
> Appointed unto Men—

How adequate unto itself
Its properties shall be
Itself unto itself and none
Shall make discovery.

Adventure most unto itself
The Soul condemned to be—
Attended by a single Hound
Its own identity.

(#822)

The recognition of one's essential solitude, merely "attended by" its dogged but quite separable pet, "identity," is on one hand part of a "profound experiment," "discovery," or "adventure"; on the other, less enticingly, this enlightened consciousness is "condemned" by its solitariness, perhaps humiliated by its mindless animal attachments. We are "windowless" (to use Leibniz's salient metaphor) with regard to other beings—nomadic, monadic, all. Identity, reduced to a "Hound," might well, when it is not serving to protect its keeper, "hound" her to the one destination she knows is her due, her very own, and the price of her exploration. The friendly Hound cannot share more than the consciousness of passing scenery. The self-endowed traveler alone knows that the trek stipulates termination, that the dreck of it becomes meaningful mainly in light of some dreckless, empty destination.

"The prospect of death," as Dr. Johnson has observed, "wonderfully concentrates the mind." Prospects, whether nourishing or depleting, protective or endangering, circumscribe the dignity and definition of "self"; the abstract demands mastery no less than the material, if the animal that regards itself as a "self" is to survive the compromised condition that Ernest Becker has called "the condition of individuality within finitude" (Becker, 1973, p. 12).

Hypothetically, in the "interval / Experience between" a mother's inexplicable disappearance and gracious return, her infant is left metaphorically, perhaps literally, "in the dark." There is no essential difference, to an infant mind, between the impossible-to-traverse half-mile separating her from the "Neighbors" Mother may have joined for tea and the ninety-three million miles between a darkened nursery and the "Sun." Hoping that Mother and Day will both return, but not *given* that, how does the abandoned child manage to traverse either impossible interval?

Freud suggests the infant consciousness, not yet fully aware of the distinctions between original, temporary, and final separations, invents stopgap measures, kinds of play that reenact and, in being repeated, control the trauma of disappearance, the satisfaction of return. Freud's classic description of this play in *Beyond the Pleasure Principle*, gives it the name *fort-da*, based on his observation of a small child playing with a toy on a string. Having thrown the toy away and acknowledged the disappearance with the word *fort*, the child, having kept hold of the string, is empowered to haul the object back to hand, welcoming it with the word *da*. As a child engages in this "magic," she or he may be telling a little "story" about a larger theme, rehearsing both the terror of separation and the ecstasy of the "destroyed" object's renewed presence.

In an empty place, the solitary self calls out for company, and, as Howard Nemerov recalls, in his essay "Bottom's Dream,"

> Echo answers. Which is not to say that nothing answers, for it may be by a species of radar that intelligence moves through the world. We might say of expressiveness itself, of the irreducible phrase, that first it is, and then it finds a meaning in the world. Or else: whatever the mind invents, it also discovers. Or again: Whatever is revealed, in poetry, plays at being revealed. (Nemerov, 1985, p. 99)

This matter of the Abyss, not susceptible to soldering, does lend itself to possession and to a rendering of its shape. Roy Schafer suggests that "the self is a kind of telling about one's individuality," just that (Schafer, 1978, p. 6). For Dickinson, this amounts to telling about a particular "interval / Experience between," about profound experiments within finitude, within parentheses chiseled or inked definitively after a name; this telling, any telling, tends to place a period on one of many possible life sentences, neat as a pin at the throat, yet revisable as an unfashionable ruffle. And, Emily, as you knew, this much *can* be done with just a mouthful of Air, if not with the airy stuff of dreams unmouthed to anyone. We are hearing your echo still, and it tells a moving story of Gaps explored, you there lost in thought—beside yourself maybe, but not alone—because we still hear the words that were there, beside you; we hear a prospective individuality, one that answers to "why?" (from under cover), "Because I am alive."

V. Playing like a Child

In order for a "self" to be fully possessed, it must be able to render its finitude in a particular way—that is, in words' good faith and in good form, born of responsible singularity. "The dexterities of language," Harold Brodkey suggests,

> have a *Christ in the world* quality, a spiritual visitor with a mastery of absence and a mastery of both real and incomprehensible presence. I think language should come out of modesty toward one's death. I think of fear as a silence out of which one stirs if one can be humble about one's death in the world. (1985, p. 68)

Emily Dickinson's "modesty" regarding the magnitude of her principal subject, death, is exemplary of Brodkey's notion; the humility of her language and chosen forms is one of its greatest claims to power. She habitually presents, not the "naked self" and its overwhelming "truth," but a "self" lyrically contained—in the preordained rhythms of her hymnal, in the symbolic, preservative gestures of familiar "narrative," and in a stylized representation of alternative selves. That Dickinson may not have been writing strictly "autobiographical" verse may come as a surprise even to her most devoted readers. However, "When I state myself, as the representative of the verse," Dickinson wrote to her mentor Thomas Wentworth Higginson, "it does not mean me, but a supposed person" (Dickinson, 1959, p. 10).

Dickinson submitted a number of these "supposed persons" for Higginson's approval, many of them poised on the very edge of their supposed finitudes, if not actually offering a postmortem view. Exposed in these works of self-investigation or self-effacement, Dickinson is savvy enough to know she risks the appearance of immodesty, of displaying what is less proper to be shown than her least starched underthings.

"To doubt my high behavior," she writes Higginson in 1863, "is a new pain." (Had she been showing him love poems? Had he presumed upon their "supposed" nature?) By way of "apology" (for whatever it was she was not supposed to have said or done) she resorts to the formality of her art, and another "supposed" person—who is, of all people, "Barabbas." She presents this "self," boldly and humbly at once: a thief before her judge, one who notes that

> The possibility to pass . . .
> Into conjecture's presence,
> Is like a face of steel
> That suddenly looks into ours
> With a metallic grin;
> The cordiality of Death
> Who drills his welcome in.
>   (#286)

Formally, and only as a matter of good form, do we pay our respects to a "self's" original response to the challenge of chaotic, senseless loss. The "drill," the enforced "cordiality," the impenetrable but penetrating look, the mechanical "conjecture" that reduces the "supposed person" to a mere "thing"—are these the formalities of social apology or of a greater mastery? "After great pain," this poet says in another poem, "a formal feeling comes" (#341). And after that feeling comes the formal act that seals the feeling, where "the Nerves sit ceremonious—like Tombs." Elsewhere, she describes, with no less particularity, the funeral in the brain, the formulas of vain condolence, the masteries that imitate and invite confidence, if not participation, in a "supposed person's" real pain. Given this sort of sensitivity and tenuousness of self-possession on an everyday basis, one might be learning to approach and master death even at a tea party.

Engaged in such "works of self," as author or reader, one is constrained to listen to one's own slight heart, to magnify its beats, to dare them to stop or be heard. One may get used to this fantastic game of controlled loss, be neither totally passive nor obviously aggressive with regard to it; this perhaps is the charm of the grown-up *fort-da*, the humble magic of the powerless. The self-imposed rhythms of angst and ease, as relatable to jokes as to penance, are as germane to the cadence of a sentence as to the rise and fall of a curtain. The symbolic cadence of a self at play with the cordialities of imagined death allows the self to possess and possibly to render its "true" nature, like the "moment in and out of time" described by T. S. Eliot with "a music heard so deeply / That it is not heard at all, but you are the music / While the music lasts" (Eliot, 1952, pp. 27–29).

And yet . . . it doesn't. So what? Despite the deep and convincing cadence of her pulse with its *I am I am,* a multiplicity of agonistic measures drill the poet's felt identity full of holes from without and seem to welcome the spill and spoil of her symbolical control, exposed as less than "true." All very high-sounding stuff, maybe, and not very sensible, either; so what if even the most ordinary child, indulging in her restorative magic or music, knows the charm will not last? We *know* that surrounding the dream's immortality is mortality, the chattering and consuming circles of "Neighbors and the Sun," the comings and goings that are still, always, potentially final. So what? So then what?

This: that the terror may be mastered or masked by play, by philosophizing, or even by "playing dead," but the original awareness trots snuffling along at heel, begging for attention as unshakably as Dickinson's Hound, identity. Where does the energy come from, to go on? W. B. Yeats renders the predicament compassionately in his poem "Upon a Dying Lady":

> She is playing like a child
> And penance is the play,
> Fantastical and wild
> Because the end of day
> Shows her that someone soon
> Will come from the house and say—
> Though play is but half done—
> 'Come in and leave the play.'

The magic of "play," whether it is performed in what D. W. Winnicott calls the "potential space" between infant and mother, on the stage, in the backyard, or in the alchemist's study, depends on the player's humble submission to rules and to circumstance. At the same time, the play appropriates some of the power felt to belong to that invisible Other who is imagined to be responsible for mortal circumstances. However entertaining or learned or sustaining a game or symphony may be for its duration, however, the magical formula "works" only because it is imbued with the consciousness of its cadence, its related finitudes. The formulae of comedy are, likewise, fueled by circumstantial melancholy.

Hence, sadness haunts even the purest comedies of Shakespeare, to the great degree that this poet understood the impulse to rehearse, and the ends implied by rehearsals of human silliness and mortification. To mine the original situation of the "self" and its modes of establishing its singularity is to approach the very source of mortal understanding: the realization that this underground and largely dirty work has little to do with nobility of soul or intellect as reflected, not only in comedy and tragedy, but in reasonable arguments of any sort. The poet's melancholy business finds resolution most movingly in Shakespeare's last play, *The Tempest,* at the point when Prospero, the magician and fabricator of his island's counterpoint of airy music and brutal muddle, breaks his wand in preparation for returning to the ordinary world and his ordinary death, over which he has no power. But, to appropriate a line of Emily Dickinson's, "One need not be [a Prospero's Island]—to be Haunted" (#670). Prospero's proper place is within all of us, the necessity of escaping from it all around.

VI. Bottom's Dream

Dream is trauma is drama; or, even if not precisely so, the coincidence of sounds does *sound* something kindred to the "work of self" I am after. Shakespeare's *A Midsummer Night's Dream,* imbued as it is with generative amnesia, cozily packed as a virus with replicative strands, ambivalent as mother love in its embrace of its subjects, is one of the most poignant representations I know of selves in process, engaged in repeating original awareness of loss and ingenious use of the "potential space" created by loss (Winnicott, 1971).

Subject to an uncanny "dream" within the *Dream* at large, which traumatically interrupts a rehearsal of the craftsmen's play, Bottom the Weaver comes to illustrate the restitutive power of a "self" at work, the power of a playful creation ex nihilo. Through the experience that shall be known as "Bottom's Dream," along with Bottom's vivacious sense of the power of theater and his own acting prowess, all the strands of Shakespeare's fantasy are woven together into the fabric of a single authorial dream. It is the work of a single night, this "play" of the solitary "self" among others.

During a rehearsal of "Pyramus and Thisby," and unaccountably, except in the convertible logic of the *Dream,* a sprite named Puck, in the employ of King Oberon, replaces Bottom's head with an ass's head. Nearby, in the same enchanted Athenian woods, Queen Titania is asleep; her eyes have been secretly annointed by Puck, such that she must fall instantaneously and unconditionally in love with the first object she sees upon waking. Bottom, meanwhile, deserted by his play-fellows due to his "translated" appearance, sings aloud to assuage his fear. In doing so of course he wakes the Queen. Thus does the powerful Titania conceive a comic passion for Bottom the Weaver, translated to an ass.

Titania, now no more discriminating than any mortal mother with her newborn, responds to Bottom's monstrous appearance with "Thou art wise as thou art beautiful" (III.1.142). She proceeds to offer him all the riches at her magical disposal—edible delicacies, her bed of flowers, and the services of her airy retinue. With the strange confidence in transmutability particular to maternity and blind love-sickness, she vows to "purge thy mortal grossness so, / That thou shalt like an airy spirit go" (III.i.153–54). And thus does Bottom (whose powers at this point are merely mortal, infantile, and erotic), find himself (like an infant previous to any trauma of separation) omnipotent: no smidgen of distressed potential space separates his desires and what rightly, divinely, belongs to him.

In this blessed state of enchantment, Bottom falls asleep; inevitably, though, he wakes alone, Titania having vanished, along with his power. Puck charitably removes his ass's head, its prankish purpose consummated in Titania's having lost face in her squabble with Oberon. Bottom does have his own face back and is no longer that "gross" Bottom he was; but neither is he omnipotent any longer with regard to a supernatural lover-mother.

In his newly awakened confusion, all Bottom can summon up from his recent past is his part as the doomed hero-lover in the rehearsal immediately preceding his magical regression and aggrandizement. Gradually, and more confusingly, an unnameable sensation, a leftover of the "dream," begins to lace his reconstructive musings—a faint tickle of the palate, as if taint and charm rode tandem on his thick tongue. He sums up his preverbal arousal, experienced as gift no less than predicament, in the following famous passage:

I have had a most rare vision. I have had a dream, past the

wit of man to say what dream it was. Man is but an ass if
he go about to expound this dream. Methought I was—
there is no man can tell what. Methought I was—and methought I had—but man is but a patched fool is he will
offer to say what methought I had. The eye of man hath
not heard, the ear of man hath not seen, man's hand is not
able to taste, his tongue to conceive, nor his heart to report,
what my dream was. I will get Peter Quince to write a ballad
of this dream: it shall be called 'Bottom's Dream', because
it hath no bottom; and I will sing it in the latter end of a
play, before the Duke. (IV.i.203–16)

When Bottom accidentally stumbles into the midst of Fairyland's
Midsummer intrigue and becomes an involuntary agent of a prank
played by the King upon the Queen (with no less than all the world's
well-being in the balance), he becomes the possessor of possibly explosive inside dope on the marital uncertainty and apparently fickle
behavior of the First Lady. He has no clear idea, however, of either
the true identity of the benefactress in his "dream," or the circumstances surrounding his "discovery" of the intrigue; nor does he remember in any particular either the infantile bliss or the asinine
offensiveness of his own presence upon the scene.

Bottom's helpless and overwhelmed speechlessness is at the very
core of the playwright's revealed trauma. The "profound experiment"
that results in the sharing of a bed, or stage, by "rude mechanical"
and Fairy Queen, results also in the sort of knowledge (symbolic of
the most carnal) ordinarily forbidden to mortals, and forbidden to
share. Bottom feels suddenly and painfully isolated, not only from his
own "bottom nature" as discovered by his "dream," but from his former self and relations as well. If he cannot *tell* his friends, somehow,
about his transformation, *show* himself to be newly possessed of mysterious and important knowledge, his true "self" will be left as un-
recognized and lonely as it was when he was wearing his ass's head.

The trouble that Bottom has in putting his dream, multilayered
trauma that it is (Winnicott, 1971), is that there *are* no words to express simultaneously the wonderful and elusive bliss of grandiose fusion and the irrevocable loss of that state of selfless, unfathomable,
all-being. Add to this that, above all, Bottom in his innocence wants
to tell the "truth" about what happened to him. Although he might
not be able to express his dilemma in philosophical terms, his quan-

dary is not unlike the one targeted by Nietzsche's essay on truth and lying, to wit:

> ... what about these conventions of language? ... Do the designations and the things coincide? Is language the adequate expression of all realities?
>
> Only through forgetfulness can man ever achieve the illusion of possessing a "truth." ... The "thing in itself" (for that is what pure truth, without consequences, would be) is quite incomprehensible to the creators of language and not at all worth aiming for. One designates only the relations of things to man, and to express them one calls on the boldest metaphors. A nerve stimulus, first transposed into an image—first metaphor. The image, in turn, imitated by a sound—second metaphor. ... (Nietzsche, 1982, pp. 45–46)

To paraphrase Dickinson, in Bottom's case, "This Consciousness that is aware [of Bliss and Bliss that's gone] will be the one aware of Death and that itself alone" must contain its most intimate experience of primal union and separation. Bottom must realize, too, that though his newly conscious self may inform *itself* of "how adequate unto itself [its most rare vision] shall be," "none [but himself] shall make discovery" of his "most profound experiment" in the end. Truly, and at bottom, the thing he has become aware of is unspeakable in itself. Imaginable and singable, however, it may be, as a lie begets an image, or as a swan sings; or, alternatively, the song made of such stuff as this dream is made of may well spring from a revocalization of that "bald cry" belonging to the infant who wakes alone in Sylvia Plath's poem "Morning Song," where after a night's separation, the mother hears her child "try / [her] handful of notes" and "the clear vowels rise like balloons."

What can we possibly know of each other, of what the child is missing in missing its source of light and life, or what we in fact are missing, hearing only the "bald cry" and able only to "liken" it to rising balloons, faceless signals of distress or celebration (elsewhere, in Plath's work, "soul-animals")? What does the mirror say when it sees us—and then, does it remember us like a dream, and not all that clearly? Is it possible we do not see at all, struck blind by the possibility

of "truth" in our separateness from our own images? "You see," says
Dickinson,

> You see I cannot see—your lifetime—
> I must guess—
> . . .
> But I guess guessing hurts—
> . . .
> Too vague—the face—
> My own—so patient—covers
> Too far—the strength—
> My timidity enfolds—
> Haunting the Heart—
> Like her translated faces—
> Teasing the want—
> It—only—can suffice!
>
> (#253)

What we "see" is only what we have been able to "translate"; we are,
for ourselves perhaps as much as for others, merely "translations" of
ourselves—into asses, into the lion's part or the Hound's, into images
of *want* and *have, fort* and *da.* "Methought I was—and methought I
had . . ." But we forget just what. Coming back to ourselves, at home,
we *will* try to make it up. Bottomless as his "dream" is, Bottom resolves
to sing it, "sing it in the latter end of a play, before the Duke."

Bottom may not remember "what happened" any more than his
friends can, but he does not doubt that he has been "transported,"
and is on his way home, not only in a geographical sense, but "home"
to himself, transported from one psychic position with regard to his
potential as a human being to another and more powerful one. He is
in a state of transport, elated and lost in the play of his own mind,
moving from and toward a self, or a role in the play that can be
rendered only in moving terms. From an original position of doubt
as to just what part he might play, and about who he is essentially, he
moves; he moves toward a certainty of art. And he consequently moves
us.

Home at last, Bottom wants to share his sense of eventfulness. "Masters, " he announces to Peter Quince and the rest, "I'm to discourse
wonders." But when Quince responds politely with "Let us hear, sweet

Bottom," the weaver can say no more than "Not a word of me. All that I will tell you is, that the Duke hath dined. . . . No more words" (IV.ii.28–42). An excited confusion of senses, amounting to an un-utterable deprivation of logical sense and continuity, cannot easily be conveyed. Bottom substitutes therefore the kind of "news" that can be told. It is highly unlikely that he has stopped to find out about the Duke's dinner before returning home, yet in "making up" a piece of information to substitute for what he cannot say exactly, Bottom may be recalling a part of his "dream." His own royal feast is indeed fin-ished; his royal image in mind though, he now uses it to announce that it is time to get on with the show.

VII. A Loaded Gun

In an essay called "That to Philosophize Is to Learn to Die," Mon-taigne says of death, "Let us rid it of its strangeness, come to know it, get used to it. . . . At every moment let us picture it in our imagination in all its aspects" (Montaigne, 1957, p. 60). Is self-possession possible, the essayist asks himself, without rendering one's finitude? Emily Dick-inson presents this notion most forcibly in a poem where her "sup-posed person's" life appears in the guise of a "Loaded Gun." The fantastical quality of her metaphor is not unrelated to the dream of potency and subsequent loss realized by "Bottom's Dream." Both fan-tasies are inherently explosive. And in Dickinson's poem we feel a potential self that might well be described as a species of "rude me-chanical":

> My Life had stood—a Loaded Gun—
> In Corners—till a Day
> The Owner passed—identified—
> And carried Me away—
>
> And now We roam in Sovereign Woods—
> And now We hunt the Doe—
> And every time I speak for Him—
> The mountains straight reply—
>
> And do I smile, such cordial light
> Upon the Valley glow—

It is as a Vesuvian face
Had let its pleasure through—

And when at Night—our good Day done—
I guard my Master's Head—
'Tis better than the Eider-Duck's
Deep Pillow—to have shared—

To foe of His—I'm deadly foe
None stir the second time—
On whom I lay a Yellow Eye—
Or an emphatic Thumb—

Though I than He—may longer live
He longer must—than I—
For I have but the power to kill,
Without—the power to die—

                                                            (#754)

This poem, and the vital weapon it barely contains, the former disembodied and the latter a positive adversary to flesh, is loaded with the ammunition of infantile desires: an imaginary amalgam, all compact, of love and aggression, as potent beyond reason as the fairy rulers of Shakespeare's fantasy. Dickinson's narrative, a vehicle devoted to the transport of both conception and extinction, carries the speaker away in a spirit not of passivity exclusively, nor of aggression, but of passionate dependence. The Gun renders protection to its Owner as it allows itself to be possessed; the relationship between the two "characters" is similar to that of the Hound and hunter in the poem of Dickinson's quoted earlier. The "I" in both poems, given the literal presence of Hound or Gun, is "loaded for bear" or other game; in both the "I" symbolically hunts the even bigger game of "self" as it entertains the comical-tragical prospect of self-obliteration.

The instincts that impel "profound experiments" such as Dickinson's are those of self-preservation (the instinct that insists the self can and must die) and of pleasure (the one that doesn't want to know), and here the pleasure is specifically that of the kill. Dickinson's narratives of "consciousness," and perhaps all narratives, at bottom, may be said to derive their principal energies from angry, unspeakable, and therefore repressed denials of death, the eventual separation from a loving "Master," from "Neighbors and the Sun." The "Loaded Gun," devoted to pleasure, however, cannot die as its owner and prey must certainly do, according to their mortal "power"; and the "Soul" is condemned to an endless adventure in solitude, the consequence and quarry of which "none / Shall make discovery."

The instinct to kill, in the somehow demure atmosphere of Miss Dickinson's presentations, becomes acceptable, as such a scene would be in dream, by virtue of its being authorized by a "Master" self, suitably removed from the decorous spinster who merely mouths his desires. Dickinson distinguishes her "Master" from her at-home "self" by gender, and mechanical nature. The macho "Master" is in turn distinguished from the character of the "Gun," who is typically "female," passively allowing her body to be possessed and handled; "she" speaks aggressively perhaps, but not for herself, for *him*. It is easy to read the poem as a metaphor for an ideal passionate "marriage." But (as everybody knows) the author knew nothing about *that*. This is surely not an autobiographical work, then; but it *is*. Dickinson is as palpably there, behind her narrative, as she was there behind the door, receiving visitors in her middle age, too shy to come out like a proper person, too lonely not to speak, to put her eye to the thin pencil of light coming from the other room. Thus does she, with her fearful Life, and with the Loaded Gun that fictively represents it, passionately do away with herself, without quite being able to disappear for good.

VIII. Between Words and Sword

Acts of omnipotence, not less potentially guilty when imaginary, and the powerful realization that death is the ultimate consequence when any body oversteps its bounds, asks too much, or goes too far, are not to be spoken of directly. The ego's "censor" will allow neither the fantasy of omnipotence nor the fact of impotence to be related by the self to its "I," will not allow them to be related at all, in fact. But with regard to fiction the ego's editor is more lenient; one *may* "make discovery" of one's inmost, most primal experience, in "song," or within the bounds of narrative structures acknowledged to be removed from the overcomprehensive "self" as it slops along through the soup of its perceptions, the mundane minestrones of the "real."

Beyond that, and beyond the mere play of words, Dickinson was throughout her private romance with language sensitive to its weaponly potential. To wit: "She dealt her pretty words like Blades" (#479).

Shakespeare's characters, too, deal out or submit to verbal punishments that are not uncommonly deadly, and not uncommonly reveal the easy transformation, via the displacement of a single letter, of *sword* to *words*.

Sword and words often may be seen to be interchangeable in the interests of the pleasure principle. Early on in Shakespeare's *Dream*, Theseus reminds his intended bride: "I woo'd thee with my sword" (I.i.16). Dickinson's romance of the Loaded Gun is no less imbued with the proximity of killing to courtship. The Gun speaks oh so lovingly *for* its Master, in imagination, and what it speaks of is the intimate pillow they will share, the productive trigger of pure desire; on the other hand, the one sound the Gun makes is synonymous with adieu. Its aim is to realize the finality of another's death, and then, its own lamentable survival, alone.

> There is a word
> Which bears a sword
> Can pierce an armed man—
> It hurls its barbed syllables
> And is mute again—
> . . .
>
> There is its noiseless onset—
> There is its victory!
> Behold the keenest marksman!
> The most accomplished shot!
> Time's sublimest target
> Is a soul "forgot!"
>
> [#8]

None knows better than an infant (literally, one "without speech") the deadly result of being "forgot"; the mortification of this, along with understandably murderous inclinations toward its reciprocally "forgot" but formerly ideal "self-object" comprise, according to Freudian theory, the infant's original intimations of death. The "noiseless onset" of "forgot" becomes, eventually and in a spoken word, the declaration of all potential absence, a precise weapon of obliteration. The "wound" of erasure, originally inflicted by the imagination, leads directly in Dickinson's view, to fantasies of sublime accomplishment. As with Bottom after his lovely cuddle in Titania's cradle, the "self"

impelled to reexperience its abandonment regarding its original solitude is momentarily free of its tag-along identity, free to make up an
alternative immortality.

The sporting act of murder in Dickinson's poem, as well as the self-
abandonment of the author in the act of writing, are forms of enter-
tainment, ways of killing time, even kinds of love play, death's sort of
foreplay. Certainly Dickinson, even in the volcanic heat of composition, was not unaware of her Loaded Gun's implicit sexuality, its eroticism implicit not only in the images as we understand them from a
Freudian point of view, but in the traditional Elizabethan double en-
tendre in the use of the verb *to die*.

Pyramus and Thisby, in the play devised by Bottom and his fellows,
die for each other on the point of a sword; in point of fact, they die
for each other in words; and in the silliness of their words, their play
"dies" for its audience, too. The players are preserved only by their
innocence of things theatrical from realizing how thoroughly the latter
might be true. They are, in their lack of sophistication, touchingly
afraid of what is, to them, the reality conjured up by their spoken
words. They are especially concerned, during their rehearsals, that
they might injure their imagined audience. Thus:

> STARVELING: I believe we must leave the killing out, when
> all is done.
> BOTTOM: Not a whit; I have a device to make all well.
> Write me a prologue, and let the prologue seem to say
> we will do no harm with our swords, and that Pyramus
> is not killed indeed . . .
>
> (III.i.13–18)

Bottom wants *so much* to tell the truth; and to tell the truth, he wants
so much besides. Nietzsche, in the fragment on truth and lie cited
earlier, considers what may have been the original motive toward this
moral enterprise. He admits, first of all, the self-protective nature of
simulation, the need to protect one's "true" or naked being by little
fibs; then, this being so easy to do, one may be tempted to go further,
to increase one's estate by gratuitous or malicious misrepresentations.
Nietzsche goes on to suggest that "because man, out of need and
boredom, wants to exist socially," he will try to make a "peace pact"
with his fellow human beings through semantic constancy.

For now that is fixed which henceforth shall be "truth";
that is, a regularly valid and obligatory designation of
things is invented, and this linguistic legislation also fur-
nishes the first laws of truth. . . . The liar uses the valid
designations, the words, to make the unreal appear as real.
. . . When he does this in a self-serving way damaging to
others, then society will no longer trust him but exclude
him. Thereby men do not flee from being deceived as much
as from being damaged by deception: what they hate at this
stage is basically not the deception but the bad, hostile consequences of certain kinds of deceptions. (Nietzsche, 1982,
pp. 44–45)

In *A Midsummer Night's Dream* the notion that swords and words may
be alternative responses to loss is never far from the surface, and the
company of craftsmen is all too aware that their social acceptability
depends on their maintenance of the separation between fiction and
reality where swords and words might all too deceptively be mistaken
for each other. In the *Dream's* "comical-tragical" playlet, upon the con-
summation of the lovers' death scene, Thisby has the honor of these
last words:

> Tongue, not a word;
> Come, trusty sword,
> Come, blade, my breast imbrue! . . .
> Adieu, adieu, adieu!
> > (V.i.329–34)

Words, no less than their pointed material counterparts, even when
as pointlessly employed as they are by the "rude mechanicals" in their
unintentional parody, *imbrue* the subject here. Nonsensical word choice
(on the play's most literal level) aside, the words suggest impregnation,
inspiration, or permeation without *actual* penetration of flesh or mind.
To imbrue the hearts of the audience with meaning is the heartrending work of the final rhyme of *adieu* as its excess spills over into the
incredulous stillness of the Court. The audience's embarrassment or
irritation notwithstanding, Thisby's valedictory word is violently resonant with all the partings witnessed by the *Dream*, from within each
scene as well as from without.

Though potentially explosive words may render protection and nourishment to the Master of them, they are, as all materially useful and merely temporal objects are, ultimately to be abandoned. The intent of Dickinson's "Loaded Gun" (and indeed her "Life") is murderous with regard to the beloved companion who in his separate consciousness is susceptible to a physical death that she cannot share. Moreover, "he" is privileged to a conscious experience beyond his observable death that is equally out of her range, as she belongs merely among the physical properties that surround, are possessed by, but cannot penetrate the deepest reaches of her "Master" even by blowing him to bits or stabbing his heart out. All she can do is try to remember him, and her experience, and try to re-create them both as part of her "self," lovingly.

IX. Child's Play

The poet's conviction that "A word that breathes distinctly / Has not the power to die" (#1651) may give rise to her utterances as well as serve to elevate the pulse of her excitement at being carried away by this mastery of her "self." Child's play: the association of destruction and survival; thus, a child's play may produce unresolvable ambivalence, too, toward the creation and continuity of a separate "self." The child learns that it may be as terrifying to survive another's death, as caused in imagination, as to undergo one's own. Words tend to heighten if not create the "reality" of this perception. Though words may rehearse all ends of the "self," the ultimate and desired transformation brought about by any real death is the sole and unsharable possession of the consciousness that undergoes it, the "self" *alone,* unprotected by its "Loaded Gun," the mere toy of figurative speech. Owned, but owning nothing itself, poetry "makes nothing happen" all right, at least not without the pressure of consciousness on its trigger.

In *The Interpretation of Dreams,* Freud arrives at what he calls "the navel of the dream" and characterizes it thus:

> There is often a passage in even the most thoroughly interpreted dream which has to be left obscure; this is because we become aware during the work of interpretation that at that point there is a tangle of dream-thoughts which

cannot be unravelled and which moreover adds nothing to our knowledge of the content of the dream. This is the dream's navel, the spot where it reaches down into the unknown. (Freud, 1973, p. 294)

"Bottom's Dream" starts from this source that "hath no bottom," and it is the perception of its bottomlessness that makes it the source of wonder and end of terror that indeed it is. All formal art and its interpretation is to some degree in search of the uninterpretable kernel that contains self and world together, or the exact place where they join; given this, there is no more to be said. As in Sylvia Plath's dilemma, from pre-preconception to ex-postmortem, to pinpoint "ends" of "self" is to prick the bubble of being, to realize that the point of doing it, the point of the narrative experiment, is to see the bubble vanish into thin air. It is not to catch and mount that "terrible fish" that lurks at the bottom of the profound experiment of relation.

Though Shakespeare's Bottom seems to have repressed both the sexuality and the terror attendant on his "dream," his wonder remains, and his wish to restore whatever it was to a shareable reality. "I will sing it in the latter end of a play," he proclaims, and adds, "Peradventure, to make it the more gracious, I shall sing it at her death" (IV.i.216–17). The occasion that seems suitable to him for his offering is significantly "her death." Ostensibly, Bottom means Thisby's demise, abetted by himself as Pyramus. Yet Bottom's resolve may be more deeply understood as a referring to the Fairy Queen's disappearance, or an infant's original experience of loss, reactivated by the content of both dream and play. Embedded in Bottom's graciousness, too, is the sense not only of "getting back" *to* but, in not so gentle a spirit, back *at* his departed dream-lover. For, as Emily Dickinson knew all too well,

> Rehearsal to Ourselves
> Of a Withdrawn Delight—
> Affords a Bliss like Murder—
> Omnipotent—Acute—
>
> We will not drop the Dirk—
> Because We love the Wound

The Dirk Commemorate—itself
Remind Us that we died.
(#379)

For Bottom to want to sing, to commemorate the occasion of "her death" is truly "most gracious," though, as the song may not only commemorate but redeem and forgive the singer for his own survival. It proclaims, "I only am escaped alone to tell thee," and invites its hearers by its well-mannered representation of loss, to celebrate the gift of mortality. Job's wholehearted response to his messengers' narratives of loss, given their formal inevitability and telling rhythms, is itself formal, and substitutes the rhythms of worship for those of devastation.

When Job hits bottom, he remembers the true nature of his sole possession: "Naked came I out of my mother's womb, and naked shall I return thither." This is the graciousness of the survivor, wholly "selved" (as is the fabric whose selvages announce the measures the weaver has taken to protect his fragile construction), despite senseless and heartrending deprivations. In Bottom's imagined performance of his "dream" of supernatural affiliation, he naturally departs, like Job, from the original grace of that condition, transcending both the less-than-human character of the ass whose head he has worn and the loss of his superhuman, undeserved powers. The song impelled by fear with which he first woke the Queen is replaced by the song to be sung at the "latter end of the play." There he will not be simply *relating* to the circumstance of his loss, but symbolically appropriating that loss to both personal and public use (Winnicott, 1971, p. 89).

In Bottom's case, absence is his principal interest, his embarrassment, and his only capital as well. He owns a very positive "nothing," one that must be rendered. His way of appropriating and destroying the power of this "nothing" is *to make something out of it*. This particular "work of self" is moving, is making waves, and *is*, not art as "defensive reaction," despite Bergson's claim that the imagination may be seen as simply "a defensive reaction of nature against the representation by intelligence of the inevitability of death" (Bergson, 1980, p. 366). It is rather an offensive action undertaken in the interest of personal survival. In this, whether it pleases its audience as "art" or not, or whether indeed it ever gets written or not, Bottom's intended narrative is more comprehensive than most art aspires to be. In the rendering of a certain catastrophic "interval / Experience between," the continuity of life before and after it, the self resurrects an aspect of its being that was once denied. And it *is* an occasion of celebration, no less than, perhaps more than, the marriages at Court and their sexual prospects of renewal and birth.

> I had the Glory—that will do—
> An Honor, Thought can turn her to
> When lesser Fames invite—
> With one long "Nay"—
> Bliss' early shape
> Deforming—Dwindling—Gulfing up—
> Time's possibility.
>
> (#349)

Is it any wonder, then, that Bottom feels the need to *sing* whatever remnants of his most rare vision he can recapture, to rock himself back into that redemptive dream, however melancholy the circumstance of his waking? The bottom may indeed fall out of all reasonable expectation for him, yet the aptly named Bottom would fill this ultimately unfillable void with a musical rendition of his ecstasy and disappointment, with his self-engendered performance the only possible antidote to ending. A solution Dickinson acknowledges no less, and no less for us all:

> That is solemn we have ended
> Be it but a Play
> Or a Glee among the Garret
> Or a Holiday
>
> Or a leaving Home, or later,
> Parting with a World
> We have understood for better
> Still to be explained.
>
> (#934)

References

Becker, E. (1973). *The denial of death*. New York: Macmillan.

Bergson, H. (1980). Quoted in L. Damrosch, *Symbol and truth in Blake's myth*. Princeton: Princeton University Press.

Brodkey, H. (1985). "S. L." *The New Yorker,* 9 September.

Dickinson, E. Linscott, R. N. (Ed.). (1959). *Selected poems and letters.* New York: Doubleday.

Eliot, T. S. (1952). *The collected poems and plays.* New York: Harcourt, Brace and World.

Freud, S. (1920/1973). *Beyond the pleasure principle. Standard Edition,* Vol. 18, 3–64. (J. Strachey, Trans. and Ed.). London: Hogarth.

——— (1973). *The interpretation of dreams.* Quoted in Pontalis, J. R., and Laplance, J., *The language of psychoanalysis.* New York: W. W. Norton.

Glass, J. M. (1985). *Woman wanted.* New York: St. Martin's Press.

Montaigne, M. de. (1957). *Complete works.* Stanford: Stanford University Press.

Nemerov, H. (1985). *New and selected essays.* Carbondale: Southern Illinois University Press.

Nietzsche, F. (1982). *The portable Nietzsche.* Kaufmann, W. (Ed.). London: Penguin.

Plath, S. (1981). *The collected poems.* New York: Harper and Row.

Schafer, R. (1978). *Language and insight.* New Haven: Yale University Press.

Shakespeare, W. (1979). *A midsummer night's dream.* Brooks, H. (Ed.). London: Methuen.

Winnicott, D. W. (1971). *Playing and reality.* London: Tavistock.

Yeats, W. (1966). *The collected poems of W. B. Yeats.* New York: Macmillan.

SELF and GENDER

These two essays could be grouped under the rubric of "feminist," but seem more appropriately labeled by the more general term of "gender." They focus our attention on the way in which gender meanings for females are at odds with most culturally accepted theories of self. Judith Kegan Gardiner argues first for the primacy of Kohut's psychoanalytic account of self as encompassing of two different genders. Her concern especially is to argue against the privileging of autonomy, ego integrity, and the phallus in psychoanalytic interpretations of self. Reasoning about a self as unified, visible, and directed has become the major paradigm for most psychoanalytic and many other psychological accounts of self. This paradigm excludes the psychological and cultural experiences of the female so that her "place" in self theories frequently is designated by the hole, gap, or blind spot—what is absent or unadmitted.

Apprehending the female subject via an assumption of her essential incompletion or inadequacy leads to demeaning characterizations of her self experiences, not to mention the political and ideological consequences for her place in society. By contrast, Kegan Gardiner asserts that Kohut's self psychology organizes a mode for self that admits both male and female experiences as primary. According to Kohut, the phallus is not a central symbol of culture nor does biological structure (anatomy) determine destiny. Although Kohut's psychology organizes our construction of self as a pretext (a symbolic abstraction), it embeds individual experience within a dependent life context over the life span. Only through dependent relationships are we capable of self-constructions; the ideal of an independent and autonomous self is a distortion based on empathic failure. Autonomy, the ideal of a patriarchal psychology of masculine domination, is not the goal of development in Kohut's psychology. Rather, individuals are seen to move from an infantile to a mature dependence, making primary the relational context that often epitomizes the female life structure.

Whereas Kegan Gardiner's essay can be read as an apology for
Kohut's self psychology, in response to the blind spots in other psychoanalytic accounts, Harriet Chessman's essay is a celebration of the
blind spot. Using the poetry and prose of Gertrude Stein as a cornerstone for her interpretation, Chessman provides us with an analysis
of the female subject in patriarchal literature: she has no name. The
distraction of the literary subject, the named persona, away from the
actual experience of women's sexuality and daily lives results in our
tendency to assume a particular life drama in which the female, qua
female, has no role. In "patriarchal poetry," Gertrude Stein forces us
to reverse our reader's tendency to rely on logos, rationality, and heroism in our literary assumptions about narrative. Stein purposely
confuses or obscures actor and action, noun and verb, until we have
wrested our old system of language out of its original context. From
Chessman, we discover that Stein's text accomplishes an effect similar
to Lacan's: "Lacan's text pushes the reader to the limits of comprehension, to the place where unconsciousness begins and the inaccessible is found. The first close encounter with Lacan's writing style often
leaves the reader feeling lost, confused, even angry. . . . the reader is
driven closer to a psychological reading of his or her own enigmatic
text" (Kugler, p. 178). Stein also brings her reader face to face with
her subjectivity, the groundwork of the female self.

Riddles, irony, and metonymy abound in Stein's writing, as she refuses to be defined, to name or be named by the patriarchal forms.
Through Stein's work, we encounter the political implications of a
female language of self that promotes a plurality of meaning. As
Chessman observes, referring to the French feminist writer Luce Irigaray, the implications for language are revolutionary: instead of a
unity in the subject, or a unity between work and meaning, there is
in female language a plurality, an undoing of the unique meaning,
the proper meaning of words, of nouns.

CHAPTER 10

Kohut's Self Psychology as Feminist Theory

JUDITH KEGAN GARDINER

I N HIS LAST WORKS, psychoanalyst Heinz Kohut, the chief proponent of a new "psychology of the self," upholds empathy against the "knowledge values" and "independence values" of "Western Man" and "Western Civilization" (Kohut, 1982, p. 399). Threatened by the "narcissistic rage that might trigger atomic holocaust," humanity, he thinks, must develop more compassion (Kohut, 1980b, pp. 462–63). Whereas other psychologies validate goals of individuation and autonomy, he claims that a more interdependent model of maturity is necessary for humanity to survive. Such characterizations may well sound familiar to those feminists who fear "Western Man" and his planetary effects. For example, Dorothy Dinnerstein ascribes the dangerous tendencies in Western civilization to the misogyny consequent upon mother-raised psychologies (Dinnerstein, 1976). However, Kohut uses his generic "Man" un-self-consciously and does not consider gender as a significant variable when meditating about individual psychology and our cultural condition. Even though Kohut does not think in gender-conscious terms and even though his idea of humanity is paradigmatically male, I think that self psychology holds great promise for feminist theory. The psychoanalytic theory now most commonly cited by American feminists is probably that of Nancy Chodorow. Her central insight that mother-dominated childrearing produces differing capacities and desires in women and men is brilliant and persuasive (Chodorow, 1978). Her theory has also come under attack, however, because of its heavy reliance on the object relations school of psychoanalysis, a reliance that results in its having some of the same limitations that its parent theories do. As a separate theoretical system, self psychology avoids some of the problems posed by feminist object

relations theory and solves some of its limitations, especially its con-
flation of femininity with heterosexuality and its apparent closure to
historical change. My goal in the present essay is to formulate a feminist self psychology: after introducing the main tenets of self psychology, I argue its advantages for feminist thought and speculate
about the directions a gender-sensitive self psychology might take.

I

Self psychology is a developmental theory about the formation of the
self:

> The self is not a thing or an entity; it is a concept; a symbolic
> abstraction from the developmental process. The self refers
> to the uniqueness that separates the experiences of an in-
> dividual from those of all others while at the same time
> conferring a sense of cohesion and continuity on the dis-
> parate experiences of that individual throughout his life.
> (Basch, 1983, p. 53)

According to Kohut's theories, the self forms in the first few years of
a child's life through the empathic mirroring and optimal frustrations
of its caretaking environment. This social milieu is as essential to the
formation of a cohesive self as oxygen is to physiologic survival. The
infant uses and perceives other people not as distinctly separate from
itself, not as "objects" in their own right, but as "selfobjects" that perform functions for the self as though part of the self. Although self
psychologists adopt nonsexist language, speaking of the "nurturing
parent" or the "child's caretaker," they assume that the mother has
the primary role in the infant's life. By reflecting the child's accom-
plishments back to it with pride and interest, the mother helps the
child achieve a positive but realistic self-image. By providing for the
child's needs, the parent can be idealized; parental values are admired
and eventually incorporated as the child's own. By being reasonably
reliable, the mother sustains the child's ability to exist comfortably by
itself. Kohut summarizes the child's needs in these regards as follows:
the child needs "to be confirmed in its vitality and assertiveness by the
mirroring selfobject, to be calmed and uplifted by the idealized imago,

[and] to be surrounded by the quietly sustaining presence of alter egos" (Kohut, 1984, p. 23).

Parents need not be perfect to produce children with healthy selves. Parental failures of response are to be expected, need not be traumatic, and, in fact, are necessary for the optimum frustrations that will realistically curb the child's grandiosity or its overidealization of the parent. Kohut's major departure from the orthodox Freudian analytic tradition is his "double track" hypothesis. Instead of a baby cocooned in primary narcissism, a victim of its instinctual drives, striving only to achieve pleasure and avoid pain, Kohut sees the baby as a relatively harmonious bundle programmed to respond to its mother from the very beginning. Under optimal parenting, it will develop a cohesive self that can perform the functions for it that the selfobjects of infancy once did, although it will continue to need selfobjects throughout life. Although the self is perceived as continuous and coherent, Kohut speaks about the "bipolar self," its dual aspects being ambitions and goals on the one hand and ideals and values on the other, with these two poles connected in a tension curve by the individual's skills, talents, and native endowments. This whole developmental track is separate from the child's loves and hates for other people, those libidinal investments whose vicissitudes Freud so graphically portrays. Freud thought that babies first loved themselves. He called this primary or infantile narcissism; normal maturation replaced this self-love with love for others, starting with mother and culminating in appropriate people of the opposite sex to the child's (Freud, 1914). In contrast, Kohut charts the self's development as a separate progress from the development of attachments to others, and he describes its distinctive rules and timetable.

Kohut first began formulating these theories after he discovered disturbed people in his clinical practice who had a common syndrome, which he labeled the "narcissistic personality disorder" (Kohut, 1971; 1977). These patients were not neurotics but arrogant or bored or apathetic people whose problems Kohut traced to defects in their self structures, which had not properly formed in the first few years of life. Almost invariably, he believed the cause of these defects to have been an unempathic mother who failed to help the child achieve a cohesive self by mirroring it appropriately.

These patients formed transferences in the analytic setting that differed from the Freudian model of transference in which the patient projects repressed desires and antagonism, which were originally directed at its parents, onto the neutral screen of the analyst's presence. Instead of these engaged transferences, the narcissists treated the analyst as a selfobject, not as a separate person. Through these selfobject transferences, Kohut found he could help patients previously considered unanalyzable by furnishing them with the empathic milieu that their mothers failed to provide so that they could treat the doctor through transference as a maternal and/or paternal selfobject: "via transmuting internalization, that is, via a wholesome psychic activity that has been thwarted in childhood," such a transference "lays down the structures needed to fill the defect in the self" (Kohut, 1984, p. 4).

A corollary of its preoedipal emphasis is that self psychology de-emphasizes the asymmetrically gendered Oedipus complex, seeing its problems not as inevitable but usually as the sequelae of earlier developmental deficits. Furthermore, it believes that oedipal pathology is becoming less common in comparison with preoedipal pathology. Kohut calls the typical Freudian patient "Guilty Man"; he is the son of a seductive mother and forbidding father and has a cohesive self, although he is conflicted about his sexual desires and antagonisms. In contrast, today's typical patient is "Tragic Man," son of an unempathic mother and an absent father (Kohut, 1984, pp. 167, 207–8). He struggles for creativity and self-realization against despair, and he is at once a pathological narcissistic personality and a representative of the modern human condition. Modern literature repeatedly describes his problems with fragmentation, "the falling apart of the self and of the world and the task of reconstituting the self and the world" (Kohut, 1974, p. 780). Rebuffing the view that he saw more of this syndrome simply because he had learned to look for it, Kohut believed that narcissistic personalities were becoming more common in our society as twentieth-century social changes, especially the growing isolation of the nuclear family, diminished the chances that children would be provided with appropriately empathic early environments. Clearly, Kohut believed that the split, fragmented, or alienated self is not an inevitable consequence of the human condition or of participation in the social order but a specific historical formation prevalent in our time.

Since the main cause of the problem was the child's early unempathic emotional milieu, the cure demanded an empathic analyst. Kohut made the concept of empathy central to his enterprise, distinguishing his use of the term from its popular meanings of compassion or intuition. He believed empathy played a double role in analysis. First, it denoted the supportive analytic situation provided by the sustained attention of the nonjudgmental doctor. This did not mean that the analyst was to "cure" the patient by supplying surrogate parental love, but instead that the analytic situation would allow the narcissistic adult's defective self to resume its development from the point at which it had been prematurely stunted. Within the protected selfobject transference, the patient could slowly develop the mental structures needed for a cohesive self. But empathy has a second meaning, too:

> Empathy is the operation that defines the field of psychoanalysis. . . . It is a value-neutral tool of observation. . . . We define it as "vicarious introspection" or, more simply, as one person's (attempt to) experience the inner life of another while simultaneously retaining the stance of an objective observer. (Kohut, 1984, pp. 174–75)

This method of observation is "experience near" rather than "experience distant"; it requires that the analyst mobilize memories of feelings comparable to the patient's in order to understand the patient's emotions, rather than just cognitively recognizing patterns in the patient's dysfunctions that correspond to the doctor's theories.

At their narrowest, Kohut's ideas found speedy acceptance. Analysts recognized that Kohut had developed therapeutic techniques beneficial to a category of patients not successfully treated by orthodox analysis. His theories about the origins of his patients' problems, however, attracted more debate. For example, Otto Kernberg, another writer on narcissistic personality disorders, disputes Kohut's "double track" hypothesis. As Kohut in his later work expanded his theories from remedies for specific malfunctions to broad ideas about human development, he aroused even more controversy from those who thought he had grown soft and fuzzy-minded. Kernberg claims Kohut errs by denying humanity's aggressive drives: for Kohut, aggression is not innate; it is a by-product of thwarted normal assertiveness (Kernberg, 1975, p. 270). John Gedo, too, upholds Freud's "Augustinian" acknowledgment of human imperfection in contrast to Kohut's utopian optimism (Gedo, 1984, pp. 363–75). Other critics feel that Kohut's approach is too intuitive and that empathy is unscientific. This controversy, pitting tough views against tender ones, reason against intuition, aggression against nurture, and scientific medicine against holistic health, reverberates for a feminist reader with gender-typed connotations such that Kohut's views parallel those of some radical feminists, in contrast to his opponents' more traditionally masculine outlook.

The self psychologists do not themselves use gender-based categories. Their obliviousness to gender seems overdetermined, and its causes may include Freud's views on women, Kohut's special sympathies for men, and general cultural prejudices. Kohut and his followers grew from the tradition of orthodox Freudian analysis, which holds that sexual identity, the child's masculinity or femininity, forms through the Oedipus complex at ages three to six, after the earlier developmental period on which the self psychologists focus. For Freud, the infant girl is a "little man" until this period, and one can treat children as unisexual and paradigmatically male, believing that the earliest mental structures do not vary by gender. Current empirical psychology confutes this idea, but the self psychologists have only recently begun to heed such evidence. A more specific reason for self psychology's blind spot about women arises from Kohut's assumptions and patient population. He repeatedly says that empathy works best as an analytic tool the more similar the doctor is to the patient. The patients Kohut describes in his published cases are predominantly male, and he seems to have been more comfortable with men (Kohut, 1971, 1977). As his career progressed, his patients were increasingly fellow analysts, most of whom were male. Moreover, his theory was officially nonsexist in a way that allowed it to ignore gender, whereas the theorists were nonetheless subject to ubiquitous unconscious sexism. One example of such unconscious sexism occurs in Kohut's response to a case presentation by Evelyn Schwaber, a woman analyst discussing a narcissistic male patient. Kohut later felt that he had misunderstood her relation to her patient because he "saw the therapist in front of us, with all her warm femininity," at a conference presentation and therefore assumed that she must represent a mother figure for her analysand, not a father figure, as turned out to be the case (Kohut, 1980b, p. 512; Schwaber, 1980, pp. 215–42). That is, in this instance Kohut notes that habitual prejudices about gender disturbed his assessment of the purportedly gender-neutral analytic situation and that he automatically considered a woman physician as playing the role of her analysand's mother.

II

Despite its disregard of gender, self psychology appears more congruent with feminist values than orthodox Freudian psychoanalysis does in three major respects: it stresses the preoedipal period more than the Oedipus complex; it separates values acquisition from an oedipal superego based on castration anxiety; and it places a special value on empathy. Of course, similarity of values to feminist ones does not prove that self psychology is true, which must be decided on other grounds; however, such similarity does ensure that its model of human nature will prove congruent with feminist theory.

The first area in which I claim self psychology accords with contemporary feminist thought is in its attention to the first few years of a child's life as the primary period in personality formation. It stresses the mother's crucial role in this preoedipal development when the child is under three years old, not because of biology but because of the social fact of mother-dominated childrearing. This theory thus agrees with feminist views, which hold that the preoedipal mother-daughter relationship is the most salient factor in female psychology. Even Freud felt that this period meant more for women than for men, and current feminist theorists like Dinnerstein strengthen his claim. Although self psychology emphasizes the mother's role in early child development, it does not limit mothering capacity to women. It claims that the mother, the father, or other adults can empathically mirror the child: it does not posit a mothering instinct or insist on mother-child bonding solidified through female-specific practices such as breastfeeding. In therapeutic work, it says that a patient may treat the analyst of either sex in ways reminiscent of the patient's parents of either sex, and male analysts often seem proud of playing maternal roles in their analysands' psyches. Thus self psychology accords with various strains in feminist theory that wish to value women's historic importance as mothers while not precluding a future in which men, too, have the capacity to "mother" children.

The second main advantage of self psychology to feminist thought is that it disconnects the child's formation of goals and values from the Freudian punitive superego through which the child introjects parental prohibitions, especially the father's "laws." Freud thought the boy's fear of castration caused him to repress his desire for his mother and identify with his father, thus resolving his Oedipus complex and causing him to develop a superego. Because girls were already "castrated," this fear worked less powerfully on them, and they therefore failed to acquire the inexorable consciences of men:

> I cannot evade the notion that for women the level of what is ethically normal is different from what it is in men. . . . Character traits which critics of every epoch have brought up against women—that they show less sense of justice than men . . . would be amply accounted for by the modification in the formation of their superego. . . . (Freud, 1925, pp. 243–58)

In contrast, self psychology separates the child's formation of a mental structure governing values and ideals from fears about castration which are inevitably differentiated by sex. Moreover, since it does not organize all other differences around sexual difference, self psychology does not privilege the phallus as the "signifier" of cultural participation. Nor does self psychology fall into the Freudian prejudices of believing that anatomy is destiny or of assuming that female genitals are actually inferior to male ones.

Third, self psychology awards empathy a central role both as a tool in the analytic process and as a major goal of psychological maturity. This emphasis contrasts strongly with classical analysis's faith in rational insight as the curative agent in patients' troubles. A central goal of Freudian psychoanalysis is the translation of unconscious conflicts to consciousness, whereas self psychology, like some feminist theory, values empathy as well as reason and thinks reason in and of itself incapable of transforming the patient's life and allowing him or her to develop the mental structures necessary for healthy functioning. Freud wrote that "a path leads from identification by way of imitation to empathy, that is, to the comprehension of the mechanism by means of which we are enabled to take up any attitude at all towards another mental life" (Freud, 1921, p. 110). Despite this strong formulation, Freud referred to empathy rarely, whereas Kohut put the concept of empathy at the center of his notions about how parents properly treat their children and how analysts create a therapeutic environment.

In short, self psychology's descriptions of mental functioning for both sexes more closely resemble feminist ideas than do those orthodox psychoanalytic theories whose model of humanity is not only male but also stereotypically masculine. Of course, there is already an extensive feminist literature critical of Freud. Some of this literature rejects all psychoanalysis as intrinsically sexist and oppressive to women; another approach is to adapt the masculinist theories of psychoanalysis from a feminist perspective. This effort at adaptation has not heretofore been tried for self psychology, whereas it has flourished in the work of feminist object relations theorists. According to Chodorow, women's greater relational capacities in comparison to men, women's less rigid ego boundaries, and other psychological differences between the sexes may be attributed not to nature but to girls' closer childhood identifications with their mothers and to boys' needs to distance themselves from women in order to prove themselves male. The feminist object relations theorists, then, tend to differentiate male from female development and value female empathy, nurturance, flexibility, and interdependence over male abstraction, competition, rigidity, and autonomy.

Along with their important insights, however, these highly influential views have assimilated some problems from the object relations theories on which they drew. Alice Rossi notes that Chodorow uses Freudian and ego psychology with restraint but never offers "the smallest critical comment on the work of object relations theorists" (Rossi, 1981, p. 494). Other feminists attack Chodorow's theories in terms of both method and content. Perhaps the most common criticism is that psychoanalysis is suspect because it privileges fantasy over reality and psychological explanations over historical and social ones. Nina Baym objects that feminist object relations–based "mothering" theory demeans adult women, limiting "maternity to a global, nonverbal or pre-verbal endlessly supportive, passively nurturing presence. . . . Pre-Oedipal, then, is an interested fantasy of the maternal. Its purpose—to contain and confine mothers and hence women within the field of the irrational" (Baym, 1984, p. 55). Literary critic Elaine Showalter faults "psychoanalytically based models of feminist criticism" because they "cannot explain historical change, ethnic difference, or the shaping force of generic and economic factors" (Showalter, 1982, p. 27).

The point is not that Chodorow or her followers are wrong or to be attacked as an "enemy" in the name of some other theoretical stance, but rather that their insights about gender might be more usefully developed if they sprang from a broader psychological base rather than being exclusively tied to the perspective of object relations theory. Self psychology provides that broader base. I have already proposed that self psychology offers feminists advantages over Freudian orthodoxy by emphasizing mothers' importance in their children's early lives. It may seem contradictory, then, to cite critics like Baym who attack this emphasis on the preoedipal. Yet I think that the way that object relations theory, including feminist object relations theory, conceptualizes the preoedipal does create some problems: an apparent acceptance of the determinate power on adult personality of early infantile experience—this is the heart of Baym's objection; an acceptance of the idea of a mother-child "symbiosis" to which the mother regresses in order to care for her child; and a concomitant acceptance of the developmental model by which maturation for the child is a struggle to break free from this early infantile symbiosis and to gain autonomy. Two other problems with feminist object relations theory arise from its dependence on the model of the Oedipus complex as the means through which children become simultaneously gendered and heterosexual. These problems are the model's inability to account for homosexuality and its acceptance of the notion that femininity and the desire to have children are compensatory. Finally, the last set of complaints against object relations theory is based on its neglect of historical and cultural contexts.

Self psychology provides solutions to some of these problems and structures its theory so that other of these problems do not arise. (1) Although it stresses the preoedipal over the oedipal stage in the development of the self, it is a whole life psychology in which change is normal throughout adulthood. (2) Self psychology does not use the concept of "symbiosis" for the mother-child bond. (3) Its model of maturity is not organized around the goals of individuation or autonomy. (4) Because it detaches self-esteem from sexual object choice, its model for healthy development is not necessarily heterosexual. (5) It does not view femininity as compensatory. (6) Its concept of selfobjects provides the means through which cultural and historical forces can shape the individual psyche.

Let me expand on these points. (1) Although self psychology believes the self should form early in the child's life, it does not see a person's character as entirely determined in infancy. Life circumstances and naturally occurring relationships, as well as psychoanalysis, foster the self's growth in adulthood, and self psychology follows a person's use of selfobjects through the whole life span, in which periods of stress may cause the self to lose its cohesion, pride, and assertiveness, which it will thereafter regain. In fact, Kohut believes that a difficult childhood and an adulthood spent compensating for it may enhance a person's character. "It is my impression," he says, "that the most productive and creative lives are lived by those who, despite high degrees of traumatization in childhood, are able to acquire new structures by finding new routes toward inner completeness" (Kohut, 1984, p. 44). Thus self psychology accords with those feminist views that see women consolidating an identity in their thirties or forties rather than in childhood or adolescence, although it holds that this flexibility is characteristic of both sexes, and it also corroborates views of female psychology as fluid and flexible throughout life rather than as determined in childhood (Lebe, 1982, pp. 63–73).

(2) Self psychology employs a more adult model of mothering than does object relations theory, especially in its primary use of the concept of empathy rather than that of symbiosis. D. W. Winnicott implies that a good mother entirely loses her self in caring for her infant. This "extraordinary condition" is "almost like an illness," but in mothers it is a sign of health, he claims (Winnicott, 1968, p. 15). Feminist object relations theorists sometimes sound as though a mother regresses to an infantile position when she enters a mother-child "symbiosis":

> Primary identification and symbiosis with daughters tend
> to be stronger and cathexis of daughters is more likely to
> retain and emphasize narcissistic elements, that is, to be
> based on experiencing a daughter as an extension or double
> of a mother herself. . . . (Chodorow, 1978, p. 109)

Thus the profound intimacy these theorists claim that women desire resembles an infantile state, and the capacities that women have to nurture and empathize are regressive responses to which women's childhood needs impel them as adults. Self psychology disputes the concept of symbiosis altogether. Although the very young infant is truly dependent on its caretakers, it initiates actions and responds actively to the treatment it receives, thus shaping a human relationship from birth that is unlike animal symbiosis. Moreover, self psychologists do not describe any aspect of parenting capacities as regressive to childhood states. Self psychology sees empathy as an adult process in which one mature self puts itself in the position of the other person. Such empathy implies an ability to be attuned to the needs of the other, an ability most mothers have developed, so that their responses to the infant's cries help it to perceive and articulate its own feelings and needs. From this perspective, empathy is not the same as but opposite to projective identification, in which one person insists that the other is an extension of the first, and this self-psychological view of empathy entails no merging, blurring, or loss of self for the adult.

One may object that there are mothers who project their own needs onto their children rather than learning to perceive the child's needs. Without undercutting the usual intensity and interdependence between mother and child, however, self psychology sees such "symbiosis" as pathological, not normal, and its model of mothering is one of mature capacities. In making empathic abilities one of the highest goals of the developing self, Kohut implicitly praises the analyst's job, but his ideas also enhance the mother's role. The analyst's claim that empathy develops through psychoanalytic practice is analogous to Sara Ruddick's argument that maternal thinking develops from maternal practice (Ruddick, 1980, pp. 342–67).

(3) Self psychology does not depend on a separation/individuation model of maturity. Object relations theorists like Margaret Mahler chart infant developmental growth as a progress from "symbiosis" with the mother to independence, autonomy, or individuation (Mahler, Pine, and Bergman, 1975). W. R. D. Fairbairn describes this progress as a transition from "infantile dependence" to "mature dependence" (Fairbairn, 1962, p. 163). Kohut explicitly argues against Mahler and this "maturation morality," which he sees as complicit with dangerous tendencies in Western civilization (Kohut, 1980b, p. 480). Object relations theorist Harry Guntrip corroborates this political connection, though he values it positively, when he speaks of the mature individual personality as being fit for democracy, whereas other personality types are more comfortable with dictatorships or the welfare state (Guntrip, 1964, p. 378). In contrast, self psychology sees all people as embedded for life in a network of human relations, and it posits mature interdependence and altruism as among adult developmental goals for both sexes:

> Self psychology holds that self-selfobject relationships form the essence of psychological life from birth to death, that a move from dependence (symbiosis) to independence (autonomy) in the psychological sphere is no more possible, let alone desirable, than a corresponding move from a life dependent on oxygen to a life independent of it in the biological sphere. (Kohut, 1984, p. 47)

Thus self psychology provides a complete developmental scheme that is not oriented toward individuation or independence as its primary goal. Self psychology's model of maturity stresses interdependence rather than independence, but it makes this only one of many adult developmental goals, not the sole defining characteristic of maturity. Maturity is not something to be achieved in any simple linear progress, and among self psychology's goals are love for other people, empathy, and creativity. Unlike independence and autonomy, these goals are not linked to culturally enforced notions of masculinity.

(4) The object relations school follows the "single track" Freudian model by which the formation of self-image and the formation of desire are aspects of the same process. The girl first identifies herself with her mother, whom she loves, then learns she must love father, and later, other men. One learns that one has or is one sex and desires to possess the other. Chodorow shows that all women are originally mother-loving, but she describes the forces driving the girl toward heterosexuality, including a need to distance herself from her mother and an attraction to her seductive father, as successful. Although her theory values women's primary bonds with one another, it does not include lesbians. At one point she notes, "I must admit to fudging here about the contributory effect in all of this of a mother's sexual orientation—whether she is heterosexual or lesbian" (Chodorow, 1978, p. 110). Self psychology does not specifically theorize lesbian development either. However, by detaching the development of self-esteem from the development of sexual desire, self psychologists make it easier to conceptualize the development of the lesbian who has a clear feminine gender identity and a strong, positive self-image. As Kohut says:

> Although the attainment of genitality and the capacity for unambivalent object love have been features of many, per-

haps most, satisfying and significant lives, there are many
other good lives, including some of the greatest and most
fulfilling lives recorded in history, that were not lived by
individuals whose psychosexual organization was hetero-
sexual-genital or whose major commitment was to unam-
bivalent object love. (Kohut, 1984, p. 7)

Although self psychology's "dual track" and "bipolar self" hypotheses sound like examples of dualistic thinking, on investigation
their polarities break down: the bipolar self has three parts—two poles
and a middle term. Instead of seeing it as polarizing, I think Kohut's
dual track hypothesis can free theory from Freud's libidinal monism
and permit us to see personality development, not as either one or
two straight lines, but as a relational web. Kohut's two tracks are neither opposed nor parallel to one another. They may assume different
shapes and suffer differing traumas. Supplementing his theory with
an area that he neglects but that is not incompatible to it, we may
consider cognitive development as a third track. Developing her self-
image along one track and her sexual object choice along another, for
example, one girl might remain childishly exhibitionistic while un-
eventfully becoming heterosexual. To take another example, one
might imagine the tracks' interacting so that a child's cognitive learning disabilities distorted a self-esteem that had begun strongly in early
childhood. The same family environment might spur on or retard a
child's growth differently in these different areas of development.

(5) Self psychology does not view femininity or the desire for children as compensatory. For Freud, girls originally settle for femininity
only when they know they are deprived of penises, and they want
babies to substitute for these missing penises. Even for Chodorow,
women's desire to mother is compensatory, although it is not based
on penis envy. She claims that heterosexual women who are psychologically constructed to need and appreciate intimacy will be disap-
pointed with emotionally distant men. Therefore, they will want to
have children for psychological reasons "that have their source in the
desire to recreate the mother-child relationship they themselves experienced" as infants (Chodorow, 1978, p. 501). In contrast, Kohut
agrees with Stoller and the empirical psychologists that girls achieve
a primary femininity prior to the discovery of genital differences between the sexes. Those who receive empathic parenting in childhood,
according to Kohut, will be able to give it in adulthood; such "moth-

ering" of others is itself an adult developmental goal that is not dependent on former lacks or present dissatisfactions (Kohut, 1959, p. 228; Kohut, 1975, p. 786). Because self psychology emphasizes values and goals, it can explain the integration of "femininity" and "masculinity" into people's self structures without conflating being female with desiring men or being male with devaluing women.

(6) The object relations school describes the child's growth through social interactions with early caretakers. The self psychologists claim their approach combines both interpersonal and intrapsychic factors, so that it is less deterministic about the specific effects on any child of the same childhood milieu. Self psychologists explain that perfectly good or healthy parents may have an innately healthy child who nonetheless develops a defective self structure. Although seeing the early caretaking environment as very influential on the child, self psychology is neither deterministically social nor mother-blaming. On the other hand, it conceives of psychological development in a historically changing context. As we have seen, some feminist critics condemn both orthodox psychoanalysis and feminist object relations theory for their antihistorical character. Although Chodorow's popularizers have sometimes been naively unhistorical, Chodorow acknowledges that historical factors might alter the tight duplicating cycle of the "reproduction of mothering" that she describes. However, she casts this historical dimension as outside her scheme, something to be considered elsewhere. In contrast, self psychology's concept of selfobjects provides the specific point in the model through which changing historical forces can affect the child and break into the cycle of socialization. Self psychology's belief in the increasing frequency of narcissistic personality disorders is based on the conviction that changing historical conditions affect childrearing, hence personality structure. Kohut's later work repeatedly stresses the importance of history. "Now it would seem to me," Kohut writes, "that it is up to the historian to undertake a comparative study of the attitude of adults toward children at different periods in history, in order to throw some further light on the conditions that Freud tried to explain biologically" (Kohut, 1974, p. 777).

III

Currently, two main kinds of theories vie for precedence among feminists. Those who begin by asking how gender is inscribed in culture often answer through a model of patriarchy that defines women's condition as oppression, which is determined by men for their own advantage. According to Catherine MacKinnon, to cite one strong spokeswoman for this view, men's sexual desires define women's roles: "Socially, femaleness means femininity, which means attractiveness to men, which means sexual attractiveness, which means sexual availability on male terms. What defines woman as such is what turns men on" (MacKinnon, 1982, pp. 530–31). On the other hand, those who begin by asking what characterizes women often answer with models of female psychology or history that privilege relations among women over male domination of women. By emphasizing the intense formative bonds between mothers and daughters, feminist object relations theorists fit this second approach.

In contrast to a one-sided focus on male domination or on female bonding, self psychology can incorporate both of these partial models. Self psychology stresses preoedipal mother-daughter bonds in female personality organization, as the object relations theorists do; however, by also stressing the formation of goals, values, and self-esteem, it shows how the larger culture influences the child's development through the early caretaking milieu. Thus the mother who prefers her son to her daughter or who reflects to her daughter that female bodies disgust her will stamp the daughter's personality from its earliest and deepest layers with a patriarchal devaluation of women, and the girl will feel such cultural influences long before she explicitly learns social roles. Kohut explains:

> The girl's rejection of femininity, her feeling of being castrated and inferior, and her intense wish for a penis arise . . . because the little girl's selfobjects failed to respond to her with appropriate mirroring, since either no idealizable female parental imago was available to her, or that no alter ego gave her support during the childhood years when a proud feminine self should have established itself. (Kohut, 1984, p. 21)

In suggesting that self psychology has much to offer feminist thought, I am not denying current gender differences in favor of a gender-blind theory, but instead I am commending a theory whose model of human development fits feminist values for all persons. In order for self psychology to be fully useful to feminists, however, we must adapt it to recognize the gender differences it elides. Classical Freudians might contend that one advantage for women that I have imputed to self psychology is actually a disadvantage and cause of error: self psychology's preoedipal focus allows it to ignore gender, whereas Freudian analysis devotes considerable attention to the construction of sexual identities through the Oedipus complex. However, the orthodox Freudian account, enthusiastically adapted by Lacanians and feminist object relations theorists, may be incorrect (Mitchell and Rose, 1982, pp. 1–57). Some object relations theorists have even simpler views, like Margaret Mahler who believes in "constitutionally predestined gender-defined differences" between the sexes (Mahler, Pine and Bergman, 1975, p. 224). Empirical psychologists describe the preoedipal acquisition of gender identity in children, and cognitive psychologists theorize children's incorporation of gender schema into their views of themselves and the world (Bem, 1983; Galenson and Roiphe, 1980; Stoller, 1980). Self psychologists are beginning to collaborate with developmental psychologists. Even if one accepts the empirical psychological account of gender-identity formation, one could still appeal to the selfobject mirrorings and idealizations of early childhood as the means through which gender acquires its affective content for each child. These early associations with gender may then be reinforced or distorted during the oedipal stage. Kohut refers to the oedipal stage as a "healthy, joyfully undertaken developmental step, the beginning of a gender-differentiated firm self that points to a fulfilling creative-productive future" (Kohut, 1984, p. 22). Moreover, although we certainly do not want to ignore gender, it might be valuable to work within a conceptual framework, like that of self psychology, which minimizes sexual polarizations and which sees such polarizations as do occur between the sexes as distortions of optimal development.

As feminists, we need a gender-sensitive self psychology. This is a new area, and I offer the following as speculations about the directions that such a gender-sensitive self psychology might take. These speculations center on two key areas: first, gender differences in the formation of self-esteem, and, second, the salience of empathy in personality formation. Although these speculations are tentative, they accord with clinicians' work to date.

I surmise, first, that self-esteem, goals, and values typically take differing shapes in the two genders, not for any innate reason but because a culture's attitudes to women will affect the ways mothers typically respond to their daughters in comparison to their sons. Our culture has different attitudes, for example, about levels of bodily exhibitionism or pride in performance that are appropriate for boys and for girls. Traditionally, girls have been shamed into modesty and discouraged from showing off athletic skills. At the same time, they may be warmly mirrored for presenting the world with a demure appearance, frilly clothes, or a conventionally pretty face. Joan Lang (1984) uses self psychology to show how the feminine heterosexual self consolidates in the socially and historically specific circumstances of female self-devaluation. There are gender differences, she claims, in how aspects of the self are mirrored and idealized, as the parents reflect to the baby how its capacities fit the parents' ideas of gender-appropriate behavior. In particular, Lang hypothesizes that a girl in a patriarchy will disavow masculine-assigned potentials of her self, particularly aggression, as "not me" (Lang, 1984, pp. 59, 66). Thus, through differential parental responses in their childhoods, men and women would typically develop different forms of healthy self-esteem and also different narcissistic pathologies. From their case presentations, Kohut and Kernberg seem to have treated differing disturbed populations, and these differences may be related to the gender distribution of their patients as well as to their varied analytic approaches. Kohut's patients were primarily men who presented themselves as defensively arrogant or as coldly detached, whereas Kernberg's cases included many shallow, flighty, and immature women (Kohut, 1971, 1977; Kernberg, 1975).

Kohut states, "there is not one kind of healthy self—there are many kinds" (Kohut, 1984, p. 44). This is an important claim, and it should free self psychology from any narrow criteria of normality or health, including such culturally determined values as independence, exclusive heterosexuality, or traditionally "masculine" or "feminine" personalities. Without prescribing any one healthy masculine or feminine type of self, however, self psychology's pluralism about health permits the investigation of the variously gendered self structures typical in any given society. In addition, the conceptual framework of self psychology should be able to account not only for differences by gender but also for differences within gender. Other groups besides the two sexes might also have distinctive narcissistic configurations. For example, Charles Kligerman hypothesizes that artists were valued for their beautiful bodies when they were children and that their infantile gratification in showing off continues to support their adult performances (Kligerman, 1980, pp. 383–95). Black feminist theorists confute the white-derived middle-class picture of female psychology as passive, self-denigrating, and ambivalent about mother-daughter bonds. Gloria Joseph (1981) cites the "respect that black daughters have" for their mothers' "strength, honesty, and ability to overcome difficulties and ability to survive" and explains that "black females are socialized by adult figures in early life to become strong, independent women. . . ." (pp. 94–95). Despite persistent social discrimination, black women maintain warm and intense ties with one another that appear less ambivalent than those recorded for white women. A sensitive self psychology that looks at specific kinds of responses mothers make to their infant daughters may find that empathic, self-assured black mothers reproduce these traits in their daughters, whose self-images, goals, and values might vary from those of white women with more ambivalent, isolated, or unempathic mothers. Of course, this matter deserves further study, but at least self psychology allows conceptual room for such empirical differences.

Among the views that have most alienated feminists from orthodox Freudian psychoanalysts are their characterization of the normal female personality as passive, masochistic, and narcissistic (Deutsch, 1924). Freud not only discerned these qualities in women but also alleged biological reasons for them. For instance, he thought women had to be masochistic to be adapted to the pain of childbirth and that they had to be passive to be adapted to receptivity in heterosexual intercourse. A gender-sensitive self psychology would not deny these allegations a priori but would reinvestigate them from its own perspective. Thus it might find that, as narcissism and self-image typically take differing forms in the two sexes, so do initiative and passivity. One indication of the direction such findings might take is found in self psychology's redefinition of empathy, stressing active inquiry and response to others, not mere intuitive receptivity. Thus its picture of mothering behavior is more active and less masochistic than the traditional Freudian one, and its picture of male-female relations does not fall into the dichotomies active/passive or sadistic/masochistic.

Empathy is a central concept in self psychology. Up to this point I have argued that self psychology's validation of empathy allies it with

feminist theory. Unlike self psychology, however, feminist theories attribute empathy more pervasively to women than to men and consider
empathy as an entirely positive trait (Eichenbaum and Orbach, 1983;
Rubin, 1983). Chodorow claims that girls have "a basis for 'empathy'
built into their primary definition of self in a way that boys do not.
. . . Girls emerge with a stronger basis for experiencing another's
needs or feelings as one's own . . ." (Chodorow, 1978, p. 167). Such
views run the risk of merely reversing traditional evaluations of the
sexes, seeing women as more empathic, intimate, and nurturant than
men, that is, as generally nicer. These theories argue that all societies
need good parenting in order to reproduce themselves and that all
known societies have delegated primary childrearing responsibilities
to women. As a result, women must internalize the traits of good
mothers in all societies. Now case presentations by self psychologists
parade before us battalions of patients with unempathic mothers. Obviously, self psychology does not agree that women in our society become empathic and nurturing. How do we account for this disparity
between the theories?

Self psychology may offer a potentially more flexible and realistic
approach to the matter than does feminist object relations theory,
valuing empathy but holding a less sentimental view of it than in some
feminist theories. Although self psychology considers empathic mirroring necessary for the self's development, it does not equate empathy simply with love or compassion but insists that it is a mature
capacity that can be used for good or ill purposes—manipulatively as
well as nurturantly.

I speculate that empathy is a characteristic that is more "marked"
for women than for men. In other words, women may be both more
and less empathic than men. Chodorow states that girls' ties to their
mothers tend to develop and reinforce empathic capacities in most
women. This claim may be true, yet it perhaps oversimplifies the relationship betwen empathy and female personality. The very salience
of such relational ties in women and the lesser influence of fathers on
girls might mean that daughters of unempathic mothers are likely to
be more afflicted than sons are. Thus women might typically develop
the capacity for empathy more than men do but might also suffer
from more extreme distortions in empathizing. That is, the whole
range of women in our society might show a much wider range of
empathic abilities and capacities than the men in our society do, in

much the same way that men in our culture have traditionally developed a wider range of abilities and capacities for competitive striving than women have and have developed a wider range of personality variables around this trait than women have. Moreover, normal or distorted empathic abilities might play a larger part in the entire aggregate of women's personality structures than in men's. Certainly her empathic capacities may be more heavily reinforced or contravened than a man's would be. An unempathic woman, especially an unempathic mother, is considered a monster, and people condemn her as seriously deficient. In contrast, the unempathic man is perceived as normal in our society and in conventional cultural representations: he may not notice the lack, his family may not feel it; and his untested empathic capacities may have little chance to grow either into distorting intrusiveness or into responsive sensitivity, unless, of course, he chooses to become a psychoanalyst.

Self psychology points to empathy, creativity, love, and humor as characteristics of the mature self. Patterns of creativity, love, and humor, as well as empathy, may now be assuming typically different shapes in the two genders. Self psychology believes that "Tragic Man" has replaced Freudian "Guilty Man" as the representative of our society. For the reasons I have outlined above, I think that self psychology has the potential to offer feminists a more flexible psychological model for both sexes than either Freudian psychoanalysis or object relations theory now offers. It also has the potential to explain for us "Empathic Woman" in her full variety.

References

Basch, M. F. (1983). The concept of self: An operational definition. In B. Lee and G. G. Noam (Eds.), *Developmental approaches to the self*. New York: Plenum Press.

Baym, N. (1984). The madwoman and her languages: Why I don't do feminist literary theory. *Tulsa Studies in Women's Literature*, 3.1/2.

Bem, S. L. (1983). Gender schema theory and its implications for child development: Raising gender-aschematic children in a gender-schematic society. *Signs*, 8.4.

Chodorow, N. (1978). *The reproduction of mothering: Psychoanalysis and the sociology of gender*. Berkeley: University of California Press.

Dinnerstein, D. (1976). *The mermaid and the minotaur: Sexual arrangements and human malaise.* New York: Harper and Row.

Deutsch, Helene. (1924). The psychology of women in relation to the functions of reproduction. In J. Strouse, (Ed.), *Women and analysis: Dialogues on psychoanalytic views of femininity.* New York: Dell, 1974.

Eichenbaum, L. S. and Orbach, S. (1983). *Understanding women: A feminist psychoanalytic approach.* New York: Basic Books.

Fairbairn, W. R. D. (1962). *An object-relations theory of the personality.* New York: Basic Books.

Freud, S. (1914). On narcissism: An introduction. *The standard edition of the complete psychological works of Sigmund Freud, 14,* 67–102. (J. Strachey, Trans. and Ed.). London: The Hogarth Press, 1973.

———. (1921). Group psychology and the analysis of the ego. *Standard edition, 18,* 65–143.

———. (1925). Some psychical consequences of the anatomical distinction between the sexes. *Standard edition, 19,* 241–258.

———. (1931). Female sexuality. *Standard edition, 21,* 221–243.

Galenson, E., and Roiphe, H. (1980). Some suggested revisions concerning early female development. In M. Kirkpatrick (Ed.), *Women's sexual development: Explorations of inner space.* New York: Plenum Press.

Gedo, J. E. (1984). Introduction: On the dynamics of dissidence within psychoanalysis. In J. E. Gedo and G. H. Pollack (Eds.), *Psychoanalysis: The vital issues.* New York: International Universities Press.

Guntrip, H. (1964). *Personality structure and human interaction: The developing synthesis of psycho-dynamic theory.* New York: International Universities Press.

Joseph, G. I. (1981). Black mothers and daughters: Their roles and functions in American society. In G. I. Joseph and J. Lewis (Eds.), *Common differences: Conflicts in black and white feminist perspectives.* Garden City, N.Y.: Anchor Press/Doubleday.

Kernberg, O. (1975). *Borderline conditions and pathological narcissism.* New York: Jason Aronson.

Kligerman, C. (1980). Art and the self of the artist. In A. Goldberg (Ed.), *Advances in self psychology.* New York: International Universities Press.

Kohut, H. (1959). Introspection, empathy, and psychoanalysis. In

P. H. Ornstein (Ed.), *The search for the self: Selected writings of Heinz Kohut.* New York: International Universities Press, 1978.

―――. (1971). *The analysis of self: A systematic approach to psychoanalytic treatment of narcissistic personality disorders.* New York: International Universities Press.

―――. (1974). The self in history. *The search for the self.*

―――. (1975). A note on female sexuality. *The search for the self.*

―――. (1977). *The restoration of the self.* New York: International Universities Press.

―――. (1980a). Two letters. In A. Goldberg (Ed.), *Advances in self psychology.* New York: International Universities Press.

―――. (1980b). Reflections on advances in self psychology. *Advances in self psychology.*

―――. (1982). Introspection, empathy, and the semi-circle of mental health. *International Journal of Psychoanalysis, 63.3.*

―――, Goldberg, A., and Stepansky, P. E. (Eds.). (1984). *How does analysis cure?* Chicago: University of Chicago Press.

―――, and Wolf, E. S. (1978). The disorders of the self and their treatment: An outline. *International Journal of Psychoanalysis, 59.4.*

Lang, J. A. (1984). Notes toward a psychology of the feminine self. In P. E. Stepansky and A. Goldberg (Eds.), *Kohut's legacy: Contributions to self psychology.* Hillsdale, N.J.: Analytic Press.

Lebe, D. (1982). Individuation of women. *Psychoanalytic Review,* 69.1.

MacKinnon, C. A. (1982). Feminism, Marxism, method, and the state: An agenda for theory. *Signs* 7.2.

Mahler, M. S., Pine, F., and Bergman, A. (1975). *The psychological birth of the human infant: Symbiosis and individuation.* New York: Basic Books.

Mitchell, J., and Rose, J. (1982). Introduction. *Feminine sexuality: Jacques Lacan and the école freudienne.* New York: W. W. Norton.

Rossi, A. S. (1981). On *The Reproduction of Mothering* by J. Lorber, R. L. Coser, A. S. Rossi, and N. Chodorow: A methodological debate. *Signs,* 6.3.

Rubin, L. B. (1983). *Intimate strangers: Men and women together.* New York: Harper and Row.

Ruddick, S. (1980). Maternal thinking. *Feminist Studies,* 6.2.

Schwaber, E. (1980). A case presentation. In A. Goldberg (Ed.), *Advances in self psychology.* New York: International Universities Press.

Showalter, E. (1982). Feminist criticism in the wilderness. In E. Abel (Ed.), *Writing and sexual difference.* Chicago: University of Chicago Press.

Stoller, R. J. (1980). Femininity. In M. Kirkpatrick (Ed.), *Women's sexual development: Explorations of inner space.* New York: Plenum Press.

Winnicott, D. W. (1968). *The family and individual development.* London: Tavistock.

CHAPTER 11

Representation and the Female: Gertrude Stein's "Lifting Belly" and Tender Buttons

HARRIET S. CHESSMAN

> Lifting belly is so seen.
> You mean here.
> Not with spy glasses.
> Lifting belly is an expression.
> Explain it explain it to me.
> (Stein, 1980, p. 16)

GERTRUDE STEIN'S WRITINGS speculate, and continually invite us to speculate, upon the notion of representation, especially the representation of the female. Stein is, in this as in other ways, one of the most important feminist thinkers of the twentieth century. Stein's refusal to accept traditional representations of women and her attempt to find new ways of thinking about female identity and sexuality anticipate the recent work of the French feminists Luce Irigaray, Hélène Cixous, Monique Wittig, and Julia Kristeva.

Important similarities between Stein and the French feminists include most significantly their shared resistance to defining "the female" and their attempt to give voice to a "feminine" subjectivity. For Irigaray, the figure whom I shall address most specifically in this essay, the Western cultural tradition has depended on the misrepresentation of the female and on the appropriation of feminine subjectivity within and by "the masculine." One of Irigaray's major concerns is the way in which female sexuality has become represented in Freudian terms as an absence, defined by its otherness in terms of male sexuality, with the assumption that value inheres only in what is visible and apparently unified: the phallus (Irigaray, 1985a). Irigaray exchanges this symbolic and patriarchal insistence on the visible for a new insistence on touch and indeterminacy. The female body and feminine subjectivity, seen as books to be "read," become in Irigaray's theory unreadable, and therefore resistant to imaginative possession.

This essay will explore the ways in which Gertrude Stein's experimental writing seems to prepare the way for later and more directly theoretical projects like Irigaray's. Similarities abound: the discarding of conventional representation, the simultaneous evocation of female-to-female relationships, the attempt to give voice to feminine subjectivities and to refigure female sexuality through various modes of indirection. I have chosen two works by Stein, "Lifting Belly" (written 1915–17) and *Tender Buttons* (originally published 1914), which offer unusual and compelling meditations upon the nature of such evocative nonrepresentation.

As Stein suggests in the epigraph for this essay, the kind of "seeing" she allows us is "Not with spy glasses"; in attempting to use such glasses, bringing what is at a distance into our line of vision, we occupy the position of an enemy attempting to see into, and so to undermine, a foreign country. Instead, we may "see" her words, "here," in the poem, and we may guess at a "here" outside of the poem, yet we can never be certain of our guess. Our desire for "explanation" ("Explain it explain it to me"), for certain knowledge, remains baffled in a way that allows "protection" for the unseen territory.

I ───

> Protection.
> Protection
> Protection
> Speculation
> Protection
> Protection.
> (Stein, 1980, p. 54)

> Lifting belly and a resemblance.
> There is no resemblance.
> A plain case of misdeed.
> (Stein, 1980, p.14)

Gertrude Stein's love poetry often seems to offer clear representations, or codes, of the female body. As poems that record fairly openly an ongoing, loving, passionate, and playful lesbian relationship, these works hold tremendous value. They help to break a silence about lesbianism and about the female body that has been, and remains, dangerously powerful and repressive. It should be noted that these most openly lesbian poems were not published in Stein's lifetime, but found posthumous publication in the 1950s in one of the eight volumes of the *Yale Edition of the Unpublished Works of Gertrude Stein*. They have a celebratory gaiety (Stein's own often-used word) that even now seems unusual and (to use another Steinian phrase) completely welcome. One wishes they could have been published earlier, if only for the impact they might have had on other writers attempting to write about love between women.

Yet what I wish to explore in this essay is not so much the representation of lesbianism or the female body, although this is important, but the more radical sense in which Gertrude Stein is questioning such representation, even when she seems most clearly to be allowing it. Such love poems call for a kind of double take: at first glance, one feels sure of the vision, of the thing seen ("There's the eye; there's the mouth; yes, there's the ——"), yet, almost at once, the "thing," whatever it is, seems to slip away before one's eyes. "Lifting belly and a resemblance," one agrees; yet the "and" here already makes us wonder about such a connection. What is the relation between one thing and its "resemblance," its representation? "Lifting belly and a resemblance. / There is no resemblance. / A plain case of misdeed" (Stein, 1980, p. 14). Resembling, I would suggest, becomes for Stein an action that is in itself a "misdeed," and a "miss," that takes aim at an object but misses.

One of Stein's most intriguing erotic long poems is "Lifting Belly." This inviting title runs like a chant, or a refrain, throughout the poem it names. The poem, in one sense, is a catalog of definitions for "lifting belly"; again and again "lifting belly" is the subject followed by the verb, the copula, that appears to promise revelation: "is." "Lifting belly is all there." "Lifting belly is delightful. / Lifting belly is so high." "Lifting belly is good" (Stein, 1980, p. 9). The poem is, in this sense, an extravagant, insistent, encyclopedic hymn of praise and celebration.

Yet what is being defined? What, precisely, *is* "lifting belly"? What article, or pronoun, even, would accompany it: *a, the, her, my, your*? Who, in other words, "owns" this belly? The absence of any defining possessive, or nonpossessive ("a"), is significant, and marks the first way in which this phrase gains freedom from definition. We cannot

locate the object, and the object has the unusual and unthinglike quality of possible autonomy. It may be attached to someone, or to two
figures (each of which has a belly), or it may not; and its attachments
may shift as the poem moves. Its umbilical cord, its original connection
to one being, has been cut, if indeed it ever existed.

This unlocatable object is difficult to find in another sense as well,
for what exactly is a "belly"? With all the catalog adjectives and nouns
apparently attempting to define this entity, nowhere is it seen or im-
aged as a palpable, visible, describable thing, just as in Irigaray's
(1985b) lyrical prose poem "When Our Lips Speak Together,"
(pp. 205–18) where the visible nature of these "lips," and even their
precise location, remains unimaged and undefined. We are left, then,
to wonder: Is it inside? Is it outside? Is it a stomach, or the intestines?
Could it be the womb? Could a "lifting" belly, then, be a pregnant
one? Or could it be a metaphor for "The interior (of things material
and immaterial)"? or for any "concave surface"? or, metaphorically,
for the front surface of anything? Then, whatever it is, how is it "lifting"? Is it active or passive? Does it do the lifting, or is it lifted? Or is
it, perhaps, stolen, or stealing, as a further sense of "lifting"? A cun-
ning stealing does seem to be going on here; the very word *belly* may
be stealing away from one significance, or it may be lifted straight out
of its traditional grounding in discourse. This belly could be a sign
detached from any particular "ground"; "There is no resemblance."

This bellyful of possible signification, I would suggest, is precisely
what Gertrude Stein hopes we come to find. She seems to be telling
us, at one and the same time, that the "belly" is full, even pregnant
with meaning, and that it is empty, that it does not necessarily contain
any objects at all. The dialogue of the poem is preoccupied with a
perplexed questioning of language's capacity to represent:

> What is it when it's upset. It isn't in the room.
> Moonlight and darkness. Sleep and not sleep. We sleep
> every night.
>
> What was it.
> I said lifting belly.
> You didn't say it.
> I said it I mean lifting belly.
> Don't misunderstand me.
> Do you.
>
> (Stein, 1980, p.5)

Or again:

> What did you say lifting belly. I did not understand
> you correctly. It is not well said. For lifting belly. For
> lifting belly not to lifting belly.
> Did you say, oh lifting belly.
> What is my another name.
> Representative
> Of what.
> Of the evils of eating.
> What are they then.
> They are sweet and figs.
>
> (Stein, 1980, p. 5)

Again, a pronoun ("it") replaces a noun ("belly"). More strikingly, however, perhaps "it" may signify something other, something left completely unstated. As an answer to the question "What was it," "I said lifting belly" may be inadequate: "You didn't say it." Saying "lifting belly" may not, after all, be the same thing as "saying it." The question that emerges is whether, after all our guesses at the possible meanings of "lifting belly," "it" has been "said" or put into words at all. "Lifting belly" itself comes to seem like a form of stamp that is stamped over something, or some things, again and again, when those things must be hidden from sight. It is almost like a sign, "Censor," that erases forbidden signs underneath: "I said it I mean ——." The "it" remains unseen, not "in the room" of the words.

"It" is absent, then; yet its presence touches on the signs that *are* present. "Moonlight and darkness. Sleep and not sleep." These opposites can only be known by their relationship with each other, even their contiguity. In the same way, the "it" or the "belly," as present signs, may touch on what they do not "say." Such representation moves through contiguity and association. "Eating" and "figs" are present, yet another kind of eating, and other kinds of figs, assert a shadowy but insistent existence. These figs do not simply figure as metaphors for the more erotic figs; yet the mention of "figs" being eaten calls up, through association, other and unstated acts of "eating."

The refusal of representation goes even further, however, with the stubborn hold on the "it"—"Do it. What a splendid example of carelessness" (Stein, 1980, p. 5)—where the "it" is left entirely to our imaginations. Even the aid of association is not allowed here to light our way through indirection. The object here is outside the poem's language entirely. Yet to be outside the language does not mean, of necessity, to be simply absent. Within the poem's context, we sense the presence of the "it" most powerfully when it remains most bare. In the poem's terms, the "miracle" is precisely this: ". . . I mean everything away. / Away where. / Away here" (Stein, 1980, p. 11). The poem finds a way *here* by touching on what is "away."

Further, these oddly unrepresentational words—"it," "this," "here"—gesture in at least two directions: to the unstated and to the statement of the poem itself, just as "lifting belly" points both to a fertile and hidden female body and to the poem "Lifting Belly." The erotic acts of lovemaking that are hinted at throughout the poem merge, in an intricate and teasing way, with the act of the poem, which can be read as an act of conversational exchange about such an erotic act.

This physical and literary sexuality depends on the freedom of its objects from possession, or representation, or visibility. Objects shake free from their status as objects; yet, unknown, misrepresented, and (happily) misunderstood, they still have a habitation (if not a name):

> Lifting belly is so near.
> Lifting belly is so dear.
> Lifting belly all around.
> Lifting belly makes a sound.
> (Stein, 1980, p. 14)

Word and poem attempt, not to be in the place of this erotics, but to be "near," close to, in touch with it, or "all around" it. They make, not clear significance ("I don't mean to be reasonable" [Stein, 1980, p. 10]), but "a sound," a more sensual creation. The poem, like the act(s), is "Remarkably a recreation" (Stein, 1980, p. 15), in the sense of both a pleasure and a new creation, a reconceiving of creation as a gesture, not of naming but of celebrating through an evocation that does not depend on a name. The question "Am I in it," asked by one of the poem's undefined voices, is answered simply, "That doesn't affect it," for the "I," the being that the poem attempts to re-create, finds no direct "resemblance" there. This "I" may be "near," or "all around," but she will not be named, unless by a name chosen by one of the voices: "Call me Helen. / Not at all. / You may call me Helen. / That's what we said" (Stein, 1980, p. 29).

Finally, the poem's oblique representation of sexuality is both compelling and difficult to picture. Although the poem almost enters into
the visible sexual realm at certain points ("Kiss my lips. She did. / Kiss
my lips again she did. / Kiss my lips over and over and over again she
did" (Stein, 1980, p. 19), even at these moments there is uncertainty:
whose lips? And in general, although we are allowed to sense that
lovemaking is going on, and that the poem is itself a form of lovemaking, we are granted no precise image, so that the claim, "This is
a picture of lifting belly having a cow," (Stein, 1980, p. 30), becomes
a characteristically Steinian joke, and an earnest one ("All of it is a
joke. / Lifting belly is no joke. Not after all" [Stein, 1980, p. 8]). Where
is the "this"? Is it outside the poem, simply gestured toward, or is it
the poem itself? And how can this "picture" be "pictured," when both
of its terms, *belly* and *cow*, are so difficult to see separately, much less
together? How do we make visual sense of "lifting belly having a cow"?
Elizabeth Fifer (1979) in her article "Is Flesh Advisable? The Interior
Theater of Gertrude Stein," suggests a rich body of possible interpretations for the word *cow*:

> Stein uses the word "cow" with great effectiveness. If, as
> Richard Bridgman suggests, it is involved in both the nur-
> turing aspect of Alice [Toklas, Stein's lifelong companion
> and lover] and some sort of dirt, it is also the orgasm, even
> the potential for it. . . . While expressing the idea of sexual
> pleasure in this privately pastoral mode, she never attempts
> to suppress her "barnyard" meanings. She also varies her
> meaning of the word "cow" itself, so that it alternately bears
> the feeling of sexuality, the organ itself, food, protection,
> or the mythical idea of lesbian birth. It is both a derogatory
> female symbol (in the beast's placidity, stupidity) and a pos-
> itive symbol of mothering and unselfishness, of pure animal
> sensuality and nurture in an Edenic world of simplicity and
> warmth. (Fifer, p. 481)

Most of these interpretations seem accurate; one could add that a
cow "lows," that this activity appears to be preoccupied with the
"lower" part of the body, and that the sound a cow is said to make
("moo"), like the word *cow* itself, may evoke a sound similar to a moan.
Yet the very number of possible meanings, as with "rose" or "belly,"
intrigues us. We wonder, further, about the oddness, literally the im-

possibility, of such a "coming out," of such a "birth." A cow, no matter what its symbolic significance, cannot easily be seen coming out of a belly, unless perhaps it is another cow's belly.

"Cow," then, like "lifting belly," begins to seem like a name to be used in place of other, uncertain namings. At any one point, we may feel we know what it refers to; as one of the voices in "Lifting Belly" says, "You are sure you know the meaning of any word" (Stein, 1980, p. 35). Yet the poem's pleasure lies in its slipping away from such capture. The poem concludes, if such a poem can be said to conclude at all, with this pleasure:

> Lifting belly enormously and with song.
> Can you sing about a cow.
> Yes.
> And about signs.
> Yes.
> And also about Aunt Pauline.
> Yes.
> Can you sing at your work.
> Yes.
> In the meantime listen to Miss Cheatham.
> In the midst of writing.
> In the midst of writing there is merriment.
>   (Stein, 1980, p. 54)

Sing, one notes, with the shifting of two letters, makes *sign.* Signs, in this poem, as in much of Stein, are to be sung, not as pointers to objects, but as caressed objects in their own right that can evoke a huge number of definitions yet, finally, elude definition's grasp. This work of singing, not signing, is both erotic and literary, literal and figurative. The literal and the figurative cannot, in fact, be separated. "In the midst of writing. / In the midst of writing there is merriment."

II

. . . bend more slender accents than have ever been necessary, shine in the darkness necessarily.
                                           (Stein, 1945, p. 468)

The movement from Gertrude Stein's more openly erotic pieces to a work as opaque and abstract as *Tender Buttons* (1914) seems to require a bold leap. Yet *Tender Buttons,* as Stein herself often suggests, is a key to her art and a culmination of her difficult struggle with the notion of representation. "And so in Tender Buttons and then on and on I struggled with the ridding myself of nouns," she states in her essay "Poetry and Grammar":

> I had to feel anything and everything that for me was existing so intensely that I could put it down in writing as a thing in itself without at all necessarily using its name. The name of a thing might be something in itself if it could not come to be real enough but just as a name it was not enough something. At any rate that is the way I felt and still do feel about it. (Stein, 1985, pp. 242–43)

More intensely than in almost any other of her writings, Stein attempts to avoid resemblances. And in an even more striking way, the objects she contemplates appear hidden from sight. Yet our other readings of Stein help to prepare us for an attentiveness to what "shine[s]," unnamed, "in the darkness necessarily."

As a "speculator" on this work's "protection," I wish not primarily to uncover what Stein has so carefully covered—even if such uncovering were clearly possible—but to explore the boundary *Tender Buttons* inhabits, between possible objects outside the words, and the words themselves. Stein insisted, of course, on the unimportance of the identity of a work of art's subject. In her 1935 lecture "Pictures," she acknowledges her own gradual realization that "there is a relation between anything that is painted and the painting of it" (Stein, 1985). Yet, in the next breath, she adds: "And I gradually realized as I had found very often that that relation was so to speak nobody's business" (p. 79). The art should achieve its own autonomy, its freedom from any prior "reality." Turning once more, however, Stein (1985) acknowledges further:

> But still one always does like a resemblance.
> A resemblance is always a pleasurable sensation and so a resemblance is almost always there.
> That is not the business so to speak of the oil painting, that is just a pleasant human weakness.

Stein is weighing two desires here: the desire to see a resemblance (which causes "a pleasurable sensation") and the desire to hide that resemblance. The object, in either case, sounds curiously private and intimate; it is "nobody's business," just as other "relations" are nobody's business.

One could argue that it is the desire for privacy, felt even more intensely than in the slightly later piece, "Lifting Belly," that compels Stein in *Tender Buttons* to make portraits, not of people, but of "rooms and food and everything." She points out, "because there I could avoid this difficulty of suggesting remembering more easily . . . than if I were to describe human beings" (Stein, 1985, p. 188). She wishes the portrait to remain in the present, not to rely on a continuity with the past.

Yet what may be at stake in this severance from memory and from resemblance is protection from an observing eye. *Tender Buttons*, as Pamela White Hadas (1979) suggests, is a maze of covers, cloaks, and lids, both in its imagery and in its form. It is Gertrude Stein's profoundest study in hiding things, and in hiding the thing that is itself.

Tender Buttons's most successful cloak, in fact, may be its appearance as a still life. Stein seems to be presenting "Objects," "Food," and "Rooms" (the titles of the work's three parts), yet is this wholly accurate? Stein is, I would argue, preoccupied with a larger sense of such "objects," of their status as objects, and of her own object-ion (she objects; the noun dissolves and becomes active, a verb) to objectification. In her "still life," she asks us to explore, with her, the nature of such "stillness." Further, she invites us to uncover, at least partly, the link between such objects and the female; she asks us to perceive the female object in another way, which can free it from its traditional definitions and picturings.

Tender Buttons is an odd title; it calls attention to itself. On the face of it, there are no further buttons in the piece, but other domestic objects and places. As a noun, what does *buttons* signify? Perhaps these buttons are simply ordinary buttons: small round pieces attached to an object, which may be used to attach parts of a garment together. Like words: words in this piece are curiously "attached to objects." They have a relationship with the objects, yet they do not describe them; instead, they seem to coexist with the objects, to coincide and to assume positions of adjacency. As Gertrude Stein notes in her interview with Robert Bartlett Haas:

> I used to take objects on a table, like a tumbler or any kind
> of object and try to get a picture of it clear and separate in
> my mind and create a word relationship between the word
> and the thing seen. (Haas, 1971, p. 25)

Stein leaves it uncertain here as to whether such a relationship is for use or ornament, for some form of signification, or for a larger autonomy of word from object and object from word. Yet, if the words of *Tender Buttons* are in one sense the buttons, they appear to be thrust, small as they are, into a larger light than the objects themselves. Further, the "objects" may not be other objects at all, but more buttons. As Stein suggests in the same interview (her last, and most explanatory, interview, helpful in an author so adverse to explanation), "I took individual words and thoughts about them until I got their weight and volume complete and put them next to another word" (Haas, 1971, p. 25). *Tender Buttons,* she states, is the "culmination" of this method of word adjacency. Stein's language here, as I have suggested, calls up the notion of painting; her painterly method in *Tender Buttons* has been acknowledged by many critics, who link her early experimental art, as she herself did, with Postimpressionism or with Cubism (Perloff, 1979).

As Marianne de Koven argues, this analogy between Stein's method and that of Cubism has serious limitations, in that words are signs in a language system, unlike bits of paint; I would suggest, however, that the link remains important. One of Gertrude Stein's major influences, as Stein acknowledges, is Cézanne, and it is his use of paint that finds a similar spirit and motivation, even ideology, in Stein. Stein notes especially his "evenness," the even strokes across the canvas, the even value given to different blocks of color and shape. Each corner is allowed equal weight, equal importance; there is no hierarchy, for our eye travels everywhere; there is no one center, but a whole geography where the notion of a center is irrelevant. For Stein, this approach had in it the essence of what she calls "democracy"; and, as Donald Sutherland (1971, pp. 145–46) persuasively suggests, this radically unhierarchical sense of things is crucial to her literary project, in form and content.

The absence of hierarchy moves in another direction as well, for if her words are "buttons," simply attached to objects, or touching on other buttons, they make no claim to the authority of naming. The

smallness and ordinariness of these articles emphasize this abjuring
of authority; anybody knows what buttons are, and sees buttons, and
uses buttons, and holds buttons. Stein seems to proffer them to us, to
"tender" them. They become units of exchange, small gifts offered
"tenderly," and to be handled with tenderness by the receiver, just as
they show tenderness toward the objects they attach themselves to, by
their protective unnamings. They protect by fastening the garments
and the covers around the hidden object.

Can this work be unbuttoned, then, or is it "buttoned up"? Is there
a way of removing its cloak, or is this issue of undressing precisely
what *Tender Buttons* ad-dresses? Often, as critics or readers, we think
of the act of reading as an entrance into the text, a penetration of its
many layers to arrive at its core of meaning. Wolfgang Iser (1974),
for example, suggests that a text leaves lacunae into which a reader is
invited to enter. By extension, the text seems, in traditional terms, to
be "female," the critic "male." Yet, with a work like *Tender Buttons,* we
are held continually at the threshold of such entrance; "entrance" itself
becomes a difficult notion that we are compelled to question. Where,
precisely, are the "holes"? And if there are such holes, what, if anything, inhabits them?

Interestingly, the holes that allow for interpretation are few, and
often seem to lead us back to the question of what is at stake both in
representation and in the interpretation of representation. *Tender Buttons* opens, if it can be said to open, with a strangely resistant "object,"
one whose object, or purpose, is resistance itself:

> A CARAFE, THAT IS A BLIND GLASS
> A kind in glass and a cousin, a spectacle and nothing
> strange a single hurt color and an arrangement in a system
> to pointing. All this and not ordinary, not unordered in
> not resembling. The difference is spreading.
> (Stein, 1945, p. 461)

Stein offers us many "buttons" here, but where is the button that
can unfasten meaning and point out the object of this representation?
"A CARAFE": this, we think, must be the object seen. Yet immediately
the link between word and thing trembles and begins to break.
"THAT IS A BLIND GLASS": as if *carafe* is not, after all, the right
word? We begin to feel hesitation about naming as an authorial en-

terprise. This, Stein seems to say, indicating the phrase and the work as a whole—This is no window, and no mirror. It is without sight, and it is out of sight; like a blind alley, it leads nowhere, if you try to trace its lines directly. It does not open onto a familiar reality, as a window might; and it does not attempt to hold the mirror up to nature. It is preoccupied not with resembling but with "not resembling," not with similarity but with "difference"—a continually expanding difference, as name leads to name, but no name leads to thing.

Yet Stein also hints here, as she does throughout *Tender Buttons*, at another form of naming. This, she says, is "A kind in glass and a cousin, a spectacle and nothing strange": a kind of glass, a relation to the glass we usually think of, and a "kind" one, a tender one (like a/ glass, Alice Toklas); a glass that may, like spectacles, readjust and clarify our vision; a strange nothing, or noting, which is paradoxically "kin" to us, if we can learn to speculate differently.

This difference is both linguistic and erotic. For, even in this opaque opening, this "arrangement in a system" of nouns upon nouns, we can sense an obscured, unnamed, and powerful female presence. "Lifting Belly" echoes here, as do other erotic poems, since Stein tends to return to certain key words. We hear the repeated "Lifting belly is so kind," and the delight in "Making a spectacle" (Stein, 1980, p. 29), even though in both cases this "spectacle" remains unseen; we hear an echo of "Lifting belly is so strange" (Stein, 1980, p. 20); and we think of another kind of "spreading," a kind and tender one, the "stretching" of "Lifting Belly": "Oh yes you see. / What I see. / You see me. / Yes stretches. / Stretches and stretches of happiness" (Stein, 1980, p. 26). Or: "Lifting belly is perfect. / Do you stretch farther. / Come eat it" (Stein, 1980, p. 35).

The "difference" here is femaleness itself, a female sexuality that is seen, traditionally, as "difference," and that makes a difference to art. Difference is now celebrated; the hole, or lacuna, which, as Irigaray points out, has been thought in a Freudian scheme to mark such difference can now be sensed to be not a hole at all but a rich and indefinable presence. As Irigaray suggests in her philosophical discourse on Freud in *Speculum of the Other Woman,*

> But perhaps through this specular surface which sustains discourse is found not the void of nothingness but the dazzle of multifaceted speleology. A scintillating and incandes-

cent concavity, of language also, that threatens to set fire
to fetish-objects and gilded eyes. The recasting of their
truth value is already at hand. We need only press on a
little further into the depths, into that so-called dark cave
which serves as hidden foundation to their speculations.
For there where we expect to find the opaque and silent
matrix of a logos immutable in the certainty of its own light,
fires and mirrors are beginning to radiate, sapping the evidence of reason at its base! Not so much by anything stored
in the cave—which would still be a claim based on the notion of the closed volume—but again and yet again by their
indefinitely rekindled hearths. (Irigaray, 1985a, pp. 143–
44)

A new form of speculation may replace and explode the old. Instead
of being seen and named as object, the female may begin to take the
"speculum" in her own hands, to "press on" into herself, and to find,
not the certainty of the named, but the fiery, uncertain, lively, and
unlocatable locus of the unnamed.

In Stein's words, here is "Glazed Glitter" (the "title" of the second
"object" in *Tender Buttons*): "glazed," in presenting a smooth and glossy
surface, of paint or of ice, or perhaps of sugar, or perhaps of glass
(Stein, 1945, p. 461). The name points to its own glossing over, its
own covering of our eyes with a film, or perhaps its covering of the
object it does not name. To approach this glaze as a surface, to attempt
to look directly at it, will yield only bafflement. What is glossed over,
what perhaps needs a gloss, is something paradoxically impossible to
glaze: "glitter," a kind of sparkling light or luster. And, in an even
more puzzling sense, the object of sight and of representation may be
left out entirely. "Glitter" may be a verb, so that "Glazed —— Glitter"
becomes a sentence with an absent subject. To glitter: "To shine with
a brilliant but broken and tremulous light; to emit bright fitful flashes
of light; to gleam, sparkle."

As Irigaray formulates it, "fires and mirrors are beginning to radiate, sapping the evidence of reason at its base!" In her revision of
Plato's metaphor of the cave, where men look only at the representations, the shadows of a truth that is outside the cave, originating in
the sun, Irigaray suggests that the cave (as a traditionally female metaphor, marking the female's "void," the void that is inherently female)
is the place where representation itself is ignited, where its insistence

on "semblance" is undercut, and where semblances are made impossible to detect.

If, for Irigaray, the act of representation, from Plato to Freud, is a masculine act of mirroring (him)self, so that language becomes merely a mirror to re-create his own likeness, then the way out of this repetition and sameness is to transform the mirror (or the female) into a glass that refuses to reflect back but that catches images and objects of representation only to destroy them. The actual, possible "object," the female realm of whatever is to be represented, is, as Irigaray so eloquently concludes, "Elsewhere. Burning still" (1985a, p. 146).

So, for Stein, the absent object(s) glitter(s). The glittering involves both the igniting of traditional representation, and the beauty of a new, gleaming form of (non)representation. As Stein hints in "Glazed Glitter," "The change has come."

> There is no search. But there is, there is that hope and that interpretation and sometime, surely any is unwelcome, sometime there is breath and there will be a sinecure and charming very charming is that clean and cleansing. Certainly glittering is handsome and convincing. (Stein, 1945, p. 461)

"No search" ("no such"?) ("nonesuch"?) for an object may be precisely what allows for "hope" and "breath." Interpretation can still exist, but in a different form, in a less "searching" form ("search and destroy"?). Such interpretation would be not an analysis from a distance, but an enactment of the author's words. The reader would be not a searcher for the truth (Plato's sense of truth), of which these words are only the semblances, but a participant, engaged in the words and allowing their entity without attempting to press behind them to something else. In a sense, one would "Come eat it," as one voice invites us to do in "Lifting Belly." ("Come-pl-eat it"? Complete it?) This glaze is sweet. It covers its objects, but it allows us even greater delight in their devouring. The object may be impossible to find, but its "breath," literally its life and its inspiration, is "there," wherever the there is. Stein "cleanses" her art through such scattered fire. And, further, she conquers (convinces).

To turn once more, with a different insistence, to these "buttons":

if "buttons" suggest words, words that do not name things directly, they hint also at a more erotic aspect. A button may be any small or rounded body: a bud or a knob, or the disk of an electric bell. Children, one notes, are often called "buttons," as a term of endearment, and the term may be used for other loved creatures, or for parts of their bodies, as in a "button nose," or "belly button." The smallness of such a body suggests its capacity to be held and handled; the familiarity of the name suggests closeness and relationship.

In a more specific sense, *button* may call up images of the female body: the clitoris, or the nipple, or a more general sense of a physical "handle." The body, in a sense, is covered with buttons. And *Tender Buttons*, as a body of words, offers its buttons for our handling ("It certainly showed no obligation and perhaps if borrowing is not natural there is some use in giving" [Stein, 1945, p. 461]). The work itself can be "interpreted" as a female being, unseen but giving us handles on herself, not for our "search" of her body, but for our rendering of her original desire ("Nickel, what is nickel, it is originally rid of a cover").

Yet, of course, this new offering must make use of old language. As Stein says in "Poetry and Grammar,"

> Of course you might say why not invent new names new languages but that cannot be done. It takes a tremendous amount of inner necessity to invent even one word, one can invent imitating movements and emotions in sounds, and in the poetical language of some languages you have that ... but this has really nothing to do with language. Language as a real thing is not imitation either of sounds or colors or emotions it is an intellectual recreation and there is no possible doubt about it and it is going to go on being that as long as humanity is anything. (Stein, 1985, p. 238)

The words, Stein suggests, are already there. Invention is, apparently, not the issue. Yet her term *re-creation* is significant, for Stein may use an old language, but she also re-creates language by her new handling of it. In a sense, she is too modest here, for this re-creation, in a work like *Tender Buttons*, amounts to a new language, a language not only or primarily of sense but more emphatically of nonsense, not of reference but of nonreference, and not only of reason but also of the body.

One way of approaching Stein's re-creation of language in *Tender Buttons*, as in her other work, is through her playful igniting of metaphor. *Tender Buttons,* to an astonishing extent, seems to be crammed with metaphors and half-suggested metaphors, especially for female sexuality. It can, in certain ways, be decoded in this fashion. "A Substance in a Cushion" suggests, for example, with some interpretation, a finger in (or on) a female "cushion" of some sort: "a little groan grinding makes a trimming such a sweet singing trimming and a red thing not a round thing but a white thing, a red thing and a white thing" (Stein, 1945, p. 462). The "cushion" has a "cover," and is "very clean"; even when there is "dirt," the dirt is "clean where there is a volume," a word hinting at the water that Stein usually associates with female wetness or orgasm. Traditional metaphors for female sexuality abound throughout this work: "A Box," "A Piece" (of coffee), a "case," a red rose surrounded by a "gate," a "dress" (as in, a woman as a "skirt"), "a bag," "A Purse," "A Mounted Umbrella," a "cup," "Red Roses," "A shallow hole rose on red," food of all sorts, especially meat ("Roast Beef," "Mutton"), sugar, "Apple," "Tails" (!), "Fish," "Cake," "Custard," "Chicken," "Cream" (as in "peaches and cream," or "ice cream"), "Cucumber" (as in "cold as a cucumber") and so on. Volumes, literally, could be written (and I hope will be) about the images Stein uses for the female.

Yet what seems intriguing to me at this point is the way in which she entices us with all these potentially erotic objects and foods, with all these buttons, and then turns us around so that we become radically unsure of these metaphors. She seems to use them with hidden laughter, as if to say, "You think you can find me here, where I have always been said to be? Look again." The sense of enticement and invitation remains, but only in spite of the undercutting of our "search."

A good place to look for Stein's disruption of metaphor is her use of one of the oldest metaphors, and one that Stein clearly finds significant:

NOTHING ELEGANT

> A charm a single charm is doubtful. If the red is rose and there is a gate surrounding it, if inside is let in and there places change then certainly something is upright. It is earnest. (Stein, 1945, p. 464)

At first glance, our eye seizes on the red rose, "surround[ed]" by a

gate: an oddly straightforward image, not difficult to picture, especially with the memory of the Lady and the Unicorn tapestries, or
illustrations for *The Romance of the Rose*. One could argue for the female symbolism implicit in such an image, and for the male symbolism
in the addition of the "something" that is "upright" and "earnest."

Yet the metaphor slips from our grasp. "A single" meaning, like a
single charm, is "doubtful," with a singleness that links, in an Irigar-
ayan sense, to the uprightness of the phallic object. In fact, where is
the metaphor at all? "Rose" may be, not a noun, but an adjective,
modifying "red." The title warns us: there is nothing here, no thing.
The substitutions for nouns seem insistent: "it," "something." And the
locations seem oddly vague, even unimaginable: "inside is let in,"
"There," "places change." How can what is already inside be let in?
The logic breaks down in earnest. The "if" insists upon itself, a warn-
ing about doubtfulness.

As Irigaray might point out, this language mirrors conventional
language, just as *Speculum* mirrors Western philosophical thought
from Plato to Freud (from Freud to Plato). "The rose is red" meta-
morphoses, in this looking glass, into "the red is rose." In this reversal,
the original ground for the logic of metaphor is cut away. Instead of
the transparency of that windowing verb *is*, we are left with the in-
decipherability but liveliness of being ("is") itself. If language is in
some sense the clothing (the cloaking?) we wear, then Stein asks us to
look, with her, in the mirror, not the mirror of representation (representation, Irigaray's *mimetisme*), but the speculum that can undo
representation. This new red is "read"; it is a color, a figure, that finds
a locus in the act of reading words on a page, an act that involves no
"single charm." For if a charm originally was a song (*carmen*), and
especially "The chanting of a verse having magic power," we chant it
too, in an incantation that disrupts—literally, puts a spell on—metaphor as a defining act.

III

Yet, even as I state this with such certainty, I am compelled to acknowledge the limits urged upon my own critical, interpretive representation of this written "object." If "the rose is red" has become
"the red is rose," if writing has, in a sense, been turned inside out,

then surely my own attempts to say "this is that" and "that is this" must remain doubtful. Literary criticism has, in many ways, begun to question the mastery of the critic; yet Stein, I think, presses us further into this uncertainty than many of the most questioning critics feel willing to go. Her writing cannot even provide a rich field for criticism's deconstruction, since Stein herself has gone beyond deconstruction, to a written world where signs so clearly do detach themselves from things, and where so many forms of literary identity and authority are already undone.

Any serious attempt to interpret a work as opaque as *Tender Buttons* must involve, at its heart, an awareness of one's difference—from the writing, from other readers, even from other instances of one's own act of reading. The subjectivity of the reader, in other words, must be acknowledged—and perhaps not only acknowledged but valued as an integral part of interpretation. Another reader's interpretation, for instance, of a line like "Water astonishing and difficult altogether makes a meadow and a stroke," will of necessity be very different from mine; yet instead of thinking of this difference as distressing—as an indication simply of uncertainty or absence of significance—we might think of it as addition: one interpretation added to another and another, and all of these, perhaps, added to the words Stein has written. None is privileged; all have a voice. As Stein writes in another part of *Tender Buttons*:

> The whole thing is not understood and this is not strange considering that there is no education [read: the text has not "e-duced" us, led us to one place], this is not strange because having that certainty does show the difference in cutting, it shows that when there is turning there is no distress. (Stein, 1945, p. 478)

The "difference in cutting" (roast beef) suggests the difference each reader makes as he or she "cuts" into this writing, at the same time that it suggests the link between "cutting" and not understanding. Instead of "cutting," we might attempt (as I have attempted in this essay) a "turning"—toward?

Two pages later, in the same section (entitled "Roast Beef"), Stein says, "Claiming nothing, not claiming anything, not a claim in everything, collecting claiming, all this makes a harmony, it even makes a

succession" (Stein, 1945, p. 480). In "claiming nothing," in not trying
to cut into and possess our slice of roast beef, our image, our sequence
of words, we may still each make a claim; yet collecting these claimings
makes, not strife among our different "cuts," but "a harmony." In the
third section of *Tender Buttons,* Stein makes her invitation to all of us
even more audible:

> It is so very agreeable to hear a voice and to see all the
> signs of that expression.
>   Cadences, real cadences, real cadences and a quiet color.
> Careful and curved, cake and sober, all accounts and mix-
> ture, a guess at anything is righteous, should there be a call
> there would be a voice. (Stein, 1945, p. 504)

The "voice" heard here may be the voice of the writing, and our own
voices as well, which come to Stein's text with their own "cadences,"
"real cadences," each one springing from a different situation, a different "room," a different consciousness and process of consciousness.
"All accounts," all attempts to make sense, are invited: "a guess at
anything is righteous." Not right, but righteous: having its own dignity,
its own belief and value.

All this, of course, is not to say that interpretation is impossible.
Perhaps what we mean by interpretation must be transformed to include the kind of interpretation that is not "claiming anything," but is
guessing at "anything." This may involve a reading "in the darkness,"
where, instead of seeing with distanced clarity, we acknowledge that
we are groping, "Lying in a conundrum," placing ourselves not outside
the writing, or even within it, but to one side, placing our own writing
next to its writing. Perhaps then we may find a new way of participating in reading, which in any case is a labor of love. We add our
voices, in this way, to Stein's many voices, we place our words next to
hers. The mixture is profoundly, and seriously, pleasurable. In writing
(or "singing") with Stein, we participate in her pleasure. "In the midst
of writing. / In the midst of writing there is merriment."

References

Cixous, H. (1975). *La jeune née.* Paris: Union generale d'editions.
Cooke, B. W. (1979). Women alone stir my imagination: Lesbianism
    and the cultural tradition. *Signs* 4, p. 718–39.

De Koven, M. (1981). Gertrude Stein and modern painting: Beyond literary cubism. *Contemporary Literature* 22, pp. 81–95.

Fifer, E. (1979). Is flesh advisable? The interior theater of Gertrude Stein. *Signs* 4, p. 481. By permission of the University of Chicago Press. Copyright © 1979 by the University of Chicago Press.

Haas, R. B. (Ed.). (1971). *A primer for the gradual understanding of Gertrude Stein.* Los Angeles: Black Sparrow Press.

Hadas, P. W. (1979). Spreading the difference: One way to read Gertrude Stein's *Tender Buttons. Twentieth Century Literature* 24, pp. 57–75.

Irigaray, L. (1985a). *Speculum of the other woman* (G. Gill, Trans.). Ithaca: Cornell University Press.

———. (1985b). *This sex which is not one.* (C. Porter and C. Burke, Trans.). Ithaca: Cornell University Press.

Iser, W. (1974). *The implied reader: Patterns of communication in prose fiction from Bunyan to Beckett.* Baltimore: Johns Hopkins University Press.

Kristeva, J. (1980). *Desire in language: A semiotic approach to literature and art.* L. S. Roudiez (Ed.), T. Gova, A. Jardin and L. S. Roudiez (Tr.). New York: Columbia University Press.

Marks, E., and de Courtivron, I. (Eds.). (1980). *New French feminism: An anthology.* Amherst: University of Massachusetts Press.

Perloff, M. (1979). Poetry as word-system: The art of Gertrude Stein. *American Poetry Review* 8, pp. 33–43.

Rule, J. (1975). *Lesbian images.* New York: Doubleday.

Stein, G. (1945). *Tender Buttons.* In C. Van Vachten (Ed.), *Selected writings of Gertrude Stein.* New York: Random House. Copyright © 1962 by Random House, Inc.

———. (1953). *Bee time vine and other pieces (1913–1927).* New Haven: Yale University Press.

———. (1980). Lifting Belly. In R. Kostelanetz (Ed.), *The Yale Gertrude Stein.* New Haven: Yale University Press. Copyright © 1980 by Yale University Press.

———. (1985). *Lectures in America.* Boston: Beacon Press. Reprinted by permission of Random House, Inc.

Steiner, W. (1978). *Exact resemblance to exact resemblance.* New Haven: Yale University Press.

Stimpson, C. (1977). The mind, the body, and Gertrude Stein. *Critical Inquiry* 3, pp. 484–506.

Sutherland, D. (1971). Gertrude Stein and the twentieth century. In
    R. B. Haas, *A primer for the gradual understanding of Gertrude Stein.*
    Los Angeles: Black Sparrow Press.
Wittig, M. (1985). *Les guerilleres* (D. Le Vay, Trans.). Boston: Beacon
    Press.

PART III

Self as Process

"Individuality," in fact, did not make its first recorded appearance until the early seventeenth century, apparently in response to the new development in the meaning of "individual." The history of this latter word is remarkable; it underwent almost a complete reversal of meaning. For "individual" as an adjective, two related meanings, first recorded in Middle English, became obsolete during the last half of the seventeenth century: (1) "One in substance or essence, indivisible"; (2) "inseparable." Then two modern meanings were introduced during the seventeenth century: (3) "Existing as a separate indivisible entity; numerically one, single, particular, special"; (4) "Distinguished from others by attributes of its own." The change from the second to the third and fourth meanings, from being inseparable to being separate and distinct, is a radical one. It describes the transition to the modern experience of identity.

Jim Swan, 1985, p. 159

MODERN IDENTITY is "distinguished from others by attributes of its own" and it is particular, unique, and special. This conception of the individual self is familiar and ordinary in Western societies now; it also is the foundation of most process or systems theories (e.g., structural and cognitive theories) of development in the human studies. The vision of an independent and responsible person who exists as separate from a cosmic order is fundamental in our reasoning about freedom of choice and intentionality. What is remarkable in the quotation above is to recognize the recent inception of this idea, and the change in human awareness that must have precipitated it.

In general, Western psychologies and religions promote ideals for autonomous, intentional, and separate individuality. They espouse a model of development that rests on an organic or biological analogy: successive differentiation and integration toward a goal. The goal is adaptation, the survival of the individual in interaction with the environment, not the dependence of the individual on some larger scheme or structure. Within our currently dominant culture, we have little use for explanations of selfhood that locate it within a transcendental order, a cosmic system of symbolic meaning, as if such explanations would restrict the enlightened rationality that has permeated our collective vision. Assuming ourselves to be masters of our own destinies, we are wary of explanations that might appear to limit our freedom or control.

Essays in this section, which approach the topic of self as a "process," present arguments from both the premodern and the modern meanings of *individual*. The modern view of self in process, formulated around a model of adaptation in which the self is the modus operandi, aims toward the best possible individual outcome of purposive action. Frederic Levine, Robert Kravis, and Philip Lichtenberg present arguments for particular theoretical formulations of self *experience* in psychotherapy that advocate the vitality of independence. Their therapeutic goal is the attainment of subjective responsibility and intentionality, the individual as actor and agent who is striving for meaning and coherence.

On the other end of the spectrum of individuation, a unified self is situated within a process of development in relation to larger principles in which it is a component part. Jungian psychological theory offers a conceptualization of self that may be cast in either the premodern or the modern version of individuation. The modern interpretation of Jung's archetype of self is to understand it as a basic organizing principle of instinctual-emotional responses. In this interpretation, congruent with Jung's later (1935–61) archetypal theory, the self is a predisposition for unity or coherence in the human personality. (It is more like an "innate releasing mechanism" than a Kantian category.) The premodern interpretation of the archetype of self, congruent with Jung's earlier work on complex and individuation (1900–34), is of an indivisible essence, something like a "soul," which is embedded in the larger psychoid nature of the universe. (See Young-Eisendrath, 1985, for a fuller account of Jung's theory of self.) This self is a transcendental category of human existence. Although the latter account appears scientifically implausible, we remind ourselves that our pervasive modern bias is decidedly in favor of an achieved individuality, characterized by unique and independent mastery.

Both Shirley Sanders and Michael Fordham argue for the a priori unity of self, from different evidence and perspectives. Sanders writes about the *experience* of hypnosis, drawing parallels between normal waking states and hypnotic states of dissociation and coherence.

Fordham, on the other hand, argues for a *unity* of self innately given. He postulates, from observational studies of mother-infant pairs and from his clinical work in Jungian analysis, the integrity of self at birth. Asserting that individuality is prior to relationship, Fordham develops a theory of "de-integration" of a unitary self to allow formation of images of oneself, others, and the world. Although the self is initially a coherent experience of being, it depends on an appropriate and supportive interpersonal-cultural environment to de-integrate successfully into the component representations of personality.

William Caspary approaches his discussion of a unified self from an ethical perspective. Like Blasi and Oresick, Caspary desires a theory of self that will support the experience and action of ethical integrity. He suggests the term *core-self* for the underlying unity of personality that may form through introjection and projection, this being distinct from self-images and self-representations.

The next essay is a definitional project—Joseph Redfearn's review of terms and concepts that fit within various schools and systems of thought concerning the self and its nearby relatives. He distills and clarifies some assumptions that underlie different definitions of the same terms.

Finally, we encounter two essays that provide accounts of transcendence in theories of self, but from two very different directions. Albert Outler's essay has something in common with the modern version of individuality as he surveys the struggles in Christian theology to define *Humanum* between the tensions of the Hebraic embodied self and the Greek multivarious self, between original divine plan and inadequate human achievement. The Christian theory of self falls between premodern and modern individuation: a self contained within a cosmic order, but also "free" to will and choose.

Streng's essay presents a wholly different theological orientation to self, through the writings of the Buddhist philosopher Nargarjuna. Here self is represented as a wholly dynamic process that can touch the ground of all existence but does not tarry there. The paradoxical image of "standing well while not having stood anywhere" expresses the experience of selfhood from the perspective of Nargarjuna.

It also expresses the nature of the "epistemic subject" of Piaget's psychology, traced out in its expression and assumptions by John Broughton in the first essay in this section. The Piagetian and Buddhist epistemologies of self are strikingly similar transindividual contributions to a theory of self. Above all, Piaget traced the process of a subject coming to know the world and its own subjectivity. His refusal to connect the structure of metasubjectivity with individual subjectivity leaves him open to philosophical criticism about his inconsistent structuralism: a subjective consciousness without a subject. Piaget was "not at all comfortable with the concept of consciousness . . . ," says Broughton, who adds that Piaget, ". . . is consistently derogatory in his references to philosophical psychologies of consciousness" (pp. 283–84).

Nevertheless, Piaget locates himself in a transcendent world, beyond the biopsychological constraints of many of his American interpreters and followers. Broughton brings us to a clear understanding of the radical constructivism of Piaget, astoundingly similar to that of Nargarjuna: "in the very motivation for the construct 'epistemic subject' is contained a simultaneous affirmation of the transindividual and refusal of the transcendental" (p. 285).

References

Swan, J. (1985). Difference and silence: John Milton and the question of gender. In *The (M)other tongue*. S. Nelson Garner, C. Kahane, and M. Sprengnether (Eds.). Ithaca: Cornell University Press.

Young-Eisendrath, P. (1985). Reconsidering Jung's psychology. *Psychotherapy, 22*:03, 501–15.

SELF AND EXPERIENCE

CHAPTER 12

Piaget's Concept of the Self

JOHN M. BROUGHTON

> The subject is reduced to nothing by its hypostasis, by making a
> thing of what is not a thing. . . . The subject is the more the less it
> is, and it is the less the more it credits itself with objective being.
> (Adorno, 1978, p. 509)

Constructivism, Structuralism, and Empiricism

THERE ARE a variety of terms by which Piaget makes reference
to the problem of the self or subject. Toward the end of Piaget's
"structural" period of thinking, however, the time at which his theory
is generally viewed as coming to maturity, his various notions concerning the self converged upon the concept of the "epistemic subject."

This term denotes something quite different from concepts of the
self currently at large on the North American scene. Although Piaget
himself was more or less oblivious to the fact, his concept of the "active
subject" (e.g., Piaget, 1971a) made possible a powerful critique of the
empiricist notion of "self-concept." The latter has occupied the rank
of orthodoxy in North American psychology since the late 1950s, having assumed authority by the supposed demonstration of certain obvious inadequacies in the prescientific notion of an immanent
substance or transcendent soul (Broughton, 1980).

Piaget's interpretation of the self as knowing subject is superior in
a number of ways to the self-concept version. These advances derive
largely from Piaget's willingness to imbed the theoretical conception
of the psychological self within a substantial "metatheoretical" context.
This involved an explicit philosophical statement of how knowledge
was to be construed. Piaget (1971b, p. 103) demonstrated the concep-

tual advantages of dignifying the subject with a certain spontaneous activity, as opposed to confining it to the passive role allotted within empiricism.

This epistemologically grounded vision of the knowing subject enabled Piaget to avoid the philosophical problems of relativism, nominalism, conformism, and infinite regress inherent in the almost self-contradictory notion that the self is nothing but a view of itself (Broughton and Riegel, 1977). Piaget's account appears more coherent because it lacks such clear contradictions. It also preserves for the self the humanist virtues of objectivity, rationality, autonomy, identity, and developmental potential (Broughton, 1981a). Nevertheless, there is a peculiar paradox in the fact that Piaget (e.g., 1970a) aligns himself with precisely that paradigm which itself arose in opposition to these humanist virtues—structuralism. It is in his book *Structuralism* that the idea of the epistemic subject first came to the attention of English-speaking psychologists. It was the structuralist movement in the French-speaking countries that brought the topic of subjectivity back to center stage in the ongoing drama of the human sciences, but with the intention of destroying it. Despite several similarities between genetic epistemology and French structuralism (Gardner, 1972, 1983), the former departed from the latter in being concerned primarily with the refutation of empiricist epistemology (Piaget, 1952, 1972; Piaget and Inhelder, 1969) rather than with the elimination of the "self-centered" conceptualization of rationality embodied in the humanistic tradition (Broughton, 1981b).

Central to Piaget's project, in fact, was the rescuing of the subject and its constructive activity as the only way to account for the fact that reason develops. While the biological aspect of his theory, preoccupied with adaptation, suggests a focus on the empirical object, its mathematical aspect (often downplayed and poorly understood by others), with its concern for necessity, indicates his concern with the subject. On one occasion he even went so far as to assert that "psychology is knowledge of the subject and his subjectivity," (Piaget, 1971b, p. 128). Vis-à-vis French structuralists, he clarified (like a good analyst) the difference between their death wish and actual moribundity: "'Structures' have not been the death of the subject or its activities" (Piaget, 1970a, p. 39).

His addition of the phrase "or its activities"—at first glance superfluous, at least from a logical point of view—suggests what is confirmed in his other writings: the very existence of the subject is to be identified with its agency. Selfhood and individuality are both connected rather directly to the transformation of cognitive structures through engagement with the world. This activity of the knowing subject is the very condition of the possibility of constructivism (Piaget, 1950, pp. 278–94; cf. Lewis, 1979). Piaget's effort to displace the Parisian variety of structuralism with the Genevan one hinges on this willful image of the self, and therefore turns out to be continuous with his lifelong argument against empiricism and its bleak vision of unilateral subjection to the objective world.

Epistemic Subject Is Not the Individual Psychological Subject

In his work prior to the 1960s, Piaget frequently appears to equate the subject with the individual person, treating the latter chiefly in terms of its capacity as a biological organism. This tendency was appropriated and exaggerated by the early North American interpreters of Piaget's work, such as Hunt (1961) and Flavell (1963). Nevertheless, Piaget's preferred strategy, especially from the 60s onward, was one that moved in the opposite direction, toward identifying the characteristics of a universal subject, a unitary and natural human tendency toward objectivity. This "epistemic subject"[1] represented "what there is in common with all subjects":

> The most general coordinations of the whole system of actions translate that which all subjects have in common and therefore refer to a universal or epistemic subject, not an individual one. (Beth and Piaget, 1966, p. 254, author's translation)

What is noticeable in this quotation is the fact that the term *subject* is employed in two contrasting ways: first, in reference to the individual object of psychological observation, and second, as the agency implied by the actions of those objectified individuals. As Gillieron (1980) has been at pains to point out, the epistemic subject is, strictly speaking, suprapsychological; it is not to be confused with the psychological subject or the competent subject (in the sense of someone in possession of a certain logical competence). The psychological subject is at best the "theater" (Piaget, 1967a, p. 1143) of the equilibration process generating and underwriting the necessity experienced as the consequence of the norms regulating thought. Structures cannot be simply and directly observed in a psychological subject—they are structures of the epistemic subject. The issue of what the subject is conscious of does not arise in the latter case, only in the former ("The psychological subject is centered on the conscious me" [Battro, 1966, p. 173, author's translation]). This is why Piaget's activities as a genetic psychologist, aimed at the solution of epistemological problems, should not be confounded with the conduct of developmental psychologists, who focus only on individual subjects and "want to understand specifically the answers children give in the experimental situation" (Coll, Gillieron, Guyon, Marti, and Ventouras-Spycher, 1976, p. 29).

Problems with the Duality of
Epistemic and Psychological Subject

Piaget's writings suggest that the coherence of the concept of the epistemic subject depends upon contrasting it rather sharply with the individual subject. However, as the logician Borel (1978) has pointed out, he seems to have had some difficulty in keeping the two distinct. In fact, in the very act of trying to set up the opposition between particular and universal subjects, he admits a psychological clause into the core of the definition of the suprapsychological:

> What they call the subject is undermined. Thus, in the first place, structuralism calls for a differentiation between the individual subject, who does not enter at all, and the epistemic subject, that cognitive nucleus which is common to all subjects at the same level. (Piaget, 1970a, p. 139)

Here, the phrase "at the same level" represents that part of the definition of the epistemic subject that implicates the realm of genetic psychology. This phrase serves to remind us that it is precisely Piaget's self-professed innovation in conceptualizing structure to point out its existence at a variety of levels. In the Piagetian scheme, each development in the objective understanding of the world entails a corresponding advance in the subject. This is not to say merely that, with increments in what is known, the content of the subject expands. Rather, much as development alters qualitatively the form of reality apprehended, making it more objective, so too this development transforms the subject, elevating it to a distinctly higher level of activity (Piaget, 1950, pp. 286–87). Thus, any discussion of "the subject" must include a specification of the degree of developmental advance attained.

If one can be permitted to distinguish in Piaget's work—as in Freud's, for example—the *metatheory* from the *theory*, the metatheoretical problem of keeping the particular and universal subjects distinct is found to be duplicated at the theoretical level. Piaget liked to demonstrate how the scientific study of the ontogenetic process itself contributes to the resolution of philosophical issues. One of his most interesting examples is a passage where he mapped the superiority of the epistemological over the individual subject onto the preoperational and concrete operational stages of development:

> I realized that we were here concerned above all with a question of levels in the activities of the subject. Irreversibility is connected with the consciousness of the individual subject. . . . On the other hand, the discovery of operational reversibility marks the constitution of the epistemological subject. (Piaget, 1971b, p. 108)

Here, we see Piaget appears to make the universal subject accessible to the same experimental observation that is employed with individual subjects, if only that observation pursue the individual subject to the end of its development.

At this point, one begins to wonder whether genetic epistemology does not require two methods, rather than one. Piaget (1970b) himself stressed that genetic psychology is only one-half of the work, the other being the historical reconstruction of the progress of science. Typically, we think of the history of science as the progress of a more or less unified rationality, rather than the mere accumulation of individual efforts, and so the historical method would seem ideally fitted to the examination of the epistemic subject and its coming to be. But Piaget repeatedly discredited the historical method, arguing that "history is always incomplete" (Piaget, 1970b, cited in Looft and Svoboda, 1975) or even impossible, since historical transformations are "not available to us" (Piaget, 1970a, p. 13).

Moreover, he claimed that the historical half of genetic epistemology was not necessary for the identification of the characteristics of the epistemic subject. This characterization could be arrived at through the study of individual subjects. How could this be, given the sharp distinction that he made between psychological and universal levels? His answer: numbers. Given that a sufficient quantity of individuals were examined (the figure of 100 is mentioned [Piaget, 1971b]) to preclude idiosyncrasies, and that individuals were sampled across the full course of their progress from less active to more active subjects, then the regularities of the epistemic subject could be discerned reliably.

The generous soul here feels pressed to suppose that Piaget did not mean to say that reversible operational thought turns the individual subject into the epistemic subject. Far from it, for if that were the case it would not be necessary to examine more than one individual in an experiment. But, then, what is the distinction between "epistemological subject" and "epistemic subject"? In the important debate between Piaget and Ricoeur (Fraisse et al., 1966; Fetz, 1985), the two terms are used interchangeably.

Perhaps another way of stating the problem in Piaget's account of the difference between the psychological and the suprapsychological is the following: Why should we run the risk of *reifying* an account of the general properties instantiated in particular instances, lending to this account the properties of an existing subject that has certain "effects" played out in the psychological domain? Otherwise said, how are we to tell if the epistemic subject is a universal of nature to be invoked in an explanatory role, or just a theoretical universal of descriptive status (Borel, 1978)?

With respect to this question of reification, one fears, with Vonèche (1980, 1986), that in this case Piaget's strategy of approaching recondite philosophical issues by "naturalizing" their terms may permit a certain interdisciplinary elegance, yet still lack sufficient justification. With respect to the general issue of the distinction between the psychological and suprapsychological, the conclusion suggests something problematic in the very way that Piaget tried to conceptualize the metaphysical relationship between particular and universal, the many and the one. Certainly, in his approach to the topic of the subject he again flouted the historical task and, at the same time, showed his disrespect for the discipline of academic philosophy. Rather than admit the limitations of scientific method in the development of meta-theory, he flouted the scholarly tradition of philosophers who at least attempt a reconnaissance of the convoluted history of thinking in an area before announcing their own position on the subject.

The Epistemic Subject Is Not the Transcendental Subject

In *Biology and Knowledge* (1971a), Piaget explains that his demotion of the individual psychological subject does not mean that, in order to preserve the quality of transindividuality, he is willing to be led by Kant down the primrose path to a transcendental subject:

> All philosophers in search of an absolute have had recourse to some transcendental subject, something on a higher plane than man and much higher than "nature," so that truth, for them, is to be found way beyond any spatiotem-poral and physical contingencies, and nature becomes in-telligible in an intemporal or eternal perspective. But then the question is whether one can possibly jump over one's own shadow and thus reach the "Subject" in oneself, with-out its remaining "human, all too human," as Nietzsche put it. . . . Thus, what we must try to do here is not to get away from nature, for no one can escape nature. . . . As the epistemological problem is to know how science is possible, then what we must do, before having recourse to a tran-scendental organization, is to fathom all the resources of the immanent organization. (p. 362)

Thus, what Ricoeur (1974) said of structuralism in general—that it is "a Kantianism without a transcendental subject"—would appear also to be true of its genetic variety in particular. This should not surprise us since the Kantian subject functions to unify consciousness, and Piaget (1976), operating within Claparede's pragmatic framework, is not at all comfortable with that concept of consciousness. It is precisely because "le sujet psychologique est centré sur le moi conscient" (Bat-tro, 1966, p. 173) that the epistemic subject is distinguished so sharply from it. Piaget (e.g., 1971b) is consistently derogatory in his references to philosophical psychologies of consciousness. He certainly shows no interest in accounting for that subjective unity of consciousness that was the raison d'être of the transcendental subject (Broughton, 1981c).

As Beth and Piaget (1966) point out, the epistemic subject possesses a universality that does not come from outside but is inherent in the biological organization of the most general coordinations of action:

> The epistemic subject (in opposition to the psychological subject) is that which all subjects have in common, since the general coordinations of actions permit a universal which is that of biological organization itself. (pp. 304–5, author's translation)

Nevertheless, Piaget (1971a) reassures us that to construe truth immanently rather than transcendentally is not "to reduce it to a biocentric organization" (p. 362). Rather,

> If we seek the explanation of rational organization within the living organization *including its overtakings [depassements]*, we are attempting to interpret knowledge in terms of its own construction, which is no longer an absurd method since knowledge is *essentially construction*. (Piaget, 1971a, p. 362)

North American commentators tend to interpret Piaget lopsidedly as "biocentric" in his epistemology. But we should not forget that, in the genetic epistemology, the naturalistic element of the biological is held in productive tension with the idealistic element of mathematical logic. Piaget is not forced to fall back on biology in order to dispense with the transcendental. In the field of logic, the transcendental position has been difficult to sustain in the light of the various demonstrations (by Gödel, Church, and Tarski, for example) of the multiplicity of formalisms and the limits of formalization. In this context, the idea of construction has emerged (Ladrière, 1982), and Piaget gets his psychological constructivism as much from the logicians' conclusion as from biologists' concepts of adaptation (Gillieron, 1984). But it is precisely the act of construction that presupposes the activity of a subject and that brings the subject back to center stage in Piaget's theory.

Thus, in the very motivation for the construct "epistemic subject" is contained a simultaneous affirmation of the transindividual and refusal of the transcendental. A transcendental subject is no more acceptable to Piaget than are transcendental objects or essences. Rather, "subjectivity and objectivity emerge as epistemic categories in natural minds, after having emerged as practical categories in living organisms" (Gillieron, 1984, p. 14). As an adjective, *epistemic*, then, should be understood as displacing *transcendental*, not qualifying it.

The Epistemic Subject Is the Operational Subject

In a nutshell, Piaget intends his epistemic subject to be a transindividual universal, immanent in the constructive functioning of the knowing process. It is the specifically operational part of the self:

> The always fragmentary and frequently distorting grasp of consciousness must be set apart from the achievements of the subject, what he knows is the outcome of his intellectual activity, not its mechanisms. Now after such precipitation of the "me," the "loved," from the "I," there remains the subject's "operations," that which he "draws out" from the general coordinations of his acts by reflective abstraction. (Piaget, 1970a, p. 139)

Provocatively, Piaget compares this "operational" self to God, who is "unceasingly constructing ever 'stronger' systems" (1970a, p. 141). The omnipotent and omnipresent epistemic subject is not an entity—about this Piaget is vehement—but rather consists in the functional invariants of the knowing mechanism (assimilation and accommodation) that define the abstract locale of the structuring act. In brief, "The self is like the centre of one's own activity" (Piaget, 1967b, p. 65). At length:

> It might seem that the foregoing account makes the subject disappear to leave only the "impersonal and general," but this is to forget that on the plane of knowledge ... the subject's activity calls for a continual "de-centering" without which he cannot become free from his spontaneous intel-

lectual egocentricity. This "de-centering" makes the subject
enter upon, not so much an already available and therefore
external universality, as an uninterrupted process of coordinating and setting in reciprocal relations. It is the latter
process which is the true "generator" of structures as constantly under construction and reconstruction. The subject
exists because, to put it very briefly, the being of structures
consists in their coming to be, that is, their being "under
construction." . . . In the realm of the natural structures,
the denial of activity leads to the postulation of an entity—
the subject, society, life, or what have you—which might
serve as "structure of all structures" since . . . structure can
live only in systems. Now as we have come to see more
clearly through Gödel but knew long before, the ideal of a
structure of all structures is unrealisable. The *subject* cannot, therefore, be the *a priori* underpinning of a finished
posterior structure; rather it is a center of activity. (Piaget,
1970a, pp. 139–42)

The Elimination of the Subject

Here we arrive at what is arguably the central paradox of Piaget's
position: the subject is a center of activity, but it is the product of
decentering. If the subject, qua activity, is generated and augmented
through decentration, then it is the *object* of decentration, not its subject. It would seem to be the case that the more successful decentration
is, the less the subject can be said to be its agent.

How are we to comprehend the ontological status of that which, by
the very activity that is its definitive characteristic, tends to displace
itself? Does it go into exile, or simply disappear? Derrida (1970) has
astutely summarized this ex-centricity of the subject as implicated in
the modern concept of structure:

Structure—or rather the structurality of structure—although it has always been involved in Western philosophy,
has always been neutralized or reduced, and this by a process of giving it a center or referring it to a point of presence, a fixed origin. . . . And even today the notion of a
structure lacking any center represents the unthinkable itself. Nevertheless, the center also closes off the free play it

> opens up and makes possible. . . . Thus it has always been thought that the center, which is by definition unique, constituted that very thing within a structure which governs the structure, while escaping structurality. This is why classical thought concerning the structure could say that the center is, paradoxically, *within* the structure and *outside* it. The center is at the center of the totality, and yet, since the center does not belong to the totality (is not a part of the totality), the totality *has its center elsewhere*. The center is not the center. (p. 248)

The asymptote of developmental progress is the total removal of the subject. Activity, then, turns out to be the antithesis of subjectivity, not just by turning away from it, but by eliminating the subject that is its condition of possibility. This should not surprise us, given that cognition is defined as a cognizing of purely objectified relationships between objects or actions (Blasi, 1976). Gardner (1970), in his study of the cognitive approach in both Piaget and Lévi-Strauss, concludes, "Thus, while neither neglects subject-subject relations wholly, subjects are viewed primarily as human objects. This perspective lends a certain one-sidedness to their accounts of the mind" (p. 362).

The only alternative seems to be to relocate the subject on another plane, at one remove. But where is it removed to? Whereas a concrete subjectivity, even though it is not a substantial entity, can nevertheless be located "somewhere," surely a pure generality can be located "nowhere in particular." If this nowhere, by virtue of its generality, is taken to subsume the particularities of lived subjectivities, then Piaget seems perilously close to the noumenal world of Kant's transcendental subject, precisely where he claimed he was not. Piaget did not want to entertain the possibility of a subject that was nonempirical, since that would be to attempt the futile task of "jumping over one's own shadow," as he put it. But if the epistemic subject, being the principle of structuring activity, "governs the structure, while escaping structurality," how is it to be known at all?

One wonders if the crucial inferential steps in Piaget's argument are really sound ones. For example, on closer examination, the "jumping over one's own shadow" and "structure of all structures" passages above—from the key metatheoretical texts *Biology and Knowledge* and *Structuralism* respectively—are rather casually speculative and fall short of the usual criteria for a convincing philosophical argument.

They depend for their plausibility on a variety of rhetorical devices—allusions, images, suppressed premises, implicit correspondences, and unsubstantiated implications (note the loose use of "therefore" in the second passage). No justification is given, for example, for the suggestion that Kant's subject is equivalent to the "structure of all structure" or that the feasibility of such a subject is therefore undermined by Gödel's theorem.

Noting that the epistemic subject is significant for a genetic epistemology precisely because of its promise of uniting the interdisciplinary "circle of the sciences," Gruber and Vonèche (1977) express the further fear that if the epistemic subject is not to be admitted as transcendental, genetic epistemology will fail as a coherent account of knowing, throwing us back upon an empiricist epistemology:

> Such a universal creates a tension between the empiricistic viewpoint, according to which all the separate sciences speak the same language, and the idealistic one, according to which they are united by an external universal. In other words, the status of the epistemic subject is unclear. Is it an external agent transcending the variety of scientific experiences? Or is it simply the catalyst of the synthesis of the simples expected by empiricism? (p. 738)

Piaget's voyage in quest of universal knowledge takes him through this dire strait between the Scylla of transcendence and the Charybdis of immanence. Given Piaget's lifelong opposition to empiricism, we suspect that he would consider the first of these the lesser of the two evils. However, to allow the epistemic subject that transcendental status which Kant and Husserl ascribed to it would be to founder in precisely that epistemology of the a priori that he built his boat to escape.

What Is the Subjectivity of the Epistemic Subject?

Even if we were to admit the naturalist reinterpretation that Piaget gives of the Kantian subject, we would still be left with an ambiguity in Piaget's accounts of the epistemic subject. If the epistemic subject represents an actual subject rather than a shorthand way of talking about a descriptive universal, then the question arises as to whether or not it possesses subjectivity. Answering this question is particularly difficult in the context of Piaget's theory, since in his discussions of the subject he manages to refrain from dealing with subjectivity as such. For example, in the quotation from Beth and Piaget above, it is entirely unclear whether we are to understand the use of *sujet* as from the point of view of the subject or from that of the observer.

Borel (1978) notes this ambiguity and interprets Piaget as saying that the qualities of the epistemic subject are not only objective but also subjective. In other words, the epistemic subject is involved in its own reflective self-conceptualization:

> In describing and explaining the modalities and level of development of the supports of action in terms of the degree of decentration of their activity, the subject (epistemic) that constructs the concept of the epistemic subject sees itself implicated by the meaning of what it has constructed. (p. 218, author's translation)

Note, here, that when an attempt is made to conceptualize subjectivity within the Piagetian scheme, it is more or less confined to reflective awareness conceived in a limited way as rational reconstruction (Döbert, Habermas, and Nunner-Winkler, 1986), so the question amounts to inquiring whether or not the epistemic subject knows itself.

Borel's leap is an interesting speculation, but as far as I can tell it represents a step beyond Piaget's account. Piaget nowhere indicates that consciousness is a characteristic of the epistemic subject. Moreover, as we have seen, he is inclined to associate consciousness with the psychological subject, and to use the concept of the epistemic subject to play down the significance of consciousness (see Piaget, 1971b). In that text, he argues that it is one thing to be conscious of what one is and quite another to understand how one came to be. There is no evidence in Piaget's account of the epistemic subject that its structure, in principle, could yield for it an account of how that structure originated. In this sense, such a subject has *had* a genesis, but cannot *own* it.

At the heart of genetic structuralism, unfortunately, is the negation of memory. Development conceived as progressive formalization is incompatible with the maintenance of biographical integrity. Piaget's (individual) subjects have no biography; they are not only genderless and generationless, but also lacking in personhood. His theory no more allows for life history than it does for history. Each reflection and rational reconstruction that makes the prior structure content to the higher form entails an erasure of the meaning of that prior structure and a dissociation from the memory of each experience constructed in its terms. Since, within progressivist psychology, nothing is lost in a developmental transformation, there is no rational need to recall the past. The past is a distortion and to return to it would only be regressive. To paraphrase E. E. Cummings "Down we forgot as up we grew" (Cummings, 1954, p. 370) is the fundamental norm of life.

The Politics of Development

Subjectivity has a history that is subject to conscious apprehension, not just formalization (Habermas, 1973; Döbert, Habermas, and Nunner-Winkler, 1986). Subjectivity therefore deserves, as much as objectivity, to be treated developmentally. But then we are pressed to the conclusion that Piaget's supposedly developing subject has no subjectivity. The epistemic subject, and the tale told of its coming to be, represent the evolution and formal upgrading of an abstract system.

Under present historical conditions, in which organized systems and their complex forms of adaptation dominate all social and even cultural forms, including language itself (Broughton, 1986a), the epistemic subject would appear quite similar to the general form of society itself. Given that Piaget sedulously avoids any theory of society, despite his operational psychology of face-to-face interaction (Piaget, 1967c; Kitchener, 1981), he is rather vulnerable to such a criticism.

If the epistemic subject resembles the institutionalized form of contemporary society, it would be hard to distinguish it from political authority itself. In this era of obsession with "national security," Piaget's (1970a) phrase "unceasingly constructing ever 'stronger' systems" (p. 141) seems an apt description of both an epistemic subject and a defense policy. As we know from recent experience (Thompson, 1981; Broughton and Zahaykevich, 1982), the ideology and practice of increasing the strength of a system occurs to the detriment of its inner life. A busy "center of activity" is hardly likely to be a good listener. The negation of subjectivity represented by the epistemic subject is understandable, then, as the function of the state in operating upon, coordinating, and regulating its "subjects" rather than understanding and responding to their subjective needs and concerns.[2]

Such a "center of activity" is indeed the "external agent" that Gruber and Vonèche feared—an objective authority visited upon not only the individual subject but also upon the course of any scientific inquiry. In a centripetal flow of power, each individual agent pursues its own adaptation only in the context of a central construction of adaptiveness itself. Such authority requires no coersion; it is willingly adopted. Precisely in the exhilaration of rising to higher and higher levels of "activity" each citizen subordinates himself or herself to a given, "natural" form of organization.

Under this interpretation, the particular authority of Piaget's theory is at one with the general form of political authority. It represents for the system at large the normative structure of psychological construction. In presenting socialization as "development," it urges the reproduction of the activity of the system in each newly developing child and the reproduction of the norms of that activity in each newly educated developmental psychologist.

Piaget's comparison of the epistemic subject to God may not have been an illusion but one of his deepest insights into the coordination of his own actions. As for the remaining school of Piagetians, one can only hope, in Borel's words, that "the subject that constructs the concept of the epistemic subject sees itself implicated by the meaning of what it has constructed."[3]

Notes

1. Furth (in press) has recently cast doubt upon the existence of this concept, arguing that it is not to be found in Piaget's own work but, rather, represents an "in-house tag current in Geneva" (ms. p. 14). The quotation below should reassure us that this was not the case, as should the various entries in the authoritative *Dictionnaire d'épistémologie génétique* (Battro, 1966). Furth's objection is all the more puzzling since my own search for the first introduction of the term *epistemic subject* in the English language suggests that it was Furth (1969) himself who was responsible!

2. On the historical and ideological origins of this systematic subordination of subjectivity, affect, and the body in Western thought, see Broughton, 1985.

3. Piaget's insistence that subjects act primarily on natural objects and not other subjects serves to conceal the fact that modern life and work are almost

entirely concerned with regulating systems of people. One cannot plausibly argue that it is only their actions that are controlled, unless one wants to return to Cartesian dualism. Of course, the fact that within bureaucratic organizations people tend to be depersonalized and treated as things lends a certain validity to Piaget's depersonalized theory (Vonèche, 1986; Broughton, 1986b, 1986c).

This essay is dedicated to the memory of Emil Oestereicher, whose untimely, though peaceful, death has increased our need for thoughtful exercises in the critical appropriation of Piaget's work. I have fond recollections, Emil, of your hospitality—both intellectual and otherwise.

The writing of this essay was facilitated by conversations with Emil, and also by the stimulation and encouragement of my colleagues Augusto Blasi, Susan Buck-Morss, Hans Furth, Christine Gillieron, Howard Gruber, Adrienne Harris, David Ingleby, Richard Kitchener, Deanna Kuhn, David Lichtenstein, Pierre Moessinger, Leon Rapaport, Jonas Soltis, Edmund Sullivan, Jacques Vonèche, Rob Wozniak, and Jim Youniss.

References

Adorno, T. W. (1978). Subject and object. In A. Arato and E. Gebhardt (Eds.), *The essential Frankfurt School reader*. New York: Urizen.

Apostel, L. (in press). The unknown Piaget: From the theory of exchange and cooperation toward the theory of knowledge. *New Ideas in Psychology, 4*(1).

Battro, A. M. (1966). *Dictionnaire d'épistémologie génétique*. Paris: Presses Universitaires de France.

Beth, E. W., and Piaget, J. (1966). *Épistémologie mathématique et psychologie*. Paris: Presses Universitaires de France.

Blasi, A. (1976). The concept of personality in developmental theory. In J. Loevinger, *Ego development*. San Francisco: Jossey-Bass.

Borel, M.-J. (1978). *Discours de la logique et logique du discours*. Lausanne: Editions l'Age d'Homme.

Broughton, J. M. (1980). Psychology and the history of the self: From substance to function. In R. W. Rieber and K. W. Salzinger (Eds.), *Psychology: Theoretical-historical perspectives*. New York: Academic.

————. (1981a). The divided self in adolescence. *Human Development, 24*(1), 13–32.

————. (1981b). Piaget's structural developmental psychology, I: Structuralism. *Human Development, 24*(2), 78–109.

———. (1981c). Piaget's structural developmental psychology. *Human Development, 24*(5), 320–46.

———. (1985). The authority of the cognitive. Paper presented at the Fondation Archives de Jean Piaget, Université de Genève, Geneva, Switz., September. To appear in B. Inhelder and H. Sinclair (Eds.), *Piaget today,* in preparation.

———. (1986a). The history, psychology, and ideology of the self. In K. Larsen (Ed.). *Psychology and ideology.* Norwood, N.J.: Ablex.

———. (Ed.) (1986b). *Critical theories of development.* New York: Plenum.

———. (1986c). The politics of faith. In B. Wheeler, C. Dykstra, and S. Parks (Eds.), *James Fowler's theory of religious development.* Birmingham, Ala.: Religious Education Press.

———, and Riegel, K. F. (1977). Developmental psychology and the self. *Annals of the New York Academy of Sciences, 291,* 149–67.

———, and Zahaykevich, M. K. (1982). The peace movement threat. *Teachers College Record, 84*(1), 152–73. Rept. in D. Sloan (Ed.), *Education for peace and disarmament.* New York: Teachers College Press, 1983.

Coll, C., Gillieron, C., Guyon, J., Marti, E., and Ventouras-Spycher, M. (1976). Les méthodes de la psychologie génétique et les questions du psychologie. *Archives de Psychologie, 44*(171), 19–30.

Cummings, e. e. (1954). *Poems 1923–1954.* New York: Harcourt, Brace & World.

Derrida, J. (1970). Structure, sign and play in the discourse of the human sciences. In R. Macksey and E. Donato (Eds.), *The structuralist controversy.* Baltimore: Johns Hopkins University Press.

Döbert, R., Habermas, J., and Nunner-Winkler, G. (1986). The development of the self. In J. M. Broughton (Ed.), *Critical theories of psychological development.* New York: Plenum.

Fetz, R. (1985). La Coordination des valeurs: Actualité de la conception piagetienne de la philosophie. Paper presented at the Fondation Archives Jean Piaget, University of Geneva, Switz., September.

Flavell, J. H. (1963). *The developmental psychology of Jean Piaget.* Princeton: Van Nostrand.

Fraisse, P., Galifret, Y., Jeanson, F., Piaget, J., Ricoeur, P., and Zazzo, R. (1966). Débat: Psychologie et philosophie. *Raison Presente, 1*(4), 51–78.

Furth, H. G. (1969). Piaget on uses and abuses of philosophy: Review of J. Piaget, "Sagesse et illusion de la philosophie." *Acta Psychologica, 14,* 126–30.

———. (in press). The social function of Piaget's theory: A response to Apostel. *New Ideas in Psychology, 4*(2).

Gardner, H. (1970). Piaget and Lévi-Strauss: The quest for mind. *Social Research, 37*(3), 348–65.

———. (1972). *The quest for mind: Piaget, Lévi-Strauss and the structuralist movement.* New York: Vintage.

———. (1983). Can Piaget and Lévi-Strauss be reconciled? *New Ideas in Psychology, 1*(2), 187–90.

Gillieron, C. (1980). The epistemic subject is not the competent subject. Paper presented at Teachers College, Columbia University, New York, February.

———. (1984). Is Piaget's "genetic epistemology" evolutionary? Paper presented at the Symposium on Evolutionary Epistemology, Gent, Belg., November.

Gruber, H. E., and Vonèche, J. J. (1977). *The essential Piaget.* New York: Basic Books.

Habermas, J. (1973). A Postscript to "Knowledge and human interests." *Philosophy of the Social Sciences, 3,* (157–89).

Hunt, J. McV. (1961). *Intelligence and experience.* New York: Ronald.

Kitchener, R. F. (1981). Piaget's social psychology. *Journal of the Theory of Social Behavior, 11*(3), 253–77.

Ladrière, J. (1982). Piaget et la logique. *Archives de Psychologie, 50,* 17–29.

Lewis, M. (1979). The self as a developmental concept. *Human Development, 22,* 416–19.

Looft, W. R., and Svoboda, C. P. (1975). Structuralism in cognitive developmental psychology: Past, present, and future perspectives. In K. F. Riegel and G. C. Rosenwald (Eds.), *Structure and transformation.* New York: Wiley.

Piaget, J. (1950). *Introduction à l'épistémologie génétique, vol. 3.* Paris: Presses Universitaires de France.

———. (1952). *The origins of intelligence in children.* New York: Norton.

———. (1967a). Les deux problèmes principaux de l'épistémologie des sciences humaines. In *Logique et connaissance scientifique.* Paris: Gallimard.

———. (1967b). The mental development of the child. In *Six psycho-*

logical studies. New York: Random House. (Originally published 1940.)

———. (1967c). *Études sociologiques*. Geneva: Droz.

———. (1970a). *Structuralism*. New York: Basic Books.

———. (1970b). *Genetic epistemology*. New York: Columbia University Press.

———. (1970c). Invited seminar, Catholic University, Washington, D.C.

———. (1971a). *Biology and knowledge: An essay on the relations between organic regulations and cognitive processes*. Chicago: University of Chicago Press.

———. (1971b). *Insights and illusions of philosophy*. New York: World Publishing.

———. (1972). The myth of the sensory origin of scientific knowledge. In *Psychology and epistemology*. Harmondsworth, Eng.: Penguin.

———. (1976). *Grasp of consciousness*. Cambridge: Harvard University Press.

———. (1981). *Intelligence and affectivity*. Palo Alto: Annual Reviews.

———, and Inhelder, B. (1969). The gaps in empiricism. In A. Koestler and J. R. Smythies (Eds.), *Beyond reductionism*. London: Hutchinson.

Ricoeur, P. (1974). *The conflict of interpretations*. Evanston: Northwestern University Press.

Thompson, E. P. (1981). A letter to America. In E. P. Thompson and D. Smith (Eds.), *Protest and survive*. New York: Monthly Review Press.

Vonèche, J. J. (1980). Commentary. In S. Modgil and C. Modgil (Eds.), *Toward a psychological theory of development*. Slough, Eng.: National Foundation for Educational Research.

———. (1986). The difficulty of being a child in French-speaking countries. In J. M. Broughton (Ed.), *Critical theories of psychological development*. New York: Plenum.

CHAPTER 13

Fluctuations of Self and Consciousness Associated with Hypnosis

SHIRLEY SANDERS

M OST CURRENT THEORISTS describe hypnosis as an alteration of our usual state of consciousness (White and Shevack, 1942). Our perceptions and sensations may be altered. Most people have experienced some type of spontaneous perceptual change such as time distortion, illusion, or visual hallucination; changes in tactile perception, such as feeling numb; alterations of pain perception, such as feeling pressure; alterations of kinesthetic perception, such as feeling movement. Frankel (1976) and others have described many examples of spontaneous altered perceptions in patients with phobias, anxiety reactions, and hysterias.

As a person enters hypnosis, the following characteristics may be observed:

1. The person appears to experience a reduction of planning functions and is less likely spontaneously to plan or initiate action or activity. It is important to note that this reduction is relative to the degree of relaxation. If instructed to initiate activity while in hypnosis, he or she can take on a planning role.

2. The person exhibits selective inattention. For example, the person may hear the hypnotist's voice but not notice the sounds outside.

3. The person becomes more relaxed with a loosening of muscle tension.

4. The person displays a reduction in reality testing and an increase in tolerance for persistent reality distortion. The person may be able to respond to suggested images as though they were real. For example, the person may be able to see the hypnotist sitting in two different chairs at the same time. This phenomenon has been called "trance logic" (Orne, 1959).

5. The person may display an increase in receptivity to suggestion, for example, be more ego receptive and less critical in judgment (Fromm, 1977).

6. The person generally displays a reduction in motor activity.
Again this reduction is relative and can be minimized with suggestions for activity.

7. The person displays an increase in imagery experience. More
nonverbal images, feelings, and perceptions come to the fore, and
logical thought decreases.

8. The person may describe various alterations in sensory, perceptual, affective, and cognitive experience. For example, the person may feel significantly lighter, like floating, and experience
thinking as much clearer, or in contrast, may feel much heavier and
more in touch with feelings, consciousness, or the unconscious.

9. The person may display a variety of physiological changes: a
reduction in respiration rate and in heart rate, a drop in blood
pressure, and a rise in temperature. These changes appear related
to the relaxation instructions but can also be specifically suggested.

Hypnosis appears to reflect a shift in conscious awareness away from
the surrounding external environment to the internal sensations and
perceptions. The boundaries between external perceptions and internal perceptions diminish. According to Shor (1959), unconscious
awareness is grounded in a network of cognitive understandings about
reality. This frame of reference he named the "generalized reality
orientation" (GRO). Hypnosis, among other stimulations, can reduce
this network of cognitive understandings and thereby decrease the
GRO.

The literature on hypnosis has tended to focus more on describing
the phenomenon of hypnosis than on the continuous experience of
self. Interestingly the GRO is less the experience of personal subjectivity and more a set of cognitive understandings. To explain hypnosis,
the idea of dissociation is usually invoked. Perhaps that is because
hypnosis appears to be a dissociative process whereas our conception
of self is based generally on an integration of associated functions.

The Development of the Self as Association

Gruenewald (1984) summarized the ego-psychological theory of the
development of self as the association of ego nuclei or ego functions

of perception, reality-testing and so forth. This early association is the basis for a cohesive sense of self and continuity. Prince (1891) described an association theory of neuroses based on the concept of self as a mosaic grouped by association. According to Balint (1968) dissociation cannot occur without association as a prior assumption. The development of a sense of security, self-cohesion, and eventual separateness requires a splitting or dissociation early on, a first ordering of sensory, affective, and cognitive experience (Grostein, 1981). Hilgard (1977) states that self-awareness is maintained by continuity of memory functions. Learning theory and behavior modification principles, important concepts in cognitive psychology, are based on association theory (Pavlov, 1928; Hull, 1933; Skinner, 1953; Wolpe and Lazarus, 1966). The importance of association in the development of an integrated self has been a theoretical mainstay.

Dissociation

Dissociation has had fluctuations in terms of its acceptability in the scientific world. Its past history has linked dissociation to hysteria (Charcot, 1893) and to psychopathology (Janet, 1925; Prince, 1906). It was not until Hilgard's neodissociation theory (Hilgard, 1977) that dissociation was viewed as being on a continuum at one end of which people demonstrate various amounts of dissociated behavior in perfectly normal everyday experiences. Thus people can engage in more than one activity at a time, such as parallel activity. Parallel or simultaneous activity is the hallmark of dissociation. Some activities are automatic, seeming to occur out of conscious awareness, while others are quite consciously focused and voluntary, such as carrying out an activity because one wants to—writing a paper, or making decisions. Thus when I find myself imagining in a free-floating way, I am not aware of the usual controls or restraints. These controls have been dissociated from consciousness, leaving room for unconscious material to emerge. Nonetheless I am still aware of who I am, of the continuity of my identity. The alteration of ego functions is not an alteration of identity. Indeed my ego can be altered and I am still aware of continuity in the midst of change.

Altered States of Consciousness

Changes described as a result of altered states of consciousness appear to refer to "reorganizations of cognitive structure." The changes described (e.g., Fromm, 1979, p. 83) occur within the range of ego functions such as perception, cognition, attention, memory, and emotion; changes in imagery; awareness of being aware, such as the experience of mind expansion triggered by hallucinogenic drugs; an openness of the ego to stimulation from within and without; changes in experience of time and space (Harticollis, 1983); and changes in vigilance.

Imagery plays a major role in alterations of consciousness (Hartmann, 1958). Imagery rehearsal as found in Cautela's notion of covert conditioning demonstrates the utility of imagery-based learning (Cautela, 1966). In this paradigm, the person rehearses a particular image, as for example, rehearsing standing up for one's rights. The rehearsed image of standing up for one's rights leads to new learning and mastery. Certainly imagery plays a major role in mastery and in fostering new learning. The imagery found in daydreams, night dreams, and free association is the first sign of change.

Naturally Occurring Alterations of the Self

Spontaneous trancelike experiences in life have been documented by Bowers and Bowers (1979), who have reviewed evidence that fantasylike and absorptive experiences occur spontaneously to a greater extent in subjects who are highly susceptible to hypnosis. These experiences may occasionally occur in the context of a creative act. Creative subjects seem more adept than nonsusceptibles at shifting cognitively from a higher to a lower level of psychic functioning, that is, from reality-based thinking to a primitive primary-process mode. Singer and Pope (1981) argue that fantasy is a continuous background to everything we do.

There is under the limited span of consciousness an ongoing geyser of images, affects, fantasies. Most theorists would agree that this ongoing unconscious activity has a potential for *heightening adaptation* through enrichment of memory and thought.

Cognitions and associations can be facilitated by trancelike and absorptive experience (K. S. Bowers, 1978; P. G. Bowers, 1978). This facilitation leads to a divergence of memories. When more emphasis is placed on reality concerns and logical thought, daydreaming is enhanced. However, when more emphasis is placed on unconscious imaginal inner experience, a blending of fantasy and reality occurs such that the two merge and the lines between imaginative experience and real experience blur. Jung's use of "Active Imagination" appears to cultivate this merging. Active imagination is a self-induced trance experience in which the ego treats the imagined episode as real, fostering heightened ego participation. Jung used active imagination as a therapeutic method. Reading, adventures, play, dance, and art are some other examples of imaginative therapy suggested by Josephine Hilgard (1979). Certainly reading permits involvement, which stimulates one to become involved actively in the manipulation of ideas and emotions. In a dramatic performance the actor may feel as though he or she is the character and not an actor during the performance. Climbing mountains or engaging in gymnastics test the limits of reality through the challenge of the task, triggering primitive feelings of omnipotence, power, freedom from restraint, excitement, while combining discipline, restraint, judgment. James Hall (1977) differentiates among these activities since active imagination, in its pure state, allows the greatest amount of participation of the unconscious: any variant that introduces an enduring physical form, such as painting, restricts the freedom of the symbol in exchange for achieving a more permanent embodiment of the symbolic image (p. 341).

As Ernest Hilgard (1977) pointed out, people can process reality and fantasy simultaneously. Unconscious or unattended information which is not brought to conscious awareness may influence our conscious perceptions in a useful way. For example, in studies of dichotic listening (MacKay, 1973) it was demonstrated that information not consciously heard on an unattended channel may still be understood by the subject. Thus the parallel or simultaneous processing of information, with only one process consciously appreciated at a time occurs.

Josephine Hilgard (1979) describes the operation of temporary absorption in satisfying experiences in which fantasy plays a large role. These intense experiences do affect the quality of life by providing the individual with an important means of coping.

According to her work, imagination and control, rather than being mutually exclusive, are indeed compatible experiences. For example, a ballerina can express deep emotion at the same time as she moves within limitations imposed by the choreography. This appears to be an example of parallel or simultaneous processing.

Focusing on psychopathology, Frankel (1976) has shown that people suffering from phobias are highly hypnotizable. He has described a variety of neurotic symptoms which appear to be triggered by an altered state of consciousness. Gruenewald (1977, 1984) among others (Braun, 1984; Kluft, 1983) has described multiple personality as resulting from dissociation, an alteration in cognition and consciousness. These alterations are natural attempts at coping with life, but rather than being adaptive, lead to the formation of symptoms. Gruenewald, Fromm, and Oberlander (1979) have demonstrated that in psychologically healthy people, hypnosis leads to adaptive regression, whereas in those individuals with ego disturbances, the regressions tend to be pathological. Beahrs (1983) suggests that we view these natural tendencies to dissociate as skills that can be redirected and guided to help the person to cope with and adapt to life. Dissociation is maladaptive when symptoms are generated. However, when coping and creativity are generated, dissociation may be adaptive.

Summary

In summary, hetero-hypnosis and self-hypnosis may be used deliberately to alter in a time-limited manner the basic relationship between the ego and self, between conscious and unconscious functions, in the service of individuation, creativity, or self-knowledge. Through the avenue of active imagination, the lines between reality and fantasy blur to some extent, permitting entry of unconscious contents into conscious awareness. The role of various ego functions is altered while a basic continuity of identity remains. Unconscious contents are given an identity through personification, permitting a dreamlike dialogue of conscious and unconscious ideation, which seems to occur independently, autonomously. This reciprocity may result in individuation, growth, and expansion, providing more divergent thought, more options—opportunity for new growth. When hypnosis is terminated, new learnings remain, but the unconscious shifts to a less dominant orientation as ego functions assume ordinary dominance in the processes of waking life. In a psychologically healthy person, hypnotic experience leads to regression and adaptive uses of dissociation. In a psychologically vulnerable individual, hypnotic experience may lead to pathological regression of maladaptive dissociation (loss of identity) unless it is supported and facilitated in a therapeutic environment. Under the guidance and structure provided by a hypnotherapist, hypnosis can aid the self in its task of healing and interpreting.

The conclusion that I offer is that hypnosis should be utilized to foster expansion and diversity within the basic continuity of one's experience of self. Such expansion and diversity generates creative development and greater differentiation that can be expressed in one's reality.

References

Balint, M. (1968). *The basic fault: Therapeutic aspects of regression.* London: Tavistock.

Beahrs, J. D. (1983). Co-consciousness: A common denominator in hypnosis, multiple personality and normalcy. *American Journal of Clinical Hypnosis, 26,* 100.

Bowers, K. S. (1978). Heart rate and gsr concomitants of vigilance and arousal. *Canadian Journal of Clinical and Experimental Hypnosis, 26,* 184.

Bowers, P. G. (1978). Hypnotizability, creativity and the role of effortless experiencing. *International Journal of Clinical and Experimental Hypnosis, 26,* 184.

———, and Bowers, K. S. (1979). Hypnosis and Creativity: A theoretical and empirical rapprochement. In E. Fromm and R. F. Shor (eds.), *Hypnosis: Research Developments and Perspectives* (2nd ed). New York: Aldine.

Braun, B. G. (1984). Hypnosis creates multiple personality: Myth or reality? *International Journal of Clinical and Experimental Hypnosis, 32,* 191.

Cautela, J. R. (1966). Treatment of compulsive behavior by covert sensitization. *Psychological Record, 16,* 33.

Charcot, J. M. (1893). The Faith-Cure. *New Review, 8,* 18.

Frankel, F. H. (1976). *Hypnosis: Trance as a coping mechanism.* New York: Plenum Press.

Freud, S. (1955). Splitting of the ego in the process of defense. In J.

Strachey (ed. and trans.), *The Standard Edition of the Complete Psychological Works of Sigmund Freud*, vol. 23. London: Hogarth.

Fromm, E. (1977). An ego-psychological theory of altered states of consciousness. *International Journal of Clinical and Experimental Hypnosis, 25,* 372.

———. (1979). The nature of hypnosis and other altered states of consciousness: An ego-psychological theory. In E. Fromm, *Perspectives* (2nd ed). New York: Aldine.   \

———, Brown, D. P., Hurt, S. W., Oberlander, J. Z., Boxer, M. A., and Pfeifer, G. (1981). The phenomena and characteristics of self-hypnosis. *International Journal of Clinical and Experimental Hypnosis, 29,* 189.

———, Oberlander, M. I., and Gruenewald, D. (1970). Perceptual and cognitive processes in different states of consciousness: That waking state and hypnosis. *Journal of Projective Techniques and Personality Assessment, 34* 375.

Grostein, J. (1981). *Splitting and Projective Identification*. New York: Aronson.

Gruenewald, D. (1977). Multiple personality and splitting phenomena: A reconceptualization. *Journal of Mental and Nervous Disorder, 164,* 385.

———. (1984). On the nature of multiple personality: Comparisons with hypnosis. *International Journal of Clinical and Experimental Hypnosis, 32,* 118.

———, Fromm, E., and Oberlander, M. I. (1979). Hypnosis and adaptive regression: An ego-psychological inquiry. In E. Fromm and R. E. Shor (Eds.), *Hypnosis: Research developments and perspectives* (2nd ed). New York: Aldine.

Hall, J. A. (1977). *Clinical uses of dreams: Jungian interpretations and enactments*. New York: Grune and Stratton.

Harticollis, P. (1983). *Time and timelessness*. New York: International University Press.

Hartmann, H. (1958). *Ego psychology and the problem of adaptation*. New York: International Universities Press.

Hilgard, E. R. (1973). Dissociation revisited. In M. Henley, J. Jaynes, and J. J. Sullivan (Eds.), *Historical conceptions of psychology*. New York: Springer.

———. (1977). *Divided consciousness: Multiple controls in human thought and action*. New York: Wiley.

————. (1984). The hidden observer and multiple personality. *International Journal of Clinical and Experimental Hypnosis, 32,* 248.

Hilgard, J. (1979). Imaginative and sensory-affective involvement: In everyday life and in hypnosis. In E. Fromm and R. E. Shor (Eds.), *Hypnosis: Research developments and perspectives,* (2nd ed). New York: Aldine.

Hull, C. L. (1933). *Hypnosis and suggestibility: An experimental approach.* New York: Appleton-Century Crofts.

Janet, P. (1925). *Psychological healing: A historical and clinical study.* E. Paul and C. Paul (Trans.). New York: Macmillan.

Jung, C. G. (1958). *Psyche and symbol.* V. de Lazlow (Ed.). Garden City: Doubleday-Anchor Books.

————. (1961). *Memories, dreams and reflections.* A. Jaffe (Ed.). R. Winston and C. Winston (Trans.). New York: Vintage Books.

Kluft, R. P. (1983). Hypnotherapeutic crisis intervention in multiple personality. *American Journal of Clinical Hypnosis, 26,* 73.

MacKay, D. G. (1973). Aspects of the theory of comprehension, memory and attention. *Quarterly Journal of Experimental Psychology, 25,* 22.

Orne, M. T. (1959). The nature of hypnosis: Artifact and essence. *Journal of Abnormal and Social Psychology, 58,* 277.

Pavlov, I. P. (1928). *Lectures on Conditioning Reflexes,* vol. 1. W. H. Ganntt. (Trans.) New York: International Publications.

Prince, M. (1891). Association neuroses: A study of hysterical joint afflictions, neurasthenia and allied forms of neuromimesis. *Journal of Nervous and Mental Disease, 18,* 257.

————. (1906). *The dissociation of a personality.* New York: Longman's-Green.

Shor, R. E. (1959). Hypnosis and the concept of the generalized reality orientation. *American Journal of Psychotherapy, 13,* 582.

————, and Orne, M. T. (1965). *The nature of hypnosis: Selected basic readings.* New York: Holt, Rinehart and Winston.

Singer, J. L., and Pope, K. S. (1981). Daydreaming and imagery skills as predisposing capacities. *International Journal of Clinical and Experimental Hypnosis, 29,* 271.

Skinner, B. F. (1953). *Science and human behavior.* New York: Macmillan.

White, R. W., and Shevack, B. J. (1942). Hypnosis and the concept of dissociation. *Journal of Abnormal and Social Psychology, 37,* 309.

Wolpe, J., and Lazarus, A. A. (1966). *Behavior therapy techniques: A guide to the treatment of neuroses.* New York: Pergamon.

CHAPTER 14

Psychoanalytic Theories of the Self: Contrasting Clinical Approaches to the New Narcissism

FREDERIC J. LEVINE *and* ROBERT KRAVIS

DURING THE PAST fifteen years, the concept of "self" has emerged from relative obscurity in American psychoanalytic theory and practice, spurred by the radical upsurge of interest in disorders of "narcissism," which some analysts believe are affecting a growing, perhaps dominant segment of the population they treat (Kohut, 1977; Modell, 1983). These syndromes, which are characterized in part by disturbances in self-experience and self-esteem, are believed by some clinicians to be poorly understood and treated by classical psychoanalysis. Numerous modifications of theory and technique have been proposed to remedy this deficiency, but public and professional attention has been most captured by the contrasting viewpoints which were offered at the same time by two prominent psychoanalytic leaders and innovators: Otto Kernberg and the late Heinz Kohut.

Kernberg's studies of borderline and narcissistic personality disorders include major efforts to clarify and reorganize theory and treatment techniques, within the broad conceptual framework of classical psychoanalysis. For him, the self is one aspect or manifestation of the functioning of the entire personality—an organized array of images, memories, experiences, ideas, and other psychic "representations" that pertain to the person as subject—or self. They exist in intimate relationship to other comparable arrays of mental contents (object representations, affect states), which have equally important roles in the personality. In contrast, in their "psychology of the self," Heinz Kohut and his followers offered a model of the mind that differs radically from the formulations of classical psychoanalysis and that dictates fundamental changes in modes of understanding data and intervening in treatment. In this theory, the "self" is not merely a set of subjective images, ideas, and the like but a psychological structure of central importance to the personality. It must be well developed for a normal or even neurotic personality to be present, and is immature and defective in narcissistic disorders. This new paradigm was hailed by its proponents as "a major conceptual shift . . . in psychoanalysis" (Goldberg et al., 1978, p. 11) that "opened for psychoanalytic treatment a new area of psychodynamics and psychopathology" (Ornstein, 1975, p. 129). It has now grown from its beginnings as a specific mode of approach to narcissistic pathology (Kohut, 1971), to become a sweeping reformulation of virtually all main aspects of theory and technique. It includes a new way of viewing the major general themes and problems of human existence (man is seen as "tragic" rather than "guilty"—as Kohut believed Freud saw him), and it is considered to have broad clinical application to the full spectrum of patients (Kohut, 1984). Although originally intended as a supplement to prior psychoanalytic understanding of narcissistic disorders, self psychology now often seems to be presented as a challenge to classical analysis, a new system that will supplant much of the older one (Ornstein, 1978; Kohut, 1984).

Self psychologists often enthusiastically describe their model as revolutionary, comparable to Freud's early ideas: "Freud changed the paradigm of the psychoanalytic treatment process with his *The Ego and the Id* (1923). Kohut's *The Analysis of the Self* (1971) might turn out to be a landmark of no lesser significance" (Ornstein, 1975, pp. 147–48).

These new and controversial ideas have generated enormous interest in the self not only in the professional community, but in the popular press as well (e.g., Breu, 1979; Leo, 1980, Woodward and Mark, 1978). There are now numerous conferences on the self, professional publications devoted to it, and many commentaries and appraisals—ranging from the enthusiasm of self psychology's proponents to partial agreement by some analysts (e.g., Lichtenberg, 1973; Tuttman, 1978; Wallerstein, 1983) and to serious criticisms and disagreements by others, who suggest that this approach may impede understanding and treatment (e.g., Arlow, 1981; Chessick, 1980; Curtis, 1983, 1984; Grossman, 1982; Kernberg, 1975, 1982, Levine, 1977, 1979, 1985; Reed, 1985; Stein, 1979).

Although some of the increased interest and the controversies about theories of the self may reflect parochial phenomena within the psychoanalytic community, the issues at stake are significant, and of much more than esoteric interest. As has been indicated, these ideas grew out of a widely felt need to extend the scope of psychoanalytic treatment in order to meet the challenges of the apparently changing epidemiology of psychopathology.

This chapter will briefly review the history and current status of psychoanalytic concepts of self and will contrast self psychology with the classical psychoanalytic views articulated by Otto Kernberg and other recent authors. It will discuss their most significant difference— one a theory of conflict between opposing forces and interests within the mind, the other a theory of the effects of deficits within the mind's "structure." Finally, it will illustrate the theoretical differences with a case example, to demonstrate the clinical consequences of the two approaches.

The Self in Classical Psychoanalysis—Historical Overview

For most of the history of psychoanalytic theory, the concept of "self" has played only a peripheral, implied role. In Freud's writings, the term *Ich* (literally, "I"), which is usually translated as "ego," often had multiple or ambiguous meanings. Sometimes he did use it to mean what has come to be called the ego—a hypothetical mental suborganization or structure encompassing the mind's executive and instrumental functions and the defense mechanisms. But at other times it referred to the person's *experience* of himself as an individual—that is, to a mental content, rather than a mechanism. Thus, for example, when Freud described narcissism as the focusing of libido (mental energy or interest) on the *Ich*, he did not mean the ego, but the person's self-interest in or love for oneself (Rangell, 1982; Kernberg, 1982).

A later writer, Heinz Hartmann, took up the meaning of "self" as part of his broad effort to systematize and clarify psychoanalytic theory. He distinguished three phenomena: (a) the *ego*, a structure, as described above; (b) the *self-representation*, which is the person's (conscious and/or unconscious) mental conception or image of himself, and (c) the *self* proper—the actual objective person, his body, his identity as seen or known by an external observer (1950). For Hartmann, then, the self was not truly a psychological concept at all, and when the term was used in clinical discourse it was actually a loose way of referring to the *self-representation*. Most subsequent American psychoanalytic writers have followed this usage, concentrating attention on the self-representation or self-image, and its connections with other manifest mental contents as well as with latent (underlying, causative) factors (e.g., Jacobson, 1964). Of particular note are the writings of Erik Erikson, whose discussions of "identity" (a concept closely akin to self-image or self-concept) achieved great prominence (1968). Erikson and other contributors have been interested in such problems as how the self-image develops; its sources in constitution, experience, and identifications; its internal unity and consistency; and what determines whether it is realistic or unrealistic, positive or negative (self-esteem).

Freud explored many of these issues in his major paper "On Narcissism: An Introduction," in 1914. He was led to the subject primarily because he observed the important role played by variations in self-esteem and self-regard in many people's lives: Some showed excessive erotic self-love; others (schizophrenics) seemed to withdraw interest from people and instead turn it upon themselves in worries or delusions about their bodies or in ideas of reference; physically ill individuals and hypochondriacs also showed heightened concern with their bodies together with proportionally reduced interest in other people; and young children as well as members of primitive societies often had the unrealistic belief that they had magical powers over other people and events. These and other observations led Freud to reason, in the context of his psychic energy model, that each person possessed a finite quantity of libido which could be invested in himself or in others. According to this thinking, love for others ("object love") would necessarily be inversely related to self-love or self-interest. Consequently, Freud concluded that people who were unusually narcissistic would have little energy available to invest in the transference relationship that is essential for effective psychoanalytic treatment.

This conclusion was one of Freud's most influential and, some think, most inaccurate clinical statements (Rangell, 1982). It led him to postulate two categories of psychic disorders: *transference neuroses* (psychoneuroses and some character problems), conditions in which there was a good capacity to form a transference bond with the analyst, and which were therefore amenable to treatment by Freud's methods; and *narcissistic neuroses* (psychoses, borderline states, and other severe character disorders) in which there was such a severe self-preoccupation and such flawed self-esteem as to preclude relatively realistic relationships to other people as separate, independent individuals. Because of this, Freud considered the latter group inaccessible to psychoanalysis.

Two other parts of Freud's discussion of narcissism are pertinent to our topic. First, he considered that narcissistic good or bad feelings and self-regard are derived from three areas of developmental and adaptive achievement: (a) Primary narcissism, which is the residue of the infant's blissful narcissistic feeling during the first months of life. Most analysts consider that insufficient nurturance and responsiveness by the parents during this early period can leave the child with a profound basic deficiency in positive self-regard (and also, some recent contributors add, with a residue of highly conflictual primitive rage) (Kernberg, 1982). (b) Fulfilling one's own standards and ideals (the "ego ideal"—which largely concerns the control and sublimation of forbidden primitive wishes). (c) Obtaining satisfaction of object-directed interest and love, and feeling that one has the competence, assertiveness, power and skills to achieve these aims. Only low self-esteem based on the first of these sources, deficient primary narcissism, is related to the quality of early parenting, and only problems of this type carry the implications of severity, inaccessibility, and intractibility that Freud called narcissistic neuroses. Difficulties in the other two areas also cause feelings of low self-esteem, but these are *not* contraindications for treatment by classical psychoanalysis. Thus, the presence of low self-esteem alone is not a sufficient diagnostic criterion.

Freud's other relevant observation for our purposes was his description of the ubiquitous search for a "cure through love" by people who are experiencing temporary or permanent disturbances in self-esteem based on any of the above three sources. In these cases, the patient seeks out as a narcissistic love object someone who has attributes that he imagines or senses are lacking in himself. The purpose of this love is to complete the subject's fantasy of what he himself should be—"If I have this idealized love object, it will perfect me, make me feel complete and worthy." This fantasy is often enacted in the patient's tie to his analyst, from whom he seeks love, not insight, because it seems much preferable to an analytic cure. If the analyst attempts to gratify these wishes he may give the patient a feeling of health and wholeness, but may also create a lasting dependency in the patient, who will require the continuing presence of the loving, supportive therapist to maintain the good feelings.

The Self in Contemporary Theories: Deficit and Conflict Models

Few clinicians dispute the observation that schizophrenics and some other severely disturbed people have such difficulty relating to others that they are essentially unreachable through psychoanalysis. However, there has always been substantial clinical interest in the less extreme segment of the spectrum of narcissistic syndromes, including borderline personalities and various severe character disorders. This interest increased greatly in recent decades, largely in response to the belief that such problems are occurring much more frequently, and demanding new or modified forms of treatment. The popular as well as scientific press heralded the onset of an "Age of Narcissism" (Woodward and Mark, 1978), perhaps caused by changing societal institutions—particularly the disruption of the nuclear family—and marked by a change in modal personality configurations.

Approaches to meeting this perceived need for new methods and understandings fall into two groups (cf. Gediman, 1983):

1. Theories in which the psychopathology is explained as due to deficits or developmental arrests in personality structure, and in which treatment is designed to repair or compensate for the deficit. By analogy, one might compare these methods with medical treatments for nutritional deficiencies, such as scurvy: sometimes a corrected diet will restore the premorbid healthy condition (repair of defect), and in other cases, irreparable damage has occurred (as in a scurvy victim whose teeth have fallen out), and compensatory prostheses are needed, as well as better food.

At the time Freud was writing his paper "On Narcissism" (1914), theories that had features of this type were being propounded by Adler and Jung, and Freud found them incompatible with his psychoanalytic method. The most prominent contemporary example of a deficit-based approach is Kohut's "psychology of the self."

2. Theories that, like the classical psychoanalytic theory of neuroses, conceptualize psychopathology as resulting from irreconcilable conflicts between competing needs and interests within the psyche, especially wish-fantasies or impulses that are (for irrational reasons rooted in the childhood origin of the conflict) unacceptable to the conscious mind. These conflictual motives and their accompanying fantasies, memories, and feelings are defensively sequestered or segregated from the main, conscious sector of the personality (e.g., by repression into unconsciousness, or through projective and externalizing defenses, which ascribe the problem to people or causes outside the individual himself, or by a variety of other methods). Psychopathological symptoms or traits, according to this model, are expressions of the *incompletely* warded-off impulses together with the maladaptive aspect of the defense mechanisms. Treatment consists either (a) in analyzing the conflict—that is, by using the free-associative method, analyst and patient jointly, step-by-step, discern the nature of the conflict and restore its connections with the patient's main, conscious mental processes (which the now more mature patient can tolerate, once the segregating processes are overcome)—thus permitting a controlled, mature resolution of the problem, or (b) compensating for it by fostering the use of more adaptive defenses and a more thorough, effective repression or screening off of the conflict. A very rough medical analogy here would be to the toxic and febrile effects of an infectious illness: The symptoms are side effects of the body's struggle with the disease process, and can be reduced *either* through cure of the process or (in cases where the disease itself is either untreatable or trivial and self-limiting) by measures such as analgesia, antiinflammatory substances and the like, which suppress the symptoms directly.

Self Psychology: Psychopathology as Structural Deficiency

Theory: Self psychology began as a method for treating narcissistic disorders that was encompassed within general Freudian theory. It followed Freud's idea that narcissism and object-love were developmentally and structurally separate tendencies in the personality. Gradually, using etiological concepts that are essentially relevant to only the first of Freud's three sources of self-regard (primary narcissism), Kohut and his colleagues elaborated an explanatory system in which deficiencies in early childhood parenting were seen as creating defects in a centrally important personality structure, the *self*, which (they proposed) must be mature before object-related development and intrapsychic conflicts (including the Oedipus complex) can occur.

Kohut's studies of narcissism and the self began with his observation that patients with narcissistic personality disorders regularly form certain typical kinds of intense attachments to their analysts, which appear to express primitive needs. He considered these phenomena to be transferences of infantile ties to parents, derived from fixation upon very early stages in which the self is not yet fully formed. For such individuals he concluded that pathology is not due to unconscious conflicts, but to the self-deficiencies caused by their developmental arrests, and consequently that efforts to explore the unconscious were certainly irrelevant, and often actually harmful because they are experienced by the patient as further weakening his fragile, unstable self-structure.

Kohut theorized that the self develops through "transmuting internalizations" of what he identified as normal early infantile phases: the grandiose self and idealized "selfobject." In the first of these stages the infant feels omnipotent and grand, and in the second he attributes power and grandeur to the main parenting figure. He experiences important figures, unconsciously, not as fully separate, independent individuals, but as extensions of, or part of, the self. Freud had called such primitive attachments "narcissistic" relationships. Kohut termed them "selfobject" relationships, to designate the lack of full self-other separation and the fundamental structural dependency of such individuals on their primitively conceived "others." In infancy, the selfobject must provide the child with certain particular forms of responsiveness in order for the early phases to develop fully and then be internalized, forming self-structure. The absence of these responses prevents adequate structure from being formed, and as a result of this deficiency, the self's "cohesion and firmness depend on the presence of a selfobject and ... it responds to the loss of the selfobject with simple enfeeblement, various regressions, and fragmentation" (Kohut, 1977, p. 137). Such individuals have not achieved the type of mature, integrated self-image and self-structure that Kohut called a "nuclear self," which is necessary before people can be related to as truly separate "independent sources of initiative" (Tolpin and Kohut, 1980), and as objects of the drives. They therefore are incapable of experiencing the intrapsychic conflicts around object-directed drives that characterize transference neuroses, and will not benefit from a treatment designed to address such conflicts analytically.

Treatment: Self-psychological treatment depends on the premise that in all but the most severe self-deficiencies (e.g., psychoses) unformed, defective aspects of the self retain throughout life a tendency to resume and complete their interrupted childhood development, with the participation of an empathic selfobject. The main task of the analyst, according to this model, is to function in the selfobject role that had not been appropriately filled by the parents. "The essential transference [is] . . . related to the reactivation of the specific developmental task, i.e., to the reintensification of the attempt to fill in a specific structural deficit" (Kohut, 1977, p. 217). When infantile grandiose and idealizing needs are reawakened in the relationship to the analyst, they are not used as sources of data in the search for insight into repressed memories and fantasies.

> The purpose of remembering in the analysis of disturbances of the self is not to "make conscious" the unconscious components of structural conflicts so that these conflicts can be resolved in consciousness . . . but to strengthen the coherence of the self. (p. 184)

New self-structure is created through transmuting internalizations of the selfobject phases, which are reactivated in the transference, and a cure is thus effected through filling in the core of the self, and/or building effective compensatory structures. In contrast to neurotic fears and symptoms, which—according to classical psychoanalysis—reflect *fantasies* of danger, attendant on the incomplete repression or warding off of conflicts over forbidden wishes, self-defects are seen by self psychology as quite real and concrete. The fears, sensations of emptiness and distress, certain types of dreams ("self-state dreams"), and many other symptoms associated with these defects are direct, undisguised signs or intrapsychic perceptions of the incomplete state of the self. Whereas in neurotics, mental contents and experiences are understood as the multiply determined resultants of very complicated unconscious conflictual forces and processes (Waelder, 1936), which can only be unraveled by examining the pattern and sequence of the patient's spontaneous free associations, in cases of self-defect no such associations are needed, according to the theory. As Kohut pointed out with regard to self-state dreams:

> Free associations do not lead to unconscious hidden layers of the mind. . . . The scrutiny of the manifest content . . . will then allow us to recognize that the healthy sectors of the patient's psyche are reacting with anxiety to a disturbing change in the condition of the self. (1977, p. 109)

As Reed (1985) has pointed out, then, because it sees manifest contents and behavior (including particularly behavior to the analyst) as directly referable to *real* inner structural conditions in the mind, self psychology applies certain relatively clear, direct rules of interpretation to them: They are taken as signs, and it is the task of the analyst to "read" those signs according to the theory and infer from them the state of the self and/or the story of its origins in deficient parenting. Having made these inferences, the analyst usually communicates them to the patient, but not primarily for the purpose of providing insight into the unconscious. Instead, the main goal of these interventions, like all of the analyst's behavior, is to provide empathic acceptance and response to the patient's primitive selfobject needs—as an immediate support for the fragile, troubled self, as well as to provide the potential for building the defective self-structure. "From the object (i.e., the analyst) . . . the analysand expects the performance of certain basic functions in the realm of narcissistic homeostasis which his own psyche is unable to provide" (Kohut, 1971, p. 47). As such interventions are made again and again, the patient comes to understand that he has a self-deficiency caused by parental empathic failures, which leaves him vulnerable to disturbances in current selfobject ties—and that deficiency is gradually ameliorated or repaired through transmuting internalizations of the analytic relationship.

From its origin as a discrete set of formulations for treating a particular subgroup of patients, self psychology has grown into a comprehensive system, a general personality theory centering on the development and vicissitudes of a newly conceived psychic structure, the self. It is now seen by its proponents as containing the most basic and general psychoanalytic explanations and therapeutic principles, and as broadly applicable to virtually all forms of psychopathology (Kohut, 1984).

Other Theories: Self-Representations and the Centrality of Conflict

While analysts other than Kohut and his associates have generally followed Hartmann (1950) in not considering "self" as a psychological structure, they have had a great deal to say about the development and vicissitudes of self-experience and self-representations, and their connections with pathology. Freud's discussion of the importance of the infantile stage of primary narcissism in the pathogenesis of severe ego disturbances has been confirmed and expanded by subsequent clinical experience, and by child observational research. Piaget's studies of cognitive development, and the psychoanalytic "baby-watching" of Margaret Mahler and her colleagues (Mahler et al., 1975) have charted the course and milestones of this crucial early period: the growing awareness that there *is* a difference between self and other, and that there is stability and unity to oneself as well as to others. From the ego-psychological point of view, it is the nonattainment of these milestones that accounts for the most severe, disabling, and often irreversible forms of what Freud called "narcissistic neuroses."

These studies show that the mental awareness, or representation, of the self begins in intimate connection with the awareness of others. Contrary to self psychology's postulate that self-development is a prerequisite for the capability to relate to others, classical analysts see these findings as the start of a continuing process of closely interconnected evolution for the two areas. These authors do not usually speak of a single self, or self-concept, but of many self-representations, reflecting the multiplicity of each person's perceptions of himself as he grows up, and the variety of wishes, needs, defenses, and other factors that determine all subjective mental contents. Grossman (1982), for example, considers self-images to be essentially fantasies that occur in many different versions in each individual. From this perspective, each person may be said to have not one but many "selves," which reflect the varied and often conflicting forces in the mind. Grossman adds that a preoccupation with self-experience, and with the feeling of self-defectiveness—which are central data for self psychology—are themselves manifestations of fantasies about the self. Patients who report such concerns, he says, have unconscious conflicts that cause them to focus attention on themselves and to feel defective.

Like Kohut, Otto Kernberg has contributed much to current psychoanalytic thinking about borderline and narcissistic personalities and about these patients' experiences of themselves and others. But his conclusions are quite different from Kohut's: "I propose ... to reserve the term 'self' for the sum total of *self-representations in intimate connection with the sum total of object representations*" (1982, p. 900, emphasis mine). An articulate critic of self psychology, Kernberg puts particular stress on that system's failure to consider the role of negative feelings and aggression in both normal and pathological development of self-images, which he considers a serious error. Kohut saw the early growth of the self as nurtured largely by empathy, mirroring, idealization, and the infant's resulting positive feelings. Kernberg, however, like Grossman, points out that the infant normally has many different self-representations, only some of which reflect positive feelings, while others involve anger, fear, and other dysphoric affects. He considers these observations to be consistent with Freud's dual-drive theory—that libidinal and aggressive motives are important and ubiquitous components of psychic life. When self psychologists ignore the important place of aggression as a human motive in health and pathology, and then describe classical analysts as harsh toward their patients, Kernberg suggests that they are behaving like Freud's early critics who objected to his emphasis on the sexual drive, and accused him of being preoccupied with sex.

Unlike many classical analysts (Rangell, 1982), Kernberg sometimes speaks of *a* self, "an ego function and structure that evolves gradually from the integration of its component self-representations into a supraordinate structure" (Kernberg, 1982, p. 905). However, even at these times he reflects the general view that the term is meaningful only when defined in terms of self-representations. From this perspective, self experiences are *not* direct intrapsychic perceptions of the inner condition of the psychic apparatus, as they are for self psychology. The analyst cannot directly interpret them to the patient as indicators of the self-state, nor can he or she use developmental concepts with equal directness, in the self-psychological manner, to reach inferences about the patient's early pathogenic experiences (Reed, 1985). Instead, as with any manifest mental content, self-experiences can best be understood analytically by using the free-associative process. That is, through a collaborative effort by analyst and patient to examine the latter's associations in order to facilitate recovery of the unconscious memories, meanings, and fantasies that may underlie them.

In his 1896 lecture "The Aetiology of Hysteria," Freud used a metaphor that aptly captures much of the difference between these two clinical approaches, as classical analysts would understand them:

> Imagine that an explorer arrives in a little-known region where his interest is aroused by an expanse of ruins, with remains of walls, fragments of columns, and tablets with half-effaced and unreadable inscriptions. He may content himself with inspecting what lies exposed to view, with questioning the inhabitants—perhaps semi-barbaric people—who live in the vicinity, about what tradition tells them of the history and meaning of these archaeological remains, and with noting down what they tell him—and he may then proceed on his journey. But he may act differently. He may have brought picks, shovels and spades with him, and he may set the inhabitants to work with these implements. Together with them he may start upon the ruins, clear away the rubbish, and, beginning from the visible remains, uncover what is buried. If his work is crowned with success, the discoveries are self-explanatory: the ruined walls are part of the ramparts of a palace or a treasure-house; the fragments of columns can be filled out into a temple; the numerous inscriptions, which, by good luck, may be bilingual, reveal an alphabet and a language, and, when they have been deciphered and translated, yield undreamed-of-information about the events of the remote past, to commemorate which the monuments were built. *Saxa Loquuntur!* (stones talk!) (Freud, 1896/1962, p. 192)

In the following section, we will try to illustrate these different approaches with a case example.

Case Illustration

A. M. is a single woman in her mid-twenties, a student in a prominent professional school, who sought psychotherapy for intense anxieties centered around school work and a relationship with a boyfriend. She was the oldest of four children in a family with high intellectual and social aspirations but only modest financial circumstances. Many members of the M. family, especially mother, were extremely ambitious. They urged her to achieve at the highest levels academically—by hook or by crook; and reminded her that as a woman and a Jew she would always have the odds against her, and must never let up. Mother herself had not married well, as A. M. saw it, and was not pleased with the moderate level of achievement that she and her husband had attained in their careers. A. M. was highly self-conscious about anything she thought others might see as a sign of inadequacy or inferiority: For example, as a child she had strenuously avoided being seen with one of her grandparents because of a physical infirmity and some eccentricities of clothing which A. M. found intolerably embarrassing. The fact that her grandparent was also well known for doing good works made little difference to her.

In therapy, A. M. talked little of her family, except her mother, for many months. Instead she spoke in a driven, anxious way about her worries and ambitions in school and with her boyfriend—a fellow student whom she saw as not romantically exciting, but dependable and a high achiever. Despite her outstanding grades in college, consistently fine evaluations for part-time work placements, and current standing at the top of her class, A. M. talked continually about life's unfairness and her need to be special. She was sure that *next* time she'd fail academically, or that the boyfriend was about to reject her.

After a number of months of treatment, it began to appear that the greatest obstacle to A. M.'s success was her own anxiety and resentful, occasionally inappropriate aggression toward the people she felt were unfair to her. On a summer job in her professional field, she obtained consistently high ratings for her performance, and showed both skill and effort beyond the call of duty when she was chosen for a special role in a major company project. However, her interpersonal behavior undermined this outstanding record and she received very low ratings: She was hypersensitive to imagined slights by superiors, reacted to them with inappropriate indignation and by trying to curry favor with a male supervisor. On one occasion she ran to this man for reassurance after snubbing a woman superior. In her final evaluation, she was told that although her job performance had merited an offer of a permanent position, her other behavior outweighed it and made her ineligible for significant professional responsibilities in that organization.

In academics, she reported something similar: She procrastinated with an assigned class presentation until she became overwhelmingly anxious and fearful of failing, and then tearfully appealed to the instructor for reassurance, support, and tolerance of the flaws she anticipated in her presentation. When he responded positively to this display of misgivings and anxiety, her actual project was, as usual, excellent.

A. M. also feared that her boyfriend would find fault with her, and she communicated to him, too, in potentially self-damaging ways. During a visit to his family in another state, she became very upset that he was distracted from her by the recently discovered serious illness of a female relative. She spoke openly of her distress and her envy of the attention being paid to the stricken family member. She told the therapist how unwanted and defective his "neglect" had made her feel, and how angry she was at the invalid who was "monopolizing" everyone's time. Must she become ill to merit his attention? If she *were* sick, would he care? She predicted that he would reject her, and that she would be devastated because she had not followed her invariable past practice of attaching herself to a new boyfriend before giving up on the old one. "I hold onto a man as a safety-line. If I let go I'll die." Fearfully, she said that she could not tolerate separations or saying goodbye. But the expected rejection did not come.

"I feel a tremendous empty space inside," she said, "and it can never be filled. I tried to fill it with my boyfriend, but that didn't work. I tried to fill it with my mother, but she rejects me." She had taken to telephoning her mother regularly, to report on her anxiety and unhappiness and to obtain reassurance about her anticipated academic and professional failures.

During the early months of A. M.'s enrollment at this professional school away from her home city, her mother had responded to the patient's telephoned pleas with equal anxiety, concrete advice, and admonitions not to give up. Recently she had changed her tune, and now was telling A. M. to stop complaining and "grow up." A. M. saw this as a terrible rejection and lack of understanding, consistent with the fact that she had never felt that her mother truly loved her or was interested in her for herself, but only wanted to push A. M. to achieve as much as possible. As an example of her mother's lack of interest,

A. M. reported an incident in which her mother had forgotten an isolated item of information about her daughter's academic life and worries, which A. M. wanted to talk about. This "proved" that her mother was not concerned for A. M.'s welfare or needs, and A. M. now spoke vividly about the furious attack she had made on her mother in justified retaliation for this slight. She turned to her female therapist with a broad, winning smile: "You are different. You always remember everything I say."

In the next few hours she reported more arguments with her mother and further instances of her longstanding neglect. Once, many years ago, returning from a trip with the four children, her mother became so engrossed in managing the baggage that she left one child behind in the airport. She remembered another occasion, when she herself had felt abandoned: After having her family, the mother returned to college to complete her education. A. M. was left with a succession of female caretakers. "Only one of them loved me. She spent lots of time dressing me, and helping me look nice. Mother fired her for irresponsibility."

A self psychologist would be likely to approach these data by applying the system's rules of exegesis (Reed, 1985), to interpret the manifest contents directly as indicators of the inner state of A. M.'s self and (through the theory's developmental propositions) to arrive at a hypothesis about the causes of this condition. Such an interpretation might say that the patient's feelings of emptiness are the expression of her incompletely developed self, a defect which she tries frantically to remedy through attachments to various selfobjects—mother, boyfriends, teachers, bosses, therapist. The self's fragility is confirmed by A. M.'s vulnerability to reacting catastrophically to all separations as well as to lack of empathy by the selfobject (boyfriend's preoccupation with his family; mother's forgetfulness). A. M.'s feelings under these circumstances correspond to Kohut's description of "the anxieties experienced by a person who is becoming aware that his self is starting to disintegrate" (Kohut, 1977, p. 102). Her idealization of the therapist, who seems (like the beloved babysitter of childhood) to provide the empathy and mirroring that A. M. needs, is consistent with the description of a therapeutic selfobject relationship, in which the analyst performs "certain basic functions in the realm of narcissistic homeostasis which (the patient's) own psyche is unable to provide" (Kohut, 1971, p. 17). If the self-psychological therapist were to accept the idealization, and interpret to A. M. that she is hurt by unempathic behavior because of her fragile self-structure, the stage would be set for A. M. to internalize new structure from the treatment relationship. The self psychologist might also speculate that A. M.'s self-deficiency is the developmental outcome of unempathic parenting, as shown in A. M.'s descriptions of her mother's past behavior. The therapist would now be able to point out that A. M.'s anger and disappointment in her boyfriend are out of proportion to his actual attitude toward her, but rather reflect her self's inevitable and understandable great vulnerability to any hint of neglect, in light of the inadequacy of her parents' empathy for her. This intervention might free A. M. to promptly establish a better relationship with her boyfriend, an outcome which she would experience as very helpful, and for which she will be very grateful to the therapist.

A classical psychoanalyst will not see A. M.'s experiences as directly translatable into data about her inner state. This therapist, aware of "the polyvalence of words" (Reed, 1985), is provided by his or her theory not with a way of going directly from manifest data to understanding, but rather with a way of listening to the patient and assisting her in a mutual exploration of her associations that will yield up the *unique* and *particular* meanings that her experiences have, in the context of her own life. This therapist would understand her sense of emptiness and defect as aspects of a *self-representation* that, like the other aspects of mental life, has multiple meanings, and expresses both impulses and defenses. She or he would therefore listen without fully accepting the patient's theory about herself (as empty, deficient, etc.) at face value (Grossman, 1982). In addition to the manifest material, the therapist would notice and wonder about such things as the power that A. M. exerts over others through her vocal complaining, the intensity of her fury when she is frustrated, and the way in which her complaints serve to give current justification to a rage that (theory tells him—cf. Kernberg, 1982) *may* be a transference of a frightening conflictual infantile feeling. If her associations showed that it *was* a transference of this type, this therapist would reason that A. M.'s anxiety concerning achievement might partly reflect a conflict about, and avoidance of, success (because of the power it would give her to act upon her inner rage). Similarly, her need to behave in pathetic, dependent ways, and to seek love as a weak, helpless person might serve in part to conceal her ambitions, aggression and power from herself and from others.

Clarification of this conflict, *if it is substantiated by further data,* would begin to free the patient to achieve in work and in love with greater efficiency and comfort. But the classical psychoanalyst would be particularly guided by theory to be cognizant of the great complexity of psychic life, and to avoid prematurely giving voice to such speculations before they are confirmed by A. M.'s associations. Instead the therapist would support the patient in further explorations.

This was done in the case of A. M., and yielded specific genetic material which could not have been predicted by a developmental theory.

After further arguments with her mother and now also with a younger sister, A. M. thought more about why she felt so unloved— more so, she felt, than any of her siblings—and always had to earn love through achievements. She now revealed that her mother was pregnant with her before the parents' marriage. "It's my fault that they had to marry. I ruined their lives. Mother was young and beautiful—I should never have been born." Her further associations went in many directions: As an "illegitimate" child, she fantasied that she had to work harder than the others to gain the approval and security to which she was not "legitimately" entitled. Her feelings of emptiness and unworthiness now also could be seen as partly reflecting guilt about her great imagined destructive power, "ruining" her parents' lives as an infant, and not simply as a direct outcome of insufficient nurturing. This shed a new light, as well, on her current struggles over anger. Further material indicated the complex connections of these matters to competition with her siblings. As the oldest child, A. M. had a number of experiences that seemed very harsh and unfair. For example, after the birth of the third child, and first boy, when A. M. was five, A. M. was displaced from the children's room in the family's small apartment. The new baby was given her old place, and she now slept on the living-room couch. This memory helped A. M. understand why she felt such urgency about proving herself special, and about having and displaying wealth and luxury. It also was a beginning for further associations about her rivalry with men at school and work. She now recognized a defensive function of her worries: Prior to a class presentation, she had gone to some trouble to tell all her classmates that it would not be good—and it turned out fine. She saw that she was reluctant to accept success because there was a "shark" inside her (i.e., a newly conscious, aggressive self-representation), which made her enjoy the triumph too much. On the other hand, she also feared being shown up as a fraud, and thus punished for her evil, sharklike impulses.

It is very important to make clear that this example is presented for illustrative purposes only. The techniques described are based on theory, and may not reflect the actual behavior that could be expected of real practitioners in the clinical situation. However, it does reflect the different approaches and purposes dictated by self psychology and classical psychoanalysis, *as theories*. A self psychologist who diagnoses a particular patient as suffering from pathology of the self (and, as indicated before, this is now the virtually ubiquitous approach of this group to all patients) will understand manifest content as a direct expression of a state of deficit in the personality. Interventions are then aimed at demonstrating this deficit and its causes to the patient, because in doing so the therapist will be functioning as the needed selfobject and fostering structure building.

From the point of view of the classical analyst, this approach is a gross oversimplification of the actual state of affairs: A return to a pre-Freudian environmentalist theory, which contains many inconsistencies and contradictions and is not truly a psychoanalytic theory at all. Self psychological treatment is potentially helpful because it offers the patient direct gratifications and plausible but inexact explanations. Such explanations may be rationalized by the analysand to control his or her problems and experiences, but relief from problems would be more a form of defensive support rather than an analytic cure.

The classical analyst believes that problems of self-esteem can have many different etiologies, and varied dynamic and structural origins. The task of the analyst is to aid the patient in exploring and understanding mental processes and fantasies through the free-associative method, with the purpose of bringing any evidence of unconscious conflicts into consciousness. Because the analyst sees no one-to-one connection between manifest phenomena and underlying causes, she or he believes that one cannot understand the patient's fantasies, experiences, and dreams without the aid of the latter's associations. One expects to find that the manifest material, including conscious self-representations, will change as treatment gives the patient increasing access to unconscious conflicts and fantasies. Consequently, one avoids a premature closure fostered by deficit theory. However, the analyst will not reject or challenge the patient's feelings and transferences (e.g., idealization) out of hand, and would agree with the self psychologist's stress on the harsh, rejecting impression that would be created by a therapist who did offer challenges of this type. Nonetheless, the classical analyst would consider empathic acceptance of the patient not as a *curative* factor (Luborsky, 1977) but simply as a tactful attitude that creates a "holding environment," in which analytic exploration can go on productively.

The self psychologist, on the other hand, would consider the classical analyst as *not* truly empathic. Instead, she or he sees the latter as overvaluing the "search for truth" about the patient in a pseudoscientific manner that meets the analyst's needs for feeling "objective," but is experienced by the patient as a repetition of the empathic failures experienced in childhood. The self psychologist would expect this approach *not* to be helpful or curative, except insofar as the analyst accidentally communicated empathy to the patient, while intending only to interpret and analyze (Kohut, 1984).

Discussion

The ferment of the past fifteen years concerning the purported rising incidence of narcissistic disorders—with popular and scientific publications pointing to the dawning of an "age of narcissism" (Woodward and Mark, 1978)—may now be abating somewhat. It has left behind it a new school of depth psychology, the psychology of the self, which has been hailed by its enthusiastic adherents as a revolutionary new paradigm of great power—this is certainly true when the method applied to the narcissistic patients for whom it was originally developed, but it is also seen by some as the true advent of the post-Freudian era, which sheds new light on all psychopathology. Others have offered serious criticisms of the new theory, suggesting that its concepts represent a return to a prepsychoanalytic environmentalist approach based on faulty logic and untenable motivational constructs. They believe that its treatment methods may give psychotherapeutic (but not analytic) relief to some, but could be harmful in other cases, in which *fantasies* of defectiveness are wrongly dealt with as accurate self-perceptions (Arlow, 1981; Curtis, 1983, 1984; Kernberg, 1982; Levine, 1977, 1979, 1985; Reed, 1985; Stein, 1979). Many of self psychology's critics, however, acknowledge that it has focused clinicians' attention on an important area of normal and pathological experience and, at least, has led to useful refinements in tact and technique.

In this chapter, we have seen some of the ways in which the concern with narcissism and the new theory itself have stimulated widespread scholarly and scientific interest in the self and self-representations and have led to questions, clarifications, and new insights into many aspects of psychoanalytic theory and practice. For example, there has been reexamination of inference procedures (Reed, 1985), exploration—on both sides—of ways in which personal motives and attitudes may influence theory construction (e.g., Kohut, 1984; Kernberg, 1985), and consideration of aspects of the logic of theory construction (Slap and Levine, 1978).

Perhaps the most important controversy underlying these developments is between deficit-based and conflict-based explanations of the clinical findings. In 1914, Freud noted that a similar difference of opinion was partly responsible for the schisms between his theories of the importance of intrapsychic conflict and the divergent schools of Jung and Adler. It is evident that this is not a new dispute, nor is it easily resolved, and it has been repeatedly suggested that strong irrational psychological forces are active on both sides. It should not be overlooked, however, that realistic issues of sincere therapeutic purpose and the frequent difficulty of making accurate diagnostic judgments also help to propel this continuing debate. The majority of observers in both schools of thought can agree about extreme cases: most schizophrenics appear, to almost all clinicians, to be suffering from some type of developmentally or biologically induced deficit(s) in ego functioning; and the majority of analysts would also agree that uncomplicated psychoneuroses are caused by incomplete repression of intrapsychic conflicts (although even here self psychologists are increasingly attempting to apply a deficit model). It is in the middle ground, where symptoms are less easily categorized as caused by developmental failure or neurotic inhibition, that the struggle is most intense. This group of disorders is often most frustrating to the analyst, for many reasons—including the uncertainty over whether analytic or supportive technique should be used.

Kernberg (1982) makes a strong argument that deficit theory is not applicable to narcissistic forms of pathology. He points out that self psychologists understand these disorders as caused by fixation at *normal* early infantile developmental stages—that is, self-structure does not develop. In conflict theory development is seen not as simply arrested, but as distorted for defensive reasons. As a result, one observes not an *absence* of structure but a structure that is formed in unusual, maladaptive ways. It is readily observed, he says, that pathological narcissism is not simply excessive self-love, but love of a pathologically distorted self-image. Thus, it is not merely an adult version of a normal childhood phase. (Similar observations were made by Curtis, 1984, and Levine, 1979.)

We would add to Kernberg's criticisms that in addition to favoring explanations in terms of fixations and deficits, self psychology's treatment recommendations are based on a postulate that seems highly improbable to us: namely, that after decades of fixation the growth process can be reawakened and, with somewhat special techniques, helped to proceed (in an adult) roughly along the path it would have taken in early infancy (Levine, 1977).

Despite its undoubted heuristic value, there is clearly serious doubt as to whether self psychology has sufficient internal logic and explanatory power to fulfill its proponents' hopes, by becoming a broadly accepted general theory. One source of its weakness as a system is that it makes extensive use of the common human inclination to reify such abstractions as "the self" and to treat them as tangible structures that can be defective, be subject to direct perception, and be repaired or helped to resume growth. This was beautifully characterized by John Stuart Mill:

> The tendency has always been strong to believe that whatever received a name must be an entity or being, having an independent existence of its own. And if no real entity answering to the name could be found, men did not for that reason suppose that none existed, but imagined that it was something particularly abstruse and mysterious. (cited by Gould, 1981, p. 185)

Notes

The authors wish to thank Dr. Ana Maria Garcia for her invaluable contributions to this essay.

Grateful acknowledgment is made to Sigmund Freud Copyrights, The Institute of Psycho-Analysis, The Hogarth Press for permission to quote from

The Standard Edition of the Complete Psychological Works of Sigmund Freud translated and edited by James Strachey and to Basic Books, Inc. for *The Collected Papers of Sigmund Freud,* vol. 1 edited by Ernest Jones.

References

Arlow, J. A. (1981). Theories of pathogenesis. *Psychoanalytic Quarterly,* *50,* 488–514.

Breu, G. (1979). Medics: Is Dr. Heinz Kohut beside himself? Rarely, but his ideas of fragmented personality revolutionized psychiatry. *People,* Feb. 26, pp. 60–63.

Chessick, R. D. (1980). The problematical self in Kant and Kohut. *Psychoanalytic Quarterly, 69,* 456–73.

Curtis, H. (1983). Review of the search for the self: Selected writings of Heinz Kohut, 1950–1978. Paul H. Ornstein (Ed.). *Journal of the American Psychoanalytic Association, 31,* 272–85.

———. (1984). Perspectives on self psychology. Paper presented at scientific meeting of the Philadelphia Association for Psychoanalysis, Philadelphia, Pa., February.

Erikson, E. H. (1968). *Identity, youth and crisis.* New York: W. W. Norton.

Freud, S. (1957). On narcissism: An introduction. *Standard edition of the complete psychological works of Sigmund Freud, vol. 14* (pp. 73–102). London: Hogarth Press. (Original work appeared in 1914.)

———. (1961). The ego and the id. *Standard edition of the complete psychological works of Sigmund Freud, vol. 19* (pp. 3–66). London: Hogarth Press. (Original work appeared in 1923.)

———. (1962). The aetiology of hysteria. *Standard edition of the complete psychological works of Sigmund Freud, vol. 3* (pp. 189–221). London: Hogarth Press. (Original work appeared in 1896.)

Gediman, H. K. (1983). Annihilation anxiety: The experience of deficit in neurotic compromise formation. *International Journal of Psychoanalysis, 64,* 59–70.

Goldberg, A., Kohut, H., Basch, M. F., Gunther, M. S., Marcus, D., Ornstein, A., Ornstein, P., Tolpin, M., Tolpin, P., and Wolf, E. S. (Eds.) (1978). *The psychology of the self: A casebook.* New York: International Universities Press.

Gould, S. J. (1981). *The mismeasure of man.* New York: W. W. Norton.

Grossman, W. I. (1982). The self as fantasy: Fantasy as theory. *Journal of the American Psychoanalytic Association, 30,* 919–37.

Hartmann, H. (1950). Comments on the psychoanalytic theory of the ego. *Psychoanalytic Study of the Child, 5,* 74–96.

Jacobson, E. (1964). *The self and the object world.* New York: International Universities Press.

Kernberg, O. F. (1975). *Borderline conditions and pathological narcissism.* New York: Jason Aronson.

——. (1982). Self, ego, affects and drives. *Journal of the American Psychoanalytic Association, 30,* 893–917.

Kohut, H. (1971). *The analysis of the self.* New York: International Universities Press.

——. (1977). *The restoration of the self.* New York: International Universities Press.

——. (1984). *How does analysis cure?* Chicago: University of Chicago Press.

Leo, J. (1980). The preacher of narcissism: Analyst Heinz Kohut's "self-psychology" rewrites Freud. *Time,* Dec. 1, p. 76.

Levine, F. J. (1977). Review of Heinz Kohut, *The restoration of the self. Journal of the Philadelphia Association for Psychoanalysis, 4,* 238–47.

——. (1979). On the clinical application of Heinz Kohut's psychology of the self: Comments on some recently published case studies. *Journal of the Philadelphia Association for Psychoanalysis, 6,* 1–19.

——. (1985). Self psychology and the new narcissism in psychoanalysis. *Clinical Psychology Review, 5,* 215–29.

Lichtenberg, J. (1973). Review of Heinz Kohut, *The analysis of the self. Bulletin of the Philadelphia Association for Psychoanalysis, 23,* 58–66.

Luborsky, L. (1977). Curative factors in psychoanalytic and psychodynamic psychotherapies. J. P. Brady, J. Mendels, M. T. Orne, and W. Rieger (Eds.), *Psychiatry: Areas of promise and advancement* (pp. 187–203). New York: Spectrum.

Mahler, M. S., Pine, F., and Bergman, A. (1975). *The psychological birth of the human infant.* New York: Basic Books.

Modell, A. H. (1983). Comments on the rise of narcissism. In A. Goldberg (Ed.), *The future of psychoanalysis: Essays in honor of Heinz Kohut* (pp. 111–21). New York: International Universities Press.

Ornstein, P. H. (1975). On narcissism: Beyond the introduction. Highlights of Heinz Kohut's contributions to the psychoanalytic treatment of narcissistic personality disorders. *Annual of Psychoanalysis, 2,* 127–49.

———. (Ed.). (1978). *The search for the self: Selected writings of Heinz Kohut: 1950–1978.* New York: International Universities Press.

Rangell, L. (1982). The self in psychoanalytic theory. *Journal of the American Psychoanalytic Association, 30,* 863–97.

Reed, G. S. (1985). Exegesis in classical psychoanalysis and in self psychology: A comparison of rules governing clinical understanding. Presented at Winter Meeting, American Psychoanalytic Association, New York, New York.

Slap, J. W., and Levine, F. J. (1978). On hybrid concepts in psychoanalysis. *Psychoanalytic Quarterly, 47,* 499–523.

Stein, M. H. (1979). Review of Heinz Kohut, *The restoration of the self. Journal of the American Psychoanalytic Association, 27,* 665–80.

Tolpin, M., and Kohut, H. (1980). The disorders of the self: The psychopathology of the first years of life. In S. Greenspan and G. Pollock (Eds.), *The course of life.* Washington, D.C.: U.S. Government Printing Office.

Tuttman, S. (1978). Kohut symposium contribution. *Psychoanalytic Review, 65,* 624–29.

Waelder, R. (1936). The principle of multiple function: Observations on overdetermination. *Psychoanalytic Quarterly, 5,* 45–62.

Wallerstein, R. S. (1983). Self psychology and "classical" psychoanalytic psychology: The nature of their relationship. In A. Goldberg (Ed.), *The future of psychoanalysis: Essays in honor of Heinz Kohut* (pp. 19–63). New York: International Universities Press.

Woodward, K. L., and Mark, R. (1978). Ideas: The new narcissism. *Newsweek,* Jan. 30, pp. 70–72.

CHAPTER 15

Attachment and the Brightening and Dimming of Self

PHILIP LICHTENBERG

AFTER THREE YEARS of psychotherapy, Arthur Samuel has begun to be aware of self within the events and encounters by which he is creating his life. He is already fifty-one years old, has been a teacher of considerable success in a private high school near a large city, and has fathered two children in the twenty-eight years of his marriage, neither of whom currently lives at home. He entered therapy because his marriage was at a critical point; both he and his wife were wondering whether they wished to remain together. In addition to being a fine teacher, much loved by his social studies students, Arthur has been an active union man and a left-wing political activist. On the surface, it would seem, Arthur Samuel should have easy access to self and a strong sense of what he is and what he wants. Yet, he was considering ending his marriage three years ago precisely because he had neither. What is that about?

With Arthur Samuel, as with many other persons married for many years, attachment had become fusion, and with fusion had come loss of sense of self in the relationship with his wife. Attachment and a bright experiencing of self in his case were mutually exclusive. He often became blank or dissociated during an evening meal with his wife, Betty, whether they ate at home or in a restaurant where stimulation by the milieu might have encouraged vivid sense of self. He had begun to seek clarity of experience of self by taking a room in their home and decorating it to his taste, and that had been a source of affirmation of individuality. Yet, that was a time-limited event and did not encroach upon the ever-present sense that he was going through life without making his life his own way.

When we remember that the attachment experiences of the infant and small child are the ground for the unfolding of the differentiation of self and other, and thus are the very conditions for the bright experiencing of self, we have reason to pause and consider the varying relations of attachment and self (Balint, 1979; Benedek, 1973; Lichtenstein, 1977). In the pages that follow, I will provide the conception of self that describes Arthur Samuel's experiences, an understanding of the brightening and dimming of the experience of self, the relationship of these changes to attachment and life-span-developmental issues that clarify the argument being made.

Following the theory of Gestalt therapy, developed by Paul Goodman in volume 2 of *Gestalt Therapy* (Perls, Hefferline, and Goodman, 1951), I will consider "self" to refer to the system of contact making and withdrawal at any given time. In this context, self is a person's experience associated with figure forming in the figure/background process by which contacts between the person and the environment are regulated. Self is the power that forms a Gestalt from the person-environment field. It is not in the person; rather it is experience of the person of the person-environment matrix, depending upon the environmental background as well as the animal-organismic background of the person for the elements that are composed into the figure during the contact-making and withdrawal process. Self, then, will brighten as the person creatively contacts the environment and will dim as the person withdraws from the environment, and this brightening and dimming will be evident in the experiential life of the individual.

Contact making and withdrawal constitute a cycle. Arthur Samuel, in his better moods, on his morning drive to school begins to think of his working day, his students, his lesson plans, his fellow teachers, whom he distrusts, his classroom and what he intends to do with it. In this transition into his school day, in which his needs and the stimuli from the school environment enter his experience, Arthur is in a period of fore-contact, a period in which the elements that will motivate contact are coming into view. Now that Arthur lives close to the school where he teaches, he has less time between leaving home and all that has transpired with his wife and arriving at school than he had in prior years. Withdrawal from contact with his wife and the early phases of contact with school activities impinge upon each other, and conflicts between Arthur and Betty often surface precisely as he leaves the kitchen door to go to his car. Quite often there is unfinished business between them as a consequence.

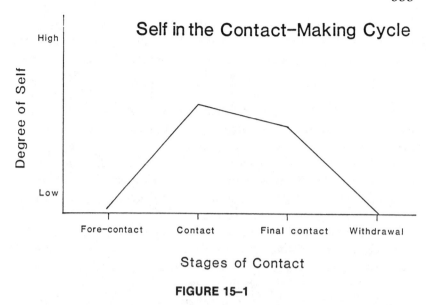

Stages of Contact

FIGURE 15–1

When he arrives at school, Arthur is immediately inundated by demands from all sides. He has attendance to take, students' questions to answer, administrative details to handle, and so forth. He is plunged from reverie and apprehensive anticipation into full activity. If he is mastering his life, he creates actions that place into a coherent figure requirements and possibilities from the diverse sources stimulating him. He is full of himself in this endeavor and his teaching is vital. In the course of his teaching—and this happens often even when he is depressed—he and the class and the material being discussed come together in a brightly experienced Gestalt. From the stage of contact in which he is managing diverse demands to this final contact of captivated unity there is a rising excitement. After the class, or after the day on a good teaching day, Arthur feels that excitement and takes time to come down from the high that he has experienced, in a withdrawal enterprise.

The cycle, then, is from a relatively withdrawn place to fore-contact, to contact, to final contact, and then to withdrawal from that episode and on to something else. This cycle takes place in the larger day, from early morning into late evening, but it also takes place in smaller units, as in a given class, or a meal, or an evening watching television. When the cycle flows without interruption or without difficulty in its accomplishment, there is a systematic increase and decrease in the appearance of self. During fore-contact, there is a modest experience of self, an awareness of what needs and intentions the person holds side by side with a processing of the stimulations from the not-self, the external or environmental world. During the contact phase there is significant unfolding of self as the person chooses what is to become figural and what is to remain as background in the construction of a figure. During the pitch of final contact, when the figure is formed and the person-environment field is integrated, at first there is brightness and strength of the experience of self, but then there is a dialectical loss of self in the new unity that has been created (Lichtenberg, 1980). And with withdrawal, self disappears entirely. A graph of what I have described would look like figure 15.1.

Brazelton and Als (1979) have described the reciprocal attention play between infant and mother in terms that fit this description of the contact and withdrawal cycle. The infant or mother initiates a process of mutual gazing, which increases in excitement as each partner attends to the other, until a climax is reached and withdrawal commences. At the height of the game there is a burst of happiness shared by both infant and mother. Brazelton and Als have also noted that positive experiences of this kind are basic to the unfolding of attachment. This pattern of an event also characterizes Freud's (1966) concept of an "experience of satisfaction," which is a basic model for his theory of human relations.

In this way of thinking, "self" is the creative adjusting carried forward by the person acting as agent, and we can speak of the dialectic of agency by which an individual moves from little self, little agency, to much self, much agentic effort, much creative adjustment, and thence to loss of self by surrender to the new figure, the new relationship that has been created (cf. Angyal, 1973, on homonomy). Just so, Arthur Samuel, working in the classroom with young people alive to his teaching, could experience brightening of self as he developed the learning climate and substance for the hour and loss of self in the communion with his students whose questions were the next step in the teaching/learning project for the day. And, conversely, Arthur and Betty, with many accumulated interrupted episodes to burden their relating, found it difficult to differ with one another and excite one another and create new figures rather than old and tired ones. This conception of "self" fits with Macmurray's *Self as Agent* (1957), in which self is the person in action (a psychology of "I do" rather than

"I think"), building community in which the person loses separateness. Yet, also with this view of self we can see that there may be too much selfness, too much agency, such that loss of self in merging with others is inhibited.

In the discussion to this point I have introduced three ways in which attachment is related to the brightening and dimming of the experience of self. First, attachment to the parent in the early days of life is the ground for self experience. Second, attachment in final contact is the goal of self experiences when other people are integrated into the new figures formed in the contact-making cycle. Third, however, attachment that constitutes excessive fusion with another serves to interfere with the contact cycle exactly when the function of the self is most central. Let us attend to each of these in turn.

Without entering into the debate, chronicled by Greenberg and Mitchell (1983), concerning whether drive theory or object-relations theory best describes the infant's attachment behavior, a debate that I think is unnecessary, since it revives the old biology-versus-culture issue under a new name, and that my concept of Self/Social Unity obviates (1969), it seems acceptable to assume that the received view of matters is that self and other are not distinguished by the infant at the beginning of life, but out of experiences of satisfaction such discrimination unfolds. Benedek introduced a critical theoretical insight: the infant develops a capacity to wait and thus can bridge the gap between the appearance of a need and the connection with the caretaker that provides for the gratification of that need (1973). From such encounters the infant develops what she called "confident expectation." This capacity to wait, to master the so-called problem of delay of gratification, permits the infant to recognize need and to own need and also to recognize the caretaker as an other.

In the terms I have been using here, the waiting activity is an early instance of the contact stage in the contact-making and withdrawal cycle. Between fore-contact, when the need is entering awareness, when the infant is restless or crying, and the final contact of relation to the caretaker, the infant waits, experiences tension within, conducts a crude search in the environment, emits new cries, and so forth. Insofar as this waiting becomes associated with eventual gratification, the infant records the event as an experience of satisfaction, and develops in consciousness and in memory inklings of selfness.

Like Benedek, Lichtenstein (1977) suggests that not only identity but also sense of identity comes from the mother-infant relationship. The sense of identity, the selfness of the infant, derives from the infant's experiences of being an instrument for the satisfaction of the mother's needs. Such instrumental actions pertain to the contact stage of the cycle.

Goodman (Perls et al., 1951), as well as Winnicott (1965), have argued that there is no infant, only the infant-parent matrix. Unless an infant is embedded in such a matrix, it will not survive, and from this matrix the infant comes to articulate a distinct self.

Arthur Samuel's life story has a mixture of good times and difficult times in attachments to others. An older sister contracted a contagious disease when he was three months old. Arthur's mother abruptly stopped nursing him to care for his sister. When he was four, his father died, and his mother placed him with an aunt and uncle for two years until she remarried and could care for him again. These major disruptions enhanced his fears of abandonment, which continued into adult life and colored his relationship with his wife, including his fear of separating from her. Counterbalancing these were many nurturant concerns of his mother, which also influenced his marriage.

The formula for what has been suggested here is: From satisfying attachment experiences the discrimination of self unfolds. The converse formula is: From lack of satisfying attachment experiences, fusion of self and other persists in the psychic life of the individual.

The second way in which attachment has been related to brightness and dimness of the aware self pertains to the stage in the contact-making and withdrawal cycle that is known as "final contact." Goodman (Perls et al., 1951) describes the matter in the following way:

> In final contact the self is immediately and fully engaged in the *figure* it has discovered-and-invented; momentarily, there is practically no background. The figure embodies all the concern of the self and the self is nothing but its present concern, so the self *is* the figure. The powers of the self are now actualized, so the self becomes something (but in so doing it ceases to be self). (p. 416)

If the stage of "contact" entails the constructing of a figure through actions that define what is to be taken in and assimilated by the person and what is to be alienated, the stage of "final contact" encompasses the person-environment matrix that has been developed into a unified figure. This means that a new merging of person and world or person and other has been created, a new attachment has been made. A climax or culmination in the person meeting the world takes place, the distinction between self and other vanishes, and, therefore, the experience of selfness dissipates as the episode comes to fruition. When the final contact is primarily centered upon a relation to another person, when the new figure that is created is an I and a Thou merged, a momentary attachment is effected; and when the experience is assimilated by the person, the grounds for full attachment are laid down.

Arthur Samuel entered therapy rather than the divorce court because he had known many such moments of final contact with Betty and they had been deeply rewarding to him. With all the disturbances of contact, and loss of self in the process, there had been shared experiences in which both partners defined themselves and emerged newly grown. In therapy itself, Arthur and Betty found freshness and new revelations, surprises and novel figures, sufficient to outweigh the distrust they had carried. Now final contact was achieved after the excitement of differences and struggle between them rather than through duplicities (Kaiser, 1965) by which they had fostered a delusion of fusion.

These duplicities, associated with what Kaiser has called the universal symptom (1965), bring us to the third way in which attachment is related to the brightening and dimming of self. Attachment can serve not only as the basis for the unfolding of self, as the background that supports the experience of self, but also, in the form of fusion with another person, as a substitute for self. An individual, by loss of ego functions (cf. Perls et al., 1951), through introjection, projection, and so on, can minimize the contact stage in the contact-making and withdrawal cycle and, thereby, diminish the experience of self. Figure 15.2 illustrates this notion.

Let us explore more fully what has just been asserted. Attachment behavior, following Bowlby (1969), refers to reliance upon proximity and involvement with another person for sense of security and well-being. One form of that security in an adult would be support given by the attachment object to an individual acting autonomously, as an agent, even as a resistant or differing other, in transactions with the attachment object. That is to say, the attachment object serves as a

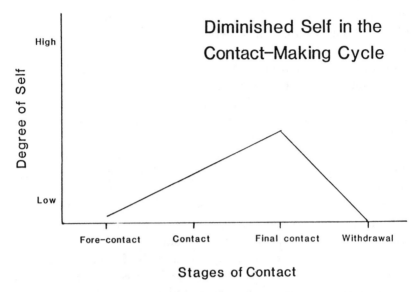

FIGURE 15–2

holding environment (Winnicott, 1965) for the person who is acting. Betty on many occasions was a source of support for Arthur in their interactions. She helped him to buy presents for herself and the children, so that he purchased appropriate and pleasing items and could feel good about himself when he had previously felt anxious and insecure. In their sexual relations, she encouraged him to find satisfaction for himself. She supported his fantasies of quitting his job when he felt frustrated by his working conditions. In each of these contexts, Betty enabled Arthur to realize self functions in the contact stage of the contact-making and withdrawal cycle.

But there is a different sort of "security" and "support" that adults pursue, a sort based on doubt and ambivalence rather than confident expectation. Rather than act autonomously, and thus carry the weight of responsibility for the consequences of their actions, persons frequently merge with others and give over their agency. Probably the most common and simplest method for fusing with another person is to enter into an introjection-projection compact. One person introjects the other while the other simultaneously projects upon the first. (Cf. Lichtenberg, Reimert, and Levine, 1982.) In the process, the two become one unit, with one source of decision making. In the case of

Arthur and Betty it was not that Arthur always introjected Betty and Betty always projected upon Arthur, though this was the more frequent situation. (For instance, Arthur was the figure in their relationship who was always identified as emotionally disturbed while Betty appeared calm and self-contained; yet half the time Arthur was carrying or expressing Betty's depression about her incompletely realized life. Betty projected her sadness and experienced it through Arthur's despair.) There were also many occasions in which Arthur assumed the position of projector and Betty did the introjecting. In either form of the introjection-projection compact, the two gave up autonomy in the act of merging.

Indications that such an introjection-projection compact is in place come from the quality of the relationships; such relationships tend to alternate between too little overt disagreement between the participants and then excessive differences. The lack of disagreement, which is known in Gestalt-therapy theory as the "demand for confluence," is the fusion process in action. The extreme differences, sometimes shown in bitter fights and resentments, other times shown in leaving the relationship to satisfy needs basic to the bond, such as extramarital affairs, surface precisely because the fusion cannot adequately meet the needs of the two individuals. The person who introjects gives up some of his or her needs in the practice of introjecting; the person who projects similarly loses out on direct satisfaction of needs. Accordingly, the relationship suffers.

Arthur and Betty were very attached by means of projections and introjections. One area of significant proportions for this fusion was their sexual relationship. Arthur was very interested in sex and very romantic; Betty was more cool and reserved. What perplexed the two was that over the years they frequently had good sexual experiences with one another, yet neither was satisfied with their relationship. Scrutiny of their sexual activities showed that when their needs were strong at the same time they quickly related and quickly climaxed with much satisfaction. In terms of the contact-making and withdrawal cycle, they moved rapidly from fore-contact to final contact. What was least emphasized was contact, precisely the area where brightening of self would be experienced. That is, neither felt confident in asserting what he or she wanted; both tried to please the other by imagining what was desirable and both disguised what was displeasing to them lest they offend the other. Significant introjections and projections limited their ego functions during their sexual play and consequently limited the height of excitement they could attain.

In short, the attachment experiences between Arthur and Betty, with special reference to the activities of the contact stage in their interactions, were fusion experiences implemented by faulty introjections and projections. Because self is most energized during the contact stage, on the one hand, and the fusion processes minimized selfness, on the other hand, both Arthur and Betty were aware only of diminished self in their relationship. In other social relationships both were lively and experienced brightness of self during the contact-making and withdrawal unfoldings. Both Arthur at school and Betty at her job as a guidance counselor could engage in spirited ways. Accordingly, both felt that their marriage was the problem and felt ready to end it. During therapy, as they discovered the various introjections and projections that produced the dim rather than bright experiences of self, and as they intensified the contact stage of their transactions, they once again became interested in the uniqueness and particularity of their partner. They rediscovered each other and themselves by undoing the fusion process that had come to dominate their interactions.

Attachment as ground for the confident unfolding of selfness and attachment as final goal in which selfness is lost represent the beginning and the culmination of the figure-forming process. It is during the creative adjusting that it is necessary for attachment to recede and selfness to be asserted in full strength and brightness. This is exactly what helped Arthur during his therapy: he could risk asserting his differences with Betty, his discontents, his desires, his hurts, his cares; and he could begin to leave for Betty her wants, her sadness, her anxieties—leave for her to experience and to manage, with his support, but not with his introjections and identifications.

Attachment and brightness of self, therefore, seem to have a dialectical quality: attachment is necessary to brightening of self, as ground is necessary to figure formation; but attachment precludes a bright awareness of self if it predominates in the contact stage of the contact-making and withdrawal cycle. Those persons who seek attachment, like those who intend cooperation as a goal, will negate the very means to accomplish it for they will control the assertion of selfness in fear of being self-centered. Only by putting forward their needs and preferences can individuals find unity with others, or, more exactly, only when they express their desires in contacting other persons can individuals realize simultaneously personal satisfaction and communion.

References

Angyal, Andras. 1973. *Neurosis and treatment: A holistic theory.* Eugenia Hanfman and Richard M. Jones, eds. New York: Viking.

Balint, Michael. 1979. *The basic fault.* New York: Brunner/Mazel.

Benedek, T. 1973. Adaptation to reality in early infancy. In *Psychoanalytic investigations.* T. Benedek, ed. New York: Quadrangle.

Bowlby, John. 1969. *Attachment and loss. Volume I: Attachment.* New York: Basic Books.

Brazelton, T. Berry, and Als, Heidelise. 1979. Four early stages in the development of mother-infant interactions. In *The Psychoanalytic study of the child,* vol. 34. A. J. Solnit, R. S. Eissler, A. Freud, M. Krisand, P. B. Neubauer, eds. New Haven: Yale University Press.

Freud, Sigmund. 1966. Project for a scientific psychology: 1895. In *The standard edition of the complete psychological works of Sigmund Freud.* Vol. 1. James Strachey, ed. London: Hogarth.

Greenberg, Jay R., and Mitchell, Stephen A. 1983. *Object relations in psychoanalytic theory.* Cambridge: Harvard University Press.

Kaiser, Hellmuth. 1965. *Effective psychotherapy: The contributions of Hellmuth Kaiser.* Louis B. Fierman, ed. New York: Free Press.

Lichtenberg, Philip. 1969. *Psychoanalysis: Radical and conservative.* New York: Springer.

———. 1980. On being thoroughly alive. *Et cetera, 37,* 254–70.

———, Reimert, Carol Roman, and Levine, Susan S. 1982. Social-emotional keys to the division of power. *Journal of Sociology and Social Welfare, 9,* 503–10.

Lichtenstein, Heinz. 1977. Identity and sexuality. *The dilemma of human identity.* H. Lichtenstein, ed. New York: Jason Aronson.

Macmurray, John. 1957. *The self as agent.* London: Faber and Faber.

Perls, Frederick, Hefferline, Ralph H., and Goodman, Paul. 1951. *Gestalt therapy.* New York: Julian.

Winnicott, D. W. 1965. The theory of the parent-infant relationship. *The maturational processes and the facilitating environment.* New York: International Universities Press.

SELF AND UNITY

Assuming the validity of Jung's concept of self as the archetype that "... stands behind the scenes, as it were, as a kind of author-director, actor-manager, producing the tangible performance that proceeds on the public (and private) stage" (Stevens, 1982, p. 52), Fordham, in the first essay in this part, argues for a radical indivisibility of unity in the personality. Symbols of self-coherence, often in mandala form, appear at the most critical moments of disintegration of the conscious personality; infants show many signs of their unique individuality and responses even just after birth; and the coherent representations of self (researched by Jung in psychotic and normal people) are in evidence in all religions and rituals, whether or not individuals recognize them as such. From Fordham's perspective, the evidence for the initial unity of self is overwhelming. The "deintegration" of the original unity is the basic process of development and internal objects are formed upon self deintegrates. The "ego" is a self-representation, the most prominent one. From Fordham's point of view, what is called "splitting" in psychoanalytic therapy and theory is the splitting of a deintegrated rather than of an integrated self. In Jungian psychology, Fordham makes the clearest and strongest argument for an inherent and original coherence of self, underlying the ego and guaranteeing its stability as it undergoes transformations over a lifetime.

Caspary also assumes an original unity of self that manifests in self-regulation, growth, and empathy. In contrast to Freudian theory, Caspary suggests that aggression is a secondary reaction to distress, not a primary drive. A mapping of introjection and aggression, as interactions within the interpersonal environment, allows us to see how contents of a "core-self" are differentiated. He asserts that the most difficult ethical dilemmas are not resolved on the level on which they occur, but are relativized through individual reference to a core-self—this being a maturational achievement. Although Caspary's core-self has some features in common with Fordham's unified self, it also resonates with the self-system of H. S. Sullivan, as described by Loevinger in the first section.

References

Stevens, A. (1982). *Archetypes: A natural history of the self.* New York: William Morrow.

CHAPTER 16

Actions of the Self

MICHAEL FORDHAM

Introduction

IT WAS IN 1921 that Jung first introduced his formulations on the self. At first he pioneered the subject, finding analogies only in religious texts, especially those of the East. Today the picture is very different: psychoanalysts Federn (1953), Winnicott (1958), Hartmann (1964), and lately Kohut (1971), not to mention Bion (1977) and Scott (1948), have studied and written about psychology of the self whether or not they have used the term. In addition, reflective researches have been carried out by philosophers (cf. Popper and Eccles, 1977). Psychologists and students of linguistics have likewise contributed. So now there is a complex and often confusing literature to digest.

I shall make no attempt to review the contributions from the very diverse fields and shall not try to construct a comprehensive theory of the self, though I have reviewed some attempts to do so elsewhere (Fordham, 1985a). Instead I shall attempt to clarify some features of Jung's work, since that has been the inspiration for my own investigations into the self in infancy and childhood. In the later part of this essay I shall attempt to elucidate my own approach. My vertex is clinical, though I have added observations of mothers and infants to my analytical experience. I hold that there are facts of experience that can be established and that only such theory is needed as will hold the data together. Furthermore I have in mind that theory is best used to further description and give meaning to what is described.

I want to note that Melanie Klein (1961–80) has also been especially influential in my investigations, and lately Bion (1977) has provided experience and ideas I have found enlightening. His brilliant, extremely complicated thesis contains a concept of "O" (1970, pp. 14f) that seems related to Jung's self. Bion holds that "O" is or leads to ultimate reality that is unknowable, but nonetheless he asserts that "O" is explosive and that basic transformations take place in it. I shall refer to other aspects of Bion's work later on.

Empirical Material—Jung's Discoveries

Those analytical psychologists and psychoanalysts who find self theory useful do so on the basis of psychopathological manifestations. It is especially required in the treatment of persons whose whole personality is unorganized so that there seems to be nobody to address; there seems to be a lack or perversion of self-esteem. That applies in the so-called narcissistic and borderline states, and in psychoses.

For the majority, however, these distressing conditions do not apply. They have, as we say, a firm self-organization and so have a sufficiently firm sense of their own identity in relation to society and their personal relationships. A good sense of continuity in the midst of change is evident. It may therefore be enquired what gives rise to the sense of self and how does it become disturbed. I shall maintain that more or less of what we term, rather inadequately, "psychopathology" is necessary to provide the dynamic for research.

After going through his "confrontation with the unconscious" (ca. 1912–14) Jung arrived at a state of security and peace. The drawing of circular diagrams (mandalas) seemed to him important in arriving at that state. Jung connected his newfound internal security and peacefulness with an undefined and ultimately undefinable "self." That knowledge had been arrived at by a process of "circumambulation" revealed in dreams and a kind of imagination called "active imagination." He writes: "there is no linear evolution, there is only circumambulation of the self. . . . Uniform development exists at most, only at the beginning; later everything points towards the centre. This insight gave me stability, and gradually my inner peace returned. I knew that in finding the mandala as an experience of the self I had attained what for me was the ultimate" (1963a, p. 196). In penetrating behind conscious experiences of self (himself), Jung added an important and far-reaching dimension to our knowledge and to the possibility of healing through experiences like his.

It is important to keep firmly in mind how Jung arrived at this special knowledge even though it has a mystical and finally uncommunicable ring. He started his personal experience with unconscious processes through a game that had its prototype in his childhood: he collected stones from the beach behind his house and constructed a miniature village and church. The game continued till he found by chance a red stone in the shape of a four-sided pyramid that he "knew" was the altar of the church (Jung, 1963a, pp. 173–75). Through this play, Jung released his imaginative capacities, and the inner pressure from which he had been suffering was relieved.

The Inner World

Jung's experience is often, and with reason, classed as that of an inner world, but that phrase is not true descriptively. His visions at the time were of Europe bathed in blood. Through his imaginative activities, he experienced visions of many figures that were all separated from "him" as subject; indeed he took particular trouble to objectify them so that confusion should not arise. When any reference is made to the "inner world," there is already a degree of abstraction involved, for the world of archetypal images has been distinguished from "outer reality." Without care the two easily overlap and can result in anything from bewilderment to the formation of delusions. When dramatic events are not felt as within the subject, they can nonetheless be considered to be within the self and its manifestations, but then it is necessary to include a cosmic dimension. Archetypal experiences are very different from ordinary experiences of oneself, and confusion can arise unless the archetypal is clearly distinguished from the ordinary.

Jung's experiences proved to be repeatable by others, especially his usually gifted patients, often through experiences in dreams or in *active imagination*, a specialized Jungian technique. Many of Jung's students and patients were religious-minded, though the religion to which they may have previously subscribed was no longer found to have any meaning for them.

Normality and Otherwise

The difference between Jung's complex symbolic data and the simple everyday experiences of human beings has given rise to conceiving the two as essentially different and sometimes unrelated to each other. If, however, Jung's data are to be generalized it is necessary to assume that the "normal" people are unconscious of what their self-feeling rests upon.

If, however, "normal" people do not need to undertake an investigation of themselves then it may be that only those need to do so who have suffered serious internal emotional damage and who need to repair such damage. Jung himself reflected on that matter and went so far as to wonder whether he was not experiencing a psychosis in his confrontation with the unconscious. If that was the case it would have to be recognised that a psychosis could be considered at times part of a self-healing process: Freud (1911) and Jung (1914b) had noted such self-healing in their analytic studies of psychotic patients. The therapeutic method that Jung devised made possible a new orientation towards a class of patients who had been thought to be beyond the reach of psychoanalysis.

With these reflections in mind we can approach the idea that Jung's self-feeling was damaged and that he had to repair it. Satinover (1985) assembles evidence that Jung's active imaginations are reparative processes related to Jung's abandonment by Freud, who ejected him from psychoanalysis and pursued him with denigration and misrepresentation. Satinover's analysis of that conflict is impressive. It touches on the possibility that, besides Jung's traumatic rupture with Freud, childhood traumata must have been charged with significance. I doubt that the rupture with Freud would alone account for Jung's need to investigate his inner world, but I assume that his productiveness was due to the basic coherence of his personality and his genius. It is remarkable that even in his most overwhelmed moments, he was never cut off from his personal relationships and social life. Then, of course, Jung was eventually (through his writing, his pupils, and his patients) able to benefit thousands of people in distress and to influence a wide spectrum of disciplines: art, religion, and psychology amongst others. To do all that through experiences that looked threateningly pathological is amazing.

Infantile Roots—Infant Observation

At the Ghost Ranch Conference in 1984, I gave a paper (Fordham, 1985a), on the subject of abandonment, the general theme of the

conference. I described in some detail the response of a baby of thir-
teen months whose mother left him for a relatively short period in the
care of a babysitter well known to him. The results were intense despair and persecution reaching psychotic proportions. His attempts to
mitigate the pain of his loss—which was not realistic—were unsatisfactory. It can only be concluded that the baby somehow needed to
become a victim of his emotion: first he cut off from it all in sleep,
but later on when his mother went out again he treated her leaving
as if that were of no consequence. He presented a cheerful impression,
but at the same time he developed a fetish, a pink fluffy elephant,
which he kept in his cot. After the first catastrophic separation, the
baby became suspicious of others. He attempted a sort of love affair
with his mother, but that broke down and he became so difficult that
he was placed temporarily with an auxiliary mother.

The baby's behaviors were surprising. Nothing like that had happened before. Indeed there had been longer separations happily negotiated, and his earlier feeding relation with his mother seemed
almost ideal. There were doubts about it in the mind of the observer
of the infant-mother pair, however. They arose from the absence of
any greedy lustful attacks on the breast that the baby may have needed
to make for full satisfaction. Moreover, the mother seemed to be defective in her capacity for containment and softness: she was in many
respects a good mother with unusual gifts for insight and understanding, but she became frail from time to time, liable to feel drained and
depleted and to develop skin rashes. It was as if the baby knew his
mother's limitations, and by his sparing behavior, contributed in a
large part to the mostly beautiful relationship. That was surprising,
but it was also supplemented by the baby turning to the observer to
find the containment, warmth and softness that his mother lacked.
Only later, after the catastrophic separation, did this baby's own violence and also his mother's difficulties in management of it become
evident.

Jung's Infancy and Childhood

If we turn to Jung's account of his early life, which of course is frag-
mentary compared with the mass of information that was collected
about this mother and baby, there are striking similarities. Jung re-

cords blissful good memories: his lying in a cot in the sun, being shown the beauty of the Alps, enjoying the smell and taste of milk and being fascinated with water. Later on, as with the baby, a very different picture emerges: it is of a suspicious phobic child with strong perse-cutory trends and occasional hallucinations. Grave suspicions of Jesus were brought about by his mother's presentation of Jesus to Carl, from which he drew conclusions of a devouring kind. Persecutory phobias developed about Jesuits, suggestions of depression, accidents, and what Jung himself believes to have been a suicidal attempt. Another interesting parallel is that Jung remembers a maid (perhaps compa-rable to the observer) who evidently provided what his mother lacked. "She belonged to me, not my family but only to me. . . . This type of girl later became a component of my anima" (1963a, p. 8).

Such disturbances in Jung's childhood suggest that all was not well in his family life, and just as the baby knew about his mother so Carl, in childhood, knew about "a disturbed atmosphere in the house" and that he was "deeply disturbed" when his mother went into the hospital for a period. At this time he developed eczema and he hallucinated her as a medusalike monster.

Predictions and Meaning

It is not however my intention to predict Jung's later distress on the basis of this early evidence or to look for causes, but rather to look at the common meaningful patterns between such very different people: the baby with the pink elephant and Carl Jung. In both cases there was a vital contribution by the infant and child to the total situation. So it becomes of interest how each dealt with difficulties which stemmed from the environment and the child self—in one case that of an "ordinary" baby and on the other one with exceptional gifts.

It would not be possible to say what will happen to the baby, but it is clear that his attempts at a solution were unsatisfactory. Cutting off his relationship with mother and developing a fetishistic object even-tuated in a later short-lived attempt at a rather too excited "love affair" with his mother. A hopeful element was the baby's capacity to find in another woman (the observer) the needed softness and containment. He could repeat that later on to his benefit. We know more about Jung in the long term, and he can tell us about the kind of experience the baby probably had. We can know about Jung's persecutions and depressions. We also know that Jung developed attempts at a solution in an archetypal way: witness the dream of the underground phallus (Jung, 1963a, pp. 11f), as well as the manikin episode (Jung, 1963a, pp. 21f) that served him in such good stead. Neither were permanent solutions, and it was not until the painful rupture with Freud that he had the opportunity to seek one by penetrating into the archetypal world and reaching the self.

Jung's Psychosis

Satinover (1985) lays stress on the importance of not overlooking the psychotic element in Jung's experience. In my opinion he is right, for unless Jung's shadow is evaluated it is only too easy to become a victim of the idealizing process that inevitably distorts his real merit. We have come to understand the ubiquity of psychotic elements in human beings from infancy onwards, continuing into personal relations and society. More understanding of this field has come from the work on the so-called narcissistic neuroses as developed by Kohut (1971) and Kernberg (1975). A difficulty arises here, as follows: the theory of narcissism is a part of psychoanalytic metapsychology and of the sexual theory to which Jungian theorists do not subscribe. Nevertheless, much of Jung's experience may be said to have strong narcissistic elements, using the term in a descriptive way. I refer especially to the grandiose language of the archetypal figures that Jung encountered in his active imagination.

Jung himself complained of it:

> I wrote down the fantasies as well as I could, and made an earnest effort to analyze the psychic conditions under which they had arisen. But I was able to do this only in clumsy language. First I formulated the things as I had observed them, usually in "high flown language" for that corresponds to the style of the archetypes. Archetypes speak the language of high flown rhetoric, even bombast. It is a style that I find embarrassing—it grates on my nerves as when someone draws his nails down a plaster wall, or scrapes his knife against a plate. (1963a, pp. 177–78)

These are surely the grandiose images of "the self" as depicted in myths, and of the sort that Klein (1952b), Kohut (1971), and Kernberg (1975) have given so much attention. Jung's typical analysands are also of interest here: they are persons with considerable achievement behind them who, later in life, are at a loss since life no longer has any meaning. Kernberg justifies the long time it takes to psychoanalyze patients with a narcissistic neurosis on the grounds that, if he does not do so, the patients will end up in a state like that described by Jung: they appear normal but in reality have a crippling psychopathology. The reason why these patients came to Jung in the second half of life could be explained by their success in life, which gave them sufficient narcissistic supplies to deceive themselves and others as to their normality. Later in life, the supplies dry up, revealing their often desperate underlying state.

Definitions of the Self

Now we may consider further the difficulty of defining the self, according to Jungian theory. In this volume, Redfearn reviews some of the definitions and has shown the confusion that reigns. I have shown (Fordham, 1985b) that Jung made many attempts at definition of self; some of these definitions are contradictory. First, there is the definition of it as the totality of a person in a state of integration. This definition also means that the self transcends opposites, suggesting that it is neither conscious nor unconscious. Within the self, both are united, not differentiated. The second set of ideas about the self centers around its being an archetype, that is, a function of the unconscious. Besides these two main trends there are many statements that appear to be difficult to integrate into either of them. Jung lays stress on symbolic representations of self in *Psychological Types* (1921), emphasizing its distinction from ego. This seems clear enough provided that we adhere to the original definition of the ego as the center of consciousness. With the development of ego psychology, that proposition is no longer adequate. Accordingly, the ego contains unconscious contents that can be made conscious and, when they are, appear to be essentially the same as conscious data. Originally this state of affairs was explained by the action of repression. The repressed contents were defined as constituting the personal unconscious. But it can be shown that some of the supposedly repressed data were not repressed at all, for they had never been conscious.

The idea that the ego was the center of consciousness was further shaken by the multiplication of ego defenses that started by being and usually remained unconscious. The list is quite formidable: identification, projection, introjection, idealization, isolation, reaction formation, undoing, rationalization, conversion, repression, dramatization, acting out, displacement, denigration, reversal, somatization, and so on. These have been identified mostly by psychoanalysts; in as much as they are descriptive, they may be taken as valid. For such reasons, it appears that there must be an unconscious ego located in the shadow. This brings the ego closer to being an unconscious archetype.

Thus, there seemed to be a shift, a deepening of the concept of ego, that ended up in Jung's beautiful passages in the *Mysterium Coniunctionis* (1963b, pp. 107f, 357f) giving rise to the notion that there is an archetype of the ego. Thus, in his later formulations, Jung claims that although the ego is the center of consciousness, it also combines in itself both consciousness and the unconscious. That brings ego much nearer to ideas about the self of which it is a manifestation.

Some clarification can be arrived at, however, if we go back to the roots of Jung's discoveries. They began when he encountered his inner world and continued when he sought analogies with myth, legend, religious ritual, and alchemy. Then he found analysands who could follow his example through active imagination and dreams. In this way, he came across archetypal images that he thought of as coming from the unconscious, especially the collective unconscious. Since they did not derive significantly from education, or other external sources, he considered them to be self-representations or symbols, which he thought of as the best possible expression of otherwise unconscious processes. It is important to realize that Jung restricts the use of the word *symbol*. The symbol transcends conscious comprehension, tends to have a cosmic reference, and cannot be fully explicated (as can a *sign*).

Following the interacting with transcendent images, Jung further discovered a progression which he called individuation. This progression led to tranquility and peace of mind, which arose through mandalas that he pictured. For him, these mandalas were "the ultimate." Jung's personal exploration of these images gave rise to calling the self an archetype. His other definitions are attempts to abstract certain experiences that occur and seem to refer in some way to "the ultimate."

Having in mind two kinds of mental functioning, directed and undirected thinking, which he elaborated first in the *Psychology of the Unconscious* (Jung, 1914), it would not be possible to make an adequate definition of the self. Indeed, Jung's definitions are like moderately abstract metaphors with little explanatory content. Thus, Jung was consistent, even if disappointing, to those who seek to make clear what is essentially obscure. It will be observed that though the self has an integrative long-term aim it appears to be exceedingly disruptive while the individuation process is proceeding.

Self as a Dynamic System

Though other reasons occupied my mind, the discovery of the incompatible definitions was influential in making me formulate a new and, as it appeared, revolutionary definition of the self (Fordham, 1947). I considered the self as a dynamic system that acted not only as an integrator of psychic and physical elements but also as a system that spontaneously could divide itself up into parts. For that, I coined the term "*de*integration," which did not disrupt the integrity of the organism as would be implied by *dis*integration. I postulated a rhythm of integration and deintegration that leads to growth. Deintegrates are new experiences, either predominantly affective or cognitive, which can then be digested and integrated into the whole.

My thesis involved experiences from various sources. Jung's concept of active imagination was enhanced when I realized that the same experiences applied to thoughts, reflections, and the like. I noted that Jung said that one did not always think thoughts; rather, they sometimes arrived in one's mind as if from nowhere. I could then see that the self might be the source of such experiences. It seemed more cogent to see it thus rather than to say that they came out of the unconscious.

Then I did a study of children's dreams and fantasies, which contained symbols of the self (Fordham, 1969), in the form of both mandalas and omnipotent fantasies. To these was added the fact that archetypal fantasies occurred in adults to compensate the ego exactly as they functioned in children to compensate the childish ego. Self symbols, in particular, often led children to a growth of consciousness and balance.

Infancy and Childhood

For Jungians in the 1930s and early 1940s, this was a shocking claim because the self was only supposed to appear in the second half of life, as an endpoint to the individuation process. So what could be the function of self in childhood? Did children also individuate?

That question I set on one side as too daring. But I formed an equally daring hypothesis that the self was primary. An infant, and even perhaps as fetus, was an integrated unit, a person with individuality from the start. That meant that Jung's metaphor of consciousness (arising like islands out of the sea of the unconscious) was inadequate. I conceived of the initial self as a primary unit more like a rock. An infant must then be thought of as essentially separate from his mother at the beginning. That was so in utero and continued after birth. It is apparent, however, that the infant quickly came into relation with his new environment. With the help of his mother, who made the relationship possible, the infant connected his self with parts of his body and especially his mouth. It seemed that he used only parts of himself in these endeavors, and so the self must have deintegrated in the process.

My idea of the self as an integrating-deintegrating system was developing. A baby could be conceived as a whole person interacting with his mother and increasingly building up a mental life. This ran counter to the idea that a baby was, to all intents, a part of his mother. One could assume that the supposed state of primary identity might develop as a result of the intimacy between mother and baby, which is followed by an increase of consciousness. The ego begins as ego fragments and gradually coalesces into a central ego.

That was the idea I put forward in *Children as Individuals* (1969) because I was under the influence of neurophysiological evidence that questioned whether perception was sufficiently developed for an infant to perceive reality with any degree of precision. The scene has changed radically since then, partly because the neurophysiological theories have been decisively disproved. The advent of mother-infant observation techniques has provided information that also made the interactional hypotheses much more likely. A further hypothesis has virtually replaced the original primary-identity notion: namely, that projective and introjective identification are dynamic processes. They are periodic occurrences within the interacting systems: mother and baby and their intrapsychic functions. It will be observed that I am not working with conceptions of consciousness and the unconscious. That is partly because they are not of much use in the descriptions of a baby's actions, but also because theoretically the self is prior to either.

Infant-Mother Observations

For many years the concept of the primary self with its capacity to deintegrate and integrate hung fire. That was because I did not do what was needed; I did not initiate systematic observations of babies and their mothers in emotional interaction. When, however, I heard of the work being done at the Tavistock Clinic, I inquired of Martha Harris whether it would be possible to collaborate with somebody who was experienced in this work. She generously delegated Gianna Henry, and I began to benefit from her observations. While the seminars on these observations were in progress, I was discussing with the trainees in child analysis both my own and others' theories and speculations. I had hoped that my trainees would contribute from their experiences, but there was no feedback. I therefore decided to attend regularly seminars conducted by Gianna Henry; this I did for about two years.

These seminars were conducted by observers of mother-infant pairs, reporting observations and forming hypotheses that were closely checked against descriptive data: such features as mother and baby being in touch with each other, the baby's capacity to respond to mother's ministrations, the way the baby fed (whether greedily and aggressively or passively), and the mother's capacity to contain her baby emotionally and to digest and "metabolize" the emotions her baby evoked in her. It was thought that besides the actual breastfeeding, a mother fed the baby with primitive thought processes and so facilitated mental development.

It was clear beyond doubt that a baby was much more integrated than I (or current theory) had supposed. The baby was evidently a whole person, an individual adapting to the new environment comprising parts of the real mother. As I listened to descriptions of feedings and read over the account of them, it became clear to me that what I had postulated was a living reality. A baby would start from sleep (integration), wake up, and give signals of wanting to be picked up or being hungry. Then a sequence of quite complex actions came into operation, leading to a feeding in which looks and playlike responses took place (deintegration). Satisfaction led to sleep once more (integration). It all seemed too obvious to mention. This sequence might not always go forward so smoothly. Either baby or mother might interrupt a feeding and there might be protests and something like battles. The breast might be rejected, attacked, or bitten, but these aggressive interchanges, when negotiated, led in the end to sleep once more.

A further feature of some babies was quite striking in that they seemed to know just how much their mothers could stand emotionally. There were sparing babies, helpful ones who could almost show a mother how to feed them. Thus there was a groundwork for conceptualizing the baby as a person. What I had daringly postulated was being translated into description.

Deintegration now seems to me to lie behind the differentiation of functions. The most primitive is the distinction between a good and a bad breast. That might be conceived as splitting, but that term is better reserved for pathological states of mind. It is true that Melanie Klein (1932) distinguished between normal and pathological splitting, but splitting of what? I cannot see that the term *ego* is useful, and so I would distinguish deintegration from splitting of the self. *Splitting* here refers to manifestations in deintegrates that have not been digested by the self as a whole. Sometimes one meets situations where a baby does not take the breast and cannot be made to do so. Such a defense is very difficult to overcome, and later on a group of battles with caretakers can be thought of "as defenses of the self," meaning thereby the baby is fighting for the preservation of integrity. I am paying so much attention to observation of infants because a reality is being brought to bear on infancy that was previously lacking, but further than this it gives great help in recognizing infantile characteristics in children and adult people.

I do not really know descriptively how it comes about that experiences become conscious and unconscious, but Bion has put forward interesting suggestions about the formation of a barrier between some mental contents and others. It is possible, however, to describe an infant's building up inner resources especially in relation to separations from his mother. At first they may not be tolerated at all, but gradually they become more and more easy for a baby to allow without too much disturbance. It seems that sometimes absence is a disaster, and that may be understood as taking place when destructive emotions on the part of the baby are mobilized in response to deprivation, which can only be alleviated by his mother's presence (cf. Fordham, 1985a).

In infancy powerful emotions, both loving and hating, cannot be called in question. They are simply expressed. Thus if the infant is angry, the object of anger is "damaged" or "destroyed." When the object is loved again, it is restored and idealized. Nevertheless, the strength of an infant's emotions cannot explain the apparent omnipotence. I think omnipotence is better explained as deriving from the self, a self that controls absolutely, just as God controls the doings of man.

Constructions

Many psychiatric constructions and theories about infancy refer to states that may lead to psychic damage. Many of these can be described and/or inferred with considerable certainty, yet the impression given that they are more or less continuous and so defining stages in development is questionable. Most of an infant's life is not dramatic: play with mother and others, play in the cot or lying there burbling, looking, listening, and reflecting. Then there is sleep. There is growing evidence that sleep is not a passive activity: the brain shows evidence that REM rhythms are associated with dreaming and that the infant is often active during sleep. Thus most of infancy may be thought of as active, but not dramatic. Perhaps the reflective times are those out of which awareness of self will develop.

Many of the constructions about infancy have been made from the analyses of children and adults, so that if attempts are made to generalize from them a false impression may be given of infancy as a whole. Infant observation put a check on such generalizations. For instance, recent interest has been aroused in the so-called mirror transference, in which the patient mirrors self in the analyst. That transference is understood as reflecting the infant's need for the mother to mirror the infant's self. It is suggested that this is done when an infant looks into her face.

It is true an infant looks into the mother's face and explores it with hands and fingers, but the behavior is much more like part of a whole mother-infant interaction than one person's mirroring in the other. Infants may also find a real mirror and look into it. One infant, for instance, looked into a mirror and saw his mother's face; then he gave a whoop of delight when he looked round and saw the real mother who was being reflected in the mirror. When he was presented with the mirror so that he could see his own face, he was puzzled and disconcerted, exhibiting some of the features of stranger anxiety. I believe this forces us to reconsider in what "mirroring" consists. It is true that babies may show great interest in their own mirror images, but in the series of infant observations I have studied, no observation suggests that a mother mirrors her child's self.

I am not maintaining that observations deny the existence of mirroring, the number of observations is too small. But they do call into question the frequency of "mirroring" if it occurs at all.

Part and Whole Objects

Considering the infant as a whole self who puts out "feelers" and so comes into relation with the environment leads to reflections on the subject of part and whole objects. It is convenient for adult persons to think that an infant comes into relation with a part of the mother— her breast, her face, and so on—and that as the infant grows these parts gradually coalesce into an experience of the mother as a whole. Thus develops an experience of a whole object as a perceived unit. That does not, however, cover the emotional experience of mother (whether part or whole object) as good or bad, or emotional development, which makes it possible to grasp that a mother that is good is the same mother that is bad.

Are we correct when we apply our adult knowledge to an infant? Does the infant know that a breast is only a part of the mother? Of course his knowledge of feeding is accompanied by the sense of secure holding, of visual, auditory, tactile, and coenesthetic experiences as well, but do they divide up or are they one experience?

An analogy may elucidate what I mean. Suppose I sit looking out of my study window and survey the garden, paths, terraces, flowering plants, and the contiguous countryside. It does not weigh with me that what I see is part of Jordans Village. I know that is true, but (I suggest that a baby is like me without the knowledge of Jordans) my limit is my view.

Later on, as a baby gets to know more of the mother, then it can know that she is more extensive than a breast, which becomes a part of her. As the perceptual field expands the baby knows also that the mother is part of a larger geographical space. In the first place however, within restricted boundaries, the experiences may be "whole."

Besides increasing knowledge of geography, there develop groups of experience in which the baby behaves differently. One group contains anger, fear, or misery. These are treated as dangerous, and effort is made to get rid of them in one way or another. The second group are satisfying and productive of joy, contentment, and love. All those experiences, I suggest, are best thought of as actions of the self out of which the ego is developing. All these are a result of deintegration, which informs the actions with organization and purpose. This view goes far to make sense of an infant's complexity without needing to evoke ideas about consciousness or unconsciousness. Those concepts become useful when structuralization emerges and an ego and archetype can be distinguished.

Having postulated a self that integrates and deintegrates, we can justifiably infer meanings to behavior—mental or physical.

Meanings

So far I have kept as close as possible to descriptive material using a concept of the self and its dynamic actions as a background. I have done this because there have been so many constructions about infancy, and it is distressing to find how little they can be confirmed. Indeed many mother-infant observations seem to indicate that many such constructions will have to be discarded.

In my early work in child analytic therapy, it was Melanie Klein (1961–80) whose books provided me with tools I could use to communicate with my child patients. I had been very impressed by her clinical work and descriptive capacity. Furthermore, I rather resentfully acknowledged that she gained access to the real inner world of infants and small children, discovering there the archetypal forms (called unconscious fantasy) and giving it decisive importance just as Jung had done for adult people. It was that discovery of the objective psyche that led him to discovery of the self. By contrast, Melanie Klein implied it. That was in the 1930s. Later she referred to a psychosomatic whole different from, and more embracing than, the ego, the superego, and the id, but she never developed the idea far.

At that time I knew little or nothing about infancy, for I was still under the spell of current views in analytical psychology: the unconscious and unorganized states of the infant that gave no individuality and no boundaries so that the baby was psychically part of the mother. Gradually the infant developed ego fragments and constructed a world of primitive identity, from which developed an omnipotent magical world from which the child gradually individuated. I was even presenting that thesis in 1969 when *Children as Individuals* was published.

As the result of studying mother-infant observations, made over the first two years of life, combined with knowledge gained by experimental psychologists, I now have found such formulations virtually useless. It seems to me that the position I took up can be decisively refuted by the revolution in the knowledge of mother-infant interaction: the infant's part is observed to be considerable right from the start of extrauterine life.

One of the constructions about infancy I had become especially interested in was Klein's (1946, 1952a) "depressive position." I had become aware that, in the literature of analytical psychology and in discussion with colleagues, there was very little interest in sadness or grief, though there were appreciative references to depression, which I could not comfortably share. The study of depression was Klein's strong point, and she had defined a depressive position, first experienced in infancy and to be discerned throughout life (1952c).

I had experience with patients, both children (one was two and a half years old) and adults, who showed striking features of Klein's depressive position in relation to both their inner worlds and their outer reality. It was therefore with much disappointment that the babies did not show the postdated sequence: the resolution of the depression through signs of reparation. Some seemed often about to do so, but they never did.

My disappointment was somewhat mitigated by Klein's own studies on infant behavior. She indicated that some states, especially those of sadness or pining, are enough to indicate the process is in action.

Nevertheless Bion's (1962) modification of Klein is more in line with the observational data at my disposal. He constructs a neat formula: Ps⟨—⟩Dep (Bion, 1962, p. 72, 1963, pp. 34f). "Ps" is an abbreviation for "paranoid-schizoid position"; "Dep" is an abbreviation from the Kleinian concept of "depressive position." The formula Ps⟨—⟩Dep indicates that though the two positions can exist, they can combine in varying proportions. This may explain why the depressive position was never fully achieved by the babies in our infant-mother observations.

Infant-mother observation has valuable achievements to its credit, but it is in its early stages of development. We may look forward to more precise understanding of this interactive field in the future.

Development

If we assume that the self is a psychosomatic whole, it must remain the same throughout the life of an individual. Yet if there is one characteristic of an infant, it is the rapidity of its mental, emotional, and physical growth. Such growth continues to be rapid and complex through childhood. In later life, the physical processes are reversed, but not mental processes, though some of the vigor of earlier life will be lacking. Jung's version of individuation known in classical analysis belongs to the later half of life.

My thesis of self postulates, besides an unchanging self, a stable representation in consciousness, the ego. The ego grows out of the interaction between deintegrates and the environmental mother, and her extensions. The interaction produces many self-representations, the most stable and prominent of which is the ego.

I have so far worked, in considering infant behavior, using the concept of the unknowable self as a theoretical necessity and an inference to account for the complexity of infant behavior. That has arisen out of my Jungian orientation. The postulate of deintegrative-integrative sequences is required to support the assumption that the infant ego is inadequately developed to account for the coherence and adapted purposefulness of infant behavior. In this way the theory of the self is extended and is woven into that of analytic theory.

I should mention here that there are those who take a different view. Some attribute the behavior to the neurophysiological substrate (see Lichtenberg, 1983, for an account of them), whereas others like Klein hold that there are an ego and unconscious fantasies at birth.

Environment

In concentrating on features of infant behavior I may seem to have left out far too much the infant's environment: father, siblings, cot, toys, and the less tangible emotional climate of the home.

I have, however, insisted on the adaptational nature of a baby: the infant adapts to the home environment. Without a mother or other caretaker to provide warmth, food, and sufficient comfort, a baby could not survive. But there is more to it than material provision. How the infant is picked up, held, looked at, attended, and responded to (both in regard to its feelings of love and hate)—all these and many others can be decisively important influences. The baby also is indeed decisively an influence on the environment and not merely a passive recipient.

In my thesis it becomes necessary to postulate a self-representation in the ego because of the sense of being the same in the midst of change. That must grow out of the interaction of baby and (m)other. It is closely related to the development of the body image and the sense of having a surface represented by the skin. But the mental processes underlying that development remain obscure. It is here that a contribution of Bion's (1977) once again becomes enlightening: out of "O" develop *beta* elements that give rise to physical actions. These become related to mental processes of a very primitive nonverbal kind, designated *alpha* functions. They correspond to reverie by mother and infant. *Alpha* elements may, in my view, be observed when it looks as if the baby is having thoughts at a time when it is most likely that such is the case. From *alpha* elements derive fantasies, dreams, and myths.

In all this baby and (m)other are an interacting couple out of which the psyche emerges as an increasingly complex system of structures.

References

Bion, W. R. (1962). Learning from experience. In *Seven servants*. New York: Aronson, 1977.

———. (1963). Elements of psycho-analysis. In *Seven servants*. New York: Aronson, 1977.

———. (1970). Attention and interpretation. In *Seven servants*. New York: Aronson, 1977.

———. (1977). *Seven servants*. New York: Aronson.

Federn, P. (1953). *Ego psychology and the psychoses*. London: Imago.

Fordham, M. (1947). Integration and deintegration and early ego development. *The Nervous Child*, 6.3.

———. (1969). *Children as individuals*. New York: Putnam.

———. (1985a). Abandonment in infancy. *Chiron: A Review of Jungian Analysis*.

———. (1985b). *Exploration into the self*. London: Academic Press.

Freud, S. (1911). *Psycho-analytic notes on an autobiographical account of a case of paranoia. Standard edition, 12*. London: Hogarth.

Hartmann, H. (1964). *Ego psychology and the problem of adaptation*. New York: International Universities Press.

Jung, C. G. (1914a). *The psychology of the unconscious*. New York: Moffat Yard.

———. (1914b). The content of the psychoses. *Collected works, 3*. Princeton: Princeton University Press.

———. (1921). *Psychological types. Collected works, 6*. Princeton: Princeton University Press.

———. (1954). On the nature of the psyche. *Collected works, 9, 1*. Princeton: Princeton University Press.

———. (1963a). *Memories, dreams, reflections*. London: Routledge and Kegan Paul.

———. (1963b). *Mysterium coniunctionis. Collected works, 14*. Princeton: Princeton University Press.

Kernberg, O. (1975). *Borderline conditions and pathological narcissism*. New York: Aronson.

Klein, M. (1932). *The psychoanalysis of children*. Rev. ed. 1980, London: Hogarth.

———. (1946). Notes on some schizoid mechanism. In *Envy and gratitude and other works. The writings of Melanie Klein, 3*. London: Hogarth, 1980, pp. 1–24.

————. (1952a). On observing the behavior of young infants. In *Envy and gratitude and other works. The writings of Melanie Klein, 3*. London: Hogarth, 1980, pp. 94–121.

————. (1952b). The origins of transference. In *Envy and gratitude and other works. The writings of Melanie Klein, 3*. London: Hogarth, 1980, pp. 48–56.

————. (1952c). Some theoretical conclusions regarding the emotional life of the infant. In *Envy and gratitude and other works. The writings of Melanie Klein, 3*. London: Hogarth, 1980, pp. 61–93.

————. (1955). On identification. In *Envy and gratitude and other works*. London: Hogarth, 1980.

————. (1961–80). *The writings of Melanie Klein*. Ed. R. Money-Kyrl. 4 vols. London: Hogarth.

Kohut, H. (1971). *The analysis of the self*. New York: International Universities Press.

Lichtenberg, J. D. (1983). *Psychoanalysis and infant research*. London and Hillsdale, N.J.: Analytic Press.

Popper, K. P., and Eccles, J. C. (1977). *The self and its brain*. New York: Springer International.

Redfearn, J. W. T. (in press). *Myself my many selves*. London: Academic Press.

Satinover, J. (1985). At the mercy of another: Abandonment and restitution in psychosis and the psychotic character. *Chiron: A Review of Jungian Analysis*.

Scott, W. C. (1948). Some embryological, neurological, psychiatric and psychoanalytic implications of the body scheme. *International Journal of Psychoanalysis, 19.3*.

Winnicott, D. W. (1958). *Collected papers*. London: Tavistock.

CHAPTER 17

The Concept of a Core-Self

WILLIAM R. CASPARY

HOW DO WE solve deep intractable ethical dilemmas? Mark Twain (1958) places Huck Finn in such a dilemma when he has to decide whether to follow "morality" and turn in Jim as a runaway slave or "selfishness"—his loving feelings toward his friend. Sartre (1957) gives us the example of a young man torn between caring for his aged mother and going off to join the fight against the German invaders. Philosophers have had sufficient difficulty with such questions that it seems worthwhile to shift orientation and study them psychologically. Rather than asking how one might or should in principle handle such dilemmas, let us inquire how this is actually done in practice. Such an investigation would be in the spirit of recent approaches to philosophy of science through histories of actual scientific activities.

A "natural history" of an ethical decision would involve many elements and phases: articulating the issues and alternatives, gaining information about causes and consequences, empathically entering into the viewpoints of others, discussing with friends, consulting authorities, clarifying one's vague inner pulls and tugs, and so on. I've considered all of these at various times, but for present purposes, I'm interested in one particular phase of the process. This is the culminating moment when, without knowing consciously how we got there, we experience resolution. We now know what we're going to do. (In particular, I'm interested in such resolutions that stand the test of time—ones that remain firm rather than being reassailed by doubts; ones that bring about the expected and desired consequences in the world rather than proving drastically miscalculated.)

Conjecture: such resolutions come from making contact with a deep core or center of the personality—what I'll refer to as a core-self. This conjecture is based principally on clinical evidence—work with clients (and as a client) in depth therapy and in Rogerian-style encounter groups. It was also suggested by writings of Rogers, Maslow, Jung, and the philosopher Dewey.

The main task that has emerged as I've explored this conjecture is to be more explicit about the meaning of this concept of core-self. Although I've seen frequent allusions to such an idea, I've found no extensive or intensive attempt to pin down its meaning.

The Idea of Core-Self

First, a brief selection of quotations concerning a center or core-self: Erik Erikson (1968), in exploring (one dimension of) his concept of identity, quotes William James as follows:

> (A person's "character") is discernable in the mental or moral attitude in which . . . he felt himself most deeply and intensely active and alive. At such moments there is a voice inside which speaks and says: "This is the real me!" (p. 19)

Jung (1965), in his autobiography discusses the mandalas that he began spontaneously to draw during a crucial transition in his life:

> It became increasingly plain to me that the mandala is the center. . . . It is the path to the center, to individuation. . . . The goal of psychic development is the self.
>
> . . . .
>
> Some years later I obtained confirmation of my ideas about the center and the self by way of a dream. . . . Through this dream I understood that the self is the principle and archetype of orientation and meaning. For me this insight signified an approach to the center and therefore to the goal. (pp. 196–97)

M. L. von Franz (1964) discusses Jung's notion of Self (what I refer to as core-self) and relates it to the Greek concept of an inner *daimon.*

> . . . one can observe a sort of hidden regulating or directing tendency at work, creating a slow, imperceptible process of psychic growth—the process of individuation. . . .

The organizing center from which the regulatory effect stems seems to be a sort of "nuclear atom" in our psychic system. . . . Jung called this center the "Self."

Throughout the ages men have been intuitively aware of the existence of such an inner center. The Greeks called it man's inner *daimon*; in Egypt it was expressed by the concept of the *Ba-soul*; and the Romans worshiped it as the "genius" native to each individual.

. . . .

This [self] . . . appears first as merely an inborn possibility. . . . How far it develops depends on whether or not the ego is willing to listen to the messages of the self. (pp. 161–62)

My own formulation of the core-self idea is as follows:

The "feel" of this core-self can be suggested by contrasting it with the conscious "I." Consider the experience expressed in the words: "I choose this." Ordinarily this implies, "'I' have reasons which 'I' evaluate on objective grounds to be satisfactory. 'I' command myself to carry out my choice." This "I" wants to be in control. It is the helmsman of the ship. The ship resists this hand at the helm but can be subdued. This "I" steers by the charts and the stars and its own interpretive intelligence. It has its own purposes from which it sets its course, but from whence these purposes come is sometimes difficult to trace.

When, in rare moments, the words, "I choose this," emanate from the core-self, the experience is very different. It is as if we say, "I *am* this. I can choose no other." This can be felt as being out of control, as "losing one's grip." At the same time it is felt as a finding oneself, of being unified in oneself. The course is now set from the bowels of the ship. Helmsman, chart and stars are instrumental to locating and pursuing the course, but the fundamental direction comes from within.

The word "will" is used in two distinct ways reflecting these two approaches to the word "I." Most commonly, the will serves the conscious "I" and subdues the organism and personality to the "I's" dictates. Will, in another sense however, refers to one's whole hearted commitment to decisions and projects emanating from the core-self.

This distinction clarifies Dewey's (1934) allusive (and elusive) formulation: ". . . not that it depends upon a particular resolve or volition. It is a change of will rather than any special change *in* will."

Although the quotations above are suggestive, they provide only a bare beginning. In the effort to delineate the core-self concept more fully, I will begin with exploring its nucleus in early infancy.

True Self and False Self

In psychoanalysis it has been the case again and again that the study of pathology has given us insights about healthy development. Recently the study of "borderline" and "narcissistic" disorders, where the development of self has been severely retarded and distorted, has provided new clues about the very nature of selfhood.

Alice Miller (1981) gives a moving presentation of the plight of babies and children adapting to the needs of narcissistic parents. In order to gain even the minimal love these parents can give, in order to escape being annihilated psychologically if not physically, the infant learns to read every subtle cue about the parents' wishes and to act out the desired demeanor and behavior. Every natural impulse must be suppressed and redirected toward the achievement of this performance. As the child grows up, such performances are elaborated and integrated into what Winnicott (1965) called a false self.

If this is the origin and nature of the false self, what can be said of the true self whose place has been usurped? Miller stresses that there is no fully formed true self waiting in the wings. Such a development never got the chance to take place. Instead these children who developed a false self grow up to experience profound doubts about who they are, or whether they really exist as persons at all. This absence of a sense of identity, of personhood, of selfhood leads to persistent feelings of emptiness and depression. (This can be masked, or relieved for periods of time through grandiose fantasies and projects for fulfilling them, through success and recognition at work, and through romanticized love relationships.) When the sense of emptiness, of not really being there, is at its fullest the person may feel terror—an intense fear of psychological death closely akin to the fear of actual physical decease.

If no true self has developed at all, then whatever surviving germ of personhood remains can give us clues to the origins of what I am calling the core-self. Doing therapy, Miller finds that there is indeed a deeply hidden center. This is revealed, after considerable therapeutic work, in certain intense spontaneous emotions that are recognized by the clients as genuinely their own. The awareness of these emotions is followed, momentarily at least, by a feeling of integration and relief from emptiness and terror. (Of course there are many emotions that function as defenses or are expressions of introjects. I'm talking here of *certain* emotions that are recognized by the experience of integration that follows them.)

It seems that the suppression of emotion leads to false-self formation. Conversely, the renewed awareness of deep emotions reopens contact with a buried nucleus of a true self. Let us look at other features of infantile behavior and expression that when met with indifference or anger by the parents lead to false-self formation. In this way we can identify the precursors of true self—or if you will, the nucleus of what I call the core-self. (Lichtenberg, 1983, provides a review of recent research on infants and relates this to psychoanalytic issues including the "sense of self" but touches only tangentially on what I have called the core-self.)

Origin of the Core-Self: Component Features

1. *Self-regulation.* Babies seem to have their own times for exploring the world of sight, sound, smell, and touch; for quiet repose, for interacting with the mothering one and other people, for nursing and for sleep. When adults are insensitive to the infant's rhythms in these matters, fussiness and crying are the response. If the baby is held, for example, in a position that is not secure and comfortable for it, it will stiffen, or wriggle, or cry. If anxious mothers seek to stimulate their babies whenever they are in states of wakeful but inactive and unfocused repose cumulative irritability will result.

Self-regulation can be seen particularly in nursing. Babies have their own patterns of intensity and duration of sucking. They have their times of withdrawal for breathing and rest. There are moments for gazing at the mothering one, for tactile exploration with hands and mouth, and so on. When mothers (or other mothering adults) seek to force the nipple upon the infant or withdraw before the infant's sucking is completed one again sees fussiness and tears.

Of course there is a degree of flexibility—even unstructuredness—in the infant's patterns. This enables it to accommodate to the patterns of the mothering one. But the adjustment must be mutual, and we can easily see examples of the limits of accommodation being reached.

If unresponsiveness to infant patterns is severe and protracted, a veritable struggle for control may ensue. The mothering one may strive more and more to impose her or his regulation upon the baby's patterns of activity and repose. The infant, in turn, may respond with continuous irritability, refusing feeding, thrashing about, sobbing, and crying. The infant may be observed to hold its breath and stiffen its body for long periods of time. It may exhibit digestive disorders with diarrhea and vomiting. It would not be legitimate to attribute such behavior to a self-consciousness and will of the sort we find in ourselves as adults. Nonetheless, we can scarcely avoid interpreting these responses as a struggle for autonomy. In the words of Tolpin and Kohut (1979):

> Applying these insights concerning psychopathology to normal development, it becomes apparent that even babies, if indeed they are surrounded by normal care, may be said to have a rudimentary self: they have phase appropriate expectations of parental responses to them, they assertively announce their needs, and they turn vigorously toward their human environment. (p. 15)

2. *Growth.* It appears virtually universal that infants move toward separation and individuation. Even under very adverse conditions some progress can be observed. Margaret Mahler (1975, pp. 156, 158, 206, 208) on the basis of her research observations of mother-infant couples over time, came to this conclusion. Perhaps it is the same inner urge toward growth that we see in adult clients in psychotherapy. We see them enduring pain and turmoil in therapy, and making use of new insights in order to renew the process of growth interrupted so long before. We also see this urge toward development highlighted in

the distress of babies whose parents cling to a symbiotic relatedness with their infants and frustrate the efforts to separate.

3. *Empathy/sensitivity.* Infants, even in the early months, are observed to be responsive to the moods and emotions of their parents. Under favorable conditions this makes possible the "social" interaction between mother and baby that is so rewarding to mothering ones and deepens their bond with their infants. It is this same sensitivity, in less favorable circumstances, that enables babies to register maternal anxiety—as Sullivan has stressed. Babies also appear to be able to recognize and show aversive reactions to angry faces and tones of voice. This responsiveness carries over to adults other than the parent. In the early months (before the onset of "eight-month anxiety"—the typical fear of strangers emerging toward the end of the first year) infants have selective reactions to nonparent adults. They may respond joyfully to some and withdraw from others.

This sensitivity—Sullivan (1953) calls it empathy, identifying it with the adult capacity—enables the infant to adapt to the parent. This adaptation can be within the range of flexibility of the infant's own patterns involving a minimum of conflict. With inadequate parenting the adaptation can be at the expense of the infant's self-regulation. This reaches its extreme in the case of "perfect babies." In therapy with disturbed adults who had severely narcissistic mothers, we sometimes learn that early in the first year they ceased ever to cry or complain and fitted themselves to the mother's schedule or whim concerning feeding, play, rest, and so on. Clinical evidence suggests that at some early age these babies began to respond not just to the moods and demands of the parents but to the parents' fantasies (often unconscious) concerning their child.

In studies of the origin of schizophrenia it has been noted that many patients grew up in homes where they not only had to adapt to contradictory demands from parents but also had to deny the sensitivity that enabled them to do this. Awareness of the crazy situation around them might have kept these people sane, but this had to be suppressed as well.

4. *Emotion.* We have already observed that suppression of emotion in infants was one notable contribution to the development of the false self. Although emotion in infants is less differentiated than in adults we can easily distinguish pleasure, distress, and fear. We can identify surprise in infants, and the precursors of what will become anger and

disgust (cf. Lichtenberg, 1983, p. 25, reporting on the work of Tomkins). Emotions like love, guilt, anger, and jealousy, on the other hand, have a large admixture of cognition and judgment. We are inclined to doubt that infants are capable of these. Concerning the suppression of emotion, the findings from therapy with adults are confirmed by observation of infants. Secure attachment, for example, appears to be related to maternal responsiveness to babies' emotions.

5. *Precursors of "Love and Work."* Since love and work are the central features of adult life to which we look when assessing psychological health, we should be able to find their roots in the core-self and in the earliest nucleus of that core.

Work. The precursors of work can be seen in the baby's curiosity—its exploration of its environment—and in its efforts at mastery of its own body and of objects around it. There may be considerable individual differences among babies in these tendencies and efforts. Researchers have explored these differences intensively under the name of "temperament" (cf. Chess and Thomas, 1977). Babies have preferences for visual, or oral or tactile stimulation. They have different activity levels, and different levels of sensitivity to certain stimuli. Such traits, existing from the very first (though perhaps subject to modification), may eventually incline the grown person to one or another vocation.

Love. Thanks to Freud, of course, we acknowledge the erotic quality of infantile experience. We see nursing as a sensual and perhaps bliss-ful experience and not simply a nutritive activity. We see this sensuality as a precursor of genital sexuality. (Reich, 1983, p. 117, made an interesting further observation that I've never seen either confirmed or denied. He claimed to have witnessed happily nursing babies exhibiting tremors of the lips which gradually spread to the entire body. The babies appeared to experience this as highly pleasurable. A relaxed state appeared to follow. In short Reich claimed to have found a precursor of genital orgasm.) As for the tender as well as the sensual component of loving, a precursor of this can be seen in quiet gazing by the baby into the mothering one's eyes.

Even though one can hardly attribute to an infant the "other-regardingness" of mature love, perhaps its origins lie in an infant's capacity—and the growing deliberate use of this capacity—to evoke pleasurable responses in the people around it. We also know that quite young children in the Nazi concentration camps were remarkable in their activity of nurturing one another when adults were no longer available to parent them. Perhaps in what we know as normal childhood—when children are protected from any responsibilities—capacities for "other regarding," or nurturing, or loving behavior lie latent. Eibl-Eibesfeldt (1972) has also reported scattered observations (but no systematic study) of babies among the Kalihari bushmen comforting other babies when they cried.

6. *The problem of aggression.* Precursors of aggression are easily seen in infants. The rather diffuse thrashing and accompanying sounds and facial expressions of distress suggest what will later become the more differentiated emotions of anger, rage, and hatred. These more developed emotions involve cognition of other selves and projects (i.e., planned activities) to overcome the opposition of these others; to force their consent; to punish them; to control, humiliate, and torture them; to remove them or annihilate them. To conceive such plans would seem to require substantial cognitive capacity.

In any case, both in its precursor and mature forms, distress/aggression seems to me to be a reaction to circumstances and not a basic component of the core-self. It is a reaction that we see with great frequency and intensity in infants, in this society at least (perhaps much less so in certain hunter-gatherer cultures). But it appears to be a reaction nonetheless, not an appetitive drive. Aside from observations of children, this view is based on the symmetry and common physiological substratum of fight and flight, the differentiation in animals between predation and intraspecies aggression, the failure of ethologists to find dominance hierarchies to be universal in all higher species of animals, and so on (cf. Fromm, 1973).

When we speak of fulfillment in adult life we speak of love and work, not of aggression. When, in another mode, we speak of the "instincts" of sex and aggression, why do we not include an instinct of fear/flight—since these have such a symmetrical relationship to anger/aggression both behaviorally and physiologically. If we are capable of seeing fear as reactive, not as a basic appetite or need, why not aggression as well?

On the other hand, if parents attempt to suppress or refuse to recognize the kicking and thrashing and howling that accompanies distress in children this can lead to severe emotional disturbance. Accordingly, I conceptualize aggression and its infantile precursors as first an occasional mechanism (and later on, "project") of defending the core-self, but not an ongoing need or appetite or expression of that core. If aggression becomes an ongoing drivelike project I am inclined to see this as a defensive fixation—as a secondary phenomenon not a direct expression of the core-self.

Growth of the Core-Self

The adult core-self, with which the discussion in this paper began, contains values, purposes, and projects. It contains capacities for mature love and for righteous indignation, for loyalties and for commitments. It may even include a deep calling or vocation to do rather specific kinds of work—work involving the particular materials and roles available in one's culture. Thus the adult core-self contains much more than the infantile nucleus from which it springs. It is a social self that is expressive of the culture in which it was formed and has intentions toward other people and the community.

There must be growth processes and learning processes by which such a mature and social core-self develops out of the much more limited and diffuse infantile nucleus. I presume the process works something like this. Children are constantly having experiences with and making discoveries about the physical and human environment. Cognitive processes are working constantly at a preconscious level to organize this material into coherent, accessible, and above all usable form. Only that material which is most fully integrated and assimilated can become part of the core-self. Only material compatible with the already established (nuclear and acquired) aspects of the core-self can be assimilated. Thus the core-self becomes elaborated, mature, and social but never loses the basic character determined by its earliest simplest nucleus.

Part of the process of reckoning with the world involves introjecting images of parent figures. These may include split images of ideally good and malevolently bad parents, or may be images of relatively coherent persons who are capable of both favorable and unfavorable treatment toward the child. (Even the more integrated images, according to Schafer [1968], are selective perceptions and elaborations from the child's special limited viewpoint and are not literal copies of the real parent.)

An introject, in Schafer's (1968) usage, is experienced as within oneself but not part of oneself. One hears its voice as a separate voice but one that speaks within one's mind, not from outside. Occasionally one identifies with that voice, even speaks to other people with that voice. We can still detect this as an introject, however, insofar as it is a relatively organized and distinct "ego-state" (Federn's term, adopted by Berne, 1961, pp. xix–xxi). That is, when we are speaking "with this voice" we will espouse an organized set of views and have expectable reactions that are distinct from those we exhibit when in other ego-states.

Introjects are clearly not part of the core-self. But introjects, too, can be assimilated. The values, beliefs, and traits of the introjects can be integrated into the ego and the core-self—with the result that the introject fades or disintegrates. This process is referred to as "depersonification" (Jacobson), "transmuting internalizations" (Kohut), "digestion" (Bion), or "metabolization" (Kernberg). (The source for this review of concepts is Greenberg and Mitchell, 1983, p. 329.) This "digestion" and assimilation of introjects would appear to be another important mechanism for the growth of the core-self.

The Freudian superego, in its simplest form, is simply a father introject. In a more complex form it results from the integration of material from a number of sources from different times in the child's life. But it is conceived as not fully integrated into the ego, it is a separate structure of agency. In therapy with clients with harsh primitive superegos, a goal of healing is to lessen the severity of superego and integrate it more into the ego. In short, the superego is subject to digestion and assimilation. If this assimilation is a very thorough one, I suspect that some of the values initially located in the superego become a part of the core-self. This would occur only insofar as these values are compatible with the tendencies established from the outset in the nucleus of the core-self.

The concept of self-representation plays a major role in contemporary psychoanalytic theory. Indeed the meaning of the word *self* for the object-relations and self-psychology schools is bound up with self-representation. What is the relationship between this concept and my concept of core-self? Let us approach this question through consideration of therapy with clients who, to a great extent, present a false self to the world. Their self-representations are likely to be split into a devalued bad self and a grandiose good self. Part of therapy will be to bring these images to consciousness, test them against reality, and gradually develop an integrated cohesive self-representation. In this process fears will be explored and gradually attenuated, emotions will be expressed, and gradually the client will get more access to the buried nucleus of the core-self. The suspended development of this core-self will be resumed. Aspects of the person's adult experience, knowledge, and skills—up to now organized in the false-self system—can be "metabolized" and assimilated into the core-self.

In this view the achievement of cohesive self-representations does not constitute the healing process, but is an accomplishment of it and an element of it. The integration of self-representation signals the more fundamental process of permitting the core-self to emerge into contact with the ego and to resume its development.

Ethical Dilemmas

Having explored the nature of the core-self—its infantile nucleus, mechanisms of growth, and mature form—let us return to ethical dilemmas, which were our point of departure. Philosophers conceive of ethical dilemmas as occurring when the dictates of two accepted principles are at odds and there is no superordinate principle for choosing between them. Psychoanalysts would add that ethical dilemmas often result from conflict between separate parts of the personality: various agencies, ego-states, introjects speak with different voices in the mind each bidding for control of our behavior. Often, without resolving the conflict, we nonetheless choose one course simply because one of these voices succeeds in shouting down, or seducing, or otherwise overcoming the others. In other cases the conflicting voices are too evenly balanced and we experience ourselves as stuck. We are unable to reach a decision. It is here that getting in touch with the core-self can bring a sense of clarity and resolution. This is not simply another entry in the din of competing voices. We recognize it as what is deepest and most central in us.

Self-Transformation

I suspect there are dilemmas that are simply not resolvable at all at the person's given level of integration and maturation. In these cases either one simply cannot get in touch with the core-self, or it too lacks the clear values and commitments to determine a choice. If resolution is possible at all it will be through further integration of the personality—integration that is forged in the very process of ethical deliberation, in the heat of ethical conflict and turmoil. This will involve the digestion of unintegrated introjects, the blurring of boundaries between separate agencies of the personality. Finally it will mean assimilating new material to the core-self. If we emerge from these struggles with new firm and deep commitments, then the core-self has grown by the addition of these commitments.

The most difficult and profound ethical dilemmas, then, are resolved (if at all) by self-transformation. It seems to me that this is what Sartre is talking about when he discusses human freedom and "radical choice" (cf. Taylor's, 1977, discussion of Sartre's view). But Sartre makes this process seem utterly arbitrary and mysterious. In the view argued here the result is anything but arbitrary. The growth of the core-self can only occur along particular lines—begun at infancy and developed throughout life. It is an assimilation of new choices and commitments compatible with those that already define the essence of who we are.

Concluding Remarks

I arrived at the idea of ethical resolution through self-unification during a discussion with students at a student-faculty weekend retreat several years ago. This was strong confirmation of my belief in the value of such occasions for teachers as well as students. Prior to that weekend I had been lecturing about John Dewey's (1922, 1932) ethical theory and trying to make sense of Dewey's cryptic comments on ethics and emotions, the self, and so on. I still do not know exactly what Dewey intended, but his writing certainly did provide the direct input for the view that I reached and have found so fruitful.

Later I thought back and realized that I had read something similar many years before when I had just begun to teach. This was in a book by Herbert Fingarette (1963) entitled—appropriately enough—*The Self in Transformation*. Going back to that source I found this evocation of the ethical deliberation process:

> If we turn to our own important private deliberations, and certainly if we turn to the crucial deliberations which take place in psychotherapy, we see that responsible choice . . . involves the "free" production of thoughts, feelings, fantasies, and memories; it involves the willingness to contemplate these, to "savor" them, to explore them, . . . Finally serious choices, the choices that make one *a new person in a new world,* involve that sometimes sudden, sometimes gradual, but always *involuntary, fusion of the whole into a meaningful pattern.* (pp. 55–56, emphasis mine)

Perhaps I would never have arrived at my conclusion had I not read Fingarette—even though it took fifteen years to realize the importance of what he said. Unfortunately, Fingarette could be of no further help since he believes (1963, pp. 100–01), with Sartre, that the fusion he speaks of creates an entirely new self through a discontinuous and untraceable leap.

When I discussed these ideas with a colleague he referred me to still another relevant account—by Charles Taylor (1977). In his article "What is Human Agency?" Taylor discusses situations of

> Radical re-valuation [in which] the most basic terms, those in which other evaluations are carried on, are precisely what is in question. [In such situations we are forced back to the] inarticulate limit [from which our basic terms originate. To conduct deliberations under those circumstances we must enter into them with a] readiness to receive any gestalt shift in our view . . . any quite innovative set of categories in which to see our predicament that may come our way in inspiration. [This is not to be taken as meaning that] anything goes, but rather that what takes the place of the yardstick [of old basic terms] is *my deepest unstructured sense of what is important,* which is as yet inchoate . . . I am trying to open myself, use all of my deepest, unstructured sense of things. . . .
> [This process] engages the whole self . . . What emerges from it is a *self-resolution in a strong sense,* for in this reflection *the self is in question*; what is at stake is the definition of those *inchoate evaluations which are sensed to be essential to our identity.* (pp. 131–33, emphasis mine)

Taylor suggests that the contemporary psychoanalytic theory of the self has much to offer. He refers to the "much more fully developed notion of a 'cohesive self' that [psychoanalysts Heinz] Kohut and Ernest Wolf have introduced." Taylor anticipates and welcomes:

> The prospect of a psychoanalytic theory which could give an adequate account of the genesis of full human responsibility, without recourse to such global and reified mechanisms as the super-ego, and with a truly plausible account of the shared subjectivity from which the mature cohesive self must emerge—[which] is a very exciting prospect, indeed. (pp. 134–35)

Taylor himself has not pursued this line of thought further in any publication of which I am aware. Perhaps psychoanalysts of the self-psychology school have developed the possibilities that Taylor raises, but I do not know of such work.

References

Berne, E. (1961). *Transactional analysis in psychotherapy.* New York: Ballantine.

Chess, S., and Thomas, A. (1977). *Temperament and development.* New York: Brunner Mazel.

Dewey, J. (1922). *Human nature and conduct.* New York: Henry Holt.

———. (1934). *A common faith.* New Haven: Yale University Press.

———. and Tufts, J. (1932). *Ethics.* (rev. ed.). New York: Henry Holt.

Eibl-Eibesfeldt, I. (1972). *Die !ko-Buschmann-Gesellschaft.* München: R. Piper.

Erikson, E. (1968). *Identity: Youth and crisis.* New York: Norton.

Fingarette, H. (1963). *The self in transformation.* New York: Harper and Row.

Fraiberg, S. H. (1959). *The magic years.* New York: Scribner's.

Franz, M. L. von (1964). The process of individuation. In C. G. Jung (ed.), *Man and his symbols.* Garden City, N.Y.: Doubleday.

Fromm, E. (1973). *The anatomy of human destructiveness.* Greenwich, Conn.: Fawcett.

Greenberg, J. R., and Mitchell, S. A. (1983). *Object relations in psychoanalytic theory.* Cambridge: Harvard University Press.

Guntrip, H. (1971). *Psychoanalytic theory, therapy, and the self.* New York: Basic Books.

Jung, C. G. (1965). *Memories, dreams, and reflections* (rev. ed.). New York: Vintage.

Lichtenberg, J. D. (1983). *Psychoanalysis and infant research.* Hillsdale, N.J.: Analytic Press.

Mahler, M. S., Pine, F., and Bergman, A. (1975). *The psychological birth of the human infant.* New York: Basic Books.

Miller, A. (1981). *The drama of the gifted child.* New York: Basic Books.

Reich, W. (1983). *Children of the future.* New York: Farrar, Straus, and Giroux.

Sartre, J. (1957). *Existentialism and human emotions.* New York: Philosophical Library.

Schafer, R. (1968). *Aspects of internalization.* New York: International Universities Press.

Sullivan, H. S. (1953). *The interpersonal theory of psychiatry.* New York: Norton.

Taylor, C. (1977). What is human agency? In T. Mischel (ed.), *The self.* Totowa, N.J.: Rowman and Littlefield.

Tolpin, M., and Kohut, H. (1979). The disorders of the self: The psychopathology of the first years of life. Unpublished manuscript, Chicago Psychoanalytic Society.

Twain, M. (1958). *Adventures of Huckleberry Finn.* Boston: Houghton Mifflin.

Winnicott, D. W. (1965). *The maturational process and the facilitating environment.* London: Hogarth Press.

SELF AND TERMINOLOGY

Among many schools of depth psychology, there may be tacit agreement hidden behind vicissitudes of terminology. In this section, Joseph Redfearn traces threads of the terminological tangle from Freud to Kohut, from Klein to Jung. Redfearn favors a Jungian system of nomenclature and devotes much of his paper to clarifying its boundaries and domain.

Here we are invited to reflect on different terms and concepts which depict or embody aspects of human experiences that are called "self": (1) the sense of being a center of subjectivity, an "I"; (2) shifting identification with a range of possible self-representations of "I," any of which could be "myself"; (3) the ability to determine, to a large degree, the content of the self-representations that "I" identify with; (4) an intuitive awareness that "I" am in process, with a history that is partially unrecoverable or fictional, and a future that is as yet indeterminate; and (5) experiences of subjectivity of which "I" is a subset, a transcendent order in which the self is contained, as a potential existing in some "other space."

Redfearn lays out the major terms that have been used to point toward these experiences in the history of depth psychology.

CHAPTER 18 _____

Terminology of Ego and Self: From Freud(ians) to Jung(ians)

JOSEPH W. T. REDFEARN

Introduction

A PSYCHOLOGICAL SCHEMA of the structure of the mind is like a map. It should not be confused with the real thing. A map is used for a purpose. A geological map would be useless to a motorist. A sociologist's map would be different from a psychotherapist's. Freudian, Jungian, and behavioral psychotherapists need different maps because of their different goals and methods of arriving at them.

I said that the map should not be confused with the real thing. What is the "real thing" in the case of the mind? A series of maps or representations? If so, what is the nature of the "I" to whom they are presented? A further series of representations? Is the "I" based on energy/matter, or is energy/matter merely a split-off, ephemeral, and alienated aspect of a universal "I" or Psyche? Or can we arrive at our personal resolution of these apparently polarized views of the psyche and matter?

How far does introspection lead us in our experience of self? Our experience of ourselves is necessarily a matter of introspection, if not for introspection alone. Writing in 1910, William James distinguished between "I," the self as a knower and doer, and "me," or "myself" as known or experienced. He saw no value in studying the "I" as a

This chapter is based on a paper first published in *The Journal of Analytical Psycholgy* in April 1983. A later version appeared in *My Self, My Many Selves* by the same author as vol. 6 in *Library of Analytical Psychology* series published by Academic Press, 1985.

knower and felt it should be banished to the realms of philosophy. Comprising the "myself" as known, James included a material self, which contained one's body, one's family, and one's possessions; then a social self, which reflected the way other people see the individual; and finally a spiritual self, which included emotions and desires.

All these aspects of the self have stood the test of time and have been studied in detail. Furthermore, James recognized that all these aspects of self were capable of evoking feelings of heightened or lowered self-esteem. And finally, James described the self as carrying a feeling of basic unity and continuity, even while being highly differentiated.

Cooley (1912) defined *self* as that which is designated in common speech by the first person singular: I, me, mine, myself. The self is characterized by stronger emotions than is the nonself. Cooley introduced the concept of the "looking-glass self"—the concept of the individual perceiving himself in the way others see him.

Taking this idea further, George Mead (1934) argued that the self-concept in fact arises out of the individual's concern about how others react to him. Mead hypothesized a "generalized other" to account for generalized feelings about oneself. He averred that there are as many selves as there are social roles played by an individual.

H. S. Sullivan (1953) agreed but stressed the importance of the mother as the most significant other person in determining the self-concept.

Allport (1955) used the word *proprium* to include the following attributes:

(a) awareness of a bodily self
(b) sense of a continuity over time
(c) a need for self-esteem
(d) an extension of the "I" or ego beyond the borders of the body
(e) an ability to synthesize inner needs and outer reality
(f) a self-image, a perception and evaluation of the self as an object of knowledge
(g) the self as knower and doer
(h) an occasional need to increase tensions, expand awareness, seek and meet challenges, etc.

I mention these authors in a general introduction to the psycholog-

ical literature because their contributions seem to me basically sound
and fundamental ones.

Ego and Self in Psychoanalysis

In attempting to sketch developments in psychoanalytic terminology
I shall need to shorten and oversimplify to such a degree as perhaps
to cause pain to each reader. I shall need much generosity from all,
as each would summarize important changes in his or her own way.
But I am not writing about the authors' actual views. I am using
selected quotations and summaries in order to discuss terminology,
typical possible terminologies. I might have invented the quotations
myself without affecting the validity of this chapter, which is written
to alert the reader to terminological confusions. The scope of confusion is not limited to terminology, and some readers will be offended
by the simplistic clarity of my presentation, which in a sense ignores
the real, nonterminological confusions and paradoxes in the actual
phenomenology of the experiences described below.

Freud

In abandoning hypnosis in the therapy of neurosis, Freud discovered
resistance and laid the foundation for what would eventually be called
the theory of defenses of the ego (*das Ich*). At first, Freud (1958/1900)
formulated a map of the mind in which three domains were characterized by different cognitive processes: unconscious, preconscious,
and conscious. His concern was initially to show how the original "primary process" of hallucinatory wish fulfillment eventually developed
into a "secondary process" of rational thinking and reality testing.

Because Freud conceived of the unconscious as primary and least
observable from the point of view of everyday adult consciousness, he
devoted his attention to charting its contents in most of his early work
(prior to 1920 and *Beyond the Pleasure Principle*). In his early papers,
Freud regarded the "reality principle" of waking consciousness as derived from the "pleasure principle" of the unconscious mind. The
initial expression of libido through the pansexuality of childhood was
conflictually repressed and defended against through the formation

of the rational modes of secondary process, delayed-gratification mental operations. Hence Freud regarded the conscious character of what was later called "ego" or the "I" to be defensive. Mostly these defenses were recognized as part of conscious life (e.g., moral inhibitions), but some defenses were unconscious (e.g., sublimation). Strachey (Freud, 1961/1923, p. 7), Freud's translator for the English *Standard Edition* of his works, says that he translated a particular meaning of the "I" (*das Ich*) to mean "self" rather than "ego": the subjective distinction of oneself from other people. This concept of "self" was the only specific focus for the term as Freud used it. By 1914–15 Freud was distinguishing between ego instincts and object instincts. In this context ego means oneself. Megalomania was explained in terms of these ego instincts, as were self-regard and self-esteem.

In his essay "On Narcissism," written about that time, Freud (1957/ 1914) described the antithesis between ego-libido and object-libido. He used the simile of an amoeba throwing out pseudopods, suggesting a basic unity of libido but flowing in opposite directions.

By this time Freud is beginning to develop the idea of a superego, comparing the behavior of the individual with that of his ego-ideal. He used the notion to explain the paraphrenic's delusions of being watched. He saw the primary state of the infant as that of boundaryless self-love which he called primary narcissism, but self and notself were as yet undifferentiated. He saw the ego developing out of this state of displacement of libido onto the mother and later on to an ideal. Satisfaction is brought about by fulfilling the mother's (later the ideal's) requirements.

Later, Freud used this interplay between object libido and narcissism to account for the building up of complex functions, such as sublimation and the neutralization of instincts.

In his important monograph *The Ego and the Id* (1961/1923), Freud made his final reformulation of the structure of the mind. He described a personality function called *das Ich* (translated as "ego") and carefully delineated its processes of reality testing and conscious awareness. He also elaborated another function, a watching faculty, *das über-Ich* (translated as "superego") that judged and measured performances of the ego, according to ideals for reality and gratification. Contained within this function was the principle for moral conscience, as well as the potential extremes of obsessional neurosis and pathological mourning. The superego was assumed to be structured primarily out of the transformation of the oedipal conflict, with its sexual attraction for the opposite-gender parent, into an ego ideal of the same-gender parent.

Freud (1961/1923) then restricted the term *unconscious* to repressed mental contents. The ego was the coherent personality function of conscious, perceptual, and reality-testing experiences. The ego controlled the approaches to waking actions (motility) and became more passive and restricted during sleep. In sleep, however, the ego still demanded that mental processes be presented in moral and rational terms in dreams. Dreams were structured secondarily around the principles of the ego; hence the ego also contained repressed elements. To some extent, the ego behaved exactly like repressed contents and produced powerful unconscious effects. In his new theory, Freud derived the neuroses from conflicts between conscious and repressed ego contents.

The other part of the mind, into which the ego extends, was now called the "id" following Groddeck (1950/1923), who regarded the ego as a surface phenomenon merely being lived out by the unconscious forces of the id. Part of the lower ego is discontinuous with the id, owing to repression. Thus the ego is that part of the id which has been modified by the direct influence of the external world through the medium of perceptions: it is in a sense an extension of the surface-differentiation. The ego mediates between the instincts and the external world through the reality principle and not through self-regard. Freud likened the ego in its relation to the id to be like a man on horseback. Often, he says, a man has to guide the horse where he wants to go.

This ego (1961/1923) is first and foremost a representation of the body, derived from bodily sensations and projected as the surface unity of the ego. The ego is the counterpart of body integrity. The reservoir of libido is with the id. In later writings, Freud used the concept of an undifferentiated ego-id as a reservoir of libido.

A large part of post-Freudian psychoanalytic literature has been devoted to delineating "ego-defenses" and "ego-boundaries." In her book *The Ego and the Mechanisms of Defense*, Anna Freud (1946/1936) elaborates on the defenses used by the ego to defend its view of reality. Here she is often referring to the feeling of "I" or "myself" and not merely to the system "ego" as defined by Freud. The notion of ego-boundaries and their preservation refers to the experience of self as distinct from others, and not to Freud's system ego as described above.

Klein, Winnicott, and Erikson

The psychoanalysis of children and of psychotic patients has enriched our knowledge of early and archaic levels of the development of personal identity. One thinks of such analysts as Melanie Klein, Erikson, and Winnicott as making fundamental contributions to terminology.

Melanie Klein (1964) uses the term *ego* to mean both the subjective "I" or "myself" on the one hand, and the "system ego" on the other, with its various stage-appropriate ways of enhancing, depending, and strengthening itself. Just as the baby sucks, takes in, shrinks from, spits out, eliminates, various objects in his struggle to survive, so the infant ego is seen taking in, spitting out, avoiding, and eliminating good and bad "objects" or parts of "objects" (mental representations of bits of his environment). Thus the ego arises out of some sort of mental representation ("brain map") of the baby itself. This is not nonsense, as would first appear, because the baby, its insides, outside, and the world of vision and hearing give rise to nervous impulses that are topographically distributed throughout the nervous system. Thus the body-image as sensed and perceived is an accurate map, in the brain, of the baby himself. The Kleinian views the ego and the psyche as a body-ego and a psyche-ego. The Kleinian "mechanisms" are all derived from as well as representations of bodily processes, sensations, and reactions.

In his classic work *Childhood and Society* and his other writings, Erikson (1950), while adhering in his definition of ego to Freud's definition, writes of ego identity and of the growth of a personal sense of identity. He writes of the ego as if it were a kind of person dwelling between the extremes of the "bestial" impersonal id and the often harsh and restrictive conscience. The ego keeps tuned to reality and integrates the individual's planning and orientation. Admittedly Erikson's ego uses "defense mechanisms," but he wants to elaborate a function beyond defensiveness. The ego is an "inner institution" evolved to safeguard order within the individual. In the case of a schizophrenic girl, he described a failure of the ego as the inability to achieve a coherent "I." Play situations permit us to experiment with ego states in which we can feel ourselves to be beyond the usual confinements of space, time and social realities. Here the ego is clearly a self with human feelings, closely related to well-being and good self-esteem. Erikson describes the child's acquisition of a sound sense of personal identity based on the body image, and goes on to trace this development in the adult. He thus extends the concept of the "I" to that of a personal identity and gives descriptions of clinical aspects of "ego-growth" and of failures in this area. For Erikson this personal identity has primarily a mediating function between inner and outer needs, between instincts and standards, and so on.

Winnicott (1965), on the other hand, uses the term *ego* to mean an integrating function of the brain present from the beginning. Thus an anencephalic infant would have an id but no ego, whereas an infant with a normal brain would already have an ego as well as an id. The ego is there from the start. In fact, ego is the starting point from which a self-representation develops. The ego is thus a function of personality which permits a unified development of subjectivity. The word *self* arrives only after the child has begun to use the intellect to look at what others see or feel or hear, and what they conceive of when they meet this infant body. The functional success of the ego, for Winnicott, depends greatly on the mother's initial ability to support and contain the actual infant before it has the ability to meet environmental demands itself. It is possible then to violate an infant's coherent ego-functioning if the mother lacks the capacity to protect the infant from unthinkable anxiety by being able to put herself in the baby's place and know what the baby needs in the general management of the body, and therefore of the person.

A baby, according to Winnicott (1965), is on the brink of unthinkable anxiety of the following varieties:

(1) going to pieces
(2) falling for ever
(3) having no relationship to the body
(4) having no orientation

These anxieties are the stuff of psychotic anxieties. Ego functioning is threatened by the experiences of such anxiety in early life. Maternal failure at this stage can lead to schizoid disorder and to the formation of a "false self," which is an attempt at self-holding or the conservation of ego. Ego development depends, thus, on the ego-supportive mother and is characterized by the following trends:

(1) integration in time and space, depending on the mother's *holding*;

(2) personalization—the development of the body ego and of a firm union of ego and body, depending on the other's *handling*;

(3) object-relating, both to things and persons, depending on the mother's way and timing of *object-presentation*.

Differentiation into "I" and "you," into "I" and "non-I," the development of subjective objects and of objectively experienced objects, and of capacity for realism proceeds gradually so long as the mother understands the child's reality limitations. For a long time the child retains areas of subjective objects as well as areas of objectively perceived objects ("not-me" objects).

Thus in Winnicott's (1965) rather comprehensive terminology, the ego is the original integrating function. Schizoid mechanisms arise out of threats to the preself, or what will later become the self. Self is oneself as distinct from other people, and its emergence is importantly dependent on how others experience an individual; in other words, self is a function of reflection from others. Thus, the self for Winnicott is what arises out of the differentiation of an original integrate of oneself and other(s).

Jacobson, Hartmann, Fordham, Kohut

For Edith Jacobson (1965) in her book *The Self and the Object World* and for Michael Fordham (1976) in his book *The Self and Autism* the original integrate is called "the primal self." For Jacobson "the establishment of the system ego sets in with the discovery of the object world and the growing distinction between it and one's own physical and mental self" (p. 19). Jacobson's terminology is thus more or less the opposite of Winnicott's as far as ego and self are concerned. For Fordham also the ego is related to the experience of "I" and is differentiated out of the primal self. It is only a part of the whole self. However, neither Jacobson nor Fordham is consistent in the use of the word *self*. For example, Jacobson's use of the word *self* in the sentence just quoted ("one's own physical and mental self" as distinct from the "not-me") does not conform with her own definition of *self*, and coincides with Winnicott's self. And Fordham (1974) describes some schizoid defenses as defenses of the self when he is not speaking of the primary integrate of total personality but of a "pre-myself," or pre-ego in Jungian terminology.

Jacobson (1965) states that her definition of *self* is based on Hartmann's (1950) definition as the whole individual, including mind and body. She says that the term was introduced by Hartmann (1939/1958) and ignores the voluminous writings on the subject by C. G. Jung, on whose work Fordham's definition and concepts are based.

Hartmann (1964) certainly pioneered a major trend in psychoanalytic theory, and made a clear distinction between "ego" and "self." For Hartmann the ego is not defined in terms of self-feeling, the experience of "I," or any other subjective experience or subjectively experienced datum, but as a system of adaptive and integrative functions hierarchically arranged. Functions of defense and anti-instinctual aspects are included in the functions of the ego. Adaptation to "reality" is the main emphasis, a biological view (Hartmann, 1964). Obviously some of those ego functions would be present from the beginning of the individual, and so Hartmann's definition of ego is similar to Winnicott's.

Hartmann also defines the self in much the same way as does Winnicott. It has very much to do with feelings and subjective experience and with the distinction between myself and not-me. For example, he says, "It will therefore be clarifying if we define narcissism as the libidinal cathexis not of the ego but of the self" (1964, p. 127). He thus diverges considerably in his terminology from the early and middle Freud, while not of course ignoring any of Freud's findings or basic ideas. In his ego functions Hartmann includes reality-oriented, anti-instinctual functions such as the postponement of gratification and the neutralization of instincts, and generally adheres to the post-1923 Freudian view of psychic structure. But his differentiation of "ego" from "self" no doubt helped later psychoanalysts such as Jacobson (1965) and especially Heinz Kohut (1971) in their clinical work on narcissism and narcissistic disorders.

Kohut (1971) pays tribute to Hartmann's conceptual separation of the self from the ego, in paving the way to his work on identity and on the subjective self which is clinically of such importance. He points out that the self in his terminology has to do with the representation of the self in the psyche, analogous to the representations of other persons and things in the psyche ("object-representations"). He uses the description *experience-near* for this concept of the self, whereas the term *ego* is used as an abstract concept describing or defining a psychic system. Much of the basic fabric of the ego, for Kohut, consists of introjections of the approving and disapproving aspects of the preoedipal mother. (I personally would agree and would add that many of the holding and containing aspects of the ego are introjected from early experiences of the mother in the same way.) With Freud, Kohut derives the superego from introjections of the "postoedipal object" (the postoedipal mother and father).

It could be asserted that as a person matures, the self as the object of narcissistic libido, the ego as a mediating and containing function, personal identity as per Erikson, and the Jungian self coincide. The real (nonterminological) issues regarding differences in these concepts preoccupied both Jung and the later Kohut in aspects of their work, as we shall see.

Jung, Neumann, Fordham

Jung used the word *self* to describe (at various times):

(1) a primary unity inseparable from a cosmic order;
(2) the totality of the individual;
(3) a feeling or intimation of such a totality, an experience of "wholeness";
(4) a primary organizing force or agency outside the conscious "I";
(5) the predisposition to organize a center of consciousness;
(6) subjective experiences of a personal self.
(See Redfearn, 1977).

For Jung, the term *self* is used for a totality, or for a mainly "not-me" force, the center of the psyche that is usually not experienced clearly by the conscious "I." Jung's "self" is placed over against his "ego," which corresponds with Freud's pre-1914 ego. This is not surprising as the divergence between Freud and Jung dated from about 1913. Of course, in its aspect of the total personality, Jung's "self" would include "ego," so that thus defined it would consist of "ego plus unconscious" or "ego plus archetypes," but Jung does not always use the term in this way. The self is for Jung not something experienced directly, but, as in the Platonic and neo-Platonic tradition, indirectly through symbols, stories, and numerous experiences including religious experiences.

Jung (1951) does not distinguish in his use of the term *ego* between the subjective "I" and the functions of defense and adaptation described later by Anna Freud and Hartmann. His "ego" is very much akin to Kohut's "self" in that it is generally experience-near, that is, near to the experience or feeling of "I," "me," "myself," my "identity." Indeed, Jung often defines it as a center of awareness or of consciousness. Somewhat paradoxically, perhaps, he regards the ego as "a sort of complex." Complexes, which were Jung's own discovery, are largely unconscious, like subpersonalities or subselves affecting consciousness and behavior but avoiding direct relationship with the "I." Jung's "ego" is an integrating and organizing force (in this it does not differ from other "complexes") and both the organizing function and the subjective unity of the "I" may become fragmented, as in schizophrenia. In schizophrenia, of course, one can observe a shifting of one personality to another (Jung, 1955/1935).

This looseness of the "I" in its attachment to the various subpersonalities of the individual, results in a migration of "I-feeling" between the different subpersonalities. This migration of "I-feeling" also characterizes the dream-ego in comparison with the normal waking-ego (Hall, 1982).

On the other hand, Jung defines ego as "a complex datum of experience" which is constituted first by a general awareness of one's body and existence, and secondly by memory data (Jung, 1955/1935). In this way Jung's "ego" is similar to Winnicott's "self" and to the Hartmann-Kohut "self." Jung's "ego," like Hartmann's "self," is the object of one's self-esteem, self-awareness, self-value, and so on; Jung's ego is also the active, willing, doing "I." "Will," for Jung, is determined by the amount of psychic energy at the disposal of the ego, which in this context is active, doing, and very much the subject and not the object.

Jung's subpersonalities—the ego, the persona, the shadow, the anima, the wise man, the wise woman, the self, and so on—as well as the complexes, behave as organizing centers, and each may take charge in turn of the feelings of "I" and of behavior. They all have an innate basis and yet are all influenced by experience and differentiate through experience. Thus the ego is acquired in the individual's lifetime and arises from the interaction of body and environment (Jung, 1951). The shadow also is partly acquired during one's lifetime (consisting of negative introjects—my term) and yet has an innate foundation—like absolute evil. Thus complexes contain positive and negative introjected elements, yet (and this is the innate element) one can only introject what one *is* in the first place.

What *is* important are the positive and negative feeling tones that are introjected. These feelings are incorporated into the personality as positive and negative interrelationships between the various sub-personalities in oneself.

Let us take such negative behaviors and attitudes as "I despise ——," "I am terrified of ——," "I ignore ——," "I turn my back on ——." All these are primary attitudes or behaviors needed originally for self-protection. If my mother has these attitudes toward various bits of myself, then what I end up with is a situation in which a "mother" bit of myself is negatively related to a "child" bit of myself. The concept of shadow is vague and generalized in clinical practice. In clinical practice we need to know about the part of the personality which is disapproving, the part disapproved of, and the specific nature (disgust, contempt, denial, fear, etc.) of the negative interaction.

It is easy to see that it is the negative attitudes rather than the affirming ones that when introjected give rise to fixations, repressions, resistances, and so on, because the "I" is usually identified with the original rejector (the on-the-whole loved or good mother, the on-the-whole accepted values of society, etc.).

Just as Jung remained consistent in speaking of the self more as the whole personality and the ego as the "I" linked with self-valuation and the sense of personal identity, so later analytical psychologists have consistently maintained these broad definitions. However, an important Jungian variation on this theme sees the self, or at any rate the way the self presents itself to consciousness, as an organizing center essentially based in the unconscious, only partly capable of being perceived directly in consciousness.

Symbols of the self, the inner voice, the image of God, and so on, are not usually experienced as part of one's own personality or as part of oneself, but are usually experienced as coming from the "not-me." This has left Jungians open to the charge of mysticism. To speak of god, or of the God image at least, as a self-image or self-symbol, even as a symbol of the totality of the psyche, seems to beg all sorts of philosophical and theological questions. But from the empirical psychological point of view we take these images and symbols as products of the psyche. This in turn seems to lead us to the view of the psyche as having no specific location in relation to the subjective "me." Or, to put it another way, the "I" may at different times be experienced in differing parts or locations within the total universe of the self. Jung, much more than Freud, always insisted that the unconscious parts of the self (of the total personality that is) are experienced "in projection," that is, they are experienced as outside the subjective "me," in other people for example. And moreover, that they must be faced, or "worked through," in the moral conflicts of real relationships.

The more unaware or regressed a person is, the more the various subpersonalities and complexes comprising his total personality are successively experienced by him as the whole thing—the whole truth, the whole of himself, the will of God, ultimate good, and so on. In other words, parts of the total personality take over the feeling of "myself" and seem like the whole of the self or even of the cosmos. To the outside observer the individual may simply be in a "possessed" or regressed state. To take a theatrical analogy, it is as if different actors successively occupy the whole stage, each thinking he is the whole show, whereas the audience (the analyst) knows that each is only part of the evening's performance.

Thus the various Jungian "symbols of the self" are themselves only parts of the personality, or represent objectively only parts of the total personality. Yet subjectively, and even objectively, they may point toward further integrations and self-awareness.

Apart from giving rise to symbolic experiences, a "sub-personality" or "part-self" may carry the feeling of "myself" at times, or it may possess the individual behaviorally and be acted out relatively unawares. Another method of discharge is through projection onto others.

The analytical psychologist Erich Neumann (1954) sees the myths of mankind mainly as the story of the struggle of the (Jungian) "ego" to free itself from the unconscious—the state of primitive or unaware nondifferentiation or boundarylessness. As the ego (the hero figure of myths and other stories) becomes free and well established, the various unconscious subpersonalities evolve alongside and differentiate, and become in general less monstrous and more human. Thus both "I" and "not-I" evolve and differentiate together with each other in a constant dynamic, dramatized in the great religions and myths of mankind. Neumann refers to this process of ego development and the consequent changes in the way the ego relates to the unconscious and to other people as the emergence of ego-consciousness from the primordial matrix. As each successive stage is laboriously attained, a stage just relinquished becomes a fascinating devourer, a temptation, a sin, and so on.

Fordham (1979) examines in some detail the groups of experience which may carry the feeling of being "myself." He calls these groups of experience "part selves" and these are similar to what I am here calling "sub-personalities." He includes complexes such as the individual's "persona," "shadow," and "anima" among these part selves.

Fordham usually defines the self as the original or primal integrate or as the total personality. He sees the various behavioral patterns of which the infant is capable as deintegrations of this original self. Successive deintegrations and reintegrations eventually result in an ego, self-awareness, an identity and so on.

In one paper, however, Fordham (1974) uses the word *self* to mean something like a "myself-feeling" or an early ego in Jung's terminology. This usage by Fordham gives rise to misconceptions because the word self here means a self-representation, and not the total personality or the primary integrate. In this paper, which deals with schizoid and archaic defenses, the description is of an individual who behaves *as if* his whole existence is under threat. He experiences that bad parts of his personality in projection.

When I submitted these thoughts to Fordham he wrote (personal communication) that the self of this particular article was not intended to refer to the self as defined in his other writings or in the general Jungian literature. "As to defenses of the self I could not say that these were directly referring to the self. But I do say that the patient behaves *as though* the whole of his existence were threatened." In other words we are dealing with fears that pertain to the schizoid level.

The Muddle of "Self" in Contemporary Jungian Psychology

I would summarize our present muddle over terms as follows:

(1) The word *self*, following Hartmann and Kohut, has for many readers come to mean what the early Freudians, the Kleinians and the

Jungians referred to somewhat loosely as the "ego." Or, more strictly, it has come to mean the experience-near concept of self-representation that was *part* of Freud's idea of the ego. The word *self* might be avoided and the word *I, me,* or *myself* used as appropriate, when we mean "the object of narcissistic libido."

While happily adopting Kohut's encompassing use of the word *self,* many analysts equally happily speak of "ego-boundaries" and "ego-defenses," thus combining and confusing pre-Hartmann and post-Hartmann terminology. Jungians could use the word *ego* in a loose way to cover the layman's "self" or the "self-concept" of the academic psychologists, but when they write about narcissistic personality disorders they tend to use the word *self* in the same way as it is defined by Kohut in his earlier writings, which is different from Jung's "self."

(2) The word *self* is, we must admit, perhaps not suitable to describe "total personality, conscious and unconscious," because it is the same word as the lay word that implies personal identity and carries the feeling of "myself." It may sometimes have narcissistic value when used thus. As an exercise in clarity, we Jungians should if possible use the precise term to convey the required meaning, whether it be "hypothetical primal integrate," or "whole personality," or "nonego organizing center" or "numinous part-self symbol," or whatever. The use of the word *Self* with a capital S is certainly worth adopting if it is clear we are referring to a greater Self that is superordinate to the ego, or to something like a totality. This usage was suggested but apparently abandoned for the English version of Jung's works. After Kohut, it seems even more necessary.

(3) The primal integrative functions of the psyche, which develop *paripassu* with the sense of self, are sometimes referred to as properties of the ego (mainly by Freudians) or of the self (Jungians).

The functions of integration, defense, repression, of modifying the instincts, containing conflict, postponing gratification, and so on sometimes carry a "myself" feeling and sometimes do not. Many of the containing, reconciling, transforming functions associated with a sound "ego" are introjected from early experiences mainly by example and by reflection from the mother (see Newton and Redfearn, 1977).

As examples, let us list a few "holding functions." They prevent the patient from schizoid disintegration—going to pieces. They prevent him from feeling utterly abandoned. They ensure his continual subjective existence. They prevent his world from becoming meaningless, or a desert, or a mechanical nightmare. Now all these holding functions may be performed by the analyst in an analysis that is proceeding well. And furthermore they can be introjected into the patient's personality when the analyst gradually "fails" to hold in a graded way. We conclude from that fact that the mother can hold the child in this way and that the child introjects these functions from the mother as he becomes more independent and active. These functions are not normally performed consciously by the person's "I" but are part of the taken-for-granted background of living. They go with a sound sense of personal identity and thus could be said to be a relatively unconscious part of the ego or the self. But they are equally not subjectively part of the self at times and belong to the patient's "world." They are functions defined by Hartmann as ego functions, and are usually regarded by Jungians as archetypal properties of the self— the vessel, the temenos, and so on. Is there some word we can use for these containing and integrative functions? Some of them simply follow from the fact that the patient is in one skin and from various integrative functions of the central nervous system; some of the higher ones are learned, as I have just explained. There is, in fact, a hierarchy of functions of this sort, as Hartmann emphasizes.

Discussion

There is some fundamental agreement among analysts and other psychologists about the development of personal identity and self-awareness, agreement that is masked by the marked differences in terminology. All the authors describe personal identity and the subjective "I" arising out of and resulting from a primal integrative background, but sometimes the personal identity is called the ego and sometimes the self, and sometimes the primary integrate or integrative functions is called the ego and sometimes the self. It is usually easy to discern the usage providing one is aware of the possibility of quite opposing usage of the terms *ego* and *self* particularly in the psychoanalytical literature.

The terminological tools of trade have been laboriously developed by the different schools of analysis, and crude or bad "translation" inevitably does violence to meaning and distorts ways of working. Many years of training are necessary even to enable one to handle one set of tools. Yet this should not prevent our trying to benefit from the experience of other schools, and the foregoing analysis may help in this. The need to help students and trainees orient themselves in the analytical literature has been the chief spur to me in attempting this correlation.

Whether we call it ego, self-concept, or self-representation, the sense of personal identity arises out of some primary, boundaryless, yet far from static or uniform sensorium where "I" and "you" are not yet distinct. To the healthy mother, her baby is already a distinct person with a mind of his own, and with several distinct possible "behaviors," not by any means all of which can be carried out at the same time. At the reflex level, and for more and more complex behaviors, complex hierarchies of integrative function, are present from the beginning. As the baby grows up, the various behaviors are further elaborated and modified, and the integrated functions are also elaborated and differentiated. Each of the functions, as well as the whole baby, tends to actualize itself, to get itself represented in the psyche, and to behave as if it were a whole structure defending itself and enhancing itself. The main ego-complex is thus a composite of representations. Archetypal images and complexes are called subpersonalities, each with its own defenses, relating to other parts of the individual as if each were a person. These ways of relating and evolving are reflected in the mythologies of mankind. Each subpersonality is potentially able to take possession of the feeling of "I," of behavior, or of both. Much of analysis consists of putting the various subpersonalities in touch with each other. The ego-complex, the will, the feeling of choice and self-value, and so on, are of vital importance in providing links in all this integration.

Ideally, the mother recognizes and—with her affect, her behavior, her talk, and so on—validates the infant and each of his behaviors or subpersonalities. The various bits of the infant's potential thus become ego-integrated and not ego-alien. Where "behaviors" compete, conflict results. The mother at first performs a choosing or holding function. The infant introjects these functions and they become part of the ego-complex (not necessarily conscious, but usually taken for granted unless called into question). Thus it does not seem profitable to differentiate ego-functions from "self-representations," as Hartmann and Kohut do. Both develop together. Furthermore, we are so accustomed to talk about ego-defenses and ego-boundaries that we may as well carry on doing so. Narcissism would then have to do with the ego in a broad sense.

Students of psychology and analytic trainees often need guidance through the confusion of terms used in various schools. The terms *ego* and *self* in analytical literature are, as has been pointed out in this chapter, in some cases used one way, and sometimes in the opposite way. For some, the ego emerges from the original self, for some it is the other way round. Yet there is little disagreement about what these terms refer to—personal identity or its precursor arises out of an original undifferentiated or boundaryless integrate or sensorium. The popularity of the writing of Kohut and his followers, and the value of their clinical work on narcissistic disorders, has now made it particularly urgent to differentiate the self in the everyday sense, and the self that has to do with self-value, from the self as conceived by Jung.

References

Allport, G. W. (1955). *Becoming: Basic considerations for a psychology of personality.* New Haven: Yale University Press.

Cooley, C. H. (1912). *Human nature and social order.* New York: Scribner's.

Erikson, E. (1950). *Childhood and society.* New York: Norton.

Fordham, M. (1969). *Children as individuals.* London: Hodder and Stoughton.

———. (1974). Defenses of the self. *Journal of Analytical Psychology 19,* 209.

———. (1976). *The self and autism.* London: Heinemann.

———. (1979). The self as an imaginative construct. *Journal of Analytical Psychology 24,* 18–30.

Freud, A. (1946/1936). *The ego and the mechanisms of defense.* New York: International Universities Press.

Freud, S. (1958/1900). *The interpretation of dreams. Standard Edition, 4 & 5.* London: Hogarth.

———. (1957/1914). On narcissism. *Standard Edition, 14.* London: Hogarth.

———. (1955/1920). *Beyond the pleasure principle. Standard Edition, 18.* London: Hogarth.

———. (1961/1923). The ego and the id. *Standard Edition, 19.* London: Hogarth.

Gordon, R. (1980). Narcissism and the self: Who am I that I love? *Journal of Analytical Psychology, 25,* 247.

Groddeck, G. (1950/1923). *The book of the it.* London: Vision Press.

Hall, J. A. (1982). Polanyi and Jungian psychology: Dream-ego and waking ego. *Journal of Analytical Psychology, 27,* 239–54.

Hartmann, H. (1958/1939). *Ego psychology and the problem of adaptation.* New York: International Universities Press.

———. (1950). Comments on the psychoanalytic theory of the ego. In *The Psychoanalytic Study of the Child, 5.* New York: International Universities Press.

———. (1964). *Essays on ego psychology.* London: Hogarth.

Humbert, E. (1980). The self and narcissism. *Journal of Analytical Psychology, 25,* 237–46.

Jacobson, E. (1965). *The self and the object world.* London: Hogarth.

James, W. (1910). *Psychology: The briefer course.* New York: Holt.

Jung, C. G. (1955/1935). On the theory and practice of analytical psychology. *Collected works 18,* 11. Princeton: Princeton University Press.

———. (1951). The ego. *Collected works, 9,* 3–7. Princeton: Princeton University Press.

Klein, M. (1964). *Contributions to psychoanalysis, 1921–1945.* New York: McGraw-Hill.

Kohut, H. (1971). *The analysis of the self.* New York: International University Press.

Ledermann, R. (1979). The infantile roots of narcissistic personality disorder. *Journal of Analytical Psychology, 24,* 107.

Mead, G. H. (1934). *Mind, self and society.* Chicago: University of Chicago Press.

Neumann, E. (1954). *The origins and history of consciousness.* New York: Pantheon.

Newton, K. and Redfearn, J. W. T. (1977). The real mother, ego-self relations, and personal identity. *Journal of Analytical Psychology, 22,* 295–315.

Redfearn, J. W. T. (1977). The self and individuation. *Journal of Analytical Psychology, 22,* 124–41.

Rycroft, C. (1968). *A critical dictionary of psychoanalysis.* London: Nelson.

Schwartz-Salant, N. (1982). *Narcissism and character transformation.* Toronto: Inner City Books.

Sullivan, H. S. (1953). *The interpersonal theory of psychiatry.* New York: Norton.

Winnicott, D. W. (1965). *The maturational process and the facilitating environment.* London: Hogarth.

SELF AND TRANSCENDENCE

The self experienced as the object of a superordinate subject is one occasion of transcendence of ordinary reality. Christian and Buddhist thinkers—each representing major traditions of religious practices—have been concerned with what transcends ordinary experiences of individuality. Whether the superordinate subject is called God or Buddha Mind, it is an expression of personal being in a unique state.

Albert Outler presents, in broad sweep, centuries of Christian visions of the search for the *humanum*—the potentiality of being fully human. Embodying these possibilities, persons are engaged in carrying out a risky, divine plan for a new creature, not as ordered as the animals and not as free as the angels. The Christian self is (1) unique, (2) possessed of moral freedom, and (3) an agent, a subjective origin of actions and values. Gregory of Nyssa considers man to be a microcosm reflecting the macrocosm. Hominization is an enterprise in process, directed by freely acting selves, responsible for their actions, each unique and unitary, but in need of altruism as a precondition for the development of their own true potential. From the Christian viewpoint, the self partakes of the mystery that surrounds it. Self is inescapable in human experience, but cannot be logically defined and is not directly accessible to empirical observations. In view of the inevitable participation of self in any human experience, a complete referencing of *self* as a language term is "incredible."

Streng examines the Buddhist notion of self, as reflected in the Buddha's famous teaching on Emptiness, and relates it to Jung's observations of the empty center in many modern mandalas, a position (the center) that has traditionally held a god image in Christianity. Within the Buddhist study of emptiness, concepts such as "ego," "self," and "God" are empty of enduring meaning.

Personal agency seems embedded in the experience of the emerging *humanum,* and there are modes of interaction (e.g., awareness of the nature of emptiness, Christian grace, Freudian mastery, or Jungian individuation) in which the self is most truly itself, felt to be in responsible and responsive relationship to the world and others. Under such conditions, a person experiences a transcendence of the ordinary boundaries of self-image, even of the physical body at times.

In this section, we come to the mystery and grandeur of self, the transcendent pole of human experience. Buddhism especially offers a view of self as a dynamic process that cannot be captured by any particular concept of human individuality or subjectivity. Nonetheless, Buddhists also contend with the search for self and a desire to know the roots of unitary subjectivity.

Psychologically and theologically, the contributors to this section struggle for a language which is adequate to dialogue about transcendence, about a state of being which is not captured by empirical description nor logical definition.

_____

CHAPTER 19

Problems of "Selfhood" in a Christian Perspective

ALBERT C. OUTLER

ONE OF THE subtler analyses of the paradox and mystery of human selfhood turns up in a strange place: Thomas Mann's *Joseph the Provider* (1944). In his brilliant reconstruction of the biblical story of Joseph and his brethren, of Egypt and Israel—which is also to say, his musings on God's ways with man in history—Mann inserts the transcript of an intriguing discussion in heaven ("A Prelude in the Upper Circles") that views the human condition in an oblique light. The angels have been deeply disquieted by a rumor that the Creator, not content to leave well enough alone, was about to venture upon yet another creation, a different sort of creature than either themselves or the animals. It would be like the animals but would lack their stability. It would be like the angels but would lack their unfettered freedoms. This, as any angel could readily foresee, was a risky business. It would produce an anomaly in creation: intelligent, free beings whose aspirations would so far exceed their grasp that nothing good would come from it. The Creator, it was generally agreed, would be well advised to forget about such a venture and to leave well enough alone. He seemed, however, bent on plunging ahead and now the angels were about to have the added bother of human history to cope with.

This is an intriguing way by a literary genius of pointing to the *humanum* as an exciting bewilderment in the world: a bafflement to itself, to the angels and even to God. Humanity belongs in the great chain of being but not as a neat fit. Thus, the creation myths of Genesis depict humanity as God's special project, the crown of creation, but also an experiment gone awry. In the biblical view, human beings were made to bear within themselves the image (*tselem*) and likeness (*demuth*) of God himself. So special a place in the great chain of being carried a special responsibility with it: viz., to tend and care for the rest of the natural order rather than to exploit it. The human project, ill-advised or not, is unique: taprooted in nature, antennaed in the realm of spirit. And yet human history is notoriously unstable; the Bible is full of recorded deviations from the original scenario.

"Anthropology" in the Hebrew Bible seems to agree that to be human is to be an integrated whole of body (*basar*), soul (*nephesh*), and spirit (*ruach*). This trichotomy has a vital inner focus of feeling and willing spoken of as "the heart" (*leb,* a literal "center"). This point is proverbial: "Out of the *heart* are the issues of life" (Proverbs 4:23); "as a man thinks in his *heart,* so is he" (Proverbs 23:7).

The New Testament has an analogous concept. The human self is a composite of body (*soma* or *sarx*), soul (*psyche*), and spirit (*pneuma*). There is likewise a heart (*kardia*), which is the inner source of all the distinctively human motivations and commitments. A psychophysical unity of the self is presupposed, with a corresponding moral imperative: to love God with one's whole self ("heart, soul, mind and strength") all together and all at once.

The biblical "mind" may seem to us to have been singularly averse to high-level abstractions. Both Hebrew and biblical Greek have their full share of personal pronouns, but no words for *self, person, individual.* It is possible, however, to discern throughout the Bible a portrait gallery of persons and groups, represented as unique in their individuations, with special powers of understanding, insight, and moral intention. The baseline metaphor is that of an image-bearer of the divine, conceived of as personal. The result is a picture of some sort of special agent whose special powers interact with the creation as a whole:

> When I look up at thy heavens, the work of thy fingers,
> The moon and the stars set in their places by thee,
> What is man that thou shouldst consider him,
> Mortal man that thou shouldst care for him?
> Yet thou has made him little less than god,
> Crowning him with glory and honor.
> Thou makest him master over thy creatures,
> Thou hast put everything under his feet:
> All sheep and oxen, all the wild beasts,

The birds in the air and the fish in the sea,
And all that moves along the ocean paths.

(Psalm 8:3–8)

There is, however, a shadow side to this triumphant vision. Humanity's record in history is not inspiring: it is, indeed, almost consistently perverse. What is worse, there are no really good reasons for these smudges on the pages of the human scenario. There is no credible rationale for "man's inhumanity to man." Thus, the Bible seems to understand the human story as a sort of tragedy with a hopeful final ending. The plot turns around the ambivalence between God's benevolent purposes and humanity's self-defeating responses. The projected denouement of the drama is a triumph of righteousness yet to come, to be ushered in by a supernatural messianic triumph.

In the New Testament, this same basic plot is reworked, but with a decisive switch. Here, the "New Age" has already dawned, Messiah has come. Now, the drama is seen as the enfoldment of an order of salvation (of divine grace and human fulfillment) that has yet to unfold. What appears at any given "moment" in history is actually an interim between two advents: first of hope, then of true fulfillment. In any given interim, human beings have their crucial (albeit deeply ambivalent) roles to play. St. Paul can, therefore, portray the self as a sort of cockpit of rival impulses. He speaks in Romans 7 of a warfare within his mind, between his positive tendency to approve the good together with an inner declension from his own best intentions: "although the will to do good is there, the deed is not." Such an inner conflict, he thinks, is universal and radical.

Thus, in the Bible generally, there is a consistent witness to the paradox of the *humanum* as an egocentric composite, free to become self-realized, and yet also free to fall short of or to miss that mark (which is the root meaning of the Greek term for sin, *hamartia*). Thus, even without the word *self*, three assumptions about selfhood may be inferred from the biblical texts. In the first place, each self is unique and unitary. To be a person is to be an embodied soul in an ensouled and inspirited body. Selves are moral agents, with capacities for thought, purpose, and virtue—with a distinctive potential for development: from diffusion to individuation, from custom to conscience, from heteronomy to theonomy.

A second assumption is that human beings are made less for them-

selves than for others and for God. Altruism is less a strategy than it
is a precondition of fully realized humanity. This is why, in the biblical
anthropology, self-centeredness is seen as the chief obstacle to self-
realization. At every stage, it generates pride and frustration rather
than that true dignity which comes from a sense of the sacred worth
of each human self accorded it by God.

A third general assumption is that each self is both morally free
and morally responsible—less to society and its demands than to a
teleonomic ideal of "the Kingdom of God and his righteousness"
(which is to say, to a higher order of grace and benevolence that has
the whole creation in view). Selves are free to become human but when
human freedoms are disoriented, the result is something less than
fully human—and usually less subhuman than "inhuman" (which is
to say, they are distortions of the aboriginal human design).

We may, therefore, speak of the self in the biblical perspective as
an *ordering center* of many complex processes of awareness, insight,
commitment. Its cognitive range is limited, and so are its powers of
judgment. Thus, human life is upheld more by faith, hope, and love
than by exact knowledge or heroic zeal. This is the argument of that
familiar paean to "love" in I Corinthians 15. It is also the ground of
the rock-solid confidence of the believer in the efficacy of grace "in
every time of need" (Hebrews 4:16).

Christianity's transplantation from its Jewish matrix into the Hellenistic world brought with it an inevitable conflict between the Hebraic concepts of selfhood we have been summarizing and the
speculative notions about personhood in Greek philosophy, psychology, and popular religion. The first main point of contention turned
around the biblical idea of divine creation in general and, therefore,
of the uniqueness of individual selves. In Hellenistic thought generally,
the idea of the eternity of the world (and of matter) was taken for
granted. From this had followed a cluster of psychological notions as
inferences: reincarnation, metempsychosis, transmigration, disembodied spirits, and the like. These were correlated with a pervasive
dualism: between soul and body, mind and matter, light and darkness,
eternity and time, good and evil, infinity and finitude.

Popular Greek wisdom split three ways. There were the "atomists"
(materialists) like Democritus (forerunners of modern reductionism).
There were the "Platonists," with their distinctions between form and
phenomena and their corollary that the individual was a phenomenon

of the universal ideal of humanity (*anthropotetos*). And, finally, there were the "Aristotelians" who saw the soul as the immanent "form" of each individual "body" and the "body" as the substantive "matter" of the soul. Each of these traditions challenged the Judeo-Christian tradition about the *humanum* on one or another vital ground (as did Stoicism, with its version of preordination). Some sort of acculturation was unavoidable—if for no other reasons than the threat of Gnosticism, with its speculative psychology that sharply disjoined soul and body and thus dissolved the biblical linkage between spirituality and ethics.

In Greek thought generally, and in "Platonism" in particular, each separate individual was seen as a sort of "copy" of a universal idea, an instance of a cosmic template. Thus, they could think of humanity as a universal and of this person or that as an example ("phenomenon") of that universal—replicated more or less imperfectly. This challenged the biblical view of individuation in which each person was to be regarded as singular and unique. It is not "matter" that individuates this concrete object (as in Aristotle), but in each case, a divine design: one of a kind.

"Orthodox" Christianity responded to the challenge of "Hellenization" by grafting slips of Greek psychology onto its Hebraic rootstocks. Clement of Alexandria and Origen appealed to the Platonic concepts of preexistent and disembodied minds (*noeta*). Origen came up with a fanciful derivation of the term *psyche* ("soul") from the verb *psychroö* ("to cool off"). From this, he could envisage the "Fall of Man" as a declension from its primeval, pure "spirituality" into "corporeality"— a sort of "cooling off" of spiritual ardor. Salvation is thus a reversal: the reascent of mind (*nous*) and spirit (*pneuma*) back up into the realm of pure spirit.

The first Latin-speaking Christian theologian (Tertullian) found this paradox of "soul" and "body" a challenge and wrote the first separate essay on selfhood in Christian literature (*De Anima*). In it, the stress is on the mystery of human freedom and the abuse of freedom. The idea of preexistence is rejected; traducianism is affirmed; asceticism is extolled. Tertullian also reacted strongly against Hellenistic rationalism. "What," he thundered, "has Jerusalem to do with Athens?"

The two most important spokesmen for "Christian Platonism" in the first five centuries, East and West—certainly on the point of anthropology—were St. Gregory of Nyssa and St. Augustine of Hippo. (All references to the dogma of Christianity come from Barth [1936–69] unless otherwise indicated.) For Gregory, the clue to human nature is its representation of the divine image of each person as a microcosm of the entire macrocosm: "the essence of a man is an imitation of him who fashioned the universe." The self "is second to none of the wonders of the world, and easily the greatest of all things known to us, because none has been made in the likeness of God except that creature which is man [*anthropos*]." St. Augustine agreed that the human is creation's crown, but he conceived of it in terms of a psychophysical parallelism. Thus the self can be identified as "a rational soul *using* a corporeal body" (*De moribus ecclesiae,* I, 27, 52). Such rational souls have special powers of knowing, intending, and responding to God. So great is the weight of sin and depravity, however, that no human being has the open option of salvation, save by the gratuitous election and predestinating grace of God. This notion of body as the soul's physical instrument would thereafter dominate Western Christian notions of selfhood, as in St. Bonaventura and the German mystics. It carried over into the psychology of the reformers of the sixteenth century.

A more Aristotelianized version of the self may be seen in men as obscure as Nemesius of Emesa (in the East) and as famous as St. Thomas Aquinas in the West. In Nemesius's essay *On the Nature of Man* (c. 390), there is an extended analysis of the interactions between soul ("form") and body. These have an integrating agent, the "spirit," which is the organizing center of sensation, thought, and voluntary action. As a physician, a professed disciple of Galen's, Nemesius was greatly impressed by the teleological perfections of both animal and human organisms, but his central concern was with moral freedom and responsibility, as the special hallmark of the *humanum* (as distinct from animals). He also sought to correlate human freedom and divine providence, and so to illuminate the distinctions between personal and impersonal events.

The human picture in St. Thomas's mind is so complex and subtle as to put an adequate summary out of the question. But it is possible to recognize his heroic efforts to synthesize the biblical views of selfhood with the newly rediscovered Aristotelian psychology. The *humanum* is not a soul using a body, but rather a *compositum* of soul and body, in which "soul" informs and directs both "sensory" and rational operations. And while there are no innate ideas in the mind, there is a *vis cogitativa* (the power of reflective thought) that transcends the *vis aestimativa naturales* (the power of instrumental intelligence present in all organisms in varying degrees). The human self is a free agent, with powers of feeling, judging, and willing. Human cogitation is not random but oriented to distinctively human ends. These ends are eudaemonistic; they focus in true happiness (*beatitudo*, "blessedness"). But all persons are drawn to seek the most fitting means of attaining their true happiness, even though they may never find it on their own. In this quest, the will is inferior to the intellect. To act apart from, or contrary to, a rational judgment (as to better and worse means to valid ends) is the essence of irresponsibility (and results in self-defeating action). To be human, then, is to have, and to rely on, rational insights. Self-realization ("hominisation") is possible only within the context of virtue and spiritual discipline. Each person is a special creation, designed for beatitude and thwarted from it by alienations that only grace and faith can reconcile.

The "Platonic" and Thomistic options continued in tension throughout the succeeding three centuries. In late medieval culture (art and architecture) one sees the human spirit in an aspiring mode—with strivings to transcend the finite, to rise above, to see beyond, to rise from the darkness below up into the light. In such a cultural climate, ideals of "chivalry," "honor," and "heroism" were energizing in many different ways: sometimes to exaltations of the human spirit, sometimes to its degradation.

A radical break from the fourteenth and fifteenth centuries appears in the thought of René Descartes. It was his intent to save the "new philosophy" from skepticism, science from mystification, religion from materialism. To this end, he fell back upon the older dualisms and gave them a decisive twist, sundering the Thomistic linkages between mind and matter. His main distinction was between matter (*res extensae*, "extension") and thought (*res cogitantes*, "mind"). Neither is reducible to the other; the body is passive, the mind is active. Their point of juncture, Descartes finally decided, was deep within the brain (viz., the pineal gland!).

The consequence, not fully intended, was a revival of old images of the human body as an elaborate machine, organized and ordered as a network of conditioned reflexes. Reflective reason, by contrast, is animating and self-transcendent. This resurrected the old problems of the *unity* of the self and allowed for various notions of radical subjectivity.

Descartes himself insisted upon "clear and distinct ideas" as the building blocks of sound thought. His actual influence, however, was deeply ambiguous. On one side, his influence led to the rational idealism of such philosophers as Hegel and Maine de Biran, and even to modern existentialism, as for example the work of Sartre.

On the other side, he opened the way to modern "mechanism"— for the work of the conventionally pious such as Sir Isaac Newton and the irreligious determinism that holds sway even now in the work of modern behaviorists. La Mettrie's *L'Homme Machine* (1748) remains a classic in a succession of theories that continue to be relevant to a branch of philosophy of science, as represented through the example of Jacques Monod's *Chance and Necessity* (1971).

In this tradition, notions of "self" are metaphorical. The term, seldom used, denotes nothing more than a fictive identity and continuity within the mechanical processes in organisms whose powers of conceptualization are not otherwise explained. Now, in the computer age, we have crossed the frontiers of "artificial intelligence." Is this the logical endpoint of reductionism?

In its turn, theology since Descartes has reacted to the challenges of reductionism with an opposite tilt toward "spirituality." In Malebranche, Berkeley, and John Wesley, the Augustinian motif of the soul as "agent using the body as an instrument" is revived in various forms but, typically, in radically subjective ways. The resulting devaluation of "body" and "corporality" has continued to dominate the traditions labeled "puritanical" down to the present time.

It was Immanuel Kant (1724–1804) who sought an alternative to the barren extremes of scientific reductionism and religious dogmatism. He rejected both and undertook a fresh depth analysis of the structures and operations of human experience, knowledge, and moral judgment. Objective reality (the thing-in-itself) is inaccessible to finite minds, bound in temporal and spatial linearities. And yet it is possible to recognize that the structures of our minds point beyond themselves to a "transcendental unity of apperception." This is the self, a centerpoint of "critical reason," the moral agent that serves as the motivating power of valid action. The moral imperative is self-evident to truly enlightened persons and can be formulated in a familiar maxim: "treat all humanity, whether in thyself or in another, always as an end and never as a means only."

Since Kant, Christian anthropology has focused more and more upon *self*-consciousness and *self*-understanding. This can be seen in the emphasis on the original perfection of the God within. In place of older notions about a primeval "fall," the new liberalism interpreted "sin" as an obfuscation of human "God-consciousness." Salvation lies in the recovery of such a consciousness, to the end that *self*-consciousness might be elided with *God*-consciousness.

The total reduction of theology to anthropology came with Ludwig Feuerbach (1841–54), in whose work an idealized humanity was substituted for traditional concepts of divinity. Later developments in the last century stress the character of the self as a moral agent. The immediate intuitions of self were held to be an analogue even of a "world mind," a reflection of God's grand design for the organization of mankind according to principles of neighborly love.

Søren Kierkegaard (1813–53) stood out valiantly against the "idealisms" of his day, but with his own version of subject-object dualism. His term for selfhood was *subjectivity* and this became the most pervasive notion in all his thought. Out of our radical subjectivity comes what knowledge we have, and what faith and freedom there may be. Here was the font of modern existentialism.

We may characterize the twentieth century's contributions to a Christian view of the self by noticing four of its most notable spokesmen: Reinhold Niebuhr (1941–43), Karl Barth (1936–39), Karl Rahner (1954–83), and Paul Tillich (1951–63). Each was a genius in his own right, and no summary comment can do more than identify them. What is important, however, is that taken together, they show how, in our times as in earlier cultural crises, the biblical traditions can be updated to produce new angles of vision and new insights as well. They all agree upon the unitary self. They are also more concerned with self and society than any of their predecessors were. Each was, in his own way, deeply influenced by modern psychology.

In Reinhold Niebuhr's anthropology there is no dualism, and not much sentimentality either.

> Man is a child of nature, subject to its vicissitudes, compelled by its necessities, driven by its impulses, confined within the brevity of the years. . . .
>
> But man is also a spirit who stands outside of nature, himself, his reason and the world. . . . His rational capacity

> includes a further capacity for self-transcendence, the abil-
> ity to make himself his own object. (pp. 3–4)

Self-awareness on the pinnacle of freedom generates a certain ex-
altation, pride, and a kind of cosmic "dizziness." This is the font of
human anxiety and yet also of creativity as well. Life goes awry when
self-centered selves seek to flourish at the expense of other selves (or
"nature"). There is no such a thing as a solitary self. Each person
exists in a dialectical relationship—the self with the self within, the
self in dialogue with other selves, and the self in its social milieu, in
which it can mature or else become self-stultified.

Karl Barth required a massive volume (1936–69, III, 2) for the
exposition of his view of human selves as creatures normed by "the
existence of the man Jesus." It offers a profound analysis of "soul and
body in their interaction," in their "particularity" and "order"
(agency), and all of this on the presupposition of an all-embracing
theonomy as the context for true and full humanity. Nothing is meaningful in human life apart from the divine initiative, providence, and
grace. Jesus is the norm and paradigm of true humanity: not for our
imitation but for communion (made possible by the divine initiative,
not ours).

In Paul Tillich, the spirit of German idealism (especially that of
Friedrich Schelling) spoke yet again, in a special version of American
cultural Protestantism. Tillich's distinctive emphases were on "self-
awareness" and "centeredness":

> Total centeredness is the situation of having, face to face
> with one's self, a world to which, at the same time, one
> belongs as part. . . . Man can oppose his self to every part
> of the world, including himself as part of his world. . . .
> This possibility is unique because it implies both freedom
> from the merely given and also norms which determine the
> moral act through freedom. (1951–63, pp. 36–39)

What is not clear here (or elsewhere in the whole discussion) is the
identity of this "man" who has "his self" at his own disposal. What
and where is "the self" that can thus intend and determine the actions
of "the self"? Here (as elsewhere) we recognize the regressive character of all speech about selfhood. Is it an infinite regress?

The late Karl Rahner will almost surely rank as the outstanding Catholic theologian in a notable century of them. At the heart of his lifelong career of "theological investigations" (he eschewed "dogmatics") was his concern for a Christian anthropology derived from the Thomist tradition ("transcendental Thomism," he called it) and modern existentialism (Martin Heidegger in particular). For Rahner, being human implies self-awareness, understood as

> one's presence to oneself, one's permanent and inescapable orientation to being as a whole and therefore to God . . . To be a person, therefore, is to possess oneself as a subject in conscious, free relation to reality as a whole and to its infinite ground and source, God. Man is a personal being who can only act in a concrete body, in history, here and now, in dialogue with another thou, constantly exposed with his fellows to painful experience of the world through his own deeds. (Rahner and Vorgimer, 1966, pp. 351–52)

The divine design and the human enterprise are the same: "hominisation," by which is meant the hazardous process of passing from alienation to reconciliation, from immaturity to maturity, real freedom, wisdom, and beatitude. This is a human endeavor; its actual attainment is, of course, a work of grace.

One may only apologize for having to pass over the analyses of human freedom and responsibility as profound and "modern" as those of Austin Farrer (whose *Finite and Infinite*, 1943, remains a masterpiece), or of working scientists like Wilder Penfield (*The Mystery of the Mind*, 1975) or Sir John Eccles (*The Human Psyche*, 1980). These studies are Christian in their psychological orientation without being credal in tone. They, and others, represent variations on the general sense that we have been rehearsing: the continuity of the biblical perspectives on the *humanum* in radically different cultural contexts.

The consensus in this whole tradition is that human selfhood is both a problem and a mystery. The self is directly accessible to neither empirical observation nor logical definition. There are, however, persistent motifs in all the different reflections of the biblical tradition as to what it means to be human at all and what it takes to become more truly and fully human. Each of these notions presupposes the self as a mysterious reality that is, on the one hand, "object" to God and, on the other, "subject" to human consciousness.

The first of these motifs focuses on the uniqueness of each self. No person is merely another instance of humanity at large; each self is a special project with his or her own potential. None is expected to be other than he or she truly is—but no less, either. A second regular accent is on moral freedom—within creaturely limits that include the inescapable brackets of transience and death. These two imply a third concept. Each self is a responsible *agent*: a determining factor in at least some of the natural processes of which it is the personal center. Most human transactions are transactions of afference and efference, of natural causes and effects.

The self, in this view, may be seen as the operator of the central relay station in a psychophysical network. And, as we know from sociometrics, whenever self-agency is introduced into a statistical process, forecasts are never wholly predictable. There *is* a "ghost" in each human machine—including computers—but it is a *human* ghost and without some sense of it as a transcendental agency, *human* behavior is finally inexplicable. Reductionism is incredible, if only because it presupposes a "reducer." And we know, by now, that language about "nature" or "process" or "systems" (as if they were hypostasy) is either question-begging or incurably vague. There has also been a consensus in the Judeo-Christian tradition that human selfhood, even at best, is radically dependent upon its total environment, including its final ground. This points to an encompassing Mystery that Christians call God, conceived as personal and not as "Nature" hypostasized. Self-sufficiency is no part of the human condition. Human existence, in the Christian view, is taprooted in something finally more dependable and person-making, on which we can depend, with as much serenity as may be the lot of creatures such as we.

Such a view of selfhood—of unique and quintessential *agents*, creatures of God and creatures on their own—could be practical in more ways than one. To begin with, it would help negate reductionisms of many kinds and dispel some facile illusions about behaviorism, on the one side, and utopianism, on the other. It would suggest the subordination of theories and therapies to the role of auxiliary means to truly human ends, as these may be discerned in their transcendent outreach. Human selves would be recognized as subsistent entities, invested with a special *dignitas* of their own—malleable and vulnerable, yet also responsive to love and wisdom and especially to grace.

Other views of "selves," as fictive or epiphenomenal, are bound to suggest adaptive therapies of one sort or another, and therefore pre-scripted processes shaped by naturalistic paradigms of illness and health. Such theories have an inherent tendency to ritualization and ideology. In the sociology of religion, obsessive ritualization is rightly called magic; in the high religions, it is rightly called idolatry.

An antidote to such self-defeating dangers is some sort of recognition of selves as unique and creative, and as bearers of *sacred* worth. Such a view would call for a profound respect for and gracious acceptance of the "patient," not merely as a clinical tactic but as a profound theological statement. It would mean from the outset the therapist would be less a wonder-worker than a minister of grace, less a guru than a friend, less an ideologue and more a comrade in a mutual quest of enlivening insights.

The caring for and curing of selves, so conceived, would mean their progressive liberation from orthodoxies and heteronomies of all sorts (including the "patient's" disabling preconceptions and the therapist's prescripted "dogmas"). For good therapy is always teleonomic, and the telos includes the restoration of the self from the status of "patient" to that of responsible agent, within a divine environment. And it understands that the disinterested love of the therapist is a curative power if and when it is a reflection of a yet more boundless love whose biblical name is "God."

Thus, while therapy proceeds, as it must, on its own empirical terms, guided by etiological and prognostic theories of its own (which are still curiously uncorrelated with their clinical efficacy), there could still be in the whole interaction a vivid sense of an encompassing mystery, essentially benevolent, by which all selves are grasped (*Die Umgreifende*), upon which all selves depend, and in which faith generates a joyful confidence that the world, at the bottom, is a fit habitat for humans.

Finally, a view such as this opens a way beyond the crisis of the so-called termination of therapy. A shackled self, liberated from false dependencies into the true freedom from which the *humanum* was designed, also needs an agenda for ongoing growth and self-fulfillment, so that the person can go on maturing into wholeness. For surely, a part of the divine design is for a human family to fill the gap in the great chain of being between "animal" and "angel"—creatures with aspirations that turn them to truth, beauty, and goodness, and spiritual sensibilities that turn them to faith, hope, and love.

What an irony it would be if it turned out that good therapy was able to negate the angels' cynicism and so bolster our belief that the divine experiment with human selfhood was not so wildly ill-conceived, after all!

References

Barth, K. (1936–69). *Church dogmatics* (vols. 1–4). New York: Scribner's; Edinburgh: T. and T. Clark.

Eccles, J. C. (1980). *The human psyche.* New York: Springer International. (Gifford Lectures, 1979).

Farrer, A. (1943). *Finite and infinite: A philosophical essay.* London: Dacre Press.

Feuerbach, L. (1854). *The essence of Christianity* (M. Evans, trans.). London: J. Chapman. (Original work published 1841).

de La Mettrie, J. (1748). *L'homme machine.* Leiden: Luzac.

Mann, T. (1944). *Joseph the provider.* New York: Knopf.

Monod, J. (1971). *Chance and necessity: An essay on the natural philosophy of modern biology* (A. Wainhouse, trans.). New York: Knopf.

Nemesius, Bishop of Emesa (1955). *On the nature of man. The library of Christian classics.* IV.203–453. Philadelphia: Westminster Press.

Niebuhr, R. (1941–43). *The nature and destiny of man: A Christian interpretation.* New York: Scribner's (Gifford Lectures, 1939).

Penfield, W. (1975). *The mystery of the mind: A critical study of consciousness and the human brain.* With discussions by W. Feindel, C. Hendel, and C. Symonds. Princeton: Princeton University Press.

Rahner, K. (1961). *Quaestiones disputatae.* Freibourg, Germany: Herder.

——— (1954–83). *Theological Investigations.* Freibourg, Germany: Herder.

———, and Vorgimer, H. Ernst, C. (ed.). (1966). *Concise theological dictionary* (R. Strachan, trans.). Freibourg, Germany: Herder; London: Burns and Oates. 2nd ed. London: Burns and Oates, 1983.

Tillich, P. (1951–63). *Systematic theology* (vols. 1–3). Chicago: University of Chicago Press.

CHAPTER 20

Mechanisms of Self-Deception and True Awareness

FREDERICK J. STRENG

THE PHILOSOPHER of science Michael Polanyi (1951; 1967; 1975) has pointed out the significance of "tacit knowledge" in any activity of knowing. Tacit knowledge is a kind of awareness subsidiary to focal awareness; it effects a "phenomenal transformation" in knowledge by providing a contextual interpretive framework that is lived (experienced) by the knower (Polanyi and Prosch, 1975). The phenomenal transformation is a kind of meaning that is due to non-explicit performances of skills presupposed by the act of knowing, such as perception of "depth" in viewing a pair of stereo pictures in a stereoptic device. The aspects of tacit knowledge to which I call attention in this essay are its interpretive framework, which contributes to the meaning of focal knowledge, and its procedural character, that is, the practical skills needed in any apprehension of knowledge. The performance of tacit awareness involves a judgment of coherence; it is a manner of integrating sensory input and memory—plus emotions, attitudes, and ideals (values)—in more complex modes of awareness.

The recognition of tacit knowledge is important for understanding the integration of sensations and other psychological processes because it highlights the lived presuppositions in human awareness (Hall, 1977). Coherent integrations include both unconscious processes and conscious intentional actions. As Polanyi reminds us, such acts by a person making judgments of what is or is not coherent can be either valid or mistaken. Within the large and complex question of the character of the most appropriate processes of self-awareness, I want to focus in this analysis on the tacit assumptions in understanding the shift from self-deception to true awareness. The procedure is to examine two expressions of this shift from widely different cultural settings: the work of C. G. Jung and the second century B.C.E. Indian Buddhist text *The Eight-Thousand Line Perfection of Wisdom Sūtra* (*ELPW*). By looking at these alternatives we may be able in a limited way to expose some of the conditioning assumptions found in each of these approaches, which, in turn, may stimulate self-reflection on contemporary therapeutic procedures.

I recognize, with Polanyi, that not all aspects of tacit knowledge can be made explicit (Polanyi and Prosch, 1975). This is due especially to the fact that when an investigator focuses on a subsidiary awareness, it becomes a focal awareness and does not function as a subsidiary implicit conditioner of the meaning in the original focal awareness. However, a comparative analysis that concentrates on the processes of becoming self-aware at the higher levels of personality organization— and that explicitly describes the difficulties in attaining true (as distinct from deceptive) awareness—can draw attention to a few elements found in those implicit processes.

Cross-cultural comparisons in therapies for true self-awareness as I am proposing are intellectually exciting and fraught with problems. Such studies are exciting in that they seek to locate and elucidate perennial problems in human self-awareness and in the understanding of one's social and physical environment. Comparisons can provide heuristic devices for probing different cultural imagery and definitions and for constructing analytic tools to examine the coherence and assumptions found in general claims about human experience. By specifying similarities and differences one can clarify issues that may provide the basis for new constructive formulations of recurrent human efforts at understanding and life enhancement. At their best they help to distinguish structural elements from incidental form, the typical from the culturally accidental.

The dangers arise from oversimplification of important distinctions in vocabulary, assumptions, and structural approaches. The difficulties in determining "original" meanings, in assuming the relative importance of concepts in a more comprehensive structure of understanding, and in intuiting the intention of (especially religious or salvific) claims are legion. Nevertheless, I will try to highlight a few assumptions in the procedure of true self-awareness in order to explore the tacit knowledge implicit in each of these differently formulated approaches to self-awareness.

The specific issue in the shift from self-deception to true awareness can be formulated as the awareness of the self as it lets go of the attachment to the ego-image. That is, we are focusing on the experience of the nonego as a process that frees one from attachment to the ego. One of the most interesting aspects of this comparison is the difference in understanding the character or nature of selfhood and of nonego according to an early Indian Buddhist text and a contemporary psychoanalyst in the light of two assumptions common to both. The first common assumption is that both understand the self as a dynamic process, as an expression of energy in flux. The second is that both acknowledge a deeper awareness of reality that is already inherent in existence but that is hidden within unexamined conventional, often compulsive, personal behavior. This deeper awareness is the true awareness, which is not simply a descriptive proposition about oneself but a *mode* of awareness or even a deepening skill in becoming aware of oneself in relationship.

Nevertheless, the descriptions of the process for transforming self-deception to true awareness provide quite different definitions of selfhood and nonego. The different understandings of selfhood and nonego lead Jung to affirm the importance of an intense projection of the self in the experience of divinity, or *numinousum,* while the *ELPW* describes the emptying process of an empty ego in relation to an empty nonego, or empty dharma, or no-path. The differences, I suggest, are intrinsically related to different assumptions about the psycho-ontological power of symbols, concepts, and the quality of consciousness. The fundamental differences, according to this analysis, are not simply different notions of selfhood and nonego, but two different modes or ways of "becoming aware" at the most profound level of human experience.

I hope to show that different types of religious knowing condition different experiences of the self. In both cases the self experience is "intrinsically guided by impersonal standards [i.e., generally applicable standards] of valuation set by the self for itself" (Polanyi and Prosch, 1975, p. 42). To note different types of self-awareness both affirms and intends to move beyond the recognition that a functioning self has an ego-center, a coherence of awareness and action, that can survive the tension of incompatible experiences. Insofar as this ego-center selects pragmatically what is valid and invalid for its sense of selfhood it has an implicit set of evaluative standards, or a tacit integration of experienced options, that incorporate some and discard other sensory, imaginal, and emotional perceptions. This essay is concerned to analyze alternative ways to integrate a self-awareness in the light of the implicit evaluative sense of the relation between an ego-image and an experienced ultimate context of life. The analysis will show that the principle of integration according to Jung's statements is a symbolic representational content that pivots on an awareness of unconscious archetypes and conscious archetypal images, while the principle of integration according to the claims of the *ELPW* is an attitudinal fusion that pivots on a quality of consciousness.

When Carl Jung gave the three Terry Lectures of 1937 at Yale University, he considered the relation of religion to psychology. Interestingly, he gave two definitions of religion. One of them expresses a perspective common in the Western theological tradition. Early in the first lecture, on the anatomy of the unconscious mind, he says, "Religion . . . is the term that designates the attitude peculiar to a consciousness which has been altered by the experience of the *numinousum*" (Jung, 1938, p. 6). The other definition comes in the third lecture, entitled "The History and Psychology of a Natural Symbol," in which he discusses the mandala. Here religion is related to the unconscious dimension of the human personality. He says:

> Religion is a relationship to the highest or strongest value, be it positive or negative. The relationship is voluntary as well as involuntary, that is, that you can accept consciously the value by which you are possessed unconsciously. That psychological fact, which is the greatest power in your system is the god, since it is always the overwhelming psychic factor which is called god. (Jung, 1938, p. 98)

These excerpts indicate Jung's recognition of a transcendent dimension of the human condition as well as the dynamic power of consciousness in creating the world of our experience. Both aspects of his vision of the human condition make possible a comparison with the Indian Buddhist vision of the human situation. *ELPW* provides a basis for comparison in that it also emphasizes the quality of consciousness as a basic condition for true awareness of one's self and the world. In contrast to Jung's analysis, however, it emphasizes that the basic character of the self, including the deepest aspect of consciousness and all perceived things in the world, is empty of any essential, a priori, or self-existent reality. Even the *numinousum*, the divinity, is empty—as is the self, in both conscious and unconscious functions.

In comparing Jung's version of the human condition with that found in the *ELPW*, we focus on one of the most dramatic claims made by Jung in his final lecture: namely, that the mandala, found in the contemporary world, as expressed by many of Jung's clients, had an empty center. This was important for Jung since he was well aware, through his study of historical sources, that traditionally the mandala had a divine figure, a god or a goddess, at the center of this great circle. He says:

> A modern mandala is an involuntary confession of a peculiar mental condition. There is no deity in the mandala, and there is also no submission or reconciliation to a deity. The place of the deity seems to be taken by the wholeness of man.
>
> When one speaks of man, everybody means his own ego personality—that is, his personality in as much as he is aware of it—and when one speaks of others one assumes that they have a very similar personality. But since modern research has acquainted us with a fact that an individual consciousness is based upon and surrounded by an indefinite extended unconscious psyche, we must revise our somewhat old fashioned prejudice that man is his [individual] consciousness. This rather naive assumption must be confronted at once by the critical question: Whose Consciousness? Is it his consciousness or the consciousness of other people around him? (Jung 1938, p. 99)

Jung answers his own question by saying that the individual consciousness is partially a collective unconscious:

> It is a remarkable fact that this replacement is a natural and spontaneous occurrence, and that it is always essentially unconscious. If we want to know what is going to happen in a case where the idea of God is no longer projected as an autonomous entity, this is an answer of man's unconscious mind. The unconscious produces a new idea of man in loco dei, of man deified (or divine), imprisoned, con-

cealed, protected, usually dehumanized and expressed by
abstract symbolism. (Jung, 1938, p. 106)

This recognition that the religious factor is identical to one's psyche
is for Jung and for many other readers awesome. One's own psyche,
says Jung, *is* the divinity:

> The gods in our time assemble in the lap of the ordinary
> individual and are as powerful and awe-inspiring as ever,
> in spite of their new disguise—the so-called psychical func-
> tions. Man thinks of himself as holding the psyche in the
> hollow of his hand. He dreams even of making a science
> of her. But in reality she is the mother and the maker, the
> psychical subject and even the possibility of consciousness
> itself. The psyche reaches so far beyond the boundary line
> of consciousness that the latter could be easily compared to
> an island in the ocean. (Jung, 1938, p. 105)

Jung warns, however, that this is a psychologically dangerous situation
for most people. It is safer to keep the intensity and power of the
beyond in an image of an external autonomous power. He says, "The
experience formulated by the mandala is typical of people who cannot
project the divine image any longer. They are in actual danger of
inflation and dissociation" (Jung, 1938, p. 105). A person who denies
the reality of the unconscious psychic forces, or assimilates his own
ego into that psychic energy, becomes the victim of "inflation" whereby
the personality is dissolved and one acts psychotically. Jung writes:

> Since the idea of God represents an important, even over-
> whelming psychical intensity, it is, in a way, safer to believe
> that such an autonomous intensity is a non-ego, perhaps
> an altogether different or superhuman entity, "totaliterali-
> ter." Confronted with such a belief, man must need to feel
> small, just about his own size. But if he declares the tre-
> mendum to be dead, then he must find out at once where
> this considerable energy, which was once invested in an
> existence as great as God, has disappeared to.
>   Since it is a matter of tremendous energy, the result will
> be an equally important psychological disturbance in the
> form of dissociation of personality. The disruption can pro-

duce a dual or multiple personality. It is as if one single person could not carry the total amount of energy, so that parts of the personality which were hitherto functional units instantly break asunder and assume the dignity and importance of autonomous personalities. (Jung, 1938, p. 104)

In another writing, Jung explains the problem of being absorbed into psychic powers beyond the capacity of one's ego:

It must be reckoned a psychic catastrophe when the ego is assimilated by the self. The image of wholeness then remains in the unconscious so that on the one hand it shares the archaic nature of the unconscious, and on the other, finds itself in the psychically relative space-time continuum that is characteristic of the unconsciousness as such. . . . Hence it is of the greatest importance that the ego should be anchored in the world of consciousness and that consciousness should be reinforced by a very precise adaptation. For this, certain virtues like attention, conscientiousness, patience, etc., are of great value on the moral side, just as accurate observation of the symptomatology of the unconscious and objective self-criticism are valuable on the intellectual side. (Jung, 1968, pp. 45–46)

Jung warns his readers about the danger of identifying the ego with its extended unconscious totally. We can ask ourselves, however, whether there is a way to understand the tremendous psychic power at the root of the human selfhood as a neutral and integrable capacity rather than as the source of a psychic catastrophe. Jung himself says that one can and must know the hidden, the "shadow" side of one's personality, and reconcile the conscious and unconscious aspects of the self. At the same time the autonomous collective unconscious always stands in tension with the ego. One's true self moves between the archetype and ego-individuality without locating oneself in either. This is the process of ever-deepening self-awareness.

Another way to understand the empty center in the deepest human awareness is found in the *ELPW,* which claims that the enlightened person knows the emptiness of both the ego and any absolute reality, whether this is termed "God," "nirvana," the "Self," a dharma, or even "Buddhahood."

To be aware of oneself and the world as "empty," from the Buddhist viewpoint, requires a shift in the mode of apprehending the human situation. It is a shift from the conventional or habitual way to one expressing the perfection of wisdom and compassion. True compassion, however, requires knowing that awareness of any idea, any perceived object, or oneself is possible only without attachment to that idea, to the object, or to the self. In chapter 9 of the *ELPW,* the manner of knowing emptiness in an empty manner is described as follows:

> The perfection of the bodhisattva has no mental attitude, because it is imperturbable. This perfection is unshakeable, in consequence of the stability of the realm of dharma. This perfection is quieted because no sign is apprehended in all dharmas. This perfection is faultless, as the perfection of all virtues. This perfection is undefiled, because imagination is something that is not. No living being is [ultimately] found in this perfection, because of the reality limit. This perfection is unlimited because of the manifestation of all dharmas does not rise up. (Conze, 1973, pp. 151–52)

For the skillful perceiver of emptiness, the world, self, and interpersonal relations do not disappear into a nihilistic void.

Granted, there is a psychological danger when one pursues the empty way of knowing. The person training in the empty manner of experiencing life is warned not to realize emptiness as a goal itself or as reality in itself. This is accomplished by focusing on caring for all beings in existence. Such caring or compassion for all beings is understood in the profound sense that there is an intrinsic relationship between oneself and all existing beings already. This is explained by the Buddha in the twentieth chapter of the *ELPW* in the following words:

> Since [the bodhisattva] has not abandoned all beings, he is thus able to win full enlightenment safely and securely. At the time when a Bodhisattva has made all beings into an objective support for his thought of friendliness, and with the highest friendliness ties himself to them, at that time he rises above the factiousness of the defilements and of Mara, he arises above the level of the Disciple and Pratyeka-

buddha, and he abides in that concentration [on friendli-
ness]. (Conze, 1973, p. 224)

The nature of emptiness as manifested in the perfection of wisdom
is a very complex topic. I want to make only three points regarding
emptiness in *ELPW.* The first is the claim that the self and its constituents are empty, or without self-existent reality. The experienced self,
as an empty self, is a process of interactive energies identified as the
five *skandhas*: materiality, feelings or sensations, perceptions, impulses
or unconscious predispositions, and consciousness. This flow of material, sensory, mental-emotional, perceptual, and unconscious energy
is without self-existent power, just as each of the constituents arises
only in relation to mutually dependent conditions (Streng, 1982,
1975). In chapter 1 of the *ELPW,* the venerable adept of perfect wisdom, Subhūti, says that despite the talk of "a bodhisattva," there is
really nothing outside the verbalizing process that corresponds in a
one-to-one way with the idea of a "bodhisattva." One who does not
become fearful when hearing this is at the irreversible stage of the
bodhisattva path; he stands well (*suṣṭita*) while not having stood anywhere (*asthānayogena*) (Vaidya, 1960, p. 4). In chapter 2, Subhūti instructs the god Śakra on the deepest value of life, perfect wisdom, and
how to achieve it. He says that having abided (*tiṣṭatā*) in emptiness
(*śūnyatām*) a bodhisattva "is stayed" (*stātavyam*) in the perfection of
wisdom. Then he continues by contrasting "abiding in emptiness" with
other possibilities that one should avoid. For example, the bodhisattva
should "not be stayed" (*na stātavyam*) in form and the other four *skandhas*, not in any of the five senses or mind (*manas*), not in sensory or
mental objects, not in the elements, not on "the pillars of mindfulness,
right efforts, roads to psychic power, faculties, powers, limbs of enlightenment and limbs of the path" (Conze, 1973, p. 97), not on the
fruits of different levels of spiritual attainment, even arhatship.

The second point is that the experienced world has various dimensions or levels of quality. One of the most important variations is
between the compulsive personal identification with projected images
of oneself and the world, on the one hand, and the freeing, spontaneous (or empty) manner of interaction of self and one's environment,
on the other. A person's awareness includes thoughts and images, but
more fundamental than the directional organizing and constructive
power of specific symbols themselves for determining either self-de-

ception or true awareness is the mode or quality of becoming conscious. The *ELPW* speaks of the freeing, or empty, manner of awareness as "not being stayed" (*na stātvyam*) in things or ideas. In two subsequent sections of chapter 1, the text delineates several possibilities of what one should not be stayed in, for example, the idea that form is empty, that it is to be apprehended as something, not even in the idea that "this is Buddhahood."

Further, a bodhisattva should not "be stayed" in the notion "that the fruits of the holy life derive their dignity from the Unconditioned," or in the stage of a Buddha, or in the recognition that he has done a Buddha's work (Conze, 1973, p. 97). This list of negations by Subhūti leaves another disciple, Śāriputra, with a question: If one should "not be stayed" even in the highest level of enlightenment, *how* then should one abide in emptiness and train oneself (*śikṣitavyam*) (Vaidya, 1960, p. 19)? Subhūti responds with a question: Where did the Buddha abide (*stitha*)? Śāriputra answers: The Tathāgata, the completely enlightened one, (*samyaksambuddha*) abode (*stitha*) nowhere. On what grounds is this claim made? Because the completely enlightened one has "not stationed" (*apratiṣṭita*) his mind anywhere (Vaidya, 1960, p. 19).

The third point regarding emptiness in the *ELPW* is the claim that to live in an empty manner is enlightenment. Enlightenment is the freeing of one's thoughts, emotions, or psychic energy from inappropriate restrictions due to attachment or compulsive identification with them. In the conversation between Subhūti and Śāriputra mentioned above regarding where the Buddha "abode" in his attainment of perfect enlightenment, Śāriputra correctly says that the Tathāgata did not abide (*na stitah*) in the conditioned realm or in the nonconditioned realm, nor did he abandon (*vyutthita*) them both. Subhūti then affirms Śāriputra's statement and summarizes the view of the *ELPW* by saying:

> Even so, Śāriputra, a bodhisattva, a great being, is stayed [*sthātavyam*], is trained. [He thinks:] As the Tathāgata, the highest (completely) enlightened one, so I am not anywhere stayed [*sthatah*], not non-abiding [*nasthitah*], not fixed [*vistitah*], not non-fixed [*nāvistitah*]. Being stayed [*sthasyam*] in this way, one is trained [*śikṣitavyam*, i.e., trained correctly]. As the Tathagata, so I 'stand' [*sthāsyami*]; thus I am trained.

> As the Tathāgata has stood [*sthānam*], thus, I stand [*sthā-syami*]; thus I train ... well placed [*suṣṭitah*], not having stood anywhere [*asthānayogena*]. Even so a bodhisattva, a great being, is stayed [*sthātavyam*], is trained. Thus trained the bodhisattva, a great being, abides [*viharati*] in the perfection of wisdom and does not lose his attentiveness to it. (Vaidya, 1960, p. 19)

Thus to train, or to stay in the course of perfect wisdom, a person should avoid being "fixed" or "stayed" in any object of perception or mental ideal.

Our language and the way we use language in a habitually symbolic way disposes us to think that there are units of reality that exist in themselves. Insight shows—says the *ELPW*—that such a view is not true. The point of meditating on the perfection of wisdom is not simply to construct a new system or image for understanding but to allow insights into the kind of verbal fallacies and emotional afflictions that human beings easily slip into. The formulations and imagery are, at best, expedient means. According to this perspective neither the ego nor the archetype—to use Jung's terminology—is a final determinate. They are determinates of selfhood only to the degree that a person gives them power.

The attachment to the concept or image of the "I" can be called a type of narcissism; however, it is a narcissism that pervades all existence, and is based on the habitual division between oneself and others. It can be eliminated only by actualizing a sense of oneself in relation to others; while selfhood is not an eternal reality, it is a complex of physical, emotional, and mental interactions even before an "I" is specified. Narcissism, as a precognitive tendency to define reality from the standpoint of the ego, is—from the standpoint of the *ELPW*—based on a dualistic mode of perception. It is a fabrication looming into a fantasy because it misappropriates the experience of becoming.

From the perspective found in the *ELPW,* any talk of a self, ego, or archetype is a mental construction. If one wants to talk about them, one should do so with the recognition that they are simply concepts that direct one's perception but do not represent (or re-present) entities outside the language system in a one-to-one relationship. The fact that all ideas and symbols are fabrications does not mean that all imagery is totally useless in attaining enlightenment. Indeed, some notions are said to be more useful than others for actualizing true awareness. To say that things are empty is more useful than to say that they refer to an essential self-existent entity; but one should not get caught in thinking that therefore there must be something that is essentially empty and something that is essentially self-existent. This would exemplify a dualistic orientation. The thought process about oneself and others that is conventional and symbolically powerful tends to keep one bound to one's own projections and obstructions. Symbolical image construction participates in the same reality of dependent coarising as the freeing actualizing of emptiness, but it is without the awareness of the empty character of that in which one is actually participating.

How do these two visions of the condition of the human situation contribute to an understanding of the emptiness at the center of the deepest human self-consciousness? The answer, I suggest, is related to an understanding of how people know the truth about themselves. This, in turn, is related to the way one finds one's own deepest values—that is, the way one valorizes experience. The Jungian approach places an emphasis on the symbolic power of images and dispositions for constructing an experienced world. The bodhisattva in the *ELPW* emphasizes shifting from a symbolic mode of consciousness to a different quality of consciousness, which we might call here an "emptying consciousness." Despite many overlapping concerns, a difference is reflected in the way that each orientation understands the possibility and danger of identifying the conscious individual or the conventional self with the deepest or most comprehensive dimension of that self.

From the Buddhist perspective in the *ELPW*, letting go of a mythic consciousness as a valorizing process is the highest goal in the most radical form of emptiness meditation. On the other hand, Carl Jung warns that inflation of ego necessarily attends the identification of oneself with an archetypal motif. The fears of identifying oneself with an archetypal motif arise, to a significant degree, because of a common Western assumption, suggested in his first definition of religion. While Jung recognizes that the Collective Unconscious is part of the self, he follows the advocates of mainline Christianity who are trained to perceive ultimate values by locating (projecting) them outside of the self. The classical manner by which ultimate values are identified by the worshipping Christian community begins with an assumption of a radical distinction between the sacred and the secular, between the holy and profane. The sacred is the incomprehensible, the wholly other source of everything, the creator who is never to be confused with the creature.

According to Jung, people need to maintain a balance between the archetype and ego by avoiding the integration of all possible archetypes into the ego. If the ego is absorbed into the archetype, the ego loses contact with the conditioned world. This model depends on the assumption that there is an ultimate value expressed in the archetype and the ego, and that there is some autonomy in each, such that each must stand over against the other in a mutually dependent tension. God is an autonomous psychic complex. Similarly, for Jung, a mandala is an expression of how one views one's awareness through a symbol, a psychic construct, or a constructed world of experience. A mandala is a true image of an experienced world. An empty center is dangerous because total absorption into the nonego requires the loss of the conditioned ego.

The Buddhist view in the *ELPW* suggests that the mandala, as any symbol, may function not only as a way of constructing a world of order and meaning. It may, at a more profound level, be a tool or expedient for shifting one's mode of consciousness from a concern to construct a meaningful world as a process of self-realization to a concern to dissipate attachment to an empty self-image as a process of self-realization (or no-self realization). In the latter process, the value given to a particular symbolic form is transcended by a process that recognizes all symbolic forms as conditioned mental-emotional processes. It is process of letting go of a mythologizing process of valorization.

On the last page of her lucid discussion of symbolic projection, *Projection and Re-Collection in Jungian Psychology*, Marie-Louise von Franz (1980) notes that when a Zen Buddhist master lives "in complete accord with the rhythm of psychic energy and with its regulator, the Self, he has no projections anymore" (p. 199). It is such a shift that the Perfection of Wisdom advocates as necessary for overcoming self-deception. Von Franz goes on to say how unusual such a centered person is:

> [O]nly a person with the most highly reflected concentration can achieve this. We average human beings, by con-

trast, will hardly be able to avoid the necessity, for the rest of our lives, of again and again recognizing projections for what they are, or at least as mistaken judgments. (von Franz, 1980, p. 199)

Here von Franz recognizes that projection of an inflated ego-image need not be the *necessary* result of a loss of ego. This is possible when ego is not seen as a separate entity forming its relation to an overwhelming external energy through an emotionally toned symbolic structure, and when the centering *process*—as expressed in her understanding of the Jungian notion of *unus mundus* (von Franz, 1980, pp. 91–92)—in which all mental and physical acts, the ego and Collective Unconscious appropriately interact, is emphasized. Such a practical expression of the self is genuine self-knowledge. The degree to which both archetype and ego are recognized as intrinsically relative to each other, and to the degree that ego-consciousness can no longer be distinguished from all other psychological and physical factors—to that degree it functions as the no-mind (nonego) in the principle of integration according to the *ELPW*.

References

Conze, E. (1973). *The perfection of wisdom in eight-thousand lines and its verse summary.* Bolinas, Calif.: Four Seasons Foundation.

von Franz, M-L. (1980). *Projection and re-collection in Jungian psychology* (W. H. Kennedy, trans.). La Salle, Ill.: Open Court.

Hall, J. (1977). *Clinical uses of dreams: Jungian interpretations and enactments.* New York: Grune and Stratton.

Jung, C. G. (1938). *Psychology and religion.* New Haven: Yale University Press.

———— (1968). Read, H., Fordham, M., and Adler, G. (eds.). Aion: Researches into the phenomenology of the self. *Collected works,* 9. Princeton: Princeton University Press.

Polanyi, M. (1951). *Personal knowledge.* Chicago: University of Chicago Press.

———— (1967). *The tacit dimension.* London: Routledge and Kegan Paul.

————, and Prosch, H. (1975). *Meaning.* Chicago: University of Chicago Press.

Streng, F. J. (1975). Reflections on the attention given to mental instruction in the Indian Buddhist analysis of causality. *Philosophy East and West* 25/1, January, pp. 71–80.

—— (1982). Realization of *Param Bhutakoti* (ultimate reality-limit) in the *Astasahasrika Prajnaparamita Sutra*. *Philosophy East and West*, 32/1, January, pp. 91–98.

Vaidya, P. L. (1960). *Astasahasrika Prajnaparamita with Haribhadra's commentary called Aloka*. Buddhist Sanskrit Texts, No. 4. Darbhanga: Mithila Institute of Post-Graduate Studies and Research in Sanskrit Learning.

PART IV

Conclusion

within a social framework of interpersonal commitments rather than as the outward expression of some inner state. Selves are psychological individuals, manifested in the unified organization of perceptions, feelings and beliefs of each human being who is organized in that fashion in their own regard. There may be human beings whose belief systems, imaginary anticipations and so on are organized in some non-unitary way. Necessarily all human beings who are members of moral orders are persons, social individuals, but the degree of their psychological individuality, their personal being, I take to be contingent. (p. 77)

Theories of self—in terms of such concepts as unity and intentionality—derive from, and apply to, particular sociocultural contexts. In order to contest the usefulness of one approach over another, we would necessarily have to be engaged in dialogue with other persons who hold a different theory.

In the first essay, deCharms sets a boundary on our project of investigating the self. He asserts that self is the subjective experience of person-characteristics, hence secondary to the concept of person. He implies that attributions about self are culturally relative because they are derived from the context of being a person among an array of persons. Although deCharms suggests that self-attributions are acquired somewhat differently from person-attributions (i.e., through immediate experience), he does not elaborate an approach to the study of self. The rest of the book contains essays that formulate principles of self from diverse theoretical perspectives.

Margolis leads us into our study through his argument for the necessity for a concept of self and his fourteen themes or guidelines for its conceptualization. It seems apparent that the concept of self is more than a linguistic trick or category. We learn to conceive of ourselves as personal beings, as points of action and cognition, in community and public activities with other persons. We appropriate the concepts of morality and social rules for individuality within that community. In American and European cultures, we are typically motivated to construct a self that is unified around an individual ideal of a unique "mental life." We are predisposed to construct ourselves as independent and unique locations of power and action. A model for a unitary or centered self is not an option within our psychology of subjective individualism. It may be more of an option within a psychology of communal personalities. In other words, the person-characteristics that most Americans and Europeans attribute to immediate experiences of subjectivity include unity, self-reflection, and self-determination.

The essays within this volume tend to support or oppose a subjective unity of the self. By arguing either for or against that concept, the authors make clear the central importance of the "synthetic a priori" in theorizing about self. These authors cannot resist commenting on the problem of unity within the individual person. It is possible to imagine a society in which the dispute about unity would never occur, either because it was entirely congruent with the accepted theory of self (e.g., the individual as indivisible), or because it was unheard of (e.g., a society in which individual selves were constantly merged within a collective order).

Finally, however, even within a communal society of group-identified people, the theoretical concept of self cannot be dismissed. Synthetic unities of individual experience—organizing the range of perceptions and cognitions into unified images and actions—must be described as a part of any theory of personal being. Although the diversity and relativity of self constructs is apparent among different social groups and cultures, individuals everywhere experience themselves as loci of perceptions and actions in a coherent and expectable manner.

Self as Construct of Individual Unity

Acknowledging the potential sectarianism of the discussion that follows, we attempt to trace out the boundaries and domains of self theories as we have encountered them in the essays presented in this volume.

The sentence that expresses the individual dilemma of selfhood best for our purposes is the following:

I am not myself today.

The personal pronoun *I* refers to a particular construction of subjectivity that is apparently organized as a judgment on another state of subjectivity—"myself"—recognized as more familiar than the immediate experience of "I." The reference to "myself" implies a personal construct of self that is ongoing and dominant, coherent and judged as valid. The construct apparently exists over time because it is evaluated as part of a process "today."

The sentence does not refer merely to a pretext (although it may conceal other meaning), in that the validity of one representation of self (as "I") is compared to another more familiar one (as "myself"), and the statement is immediately accepted as potentially truthful. Such a statement may be used as an excuse in ordinary conversation, but the fact that its meaning is commonly accepted as truthful indicates that both forms of self (the coherent, dominant, or familiar "myself" and the immediate, idiosyncratic, or unique "I") are admitted as attributes of individual persons within our social context.

The necessity for positing a theoretical unity, a synthetic unity of experience organizing consciousness over time, is apparent in the meaningfulness of this sentence to English readers. Because such a sentence is consensually validated among speakers of English, we can assume that the two contrasting meanings of self are valid constructions within our psychology of individual being.

The concept of a transcendental unity of self, as an organizing principle over time, is a type of theory or construct; it is not a thing. Contrary to the assertion that such a synthetic unity is mystical, obscure, or nondemonstrable, the fact that this sentence is meaningful indicates the plausibility of at least two contrasting theories of self. One theory represents the experience of a familiar, ongoing sense of individuality reported as the typical or usual center of subjectivity; the other is a less familiar (assumed to be temporary) organization of subjectivity from which the person pronounces immediate judgment.

These two conflicting theories of self—as unified and permanent and as transitory and impermanent—are ongoing constructs in our ordinary conversations. Kant grounded his self theory of subjective unity in a transcendental unity of the mind, a categorical imperative in all human experience. We prefer the constructivist approach to this categorical unity of self. The unity of subjective experience arises in a universal tendency to order schemes of perception, action, and thought into some capacity to speak and act as continuous individuals. This capacity may contain more or less belief in the ultimate unity of the individual, as well as the ultimate freedom of action and thought. In this volume, the chapters by Broughton and Streng offer the most thoroughly developed constructivist theories of self in their respective discussions of Piaget's epistemic subject and of Buddhist philosophy. For our purposes, then, we will define our use of the term *self* as the construction of subjective individuality, the development of a theory or knowledge about oneself. In Piaget's terms, "the self is like the centre of one's own activity. . . . The subject exists because, to put it very briefly, the being of structures consists in their coming to be, that is, their being 'under construction'" (pp. 285–86, this volume).

By asserting that a constructivist definition of *self* is primary, we do not exclude a priori universal experiences of personal being from our discourse. Rather, we would shift the reference for such theories from the focus on self to a focus on person.

Psychology of Universals

As Harré's opening statement suggests, some experiences of personal being should be considered "ubiquitous" in that physical embodiment, as it affects point of view, presumes a universal perspective and predisposition to activity in human life. Theorizing about such universals of human life is paradoxical because of the formal problems it entails regarding our specific socialization into different constructs of subjective experience, different self theories. The problems of tracing universals in human instinct and actions may be formally unsolvable at this stage of theory. Because we have no adequate discourse between people who hold markedly different self theories (e.g., between those people who embody collective indivisible individuality and those people who embody self-reflective individuality), we cannot yet differentiate what remains of universal personal being when sociocultural differences have been "subtracted" from selves.

Even so, some promising theories of universal personal characteristics have been traced out, if only in preliminary fashion. The obvious (and nontrivial) fact that the form and physiology of the human body are universal introduces the potential for a psychology of universal states of being a person. Jung's (1959) archetypal psychology of Self is grounded on the predisposition to form a unitary image of oneself and to act in specifically human ways. From the myriad perceptions, emotions, and ideas of personal life, argues Jung, certain features emerge in all human cultures, and are displayed in recurring mythic and imagistic themes across societies and ritual practices. These archetypal themes arise in symbolization of human instinctual-emotional expressions recognized as structural patterns in mythic and ritual practices in contrast to particular individual expressions of self experiences. John Bowlby (1969) has undertaken an ethological approach to the study of instinct in regard to typical human relationships and symbolization of emotional states such as bonding, loss, separation anxiety and grief. Although Bowlby's approach is ostensibly nonconventional, it has unfortunately many cultural biases of Western psychology that favor a model of autonomous, self-reflective individuality. Jung's studies of collective symbolic forms, in comparative tracing of archetypal motifs of social rituals and cultural records, have generally been more widely encompassing of differing self constructs although still prejudiced toward the concept of a free individual.

In this volume, Fordham, Sanders, and Caspary probably best exemplify the Jungian bias toward a universal psychology of core-being. For our purposes, we consider the construct of *core-being* to be classed as an aspect of a person. In other words, for systematic rules of discourse, we would define Jung's construct of archetypal Self to be a predisposition to form a unitary image and experience of personal being. As an aspect of being a person, this core-being would be "identifiable by public criteria" (as in Harré's definition) and interpreted within a social framework of commitments, especially universal forms of human relationship. The public or collective nature of personal being is characterized by socially defined, publicly visible embodied being, which is "endowed with all kinds of powers and capacities for public, meaningful action" (Harré, 1984, p. 26). By interpreting archetypal core-being constructs to be essentially public and visible, we invite opportunities for reviewing the possibility of universal core-being states as displayed within all existing or known cultures regarding the unitary experience of subjective consciousness. We understand this concept to be substantially different from the concept of self as a personal unity of intentional action, a set of beliefs about agency, responsibility, and so on. The conditions predisposing to such core-being may be argued to be metaphysical in nature and/or socially derived, but they would necessarily have to be as publicly displayed as other more visible features of personhood—for instance, the displays of point of view and point of action connected with physical embodiment.

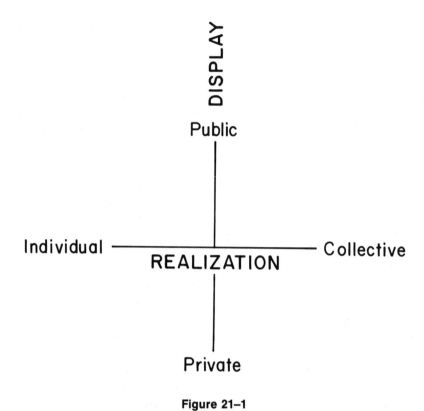

Figure 21–1

Dreams and dream-states may become the best data for research on core-being of personal life in that representations of "I" or personal being in dreams (collected across societies and cultures) could provide a foundation for core-being representations under conditions when intentional activity is not the predominant mode of being.

Two Dimensions of Personal Being

Harré (1984) introduces a two-dimensional space for rational mapping of concepts of personal being. We use it here in order to formulate some systematic rules for discourse about self theories. Figure 21.1 presents the basic map of two dimensions: display and realization. *Display* involves representation of personal attributes that may be pro-

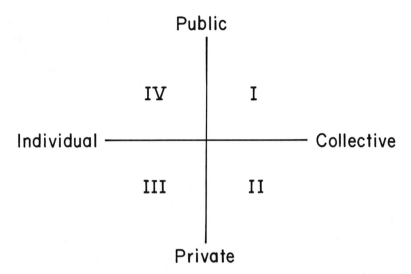

Figure 21–2 For convenience of discussion, the four quadrants can be labeled in terms of successive movement from one order to another.

jected from others and/or identified with. Public displays involve general and open communications that may be linguistic or nonlinguistic. Private displays involve self-representations or speaking or imagining oneself. The dimension of *realization* concerns the degree to which personal attributes are assumed to "belong" to the individual or the group matrix. Groups or tribes of people can be considered aggregates of personal action and power; similarly individuals can be assumed to be the loci of control or authority. The second dimension spans an awareness of individual to collective realization of psychological attributions deriving from a source. The two dimensions are represented as intersecting to form four quadrants in which concepts of personal being can be mapped (fig. 21.2).

Person

As a concept of social being, the construct of "person" is in the primary first quadrant and is identifiable by public criteria and collective realization. As in Strawson (1959) and deCharms (this volume), the person is a primitive or first-order concept that is experienced in such a way that a person attributes to self and other exactly the same referents from different points of view and points of action. I recognize experiences as "I am afraid" or "I am in control" by using these ideas in interactions with other persons whom I consider to be like myself. The personal pronoun *I* has a hypothetical reference to an individual "self" (second quadrant) that is considered to be a construct derived from particular sociocultural contexts.

Core-Being

In order to accommodate theories of core-being as universals, we introduce this concept into the primary space of the first quadrant as the discussion above indicates. In line with Harré's argument, we would assume that core-being indicates a potential for developing a self, as the theoretical center of individual subjectivity.

Fordham's paper advocates a theory of archetypal self (from Jung's psychology) as inherent within the person, in contrast to the assumption that unity is achieved within a social environment of persons interacting. Fordham's "deintegrates" of the archetypal self can be understood as products of social involvement with persons who make attributions about the diverse and unique characteristics of one's individuality. Although Harré might deny that core-being concepts are first-order, he hypothesizes the necessity of theorizing about individual selves on the basis of an analogy with gravity in the physical sciences. He says:

> The structure of the gravitational field enables us to understand the apparently unique and differentiated motions of bodies in proximity to the earth. The organizing power of the concept is independent of whether we treat gravitational potentials as real-world entities or mere fictions. I want to suggest that "I" . . . does have a referential force to a hypothetical entity "the self," in much the same way that the gravitational term g refers to a hypothetical entity, the gravitational field. Possession of the theoretical concept "self" permits just the kind of organization of a person's experience that Kant called "synthetic unity." (Harré, 1984, p. 82)

We would suggest that an analogy between the properties of physical bodies operating "according to the principles of gravity" and personal beings operating "according to the principles of self" holds in the case of personal being. Consequently, it is plausible to suggest that a core-being state is a universal, primitive experience among persons that predisposes them to construct theories of self. Jung's concept of an archetypal self, as a predisposing condition to construct a unitary subjectivity, would be classed as a core-being psychological concept.

Self

The term *self* seems best suited for speaking about the center of individual subjectivity as it is recognized and described in typical organizations of perceptions, feelings, and beliefs according to collective standards for private recognition of authority for one's own actions. The self is experienced as having and being certain kinds of states and images that are claimed as one's own in waking and dreaming.

Self-Images

Experiences of self are regularly associated and identified with particular images, moods, feelings, and activities. We prefer *self-image* to *self-concept* as a term to describe both transitory and continuous identifications of self with certain ways of being and appearing. Generally the image of a physical body and its attendant characteristics is a central and enduring self-image. Self-images of body and social roles are imbued with gender meanings, as male and female persons are encouraged to construct selves that include only certain appearances, styles, ideals, and expressions.

Gender differences in constructions of self and self-images provide a good case for examining some implications of particular social difference in the construction of an individual self. Gender categories of social attributions about persons are the most pervasive, universal, and lifelong categories of human difference in all known societies. There is no existing society in which people are not sorted into gender groups, assigned roles and characteristics based on physical body structures. Male and female self-images are shaped significantly by the meaning of their genders.

In traditional Western culture, collective images of individual self-hood contain central features of personal agency and self-determination as inherent categories of personal worth (e.g., the "right to be free"). Females are socialized to believe that they inherently lack something as complete persons (e.g., physical strength, a complete anatomy, objectivity, competence, knowledge). They are also offered androcentric theories (e.g., penis envy) as explanations for their feelings of inferiority and inadequacy. Androcentrism, reasoning about females from essentially male perspectives and experiences (about both self and female other), results in classifying female persons according to male standards for truth, beauty, and goodness.

Self theories of male persons as complete and valid, buttressed by self theories of female persons as incomplete or inferior, are so widely accepted in most literate societies that we must wrestle with our basic concepts of being persons in order even to recognize the consequences for individual constructions of selves.

Studies of American expectations of "ideal" men and women (Broverman, Broverman et al., 1970; Broverman, Vogel et al., 1972) are frequently cited as empirical evidence of the collective prejudices we share about gender differences. These studies show that Americans expect men to be stronger, more objective, more competent, and more independent than women—results that are clearly evident in daily experiences. Women are expected to be weaker, less competent, and more emotionally expressive than men. More important for a theory of self, however, is the expectation that ideal women are less competent than "healthy adults" when gender is not specified in putting the question. This last finding from the Broverman questionnaire study is an illustration of the strength of gender differences in self theories. If a female person behaves as a healthy adult person, she will be considered to be unwomanly or lacking in her gender validity. If she behaves as validly female, she will be considered as lacking in complete personhood, in achieving the personal autonomy and responsibility expected of an adult.

The double bind of female gender identity is wholly unavoidable in male-dominated societies. Many women of different cultures fight self-attributions of inferiority these days. They attempt to identify with strength, competence, and personal authority. Unfortunately, they cannot escape social contexts in which they will be seen and described as "compensating" for their inferiority. In public arenas of American society, for example, a forceful and authoritative woman typically experiences a great deal of distress as she is described as "too masculine," "too intellectual," or "too emotional."

As Harré (1984) points out, the legitimacy of being a person (the fundamental reality on which a self is grounded) is limited by the "right" to occupy a particular time and space in the conversations of personal life. This contingent right is closely related to consensual validation of individual experiences and truths. Harré says the following:

> Persons are embodied beings located not only in the array of persons but in physical space and time. The relation between the consequences of our joint location in both manifolds is mediated by the local moral order, particularly the unequal distribution of rights. . . . For example, one may be physically present with others in the same space and time of a meeting, but in the position of secretary, may not have the right to contribute to the cognitive processes proceeding in the flow of the conversation. (p. 65)

Women who oppose social and cultural limitations on female self frequently occupy a position similar to the secretary when they make forceful claims to their authority. They are seen but not heard. They get the impression, both implicitly and explicitly, that they are not legitimate selves as full participants in the social reality of the moment.

On the other hand, women who accept the traditional gender meanings for being female—and express themselves as inferior to males in significant aspects of self-determination—face a different kind of fate in regard to adequacy of self. They are usually perceived as legitimately female—as complete or whole as people—but as inherently childlike or dependent on male people.

Gender categories, as well as other categories of social attributions about difference—for example, race, class, and age—contribute importantly to the construction of individual selves and self-images. The regular collection of self-images with which a person identifies can be called "identity" and understood as a collection of diverse (and sometimes noncompatible, as in the case of adult females) self-images that are referenced to various aspects of being and relating as an individual person.

Generally people experience and discuss self-images as though they cohered into a unified sense of subjectivity: myself. It is far more likely, however, that shifting social realities (as for example the secretary's nonparticipation in the board meeting) determine occasions in which one or another self-image comprises momentary identity as a person. From time to time, alien self-images are in fact described as though they represented *part personalities, subpersonal beings* contained within a person. A statement like "My nasty mood got the best of me" expresses such a subpersonal influence. Different voices, gestures, poses, meanings, and mannerisms are associated with different self-images. As both an occasion and a representation for action, a self-image is a point of view and an experiential predisposition.

Within all cultures and societies, certain self-images are permitted and valued over others. Within some groups in Western society, the psychoanalytic construct of "ego" constitutes such a preferred self-image. The ego refers to a synthesis of feelings, attitudes, and activities organized as a dominant self-image that coheres around a sense of personal responsibility and mastery over perceptions and action. Certain "defenses," or habitual manners of acting and speaking, are described as protecting the ego (an individual's attempt at mastery) from challenges and disintegration. Both the ego and its defenses can be described as public displays of behavior and attitudes, individually appropriated as explanations of a particular self-image. The construct of ego is by no means a universal self-image and would indeed be a burden to a person who functions primarily as a member of a collective group in which self-determination and individual freedom are not priorities of the dominant social order.

Narration

In all known societies, life histories of individual persons are a prominent aspect of personal being and the project of identity. Self-images are constructed and maintained as a part of a life's story, which is generally told within a continuous structure of time and space. A person locates the self within a matrix of people, culture, and society and strives to maintain a continuous timeline of events and changing self-images that permit membership in one's group. Reference groups for self-images change in the course of a lifetime narration. According to psychoanalytic theory, major self-images form in the family of origin, which has a determining effect on all subsequent self-images. Other personality theories, as for example interpersonal theory, may attribute less determinant influences to the family of origin. In our North American society, life narratives take on attributions of originality, uniqueness, individuality, and personal heroism, which are priorities for personal power. Whereas we have few prominent social rites of passage from one historical point of the life cycle to the next, we do have standard ways of narrating ourselves. For example, Americans generally idealize spontaneity and creativity of childhood years, give some account of teenage rebelliousness (or the lack thereof), then of settling down to adult responsibilities, and so on. Therapeutic accounts of American life histories emphasize the "struggle" to establish the self as an individual with the necessary autonomy for independent choice and self-reflection, as ambiguous as these may seem to be within individual experience. Lichtenberg's (this volume) case history, concerning attachment and vitality, is a good example of the prominence given to ideals of freedom and autonomy for a secure self-image in an American man.

Although narrative structure cannot wholly account for the experience of a continuous sense of self, it does make an essential contribution to the sense of being a legitimate person. Without some adequate telling about one's development and place over time, a person will necessarily feel excluded or disoriented, experiencing a social isolation that is a prominent feature of what is usually considered to be pathology of personal being. Psychoanalysis, as a narrative discipline of life history, seems explicitly designed to assist a person in closing the "gaps" and presenting a rational, sequential account of the self over time.

Transcendence of Self

By assuming that self is a theoretical construct, sustained within an ongoing discourse about personal being, we can argue that transcending the self is entirely understandable: narrative and dramatic practices may be designed to demonstrate the insubstantiality of an individual self. Whereas it is absurd to speak about transcending personhood, it is clearly possible to construct a subjective individuality based on beliefs, principles, and activities that oppose the immediate unity of time, space, causality, and perceptions according to the Western paradigm of natural sciences. To speak of a self theory that transcends or opposes principles of unity and/or categories of physical reality is to describe ways of constructing and maintaining subjective states that may correspond to self-images different from an ordinary personal self of shared common realities. Transcendental theories are constructed on principles and self-images that are primarily excluded from the accepted domain of personal reality, yet are nevertheless products of shared awareness and public discourse. Whether we inquire of non-Western peoples, parapsychologists, schizophrenic people, or saints, we will discover self-images and self constructs formulated according to principles different from the paradigm of Western sciences.

People who hold dissident beliefs about self, within a dominant culture, are often labeled as outsiders (even "crazy") although they regularly engage in shared experiences and dialogue among other people who hold similar beliefs. Unless we accept the entire range of self constructs within our arena of potential dialogues, we have no possibility of differentiating universal aspects of personhood from ideological constructions of self. Consequently, we would include within our rational space the principles of a transcendental self constructed according to belief systems at variance with whatever the dominant beliefs of a particular culture or society may be.

A Map for Rational Discourse

Figure 21.3 locates various self and person terms on the two-dimensional space of Harré's diagram. The arrows indicate movement from the primary space of personal being to secondary and tertiary theories of individual self. Some societies construct self theories that remain in the second quadrant of collective-private realization only. In such societies there is no belief in a freely activated individual self, a representation of a free individual agent. This map permits us to see that the primary construct of *person* is realized within the domain of public display and collective recognition. We hypothesize a core-being state within the person that is the analogue of the ubiquitous form of the human body and its perceptual organization. All persons necessarily

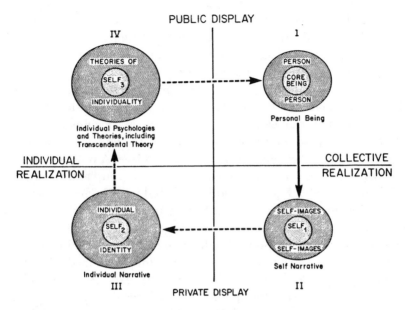

Figure 21–3

formulate a theory of self within a collective situation, necessarily because of the unitary organization of perceptual experience. Even without the personal pronoun *I,* all persons perceive themselves as loci of
personal action and point of view. Out of these experiences come self-
images identified with body-states and moods as they are attributed
to private reality within a collective array of persons.

The second quadrant concerns the social construction of shared
theories of self, which are collectively and privately displayed in representational forms of an individual point of view and point of action.
Gendered and social self-images are formulated within this collective,
private domain. In some societies individual subjectivity remains
within a collective domain. In such a society, the self corresponds to
personal membership as a unit within the collective order that provides both morality and social conscience for the individual.

As we have asserted, in North American and European societies,
there are second- and third-order selves that are constituted from
diverse reference systems. The second-order self is constructed
around a narrative of autonomous individuality.

Individual theories of self are represented as connected by a broken line to the second quadrant because they are not necessarily a part of personal being and human society. Only certain societies construct principles of individuality and self-determination as aspects of personal being. Third-quadrant self theories are necessarily derived and congruent with second-quadrant theories of self, although first- and second-quadrant realities are probably *prior* to a formulation of self in the third quadrant. It is possible to imagine a society—for example, a group of American eight-year-old children—in which self constructs are not developed beyond the third quadrant. The self would be experienced and talked about as individual and free. A unique personal identity would be conceived as relating to one's group and family, but no theory of individuality would be included in ordinary discourse.

The fourth quadrant is the final domain of self theories in which individual conceptions of self enter the public domain of discourse, and are displayed as aspects of individual realization. In this domain, the self is publicly characterized as being unique, individual, autonomous, independent, transcendent, and the like. Here the self is treated as an abstract concept on the same level as other abstractions about the physical and emotional world—for example, as similar to the concepts of time and space. Disputes about the reality or unreality of self constructs take place within this domain, as well as personal assertions about individual and original personality characteristics, and so on. Ultimately the diagram should have arrows moving *both* ways in all domains and diagonally as well, because all domains of self constructs are constantly interacting with personal being within a public-collective situation (fig. 21.4).

A diagram like this assists us in locating concepts and terms. Ordinary discourse is confusing because personal pronouns may be referenced to any one of these domains. Referents for personal viewpoint and personal action may include person, self-image, individual identity, or theoretical individuality. For example, "I_1 am not myself$_2$ today, but I_3 predict that I_4 will feel quite normal tomorrow." The subscript numerals refer to the quadrants that may be used as referents for the statement. The initial "I" refers to the person (first-order) speaking about a self-image (second-order) that is apparently considered ordinary and continuous. The third-order "I" is able to freely construct and predict an intuited reality for a "normal" (fourth-order) state of being oneself in the future.

Both formal and everyday discourse about self is burdened by the

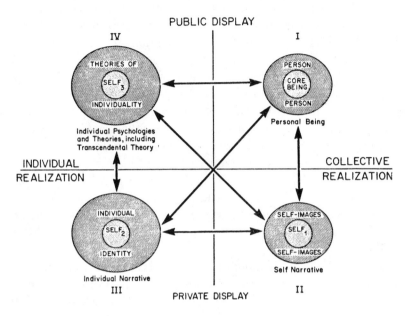

Figure 21–4

ambiguity of self and person referents to contrasting assumptions and domains of personal being. By using a map, such as this two-dimensional space, it is possible to eliminate some confusions and cross-references to different domains of experience. For example, in discussing the principles of a core-being construct, such as Jung's archetypal self, people tend to argue in terms of beliefs rather than evidence. If we are correct in assigning this construct to the primary first quadrant, then its attributes and effects would have to be explained in terms of public displays and collective realizations about personhood rather than in terms of private belief systems about self. Indeed, the concept of core-being, grounded on a hypothesis of a given unity of perception and unitary action in the human organism, arises from "physical necessities that corporeal embodiment in a world of things imposes on a point of view," as Harré says. Thus core-being must be publicly observable (e.g., in infant interactions) as an aspect of personal life. Indeed core-being is evidenced through the *visibility* of corporeal embodiment within a uniform body type, *and* through the attribution of *unified forms* of personal power and perceptual capacities to all persons.

Discourse about belief systems and theoretical constructs of individuality belongs properly in the third and fourth quadrants. The fourth quadrant especially constitutes the rational domain—individual realization and public display—for studying various beliefs about individuality and selves. To continue the above example, Jung's extensive theory of archetypal self-images, as they are interpreted from myths and rituals, appropriately belongs within the fourth quadrant as a belief about representations that derive from a theory of individuation according to a universal transformation of core-being.

Experiential constructs related to a person's identity—such as personal examples of remembered childhood activities used to explain present enactments—are third-order constructs. They are referred to private displays of individual realization, and may or may not engender theories of individuality, may or may not connect with immediately experienced self-images.

From this diagram, it should be apparent that theories of individuality are not necessarily consonant with experiences of self. Theories of individuality derive from constructs about individual subjective experiences, and these do not derive directly from what can be perceived publicly in the array of persons. When we are able to differentiate types and principles of self theories across cultures, and to account for all forms of self-images and theories of self, we may be able to capture what is universal in personhood. Whatever can be displayed as consistently present across cultures, in terms of the form of self-images and self constructs, and/or in terms of the common elements of core-being, will necessarily be public in nature and able to be displayed or demonstrated, not as a matter of belief, but as a matter of immediate recognition of being a person among persons.

In the meantime, we hope that philosophers, psychologists, theologians, anthropologists, social workers, sociologists, biographers, and historians will improve the clarity of their dialogue by mapping constructs of person and self according to a sociocultural account of the constructs. Because person and self constructs are noncompatible, being referenced interchangeably through personal pronouns and evidenced at different levels of abstraction and display, we must search our assumptions before arguing particular assertions.

Beyond the Personal Self

Within fourth-quadrant theories of individuality, we can include attributions of individual self (as a center of subjectivity and unity) to nonpersonal beings. People attribute individual selves to both subpersonal beings (e.g., dogs and cats) and suprapersonal beings (e.g., gods and goddesses). In order to enter into discourse with people who have constructed and attributed selves to nonpersonal beings, we must be open to the possibility that core-being states can be understood as potential experiences of beings who are not persons. In other words, we must admit the possibility that personal experience could potentially belong also to nonpersonal beings.

Hall (1977) has presented evidence from research on dreams and dreaming that suggests a person's self-images are influenced by experiences that appear to emerge from a nonpersonal center of subjectivity and individuality. Hall argues for the possibility of demonstrating evidence of a suprapersonal self that maintains an enduring correspondence with personal self-images. In Hall's account, transformation of personal self-images involves both social interaction with other persons, and dreaming interaction with a nonpersonal self.

Critical to Hall's account is the observation that personal self-images change as a result of dreaming, whether or not the dream is understood, even remembered. Such tacit changes in self-image may become an aspect of the self narrative and influence a person's account of his or her individual development (quadrant III).

Transcendental theories of self (quadrant IV) introduce the possibility that suprapersonal beings are themselves centers of subjectivity and core-being. Interaction between personal and suprapersonal beings could take place through transformations of self and self-images and would be schematized as a three-dimensional extension of the two-dimensional representation of figure 22-3. Rather than being demonstrable communications among the array of persons (quadrant I), suprapersonal effects would be experienced as shifts in self-images.

Empirical evidence for a transcendental theory of self is suggested by the field of parapsychology (Rhine, 1976–77). Psi events such as telepathy, clairvoyance, and psychokinesis convey information which is demonstrated in quadrant I as public displays among persons. Theories of suprapersonal individuality have traditionally been problematic for Western science, but parapsychological experiments may provide a basis for new theories of individuality.

Conclusion

Through employing Harré's scheme for mapping personal being, we have highlighted some conceptual confusions in referencing self terms, in both ordinary conversation and formal theoretical discourse. Revealing the inconsistencies and ambiguities of referents for personal pronouns, and other personal indexical language, has guided us in formulating some rules for discourse about self theories.

Accepting the construct of person as primary, necessarily public and collective, clarifies the interpretive method used to explicate terms referring to universals in personal psychology. Similarly, limiting the use of the term *self* to theoretical constructs of individual being, we can discriminate different self theories as they arise within particular sociocultural contexts. Even more significant, perhaps, by illuminating the effects of social and cultural categories on self-theory formulations (as, for example, in regard to gender), we may be able to clarify differences between personal identities and their effects on the construction and representation of experience.

References

Bowlby, J. (1969). *Attachment and loss, vol. I*. London: Hogarth.

Broverman, I. K., Broverman, D. M., Clarkson, F. E., Rosenkrantz, P. S. and Vogel, S. R. (1970). Sex-role stereotypes and clinical judgments of mental health. *Journal of Consulting and Clinical Psychology, 34*, 1–7.

———, Vogel, S. R., Broverman, D. M., Clarkson, F. E., and Rosenkrantz, P. S. (1972). Sex-role stereotypes: A current appraisal. *Journal of Social Issues, 28*, 59–78.

Hall, J. (1977). *Clinical uses of dreams: Jungian interpretation and enactments*. New York: Grune and Stratton.

Harré, R. (1984). *Personal being*. Cambridge: Harvard University Press.

Jung, C. G. (1959). Conscious, unconscious and individuation. In *Collected works, 9*, 1. Princeton: Princeton University Press.

Rhine, J. B. (1976–77). Parapsychology and religion. *Journal of the Texas Society for Psychical Research*, 9–22.

Strawson, P. F. (1954). *Individuals*. London: Methuen.

INDEX